ORIGEN

HOMILIES
ON GENESIS AND EXODUS

Translated by

RONALD E. HEINE

Lincoln Christian College and Seminary

THE CATHOLIC UNIVERSITY OF AMERICA PRESS
Washington, D.C.

Nihil Obstat:
  REVEREND HERMIGILD DRESSLER, O.F.M.
    Censor Deputatus

Imprimatur:
  REV. MSGR. JOHN F. DONOGHUE
    Vicar General for the Archdiocese of Washington

July 8, 1981

The *nihil obstat* and *imprimatur* are official declarations that a book or pamphlet is free of doctrinal or moral error. No implication is contained therein that those who have granted the *nihil obstat* and the *imprimatur* agree with content, opinions, or statements expressed.

Library of Congress Cataloging in Publication Data

Origen.
  Homilies on Genesis and Exodus.

  (The Fathers of the Church; v. 71)
  English translation of: Homiliae in Genesim;
In Exodum homiliae/by Origen; Latin translation by Rufinus Tyrannius.
  Bibliography: p. vii
  Includes indexes.
    1. Bible. O.T. Genesis—Sermons.   2. Bible. O.T. Exodus—Sermons.
  3. Sermons, English—Translations from Latin.   4. Sermons,
  Latin—Translations into English.   I. Heine, Ronald E.
  II. Origen. In Exodum homiliae. III. Title. IV. Series.
  BR60.F3068   [BS1235]   22'.1106   82-4124
    ISBN 0-8132-0071-7   AACR2

33,704

CONTENTS

SELECT BIBLIOGRAPHY

Texts and Translations of Origen's Works

Baehrens. W. ed. *Origenes Werke: Homilien zum Hexateuch in Rufins Übersetzung.* Part 1, *Die Homilien zu Genesis, Exodus und Leviticus.* Die griechischen christlichen Schriftsteller der ersten drei Jahrhunderte, vol. 29. Leipzig: J. C. Hinrichs'sche Buchandlung, 1920.

Blanc, C., ed. and trans. *Origène: Commentaire sur St. Jean.* Vol. I. Sources chrétiennes, vol. 120. Paris: Les éditions du Cerf, 1966.

Butterworth, G., trans. *Origen: On First Principles.* 1936. Reprint. New York: Harper and Row, 1966.

Chadwick, H., trans. *Origen: Contra Celsum.* Cambridge: At the University Press, 1965.

Doutreleau, L., ed. and trans. *Origène: Homélies sur la Genèse.* Source chrétiennes, vol. 7bis. Paris: Les éditions du Cerf, 1976.

———. "Le fragment grec de l'homélie II d'Origène sur la Genése. Critique du text."*Revue d'histoire des textes* 5 (1975):13–44.

Fortier, P., trans. *Origène: Homélies sur l'Exode.* Sources chrétiennes, vol. 16. Paris: Les éditions du Cerf, 1947.

Glaue, D., ed. *Ein Bruchstück des Origenes über Genesis 1,28.* Giessen: Alfred Töpelmann, 1928.

Gueraud, O., and Nautin, P. eds. and translators. *Origène, sur la Pâque: Traité inédit publié d'après un papyrus de Toura.* Paris: Beauchesne, 1979.

Jaubert, A., ed. and trans. *Origène: Homélies sur Josué.* Sources chrétiennes 71. Paris: Les éditions du Cerf, 1960.

Menzies, A., ed. *The Ante-Nicene Fathers*, vol. 10. Reprint. Grand Rapids, Mich.: Wm B. Eerdmans, 1969.

Nautin, P., and Husson, Pierre, eds. and translators. *Origène: Homélies sur Jérémie.* Vol. 1. Source chrétiennes, vol. 232. Paris: Les éditions du Cerf, 1976.

Oulton, J. and Chadwick, H., translators. *Alexandrian Christianity.* The Library of Christian Classics, vol. 2. Philadelphia: Westminster Press, 1954.

Scherer, Jean, ed. and trans. *Entretien d'Origène avec Héraclide.* Sources chrétiennes, vol. 67. Paris: Les éditions du Cerf, 1960.

Other Works

Altaner, B. *Patrology.* Translated by H. Graef. 2nd ed. New York: Herder and Herder, 1961.

———., and Stuiber, A. *Patrologie.* Frieburg: Herder, 1978.

Baehrens, W. *Überlieferung und Textgeschichte der lateinisch erhaltenen Origenes Homilien zum Alten Testament.* Texte und Untersuchungen, vol. 42.1. Leipzig, 1916.

Bardy, G. "Aux origines de l'école d'Alexandrie." *Recherches de science religieuse* 27 (1937):65–90.

———. *Recherches sur l'histoire du texte et des versions latines du De Principiis d'Origène.* Paris: Edouard Champion, 1923.

———. "Les traditions juives dans l'oeuvre d'Origène." *Revue biblique* 34 (1925):217–52.

Barnes, T. "Origen, Aquila, and Eusebius." *Harvard Studies in Classical Philology* 74 (1970):313–16.

Barthélemy, D. "Origène et le texte de l'ancien testament." In *Epektasis: mélanges patristiques offerts au Cardinal Jean Daniélou*, edited by J. Fontaine and C. Kannengiesser. Paris: Beauchesne, 1972.

Chadwick, H. *Early Christian Thought and the Classical Tradition*. Oxford: At the Clarendon Press, 1966.

─────. "Rufinus and the Tura Papyrus of Origen's Commentary on Romans." *The Journal of Theological Studies*, n.s. 10 (1959):10–42.

Courcelle, P. *Late Latin Writers and Their Greek Sources*. Translated by H. Wedech. Cambridge: Harvard University Press, 1969.

Crouzel, H. *Bibliographie critique d'Origène*. Instrumenta Patristica 8 (La Haye: Nijhoff, 1971).

─────. "Comparaisons précises entre les fragments du *Peri Archôn* selon la Philocalia et la traduction de Rufin." In *Origeniana: Premier colloque international des études origéniennes (Montserrat, 18–21 septembre 1973)*, edited by H. Crouzel, G. Lomiento, and J. Rius-Camps. Universitá di Bari: Istituto di letteratura cristiana antica, 1975.

─────. *Origène et la philosophie*. Aubier, 1962.

─────. *Théologie de l'image de Dieu chez Origène*. Aubier, 1956.

Daniélou, J. *Origène. Le génie du Christianisme*. Paris: La table ronde, 1948.

Faye, Eugène, de. *Origène, sa vie, son oeuvre, sa pensée*. 3 vols. Paris: Leroux, 1923–28.

Freedman, H. and Simon, M., eds. *Midrash Rabbah*. 10 vols. London: The Soncino Press, 1939.

Frend, W. "A Severan Persecution? Evidence of the 'Historia Augusta.' " In *Forma Futuri: Studi in Onore del Cardinale Michele Pellegrino*. Torino: Bottega d'Erasmo, 1975.

Ginzberg, L. *The Legends of the Jews*. 7 vols. Philadelphia: The Jewish Publication Society of America, 1909–1938.

Goodenough, E. *Jewish Symbols in the Greco-Roman Period*. Vol. 10. New York: Pantheon Books, 1964.

Grant, R. *Augustus to Constantine*. New York: Harper and Row, 1970.

─────. "The Case against Eusebius or, Did the Father of Church History Write History?" In *Studia Patristica* 12.1, edited by E. Livingstone, pp. 413–21. Berlin: Akademie-Verlag, 1975.

─────. *The Earliest Lives of Jesus*. New York: Harper and Brothers, 1961.

─────. "Early Alexandrian Christianity." *Church History* 40 (1971):133–44.

─────. "Eusebius and His Lives of Origen." In *Forma Futuri: Studi in Onore del Cardinale Michele Pellegrino*. Torino: Bottega d'Erasmo, 1975.

─────. *Eusebius as Church Historian*. Oxford: Clarendon Press, 1980.

Gustafsson, B. "Eusebius' Principles in Handling His Sources as Found in His Church History, Books I-VII." In *Studia Patristica* 4, edited by E. Livingston, pp. 429–41. Berlin: Akademie-Verlag, 1961.

Hammond, C. "The Last Ten Years of Rufinus' Life and the Date of His Move South from Aquileia." *The Journal of Theological Studies*, n.s. 28 (1977):372–429.

Hanson, R. "Interpretation of Hebrew names in Origen," *Vigiliae Christianae* 10 (1956):103–23.

─────. *Origen's Doctrine of Tradition*. London: S.P.C.K., 1954.

————. Review of *I Principi di Origene*, by M. Simonetti. *The Journal of Theological Studies*. n.s. 31 (1970):181–83.

————. Review of *Origène, sa vie et son oeuvre*, by P. Nautin. *The Journal of Theological Studies*, n.s. 29 (1978):556–58.

Hoppe, H. "Griechisches bei Rufin." *Glotta* 26 (1938):132–44.

————. "Rufin als Uebersetzer." In *Studi dedicati alla memoria di Paolo Ubaldi*. Milan: Società Editrice "Vita e Pensiero," 1937.

Hornschuh, M. "Das Leben des Origenes und die Entstehung der alexandrinischen Schule." *Zeitschrift für Kirchengeschichte* 71 (1960):1–25; 193–214.

Hritzu, J., trans. *Saint Jerome: Dogmatic and Polemical Works*. The Fathers of the Church, vol. 53. Washington, D.C.: The Catholic University of America Press, 1965.

Kelly, J. *Jerome: His Life, Writings, and Controversies*. New York: Harper and Row, 1975.

Koch, H. *Pronoia und Paideusis*. Berlin: Walter de Gruyter and Co., 1932.

Kraeling, C. *The Synagogue*. The Excavations at Dura-Europos. New Haven; Yale, 1956.

Lang, C., ed. *Cornuti theologiae graecae compendium*. Leipzig: Teubner, 1881.

Lange, N., de. "Jewish Influence on Origen." In *Origeniana: Premier colloque international des études origéniennes (Montserrat, 18–21 septembre 1973)*, edited by H. Crouzel, G. Lomiento, and J. Rius-Camps. Universitá di Bari: Istituto di letteratura cristiana antica, 1975.

————. *Origen and the Jews*. Cambridge: Cambridge University Press, 1976.

Levine, L. *Caesarea under Roman Rule*. Leiden: E. J. Brill, 1975.

Lewis, J. *A Study of the Interpretation of Noah and the Flood in Jewish and Christian Literature*. Leiden: E. J. Brill, 1968.

Murmelstein, B. "Agadische Methode in den Pentateuchhomilien des Origenes." *Jahresbericht israelitischtheologische Lehranstalt* 37–39 (1929–32): 93–122.

Murphy, F. *Rufinus of Aquileia (345–411): His Life and Works*. Washington D.C.: The Catholic University of America Press, 1945.

Nautin, P. *Lettres et écrivains chrétiens des IIe et IIIe siècles*. Patristica 2. Paris: Les éditions du Cerf, 1961.

————. *Origène: sa vie et son oeuvre*. Paris: Beauchesne, 1977.

Oulton, J. "Rufinus's Translation of the Church History of Eusebius." *The Journal of Theological Studies* 30 (1929):150–74.

Rist, J. "The Greek and Latin Texts of the Discussion on Free Will in De Principiis, Book III." In *Origeniana: Premier colloque international des études origéniennes (Montserrat, 18–21 septembre 1973)*, edited by H. Crouzel, G. Lomiento, and J. Rius-Camps. Universitá di Bari: Istituto di letteratura cristiana antica, 1975.

Smalley, B. *The Study of the Bible in the Middle Ages*. 1952. Reprint. Notre Dame, In.: University of Notre Dame Press, 1978.

Studer, B. "A propos des traductions d'Origène par Jérôme et Rufin." *Vetera Christianorum* 5 (1968):137–55.

Trigg, J. "The Charismatic Intellectual: Origen's Understanding of Religious Leadership." *Church History* 50 (1981):5–19.

————. "A Decade of Origen Studies." *Religious Studies Review* 7 (1981):21–27.

Vogel, C. de. *Greek Philosophy*. Vol. 3. Leiden: E. J. Brill, 1973.

Völker, W. *Das Vollkommenheitsideal des Origenes*. Tübingen: J. C. B. Mohr, 1930.

Wagner, M. *Rufinus the Translator. A Study of His Theory and Practice as Illustrated in His Version of the Apologetica of S. Gregory Nazianzen*. Washington, D.C.: The Catholic University of America, 1945.

Winkelmann, F. "Einige Bemerkungen zu den Aussagen des Rufinus von Aquileia und des Hieronymus über ihre Übersetzungstheorie und -methode." In *Kyriakon: Festschrift Johannes Quasten*, vol. 2, edited by P. Granfield and J. Jungmann. Münster: Verlag Aschendorff, 1970.

Wutz, F. *Onomastica Sacra: Untersuchungen zum Liber interpretationis nominum hebraicorum des hl. Hieronymus*. Leipzig: J. C. Hinrichs'sche Buchhandlung, 1914.

ABBREVIATIONS

ANF	The Ante Nicene Fathers
Aristotle, *Phys.*	Aristotle, *Physica*
Augustine, *De civ. Dei*	Augustine, *De Civitate Dei*
Quaest. in Hept.	*Quaestiones in Heptateuchum*
Cicero, *N.D.*	Cicero, *De natura deorum*
Clement, *Paed.*	Clement of Alexandria, *Paedogogus*
Strom.	*Stromata*
Epictetus, *Disc.*	Epictetus, *The Discourses as Reported by Arrian*
Eusebius, *H.E.*	Eusebius, *Historia ecclesiastica*
FOTC	*The Fathers of the Church*
GCS	*Die griechischen christlichen schriftsteller der ersten drei Jahrhunderte*
Jerome, *Adv. Ruf.*	Jerome, *Apologia adversus libros Rufini*
Ep.	*Epistolae*
Josephus, *Ant.*	Josephus, *Antiquitates Judaicae*
Bell.	*Bellum Judaicum*
LXX	*Septuaginta*
NCE	*New Catholic Encyclopedia*
Origen, *Cels.*	Origen, *Contra Celsum*
Comm. Jn.	*Commentary on John*
Comm Mt.	*Commentary on Matthew*
De. Princ.	*De principiis*
Ex. Hom.	*In Exodum homiliae*
Gn. Hom.	*In Genesim homiliae*
Hom. Jer.	*In Jeremiam homiliae*
Hom. Josh.	*Homiliae in librum Jesu Nave*
Mart.	*Exhortatio ad martyrium*
Nm. Hom.	*In Numeros homiliae*
Phil.	*Philocalia*
PG	Migne, *Patrologia Graeca*
Philo, *Abr.*	Philo, *De Abrahamo*
Cher.	*De cherubim*
Cong.	*De congressu eruditionis gratia*
Deus.	*Quod Deus sit immutabilis*
Ebr.	*De ebrietate*
Fug.	*De fuga et inventione*
Her.	*Quis rerum divinarum heres sit*
L.A.	*Legum allegoriarum*
Mig.	*De migratione Abrahami*
Mos.	*De vita Mosis*
Op.	*De opificio mundi*
Post.	*De posteritate Caini*
QE.	*Quaestiones et solutiones in Exodum*

QG.	*Quaestiones et solutiones in Genesim*
Sac.	*De sacrificiis Abelis et Caini*
Som.	*De somniis*
PL	Migne. *Patrologia Latina*
Plato, *Phdr*	Plato, *Phaedrus*
Rufinus, *Apol.*	Rufinus, *Apologiae in S. Hieronymum libri duo*
Apol. ad Anastasium	*Apologia altera ad Anastasium papam*
Praef. De Princ.	*Origenis de principiis Praefatio Rufini*
Praef. ad Gaudentium	*S. Clementis recognitionum libros praefatio ad Gaudentium episcopum*
Praef. ad Heraclium	*Ad Heraclium praefatio in explanationem Origenis super epistolam Pauli ad Romanos*
SC	*Source chrétiennes*
SPCK	Society for Promoting Christian Knowledge
Tertullian, *Praes. Her.*	Tertullian, *De praescriptione haereticorum*
TU	*Texte und Untersuchurgen*

ORIGEN

INTRODUCTION

Origen stands out in the third century Church like an oak on the prairie. The Church was to live for centuries in the shade of his achievements, both instructed and divided by them. Few indeed were the churchmen in the following centuries, even among those who repudiated him, who did not owe some aspect of their theology or methodology to Origen. He was able to perceive and pursue the crucial questions that touched the nerve centers of faith and religious life in his day. And, as Henry Chadwick has pointed out, "some of his most characteristic themes...have remained to this day permanently troubling questions in the history of Christian thought."[1]

Origen's written works touched nearly every discipline of the life and thought of the Church. Robert Grant has called him "the most important Christian critic in antiquity."[2] Henry Chadwick hailed the *Contra Celsum* as "the culmination of the whole apologetic movement of the second and third centuries."[3] Joseph W. Trigg refers to Origen's *On First Principles* as "the first sustained essay...that any Christian made at a comprehensive, philosophically informed presentation of the principal truths of the faith."[4] His concern for and sustained work on the text of the Bible demonstrated in the *Hexapla* was

---

1 *Early Christian Thought and the Classical Tradition* (Oxford: At the Clarendon Press, 1966), 66, (hereinafter cited as Chadwick, *Early Christian Thought*). The bibliography in Origen studies is enormous. See the monumental work by Henri Crouzel, *Bibliographie critique d'Origène*, Instrumenta Patristica 8 (La Haye: Nijhoff, 1971), hereinafter cited as Crouzel, *Bibliographie*.
2 *The Earliest Lives of Jesus* (New York: Harper & Brothers, 1961), 50.
3 *Origen: Contra Celsum* (Cambridge: At the University Press, 1965), ix, hereinafter cited as Chadwick, *Origen*.
4 "A Decade of Origen Studies," *Religious Studies Review* 7 (Jan., 1981): 23, hereinafter cited as "A Decade of Origen Studies."

1

to have no parallel for centuries. While he was not the first
Christian to write commentaries on the books of the Bible, the
scope of his achievements in this area was unmatched in the
ancient Church. His are not the earliest Christian homilies
preserved, but the size of the corpus of his homilies makes
them the earliest that can be studied in breadth and depth.
They reveal him as an accomplished preacher of the Bible and
a concerned pastor of the Church. He seems, moreover, to
have been the first Christian to conceptualize the her-
meneutical process. He devotes a large portion of the fourth
book of *On First Principles* to how the Bible should be interpreted. This issue is also raised in his homilies.[5] His approach
to the Bible prevailed in the Church among both his followers
and his antagonists for centuries. Beryl Smalley has said, "To
write a history of Origenist influence on the west would be
tantamount to writing a history of western exegesis."[6]

At the center of all Origen's work, however, burned his own
intense devotion to God.[7] J. E. L. Oulton remarked that "in his
capacity for combining as a unity in himself intellectual passion
with warm personal devotion to God in Christ and the practical
virtues of a Christian, Origen is perhaps unique among the
Fathers."[8] This combination of "intellectual passion with warm
personal devotion" is especially obvious in his homilies.

Eusebius and the Life of Origen

Eusebius of Caesarea, as Eugène de Faye said over half a
century ago, is still our principal authority for the life of

---

5 See, for example, *Ex. Hom.* 5.1.
6 *The Study of the Bible in the Middle Ages*, 2d ed. 1952 (reprint ed. Notre
  Dame, In., 1964), 14.
7 Walther Völker's study, *Das Vollkommenheitsideal des Origenes* (Tübingen:
  J. C. B. Mohr, 1930), has probably been the most important in bringing this
  aspect of Origen to the attention of modern scholars. Hereinafter cited as
  Völker, *Das Vollkommenheitsideal.*
8 *Alexandrian Christianity*, ed. and trans. J. Oulton and H. Chadwick, The
  Library of Christian Classics, vol. 2 (Philadelphia: Westminster Press,
  1954), 186.

Origen.[9] Pierre Nautin's recent monumental study of Origen, however, has taken Origen studies one step behind Eusebius' *Church History*. Nautin attempts to identify and evaluate Eusebius' sources and then to reconstruct Origen's life on the basis of these sources rather than simply following Eusebius' account of Origen's life.[10] This is an important advance, aptly compared by Trigg to "the advance Bultmann and Dibelius made over previous New Testament scholars when they applied form criticism to the gospels."[11] We shall briefly relate some of the reasons for mistrusting Eusebius' account of Origen along with the nature of his sources before sketching an outline of Origen's life.

Eusebius was, in many respects, in a unique position to compose a life of Origen. He was a devoted Origenist, bishop in the very city in which Origen had spent his last years teaching, preaching, and writing. He had collaborated with Pamphilus in composing an *Apology for Origen* in six books, the sixth of which he had completed after Pamphilus' death as a martyr in 309.[12] Pamphilus had collected an ecclesiastical library at Caesarea containing Origen's works and those of other Christian authors. Eusebius had drawn up a catalogue of this collection.[13] He had himself assembled over a hundred of

---

9 *Origène: sa vie, son oeuvre, sa pensée*, 3 vols. (Paris: Éditions Ernest Leroux, 1923–28), 1.1. Hereinafter referred to as de Faye, *Origène*. For the other sources, which are largely inconsequential, of Origen's biography see P. Nautin, *Origène: sa vie et son oeuvre* (Paris: Beauchesne, 1977), 99–224. Nautin's work is hereinafter cited as Nautin, *Origène*.

10 Ibid., 19–98, 413–41.

11 "A Decade of Origen Studies," 23.

12 *H.E.* 6.33.4. (All references to Eusebius, *H.E.* follow the numbering found in the edition of E. Schwartz.) This *Apology* has perished. We know something of its contents from two sources. The translation of the first book into Latin by Rufinus is extant (PG 17. 541–614). This first book is concerned almost exclusively with Origen's theology and provides no significant biographical information. Photius is our other source of information about the contents of this apology. He read the entire work and made notes on his reading. These notes have been preserved. For an analysis of these works see Nautin, *Origène*, 99–153. Eusebius makes three other references to the *Apology* for fuller details on various aspects of Origen's life (*H.E.* 6.23.4; 32.3; 36.4).

13 *H.E.* 6.32.3.

Origen's letters.[14] There were, in addition, stories about Origen handed down orally by some of Origen's students and by some older men of Eusebius' day.[15] It is assumed that these older men had known Origen, though Eusebius never actually says this.

There were, therefore, abundant resources available for Eusebius to utilize in composing his account of Origen. He was, moreover, a man who made extensive use of sources. B. Gustafsson says "he very seldom worked without a source."[16] He did not follow the Thucydidean practice of composing speeches for his characters.[17]

Nevertheless, Eusebius' account of Origen must be used with great caution. He wrote as a devotee of Origen's theology at a time when that theology was under attack by a large portion of the Church. De Faye recognized his tendency to excessive statements in praise of Origen.[18] Grant calls attention to certain apologetic purposes that are evident in part of Eusebius' account, and to the fact that the *Apology for Origen* written by Pamphilus and Eusebius underlies much of his account in the *Church History*.[19] Nautin thinks the first part of Eusebius' description of Origen is based, in part, on a letter that Origen had written to Alexander, bishop of Jerusalem, to defend himself against the attacks of Demetrius, bishop of

---

14 *H.E.* 6.36.3.

15 *H.E.* 6.2.1; 33.4. The Greek text in the latter reference has *hoi presbyteroi*, i.e. the elders. Nautin, *Origène*, 20, translates "*vieillards*," but raises the possibility that they may have been priests.

16 "Eusebius' Principles in Handling His Sources as Found in His Church History," *Studia Patristica* 4 (1961), 429. Hereinafter cited as "Eusebius' Principles."

17 See R. Grant, *Eusebius as Church Historian* (Oxford: Clarendon Press, 1980), 63. This work is hereinafter cited as Grant, *Eusebius*.

18 *Origène*, 1:2.

19 *Eusebius*, 81–82; "The Case Against Eusebius or, Did the Father of the Church History Write History?" *Studia Patristica* 12, Part 1 (1975), 418; "Early Alexandrian Christianity," *Church History* 40 (1971): 134; "Eusebius and His Lives of Origen," *Forma Futuri: Studi in Onore del Cardinale Michele Pellegrino* (Torino: Bottega d'LErasmo, 1975), 637–39; 641–47. The last two works are hereinafter cited respectively as Grant, "Early Alexandrian Christianity," and Grant, "Eusebius and His Lives of Origen." We will discuss these apologetic themes later.

Alexandria.[20] All of this suggests that Eusebius' depiction of Origen is skewed.

Eusebius' use of oral sources also raises a red flag. It must be said to Eusebius' credit that, for the most part, he identifies his sources as written or oral by the way he introduces them. The oral sources can be identified by such introductory phrases as "they say," or "it is said."[21] Nautin calls attention to two problems connected with these oral sources.[22] First, when Eusebius refers to the older men as being "of our day," he is not affirming that they are alive while he is writing. This phrase in Eusebius, he asserts, refers to the whole period of time since his own birth. Nor does the fact that he uses the plural necessarily mean that there were several, since he sometimes uses the plural of indetermination to refer to a single person. Second, the stories Eusebius relates from these sources are hagiological. Some of the material, Nautin thinks, was invented for edification.[23]

The majority of Eusebius' sources, however, were written. "He was," Grant says, "a man of books and libraries."[24] He mentions the extensive ecclesiastical correspondence in the library at Jerusalem founded by Alexander, as well as the library at Caesarea gathered by Pamphilus.[25] He cites letters,[26] Origen's published works,[27] a record of one of Origen's debates,[28] Porphyry's comments about Origen,[29] notes in Origen's own hand in the front of some of his works,[30] and other unidentified written sources.[31] It is these written sources, most

---

20 *Origène*, 22–24. This letter will be discussed later.
21 Indications of oral sources occur in the following passages in relation to Origen: *H.E.* 6.1.1, *ho legomenos*; 6.2.11, *phasin*; 6.2.11, *mnēmoneuousin*; 6.3.12, *legetai*; 6.33.4, *mnēmē paradidoasin*; 6.36.1, *phasin*.
22 *Origène*, 20–21.
23 Ibid., 35, 41.
24 *Eusebius*, 63.
25 *H.E.* 6.20.1; 32.3.
26 *H.E.* 6.2.1; 2.6; 14.8; 19.11; 20.1; 28.1; 31.1; 36.3; 39.5.
27 *H.E.* 6.24.1,2,3; 25.1,6,7,11; 38.1.
28 *H.E.* 6.33.3.
29 *H.E.* 6.19.8.
30 *H.E.* 6.24.3.
31 *H.E.* 6.3.1; 4.3; 14.10; 17.1.

of which have been preserved nowhere else, that make the
Church History such an important source for the life of Origen.

Even the written sources in Eusebius, however, cannot be
accepted uncritically. Gustafsson has pointed out that Eusebius did not "differentiate between primary and secondary
sources," and that "we cannot always be sure that he had seen
and directly used the writings that he mentioned."[32] Grant has
shown that the *Apology for Origen* underlies much of Eusebius'
account of Origen in the *Church History*.[33] In those places where
he is dependent on the *Apology* Eusebius probably did not
check the sources themselves behind it.[34] There are also two
adverbs which Eusebius sometimes uses in his introductions of
written sources that suggest he did not have the material
before him as he wrote. The first is the enclitic adverb *pou*,
which means somewhere. He uses it in the following phrases in
relation to Origen: "as he himself says somewhere with the
very word"; "as he himself also relates somewhere in writing";
"as he himself says somewhere"; "he himself writes somewhere."[35] The other is the enclitic adverb *pōs*, which Eusebius
joins three times with the adverb *hōde* in introducing written
sources concerning Origen.[36] The combination means:
"somewhat as follows." The use of these adverbs suggests that
Eusebius has seen the material he is citing, but that he has not
bothered, or has not been able, to check it out as he writes. This
means that in those seven passages, at least, while Eusebius
cites written sources as his authority, he is in actuality relying
on his memory.

This data about Eusebius' account of Origen's life which
recent research has brought to light envelops many of the
details of our already somewhat sketchy knowledge of that life

---

32 "Eusebius' Principles," 430.
33 See above, n. 19.
34 Pamphilus probably knew Origen's works well since he had had the
   interest to collect them at Caesarea. The fact that he was in prison when he
   composed the *Apology*, however, raises the possibility that in parts of the
   work, at least, he was relying on his memory and did not have the sources
   before him as he wrote.
35 *H.E.* 6.2.14; 3.1; 4.3; 14.10.
36 *H.E.* 6.25.1,3; 38.1.

with an impenetrable fog. It has, nevertheless, like the white lines on a pavement, made some of the boundaries and directions of his life more certainly discernible. We shall attempt, in the outline of his life which follows, to make clear where the road can actually be seen and where it is only surmised.

Origen at Alexandria

Origen was born ca. A.D. 185.[37] Though Eusebius does not mention his birth or birthplace, it is assumed, because his story of Origen's youth is set in Alexandria, that he was born in that city. We know very little about Origen's childhood. Porphyry says he was born and educated as a Greek.[38] Eusebius denies this, asserting that he was raised as a Christian.[39] That Origen's parents were either Christians when he was born or were converted to Christianity during his childhood is fairly certain since the martyrdom of Origen's father as a Christian is attested in a letter of Origen which Eusebius claims to have used.[40]

Grant has detected four apologetic themes which structure Eusebius' story of Origen's childhood: (1) his zeal for martyrdom, (2) his devotion to the study of the Scriptures, (3) his dislike of heresy and heretics, and (4) his philosophical and ascetic way of life.[41] By comparing Photius' notes on the *Apology*

---

37 Nautin, *Origène*, 363–64, 413. Eusebius' chronology is confused in relation to Origen's early years. See Grant, "Eusebius and His Lives of Origen," 641, and T. Barnes, "Origen, Aquila, and Eusebius," *Harvard Studies in Classical Philology* 74 (1970): 313–16.

38 Quoted in *H.E.* 6.19.7.

39 *H.E.* 6.19.9–10.

40 *H.E.* 6.2.6. We should not assume that Eusebius had seen the actual letter Origen wrote to his father who was in prison. What Eusebius probably saw was a reference to this event in a letter Origen wrote later. See Nautin, *Origène*, 35. De Faye, *Origène*, 3, argues that Origen's father had converted to Christianity after Origen's birth on the basis that the persecution of Severus was intended to put an end to proselytizing by both the Jews and Christians. Hence, he concludes it did not affect those who had been Christians from birth. See also W. Frend, "A Severan Persecution? Evidence of the 'Historia Augusta,' " *Forma Futuri: Studi in Onore del Cardinale Michele Pellegrino* (Torino: Bottega d'Erasmo, 1975), 470–80.

41 *Eusebius*, 81–82; cf. Grant, "Eusebius and His Lives of Origen," 641–45.

for Origen by Pamphilus and Eusebius, he has been able to demonstrate that this portion of Eusebius' *Church History* is dependent on that *Apology*.[42] The ultimate source of much of this material, furthermore, was hearsay.[43]

Without endorsing the exaggerated claims Eusebius makes, it seems that the following assertions about Origen's youth can be accepted as quite probably factual, based on their harmony with Origen's later achievements. Origen's education in the Scriptures was begun quite early and may have been supervised by his father.[44] His broad knowledge of the Bible demonstrated in his commentaries and homilies gives evidence of a mind that has lived in the Bible for years. He also received the standard education for a boy in that day.[45] We may reasonably assume that he progressed exceptionally well in both these educational endeavors. He may also have shown some ascetic tendencies in his youth since Egypt was the seedbed of Christian asceticism and Origen displayed tendencies in this direction later.[46]

Sometime around Origen's sixteenth or seventeenth year his father was martyred in Alexandria.[47] Again, given the veneration of martyrs in the ancient Church and Origen's later treatise, *Exhortation to Martyrdom*, we may tentatively accept Eusebius' assertion that Origen desired to share his father's fate, while doubting the embellishments of the story.[48] After

---

42 Ibid., 637–39; 645–47. Grant, *Eusebius*, 77, seems to have changed his mind slightly later in regard to Photius' notes on the *Apology* of Pamphilus representing a trustworthy report of the contents of that *Apology*. He appears to agree with Nautin, *Origène*, 99–108, who thinks Photius' notes on Origen blend material from the *Apology*, Eusebius' *Church History*, Jerome's *De viris inlustribus*, and some conjectures by Photius himself. Grant is still able to maintain, however, that the *Apology* is an important source for this section of the *Church History*.

43 See *H.E.* 6.2.1,11; 3.12.

44 Cf. *H.E.* 6.2.7.

45 Ibid.

46 Cf. *H.E.* 6.3.9–12.

47 See Grant, "Eusebius and His Lives of Origen," 641; *H.E.* 6.1.1; 2.2–6,12 and our note 40, above. Nautin, *Origène*, 414, thinks it was the martyrdom of his father more than anything else which kept Origen in the Church throughout his life.

48 If the persecution by Severus was directed at proselytes, however, and

the death of his father, Eusebius asserts, Origen was left destitute with his mother and six younger brothers.[49] His father's property had been confiscated. Origen was taken in by a wealthy lady of Alexandria who made it possible for him to continue his secular education to the point that he was able to begin teaching and, thereby, provide the means for his living.[50]

After he had begun teaching secular subjects, Origen was approached by certain pagans who requested that he teach them "the word of God." Eusebius says this request came to Origen because those in charge of catechetical instruction at Alexandria had fled under the threat of persecution. He claims that this information comes from some writing of Origen.[51] Eusebius then asserts that Origen, in his eighteenth year, was appointed by Demetrius, bishop of Alexandria, to preside over the catechetical school there. Nautin thinks Eusebius has erred in his chronology and that the events described took place after the death of Severus in 211.[52] This means Origen was approximately twenty-six years old at the time rather than eighteen. Sometime later Origen ceased teaching secular subjects and devoted himself to sacred studies.[53] At this same time, according to Eusebius, Origen sold his secular library for a guaranteed income of four obols a day.[54]

Gustave Bardy has shown that Eusebius' tracing of the

Eusebius is correct in his assertion that Origen was raised as a Christian, then there is little likelihood that Origen could have been martyred in that persecution even had he zealously so desired. See above, n. 40, and *H.E.* 6.19.9–10.

49 *H.E.* 6.2.12–15.

50 *H.E.* 6.2.12–15. It is in this context that Eusebius introduces Origen's refusal to associate with a heretic who also resided with Origen's patroness.

51 *H.E.* 6.3.1. Grant, "Eusebius and His Lives of Origen," 642, thinks Eusebius is alluding here to what he quotes as a letter of Origen in *H.E.* 6.19.12: "As I was devoted to the word, and the fame of our proficiency was spreading, sometimes heretics approached me and sometimes those trained in Greek studies, especially in philosophy." Cf. P. Nautin, *Origène*, 36–37, 53–54; *Lettres et écrivains chrétiens des IIe et IIIe siécles* (Paris: les éditions du Cerf, 1961), 126–34, 245. The latter work is hereinafter cited as Nautin, *Lettres*.

52 *Origène*, 364–65, 417.

53 *H.E.* 6.3.3, 8. See Grant, "Early Alexandrian Christianity," 135, for the inaccuracy of Eusebius' chronology here.

54 *H.E.* 6.3.9.

heads of the Alexandrian catechetical school from Pantaenus
to Clement to Origen is mistaken.[55] Neither Pantaenus nor
Clement, he argues, ever headed a catechetical school. They
each had independent schools on the order of Justin's earlier
philosophical school in Rome. Origen had predecessors,
Bardy thinks, but they were obscure and unknown Christians.
Trigg, following Nautin and others, thinks that "Origen did
not consider himself an official catechist, even if Bishop Demetrius may have given his teaching a belated cachet."[56]

It is in the context of this period of Origen's teaching at
Alexandria that Eusebius relates the story of Origen's self-
castration.[57] The reliability of the story is debated. Eusebius
gives no indication of his source. Nautin assumes that his
source was a letter written by bishops Alexander of Jerusalem
and Theoctistus of Caesarea to Pontianus, bishop of Rome, to
defend their action in ordaining Origen. He argues that Demetrius' letter to "the bishops throughout the world"[58] would
have been intended primarily for the bishop of Rome. In this
letter, Demetrius, Nautin supposes, accused Alexander and
Theoctistus of an impropriety in ordaining a eunuch.[59] The
two bishops responded with a letter to Pontianus in which they
admitted that Origen had made a mistake, but argued (1) that
it had been done in his youth, (2) that he had done it thinking
he was obeying Matthew 19.12, and (3) that he had wanted to
avoid charges of misconduct from the pagans regarding his
relations with the women he taught.[60] This sounds very
reasonable, but we must note that it is all conjecture on
Nautin's part.[61] Chadwick, on the other hand, regards Eu-

---

55 H.E. 6.6.1. G. Bardy, "Aux origines de l'école d'Alexandrie," Recherches de
science religieuse 27 (1937): 65–90. See also M. Hornschuh, "Das Leben des
Origenes und die Entstehung der alexandrinischen Schule," Zietschrift für
Kirchengeschichte 71 (1960): 1–3.
56 J. Trigg, "The Charismatic Intellectual: Origen's Understanding of Religious Leadership," Church History 50 (1981): 5–6.
57 H.E. 6.8.1–2.
58 H.E. 6.8.4.
59 Cf. H.E. 6.8.5.
60 Nautin, Lettres, 121–26.
61 The only fragment from the letter of bishops Alexander and Theoctistus

sebius' story at this point as based on "an unwritten tradition."[62]
He calls attention to Origen's commentary on Matthew, written near the end of his life, "in which he deplores the fanat-
icism of exegetes who have interpreted Matthew 19.12 literally." Furthermore, he notes that Epiphanius knew a tradition
that attributed Origen's chastity to drugs. "Possibly both stories," Chadwick concludes, "were generated by no more than
malicious gossip." Grant calls attention to certain incon-
sistencies in Eusebius' account at this point.[63] First, the story "is
told with reference to the literal interpretation of Matthew
19.12 . . . while in discussing his very early interpretation of the
scriptures Eusebius has described how he [Origen] looked for
the deeper meaning." Second, Eusebius asserts that Origen
performed the deed to avoid slander while teaching women,
but on the other hand he says Origen "endeavored to keep his
action secret; Demetrius heard about it only later, and then
encouraged Origen to keep teaching (vi. 8, 2–3)."

After Origen sold his classical library and devoted himself
to the study of the Bible, he became dissatisfied with the
Septuagint and wished to learn the tenor of the Hebrew text.[64]
He turned to a Christian Jew from Palestine who was living in
Alexandria who was called simply, "the Hebrew." This man,
Nautin believes, exercised a tremendous influence on Origen.
There are numerous evidences of Jewish influence in Origen's
works.[65] Although Eusebius assures us that Origen made a
careful study of the Hebrew language, the modern opinion is

---

written in their defense against charges made by Demetrius is in *H.E.*
6.19.17. They defend themselves in this fragment only against the charge
of allowing a layman to "preach in the presence of bishops."
62 *Early Christian Thought,* 67–68.
63 "Eusebius and His Lives of Origen," 643–44.
64 Nautin, *Origène,* 417.
65 See, for example, G. Bardy, "Les traditions juives dans l'oeuvre d'Origène,"
Revue biblique 34 (1925): 217–52; B. Murmelstein, "Agadische Methode in
den Pentateuchhomilien des Origenes," *Jahresbericht israelitischtheologische
Lehranstalt* 37–39 (1929–32), 93–122, (hereinafter cited as Murmelstein);
N. De Lange, *Origen and the Jews* (Cambridge: Cambridge University Press,
1976), hereinafter cited as De Lange, *Origen and the Jews.* See also the
various places noted below in our translation of the homilies on Genesis and
Exodus.

that he knew very little Hebrew.[66] De Lange's view is justified: "No one has succeeded in establishing that Origen knew Hebrew well. My own assessment. . . is that Origen could not speak, read or write Hebrew, but that he had some basic knowledge of the structure of the language and was familiar with some Hebrew words."[67]

Around 215 Origen made a trip to Rome during the pontificate of Zephyrinus. Eusebius says Origen "writes somewhere" that he made this trip out of a desire "to see the most ancient Church of the Romans."[68] Nautin thinks this statement was made by Origen in self-defense, and that the trip was actually made from a desire to hear the numerous philosophers in the capital city and perhaps even to attempt to establish himself there in what he thought might be a freer intellectual environment.[69] He returned to Alexandria, however, sometime before the death of Zephyrinus in 217 and resumed his catechetical instruction.[70]

Sometime after Origen's return from Rome the Alexandrian school was reorganized with Origen instructing only the advanced students, and one of Origen's former students, Heraclas, instructing the beginners. Eusebius says that Origen initiated the reorganization.[71] Grant, however, assumes that the school was reorganized by Demetrius.[72] This seems likely, especially if Origen's trip to Rome had been undertaken with the intention of possibly residing there permanently. That

---

66 *H.E.* 6.16.1. See D. Barthélemy, "Origène et le texte de l'ancien testament," *Epektasis: mélanges patristiques offerts au cardinal Jean Daniélou* (Paris: Beauchesne, 1972): 254–55. There is evidence in the homilies on Genesis and Exodus that Origen knew very little Hebrew. For example, in *Gn. Hom.* 12.4 he is dependent on others for the meaning of Esau's name in Hebrew, and in *Ex. Hom.* 2.1 he confuses the name of one of the midwives with the name of Moses' wife. Both names are spelled the same in the Septuagint.
67 N. De Lange, "Jewish Influence on Origen," *Origeniana: premier colloque international des études origéniennes (Montserrat, 18–21 septembre, 1973)*, ed. H. Crouzel, G. Lomiento, J. Rius-Camps (Universitá di Bari: Istituto di letteratura cristiana antica, 1975), 229.
68 *H.E.* 6.14.10.
69 *Origène*, 365, 418.
70 *H.E.* 6.14.11.
71 *H.E.* 6.15.1.
72 R. Grant, *Augustus to Constantine* (New York: Harper & Row, 1970), 204.

would suggest that the conflict between Demetrius and himself was already smouldering. The reorganization of the school by Demetrius, then, may have been his first attempt to get more control over Origen's influence. Eusebius makes the choice of Heraclas that of Origen and points out that he was one of Origen's pupils. The fact that later, however, when Heraclas succeeded Demetrius as bishop· of Alexandria, he upheld Demetrius' condemnation of Origen suggests the possibility, at least, that he may not have been a great devotee of Origen even at this point and could have been selected by Demetrius as one in sympathy with his own views.

Eusebius mentions a military official who was sent to Demetrius from the ruler of Arabia with letters requesting that Origen be sent for an interview with him.[73] Nautin thinks that Origen had become known through his treatises such as the *Stromateis* and *On the Resurrection*. Eusebius says he had seen a note in Origen's hand in the front of these volumes showing that they were written in Alexandria during the reign of Alexander Severus (222–35).[74] On this basis Nautin posits that this trip to Arabia occurred towards the latter part of the period 222–29, several years after Origen's trip to Rome.[75]

Nautin places the writing of Origen's *Commentary on Genesis* and *On First Principles* in the period after he returned from Arabia, but before he left for Palestine. Eusebius, includes *On First Principles* among those volumes written in the reign of Alexander on the basis of notes he had seen in Origen's hand in the volumes.[76] Nautin thinks these two works precipitated Origen's departure to Palestine.[77] He argues as follows. First,

---

73 *H.E.* 6.19.15.
74 *H.E.* 6.24.3. We will not attempt to mention or date all of Origen's works in the course of this brief outline of his life, but only those which contribute something significant to his biography. Many of the dates for his works are tenuous and a large portion of his works has perished. A list of his extant works is given below in our section, "The Preservation of Origen's Works." Dates for many of his works can be found in a convenient list in Nautin, *Origène*, 409–12.
75 *Origène*, 365–66, 420–21.
76 *H.E.* 6.24.3. That the early part of the *Comm. Gn.* preceeded *De Princ.* is clearly shown by the reference to that commentary in *De Princ.* 2.3.6.
77 *Origène*, 366–70, 423–25.

Eusebius' statement that Origen left Alexandria for Palestine
because "no small warfare broke out again in the city" should
not be taken as a reference to the massacre under Caracalla in
215, but as a reference to the conflict between Demetrius and
Origen.[78] This conflict, Nautin supposes, flared up over the
opening chapters of Origen's *Commentary on Genesis* which
allegorized the creation story. Origen may then have inter-
rupted his work on the commentary to compose *On First
Principles* in defense of his exegesis and doctrines. Book four of
On First Principles seeks to defend the allegorical interpretation
of Scripture, and the other books contain indications that they
were written when Origen had been accused of heterodoxy.
This treatise, the stumbling stone of Origenism through the
centuries, had the effect on the conflict with Demetrius that
gasoline has on fire. The conflict exploded. *On First Principles*
confirmed Demetrius' suspicions. Origen withdrew to Palestine and took refuge with Alexander, bishop of Jerusalem,
and Theoctistus, bishop of Caesarea. The former bishop had
already been at odds with Demetrius for some time, a factor
which may have been significant in Origen's choice of Palestine
for his retreat.[79]

Once in Palestine, Eusebius relates, Origen was invited by
both bishops to preach in the Church.[80] His source of information is a letter, written later by Alexander and Theoctistus
to defend themselves against Demetrius' charge that they had
allowed a layman to preach in the presence of bishops. Demetrius, sometime later, recalled Origen to Alexandria by
letter and by an embassy of deacons.[81] Some kind of peaceful
overture must have been made by Demetrius, for Origen
returned to Alexandria.[82] It is this interlude in the conflict,
Nautin believes, that Origen alludes to in book six of his
Commentary on John when he says, "We proceeded as far as the
fifth volume in spite of the obstacles presented by the storm in

---

78 *H.E.* 6.19.16.
79 See Nautin, *Lettres*, 120.
80 *H.E.* 6.19.16–17.
81 *H.E.* 6.19.19.
82 Ibid.

Alexandria, . . . for Jesus rebuked the winds and the waves of the sea."[83] On returning to Alexandria, then, Origen undertook the composition of the *Commentary on John* for his wealthy patron Ambrose.[84] This appears to be the meaning of Origen's remarks in the opening of the first book of that commentary when he refers to a recent "bodily separation" which he and Ambrose have experienced, and then says this commentary is "the first fruits of our activity, *since the time when we came to Alexandria*."[85] The calm in the storm, however, was short-lived, lasting, perhaps, only a few months before breaking out with new bitterness and intensity. Origen then left Alexandria permanently. He refers to his departure as his exodus from Egypt: "We emerged from the storm, we were brought out of Egypt, that God delivering us who led his people forth from there."[86]

Nautin also places Origen's visit to Antioch at the invitation of the emperor's mother in the brief interlude between Origen's return from Palestine and his final departure from Alexandria.[87] His chronology for this period of Origen's life is as follows.[88] Origen withdrew to Palestine first sometime in 230. His stay may have lasted from a few months to over a year. He returned to Alexandria in 231 where he stayed a few months and dictated the first four books of the *Commentary on John*. At the invitation of the emperor's mother, Mamaea, who was spending the winter of 231–32 at Antioch, he went to Antioch. There he composed the fifth book of the *Commentary on John* and sent it to Ambrose. In the spring of 232 Origen returned to Alexandria where the intensity of his conflict with

83 *Comm. Jn.* 6.2.(1).8, translation in ANF 10.349. (All references to Origen's *Comm. Jn.* follow the numbering found in the edition of J. Preuschen.)
84 *H.E.* 6.18.1; 23.1–2, relates that Origen had converted Ambrose from Valentinian Gnosticism, and that Ambrose provided Origen with stenographers, along with motivation, to write his commentaries.
85 *Comm. Jn.*1.2(4).12–13, translation in ANF 10.298.
86 *Comm. Jn.* 6.2.(1).8, translation in ANF 10.350.
87 *Origène*, 367, based on the reference to another separation between Origen and Ambrose in the preface to *Comm. Jn.* 5.1. Cf. Eusebius, *H.E.* 6.21.3.
88 Nautin, *Origène*, 68–69, 368. See also Grant, "Early Alexandrian Christianity," 135.

Demetrius forced him to leave. He then departed for Greece via Palestine where he was ordained at Caesarea.[89]

Demetrius' reaction to the news of Origen's ordination was swift and extensive. Eusebius makes only a veiled passing allusion to it.[90] Nautin has reconstructed a convincing schema of the events.[91] Demetrius wrote a letter to Pope Pontianus in which he protested Origen's ordination by the bishops of Palestine.[92] Pontianus concurred.[93] Theoctistus and Alexander responded with a letter to Pontianus in which they defended their actions.[94] Alexander sent a messenger to Origen at Athens who informed him of the condemnation. This prompted Origen to write a lengthy autobiographical letter in defense of himself to Alexander.[95] Alexander responded with a short note to Origen in which he reassured him of his continued friendship.[96] Origen also sent a letter from Athens to his friends in Alexandria in which he complained (1) that some of his enemies asserted that he taught that the devil would be saved, which he denied, (2) that a heretic had corrupted a transcript of a debate with himself and had published it as a verbatim copy, and (3) that another heretic had written a treatise and published it in Origen's name. This latter treatise, he says, had reached Rome.[97]

Origen went to Athens, Nautin believes, with the intention

---

89 *H.E.* 6.23.3–4; 26.1. Cf. Nautin, *Origène*, 65–70.

90 *H.E.* 6.23.4.

91 See *Origène*, 429–31; *Lettres*, 121–34.

92 *H.E.* 6.8.4. See our discussion above, p. 10.

93 See Jerome, *Ep.* 33.4: Origen "stands condemned by his bishop, Demetrius, only the bishops of Palestine, Arabia, Phoenicia, and Achaia dissenting. Imperial Rome consents to his condemnation. . . ."

94 The only extant fragment of this letter is in *H.E.* 6.19.17–18. Nautin assumes that *H.E.* 6.8.1–5 also reflects the contents of that letter.

95 *H.E.* 6.19.11–14 may be a fragment of that letter. Nautin thinks this letter provided much of the information for Eusebius' account of Origen's earlier life.

96 *H.E.* 6.14.8–9.

97 This letter is preserved in Rufinus, *Liber de adulteratione librorum Origenis* (PG 17.624A–626B), and indicates that Origen was in Athens when he wrote it. See Nautin, *Origène*, 161–68. Nautin thinks that Demetrius had died and that Heraclas was bishop of Alexandria when Origen wrote this letter.

of settling there in the famous intellectual city.[98] The questions and controversies that Demetrius had succeeded in raising, however, made him aware that it would be difficult for him to establish himself and have an effective ministry in a new place. He chose, therefore, to return to his friends of long-standing in Palestine and to reside at Caesarea where he had been ordained as a priest. This he did sometime probably in 234.

Origen at Caesarea

One of Origen's first undertakings at Caesarea seems to have been the completion of his *Commentary on John* for Ambrose. In the preface to the sixth book of that commentary, he refers, as we already noted, to his having come out of Egypt. The storm has subsided; he is again settled, composed, and ready to work.

> I now make this second beginning and enter on my sixth volume, because what I wrote before at Alexandria has not, I know not by what chance, been brought with me. I feared I might neglect this work, *if I were not engaged on it at once*, and therefore thought it better to make use of this present time and begin without delay the part which remains.[99]

The persecution which broke out in 235 under Maximin affected Ambrose and prompted Origen to write his *Exhortation to Martyrdom*.[100] This persecution ended with Maximin's death in 238. It may have been at this period, when peace had returned to the Church, that Origen began receiving students at Caesarea.[101] Eusebius mentions Theodore, whom he identifies with Gregory Thaumaturgus, and his brother Athenodore. Nautin has shown that Eusebius' identification is incorrect and that they were, indeed, two separate persons, neither

---

98 *Origène*, 431.
99 *Comm. Jn.* 6.2.11–12, translation in ANF 10.350.
100 *Mart.* 1; *H.E.* 6.27.1.
101 See *H.E.* 6.30.1.

of whom was Gregory Thaumaturgus.[102] One was the Gregory to whom Origen addressed a letter when he left his school; the other, Theodore, wrote the *Panegyric* on Origen. These two latter documents allow us to gain some idea of the nature and goals of Origen's instruction at Caesarea.

> Commencing with grammar and rhetoric, a student then moved to the sciences including physics, mathematics, geometry and astronomy. Having thus opened up the secrets of the natural world, its variety and structure as well as the reasons for change, one then progressed to the important field of philosophy, commencing with an analysis of the moral life. Origen's aim was not merely to define and classify feelings and emotions, but rather to mould a student's character.[103]

In his letter to Gregory, Origen says,

> I should like to see you use all the resources of your mind on Christianity and make that your ultimate object. I hope that to that end you will take from Greek philosophy everything capable of serving as an introduction to Christianity and from geometry and astronomy all ideas useful in expounding the Holy Scriptures; so that what...philosophers say of geometry, music, grammar, rhetoric, and astronomy, that they assist philosophy, we too may be able to say of philosophy itself in relation to Christianity.[104]

Origen made several intermittent trips during his residence at Caesarea, but they cannot be dated with any precision. He visited Caesarea in Cappadocia at the invitation of Bishop Firmilian, another of his students.[105] He was invited by certain bishops in Arabia to participate in discussions with Beryllus, bishop of Bostra, whose doctrine had gone astray.[106] Scherer

---

102 *Origène*, 81–86, 183–97.
103 L. Levine, *Caesarea Under Roman Rule* (Leiden: E. J. Brill, 1975), 123. Hereinafter cited as Levine, *Caesarea*.
104 *Epistle to Gregory*, 1, PG 11.87B, translation in Levine, *Caesarea*, 123.
105 *H.E.* 6.27.1.
106 *H.E.* 6.33.1–3.

places the *Dialogue of Origen with Heraclides*, another straying bishop assumed also to be in Arabia, tentatively in the period 244–49.[107] Eusebius places a trip to Athens in this period also, where "he finished the commentary on Ezekiel, and began that on the Song of Songs."[108]

Origen's preaching at Caesarea is of primary concern for our purposes. Unfortunately, the evidence both for the dates and places the various sermons were delivered is very tenuous. It seems quite probable that the extant homilies were all delivered at Caesarea, with the exception of those on 1 Samuel which appear to have been delivered in Jerusalem.[109] Eusebius relates that "Alexander, who presided over the Church of Jerusalem, and Theoctistus, who presided at Caesarea, continued their attendance on him the whole time, as their only teacher, and used to concede to him the task of expounding the divine Scriptures, and the other parts of the Church's instruction."[110] Nautin has reconstructed a complicated, but convincing, it seems to me, schema of Origen's preaching in which he correlates "the delivery of his homilies with what is known of the liturgical practice of the Church of his day."[111] Because of its direct relation to the subject of this volume, I shall summarize Nautin's argument in the paragraphs which follow.[112]

Drawing on bits of information in Pamphilus' *Apology*, Socrates' *Church History*, the *Didache*, the *Apostolic Tradition*, Tertullian's works, and Origen's homilies, Nautin reconstructs the weekly services of the Church at Caesarea in the first half of the third century. There were two types of services, a eucharistic and a noneucharistic.[113] The noneucharistic assembly met

---

107 J. Scherer, *Entretien d'Origène avec Héraclide*, SC 67 (Paris: les éditions du Cerf, 1960), 19–21.
108 *H.E.* 6.32.2.
109 See Nautin, *Origène*, 405, 434.
110 *H.E.* 6.27.1.
111 R. Hanson's review of P. Nautin, *Origène, sa vie et son oeuvre*, *The Journal of Theological Studies*, ns. 29 (1978): 556.
112 *Origène*, 389–409.
113 See also P. Nautin and P. Husson, *Origène: homélies sur Jérémie*, SC 232 (Paris: les éditions du Cerf, 1976), 1.100–112, hereinafter cited as Nautin, *Homélies sur Jérémie*.

every morning except Sunday for the reading of a lengthy passage from the Old Testament and a homily on the passage read.[114] These daily assemblies were for both the faithful and catechumens. The Gospels were not read in these assemblies because, in those days, catechumens were not admitted to the reading of the Gospel until the last weeks preceeding their baptism.[115] These readings and homilies proceeded systematically through the Old Testament. Based on the average number of verses covered in Origen's homilies on the Old Testament, Nautin concludes that the entire Old Testament would have been covered in approximately three years, which, according to the *Apostolic Tradition* 17, corresponds to the length of the catechetical instruction.

Eucharistic services were held every Sunday morning and every Wednesday and Friday evenings. The evening eucharistic services marked the end of the fast on those days. The Sunday services had three readings from Scripture, the Gospel reading, a reading from either the Acts or the Epistles, and an Old Testament reading. Each of these readings, Nautin thinks, was followed by a short homily. He bases this on the fact that Origen's homilies on Luke, on the average, are only about a third as long as those on the Old Testament. Since he assumes the homilies on Luke were delivered following the Gospel reading, he concludes that there would have been time for three homilies of such length.

Using the average number of verses covered by each of Origen's homilies on Luke, Nautin determines that it would have taken nine years to read through the four Gospels if they were read only in the Sunday service. He concludes that they must have been read at all three weekly eucharistic services and were, therefore, covered also in a three year cycle. The Acts and the epistles formed a separate cycle on which we have no direct information, but given the two preceeding cycles, it is reasonable to assume that this cycle, too, had a duration of three years.

---

114 See Origen, *Hom. Josh.* 4.1.
115 *Apostolic Tradition* 20.

This liturgical cycle, Nautin thinks, means that all of Origen's homilies on the Old Testament were delivered in the space of three years, for there is no reason to suppose that he was charged with the cycle twice in succession. The same was probably true for his New Testament homilies as well. In fact, Nautin thinks it is probable that Origen's homilies on the Old Testament and the New Testament were delivered in the same three year cycle, and that Origen had charge of all the preaching at Caesarea for one three year period.

In attempting to date the period in which Origen delivered his homilies, Nautin begins by dismissing as erroneous Eusebius' statement that Origen was sixty years old before he permitted his homilies to be recorded by stenographers.[116] This statement by Eusebius has long hampered Origen scholars in dating the homilies. R. P. C. Hanson, for example, who has the most extensive treatment in English of the dating of Origen's works, noticed that in the *Commentary on the Song of Songs* Origen refers to his homilies on Judges, on Exodus, and on Numbers, and to a work on Leviticus, but hesitated to date these homilies before 244, the date given to the *Commentary on the Song of Songs*.[117] He concluded that it was "safer" to assume that the reference was not to the homilies known to us, and to place those homilies we have on these books between 246 (when Origen would have been 60) and 255.

Nautin also dismisses as incorrect the identification of the allusion to persecution in the ninth homily on Joshua with the persecution under Decius.[118] His primary reason for dismissing this identification is that there are no references to any martyrs in the homily and no exhortation to faithfulness under trial, but simply an allegorization of the narrative of Joshua. This, Nautin reasonably observes, is very strange if these homilies were delivered during or near the time of the Decian persecution.

After dismissing the two previous dates usually used for

116 *Origène*, 401.
117 *Origen's Doctrine of Tradition* (London: S.P.C.K., 1954), 22. Hereinafter cited as Hanson, *Tradition*.
118 *Origène*, 401–402; *Hom. Josh.* 9.10.

dating Origen's homilies, Nautin then establishes a relative chronology for the Old Testament homilies on the basis of cross references to other homilies made in them. The series on the prophetic books, Isaiah, Jeremiah, and Ezekiel, was after the series on the books of wisdom: Psalms, Job, Proverbs, Ecclesiastes, Song of Songs, because (1) homilies eight and eighteen on Jeremiah refer to homilies on Psalms 134 and 140, and (2) homily six on Ezekiel refers to a homily on Job.[119] The series on the historical books, Genesis, Exodus, Leviticus, Numbers, Deuteronomy, Joshua, Judges, is not only after that on the wisdom books (homily thirteen on Leviticus and homily fifteen on Joshua refer to homilies on Psalms 101 and 118), but also after that on the prophetic books, since (1) homily thirteen on Joshua refers to the homilies on Jeremiah, and (2) homily twelve on Jeremiah shows that it preceeded the homilies on Numbers.[120]

These internal cross references, therefore, show that the Old Testament was read and explained in the order: (1) Wisdom books: Psalms, Job, Proverbs, Ecclesiastes, Song of Songs, (2) Prophetic books: Isaiah, Jeremiah, Ezekiel, and (3) Historical books: Genesis, Exodus, Leviticus, Numbers, Deuteronomy, Joshua, Judges, 1 Samuel. Nautin believes, from this schedule, that Origen began to preach when the liturgical cycle of readings had arrived at Psalms. He, therefore, preached successively on the books of wisdom, the prophets, and then went to the beginning of the cycle and took up the historical books with Genesis.[121]

Finally, Nautin attempts to date this three year cycle of

---

119 Nautin, *Origène*, 403.
120 Ibid.
121 Nautin, *Origène*, 405, raises the possibility that Origen may have been relieved of his preaching duties by Theoctistus before he completed the three year cycle. He bases this possibility on three pieces of evidence. (1) There is no evidence of any homilies on the historical books by Origen beyond 1 Samuel. (2) The homilies on 1 Samuel appear to have been delivered at Jerusalem instead of Caesarea. (3) The sermons show that there was criticism of Origen's exegesis and theology. Perhaps, because of the criticism, Theoctistus decided to replace Origen before he finished the cycle.

Origen's sermons on the basis of two references within them. The first is in his first homily on Psalm thirty-six, a homily which belongs to the beginning of the relative chronology Nautin established.[122] The passage reads:

> Behold who ruled thirty years ago, how his rule flourished, but suddenly "like the flower of the grass" he withered away; then another after him, then another and another, who next became rulers and princes and "all their glory" and honor withered away, not only "as the flower," but also as dry dust and was scattered by the wind. Not even a vestige remained of it.[123]

The reference to the one who ruled thirty years ago, Nautin thinks, is to Septimius Severus.[124] That would make the homily delivered, and consequently the cycle of Origen's preaching begun, sometime in the reign of Gordian (238–44), and probably towards the beginning of his reign.

The other reference which suggests a definite date for the homilies is in the *Commentary on the Song of Songs*. There Origen mentions the homilies on Judges, which would have been among the last in the series Origen preached. Nautin dates the *Commentary on the Song of Songs* in 245, and thinks it was written, as Eusebius says, in Athens.[125] Nautin then proposes that Origen's homilies were delivered at Caesarea in one of the following three year periods: 238–41, 239–42, 240–43, or 241–44. He opts for one of the first two periods on grounds that are rather tenuous. Delivery of the homilies sometime between 238 and 244, however, seems highly likely to me.

---

122 *Origène*, 404.

123 PG 12.1323AB.

124 Hanson's, *Tradition*, 17, objection to taking this as a reference to Severus seems unjustified. First, he takes it to be "straining language to describe Severus, who died a natural death, as cast down." "Cast down" seems to be too violent a meaning to give to the verb *emarcuit* ("withered away"). Origen is following the text of Is 40.6–7 which speaks of the frailty of flesh. His other objection is based on Eusebius' assertion that Origen did not permit his homilies to be taken down until he was sixty years old, which is dubious.

125 *H.E.* 6.32.2.

It should be noted that everything in Nautin's scheme depends on previous conclusions he has reached. He has constructed a house of interlocking arguments from a few scraps of evidence. It is an ingeniously constructed edifice put together from "gold, silver, precious stones, wood, hay, straw."[126] Undoubtedly portions will perish in the heat of future debates, but it seems doubtful that the whole building will be lost.

Origen's Death

In 249 Decius became emperor and undertook to revive the ancient paganism.[127] An edict was issued demanding that all people offer sacrifices to the gods. Fabian, bishop of Rome was executed. Alexander of Jerusalem and Fabius of Antioch were imprisoned for refusing to offer sacrifice; both died in prison. Chaeremon of Nilopolis, Cyprian of Carthage and Gregory Thaumaturgus of Pontus fled their cities. In Caesarea, Origen was imprisoned and tortured. He did not, however, die in prison. Decius was killed in 251. The persecution continued sporadically until 253 when Valerian came to power and a brief peace returned to the Church. Origen probably died early in the reign of Valerian.

Photius reports two traditions about Origen's death.[128] The one, coming from Pamphilus, said he was a martyr in the persecution of Decius. This would have made his death ca. 250–51 at about sixty-six years of age. The other tradition says he died at Tyre at age sixty-nine, i.e. ca. 254 or 255. Grant has shown that Eusebius originally described Origen's death as a martyrdom in the reign of Decius.[129] He thinks that Eusebius, later became aware of Origen's tomb at Tyre and rewrote the

---

126 1 Cor 3.13.
127 See Grant, *Augustus to Constantine*, 168–70; *H.E.* 6.39–46.
128 See Grant, "Eusebius and His Lives of Origen," 647–49; Grant, *Eusebius*, 78–79.
129 "Eusebius and His Lives of Origen," 647–48; *H.E.* 6.39.5.

ending of Origen's life, but without removing all the traces of his earlier view.[130]

The Preservation of Origen's Works

Origen's literary output was truly prodigious.[131] Epiphanius estimated his works to number six thousand.[132] Jerome, basing his statement on the list of Origen's works Eusebius had inserted in Book 3 of his *Life of Pamphilus*,[133] puts the number under two thousand.[134] There is a list of 786 titles of Origen's works in Jerome's letter to Paula.[135] A number of titles of Origen's works can also be found in Eusebius, *Church History* 6.

The largest portion of this vast literary production has perished. Some perished, no doubt, because of the vastness of the work itself. There was simply too much to copy.[136] Jerome

---

130 *Ibid.; H.E.* 7.1.
131 B. Altaner, *Patrology*, trans, H. Graef, 2nd ed. (New York; Herder and Herder, 1961), 225 says the quantity of his literary output surpasses "that of all other writers of Christian antiquity." For the most recent German edition of this work, see B. Altaner, A. Stuiber, *Patrologie* (Freiburg: Herder, 1978).
132 *Haereses* 64.63.
133 This work has perished.
134 *Adv. Ruf.* 2.22.
135 *Ep.* 33.
136 Rufinus, in the preface to his translation of the *Commentary on Romans*, mentions that he had been asked to abbreviate as well as translate the commentary, and that even at that time some books of the lengthy work were missing. Jerome, *Ep.* 34, laments that Origen's notes on Psalm 127 are no longer extant. In the prologue to his *Commentary on Isaiah* Jerome notes that the twenty-sixth book of Origen's *Commentary on Isaiah* is missing. It is quite probable that the huge *Hexapla* was never copied in its entirety (See Johannes Quasten, *Patrology*, vol 2 [Westminster, Md.: The Newman Press, 1953], 44). Of the thirty-two books of his *Commentary on John*, only eight have been preserved, and of the twenty-five on Matthew, only eight have been preserved in Greek plus a larger portion in a Latin translation. In both cases it is more likely that it was their size rather than their contents which caused these works to be preserved in abbreviated form. P. Courcelle, *Late Latin Writers and Their Greek Sources*, trans. H. Wedech (Cambridge: Harvard University Press, 1969), 103–4, notes the difference in the number of Origen's works referred to in Jerome's *Adv. Ruf.* where he says the catalogue in the *Life of Pamphilus* "came to almost

raised the question whether anyone had even read all that
Origen had written.[137] The heated controversies which swirled
around Origen's thought after his death and finally led to his
condemnation as a heretic in the sixth century Council of
Constantinople II may also have contributed to the loss of
some of his works.[138]

The following works of Origen have been preserved in
Greek:[139] eight books of the *Commentary on Matthew*; eight books
of the *Commentary on John*; twenty homilies on Jeremiah; one
homily on 1 Samuel 28.3–28, *Against Celsus* (entire); portions
of *On First Principles, Against Celsus*, and several shorter selec-
tions from various homilies and commentaries in the *Philocalia*
excerpted from Origen's works by Basil and Gregory of Nazianzus; the treatise *On Prayer*; *The Exhortation to Martyrdom*;
and comments on various Scriptures preserved in *catenae*. The
papyri discovered at Tura in 1941 have, in addition to providing an earlier text to books one and two of *Against Celsus* and
the fragments of the Greek text of the *Commentary on Romans*,
added two new works in Greek to our corpus of Origen's
works: the *Disputation with Heraclides*, and two books, somewhat
fragmentary in places, of a treatise *On the Pascha*.

Jerome's Latin translations of two homilies on the Song of
Songs, eight on Isaiah, fourteen on Jeremiah, and thirty-nine
on Luke are extant. The Latin translations of Rufinus which
have been preserved are: *On First Principles*; ten books of the
Commentary on Romans; four books of the *Commentary on the
Song of Songs*; sixteen homilies on Genesis, thirteen on Exodus,

2,000 items" and the 786 titles listed in his own *Ep.* 33. He suggests that
though Jerome probably compiled his list with the aid of Pamphilus'
catalogue, he suppressed "all Origen's writing that he had not himself
read. These latter works," he suggests, on the basis of Jerome, *Ep.* 34.1,
"must have been lost at the time when the papyri in Pamphilus' library
were destroyed before being recopied on parchment by Acacius and
Euzoius." If this is true, the largest portion of Origen's works perished
quite early, and primarily because of their own massiveness.

137 *Ep.* 33.4.
138 For a convenient survey of these controversies see H. Crouzel, in NCE, s.v.
"Origen and Origenism." Crouzel thinks "this condemnation occasioned
the loss of the greater part of his works in their original language."
139 See Altaner, *Patrology*, 226–9, for the following lists of Origen's works.

sixteen on Leviticus, twenty-eight on Numbers, twenty-six on Joshua, nine on Judges, and nine on Psalms. In addition, there is an anonymous Latin translation of the *Commentary on Matthew* from Matthew 16.13 to 27.63, an anonymous translation of a homily on 1 Samuel 1–2, plus fragments of other homilies.

More of Origen's works have been preserved in Latin translations than in their original Greek form. The bulk of these Latin translations which have survived, including the homilies on Genesis and Exodus, were done by Rufinus of Aquileia.

The Latin Translations of Rufinus of Aquileia

In A.D. 397, after spending twenty-five years in the East, Rufinus left his monastery on the Mount of Olives and returned to Italy.[140] He brought with him a collection of Greek Christian manuscripts. Several of Origen's works were among those manuscripts.

Rufinus was an ardent admirer of Origen and appears to have been one of the few men at that time who was thoroughly acquainted with his works and thought. Before going to Jerusalem he had spent a total of eight years in Alexandria where he had studied under Didymus the Blind, the famous Origenist, and Gregory of Nazianzus, compiler, along with Basil, of the *Philocalia* of Origen.[141] When Atarbius, Epiphanius' emissary, and later Epiphanius himself, had visited Jerusalem and Bethlehem to condemn Origenism, Rufinus refused to yield to their pressure. Jerome, who had been as fervent an admirer of Origen as Rufinus, was less resolute. Thus was born the infamous quarrel over Origen between Jerome and his life-long friend Rufinus. It is not necessary to follow the

---

140 For Rufinus' life, see F. Murphy, *Rufinus of Aquileia (345–411): His Life and Works* (Catholic University of America Press: Washington, D.C., 1945); C. Hammond, "The Last Ten Years of Rufinus' Life and the Date of His Move South from Aquileia," *The Journal of Theological Studies* n.s. 28 (1977): 372–429; *NCE*, s.v. "Rufinus of Aquileia." Murphy's work is hereinafter cited as Murphy, *Rufinus of Aquileia*; Hammond's as Hammond, "The Last Ten Years."

141 Rufinus, *Apol.* 1.43, 2.12.

tortuous path of that quarrel here, but only to point out that
Rufinus remained a staunch supporter of Origen till his
death.[142]

Rufinus launched his translation activities almost immediately on his arrival in Italy. Our brief survey will take notice
only of those works of Origen which he translated and those
directly related to Origen.[143] He began in 397, at the request of
Macarius in Rome, by translating the first book of Pamphilus'
Apology to which he appended a treatise of his own *On the
Falsification of the Books of Origen*. Next, Macarius requested that
he translate Origen's *On First Principles*. Rufinus completed the
first two books of this treatise in the early weeks of Lent in 398,
with Macarius constantly at his side encouraging him. He
began translating the last two books of this work after Easter, at
a more leisurely pace since Macarius was no longer present to
prod him. Before leaving Rome for Aquileia in the latter half
of 398, he translated nine homilies of Origen on the thirty-
sixth, thirty-seventh, and thirty-eighth Psalms for Apronianus.[144]

In Aquileia sometime perhaps late in 399 Rufinus translated the *Dialogue of Adamantius* for a certain Paul who is
otherwise unknown. Rufinus considered this dialogue to have
been written by Origen, perhaps misled because of the name

---

142 The details of that controversy have been set forth in Vol. 53 of this series,
    J. Hritzu, trans., *Saint Jerome: Dogmatic and Polemical Works*, FOTC 53
    (Washington, D.C.: The Catholic University of America Press, 1965),
    47–58. See also Murphy, *Rufinus of Aquileia*, 82ff.; and J. Kelly, *Jerome: His
    Life, Writings, and Controversies* (New York: Harper and Row, 1975),
    195–258.
143 My survey is based on the information in Murphy, *Rufinus of Aquileia*. It
    was during this same period (397–411), when he was translating the
    various works of Origen that Rufinus also translated Clement's *Letter to
    James*, Basil's *Rules*, eight homilies of Basil, nine orations of Gregory of
    Nazianzus, *The Sentences of Sextus*, Eusebius' *Ecclesiastical History*, the *His-
    toria Monachorum*, the *Sentences* of Evagrius, and the *Clementine Recogni-
    tions*. He also composed all of his own original works in this same final
    fifteen year period of his life.
144 It should be noted that C. Hammond, "The Last Ten Years," 428–29,
    assigns different dates to some of Rufinus' translations, though he dates
    them all in the same general period.

Adamantius which was sometimes applied to Origen. The controversy between Jerome and Rufinus over Origen was at white heat at this time, being fanned especially by Jerome's friends in Italy. C. P. Hammond is probably correct in his assertion that Rufinus' intention in choosing to translate this particular work at this time was "to exhibit Origen as himself a champion in the fight against heresy."[145]

Sometime between 401 and 403 Rufinus translated Origen's homilies on Joshua and Judges. These were followed, between 403 and 405 by the translation of his homilies on Genesis, Exodus, and Leviticus. The *Commentary on Romans* was translated in 406. Rufinus tells us in the peroration appended to the *Commentary on Romans* that that treatise along with the homilies on Genesis, Exodus, and Leviticus was translated for a certain Heraclius.[146] The translations of the homilies on Genesis, Exodus, Leviticus, Joshua, and Judges all lack prefaces.

In 410 Rufinus translated Origen's homilies on Numbers on the island of Sicily where he had fled from Alaric's invasion. He dedicated this work to Ursacius, the Abbot of Pinetum. In the preface to this work Rufinus expressed his intention to translate Origen's work on Deuteronomy and thus complete everything he had written on the Law. The translation of the Song of Songs may have been done next, however, in place of Deuteronomy.[147] Rufinus died in 411. No translation of Origen's work on Deuteronomy has survived. Hammond notes, however, that Cassiodorus possessed a translation of Origen on Deuteronomy consisting of four sermons, but that he does not name the translator.[148]

---

145 Ibid., 391.
146 It may be that the homilies on Joshua and Judges were done for the same man. They, too, are mentioned in the peroration to the *Commentary on Romans*, but they are mentioned in conjunction with the translation of the homilies on the 36th, 37th, and 38th Psalms, which we know were translated for Apronianus. Consequently, not all the works mentioned in this peroration were done for Heraclius.
147 See Murphy, *Rufinus of Aquileia*, 216. Hammond, "The Last Ten Years," 429, dates the translation of the Song of Songs, 408–9.
148 "The Last Ten Years," 393.

Rufinus' Assumptions, Methodology, and Reliability as a Translator

Rufinus has long been maligned as a translator by his critics.[149] Hal Koch makes the statement that Koetschau's edition of the *De Principiis* and de Faye's investigations have shown that Rufinus cannot be trusted in his translation of that work.[150] De Faye, he says, was methodologically correct when he used the Greek texts of Origen practically exclusively. Koch himself followed the principle of taking his starting point from the Greek texts.[151] G. W. Butterworth[152] and R. P. C. Hanson[153] agree with this principle. J. E. L. Oulton, in comparing Rufinus' translation of the *Church History* of Eusebius with the Greek text says, "Rufinus transgressed the bounds of freedom which every translator must be expected to observe."[154] Heinrich Hoppe says Rufinus sometimes misreads the Greek text because of the haste with which he works and his insufficient mastery of the Greek language, and that he makes additions and alterations in the areas of both theology and rhetoric.[155] Basile Studer has shown that both Rufinus and Jerome altered the Christological titles in Origen's works to bring them into line with the theology of their time.[156]

On the other hand, there has been a more positive evalu-

---

149 For an extensive bibliography of studies on Rufinus as a translator see F. Winkelmann, "Einige Bemerkungen zu den Aussagen des Rufinus von Aquileia und des Hieronymus über ihre Übersetzungstheorie und -methode," in *Kyriakon: Festschrift Johannes Quasten*, Vol. 2, ed. P. Granfield and J. Jungmann (Münster: Verlag Aschendorff, 1970), 532–47. This work is hereinafter cited as Winkelmann, "Einige Bemerkungen."

150 *Pronoia und Paideusis* (Berlin: Walter de Gruyter & Co., 1932), 322, hereinafter cited as Koch.

151 Ibid., 323.

152 *Origen: On First Principles* (New York: Harper and Row, 1966), xlvii.

153 *Tradition*, 47.

154 "Rufinus's Translation of the Church History of Eusebius," *The Journal of Theological Studies* 30 (1929): 150. Hereinafter cited as Oulton, "Rufinus's Translation."

155 "Rufin als Uebersetzer," in *Studi dedicati alla memoria di Paolo Ubaldi* (Milan, 1937), 142–49.

156 "A propos des traductions d'Origène par Jérôme et Rufin," *Vetera Christianorum* 5 (1968): 137–55.

ation of Rufinus' work paralleling that of his critics. Henry Chadwick, for example, disagrees with Scherer in several places in the *Commentary on Romans* where the latter thinks Rufinus is guilty of interpolating material.[157] In comparing the exegesis of Romans 4.14–15 in the papyrus and in Rufinus he concludes, "I think it evident that, so far as general fidelity is concerned, Rufinus emerges well from the scrutiny."[158] Gustave Bardy regarded Rufinus' translation of *De Principiis* as a paraphrase, but one which renders correctly the general sense of the text.[159] M. Simonette, according to the review of Hanson, has questioned Koetschau's text of the *De Principiis* at several points and on some occasions has preferred Rufinus' translation to the Greek text in the *Philocalia*.[160] Walther Völker used the Latin translations of Origen's homilies extensively, even starting from statements made in them.[161] Henri Crouzel, following de Lubac, thinks the translations should be used massively, by bringing together parallel passages on the same subject.[162] This assumes, of course, that some of the translated passages may be questionable. Nautin finds Rufinus' translation of the *Apology* by Pamphilus altered on the discussion of the Trinity but almost literal in other passages which can be compared with Greek fragments where the doctrine of the

---

157 "Rufinus and the Tura Papyrus of Origen's Commentary on Romans," *The Journal of Theological Studies* n.s. 10 (1959): 19–37. Hereinafter cited as Chadwick, "Rufinus and the Tura Papyrus."

158 Ibid., 25.

159 *Recherches sur l'histoire du texte et des versions latines du De Principiis d'Origène* (Paris: Edouard Champion, 1923), 118–20. See also H. Crouzel, "Comparisons précises entre les fragments du Peri Archōn selon la Philocalie et la traduction de Rufin," *Origeniana: Premier colloque international des études origéniennes (Montserrat, 18–21 septembre 1973)*, ed. H. Crouzel, G. Lomiento, and J. Rius-Camps (Universitá di Bari: Istituto di letteratura cristiana antica, 1975), 114; J. Rist, "The Greek and Latin Texts of the Discussion on Free Will in *De Principiis*, Book III," ibid., 111.

160 R. Hanson's reveiw of M. Simonetti, *I Principi di Origene*, Classici delle Religioni 4 (Turin: Unione Tipografico Editrice Torinese, 1968), in *The Journal of Theological Studies* n.s. 31 (1970): 181.

161 *Das Vollkommenheitsideal*, 17–18.

162 *Théologie de l'image de Dieu chez Origène*, Théologie, vol. 34 (Paris: Aubier, 1956), 13, hereinafter cited as Crouzel, *Théologie de l'image*.

Trinity is not discussed.[163] Annie Jaubert's conclusion regarding the reliability of Rufinus' translation of the homilies on Joshua can be regarded as representing the general conclusion of the various scholars who have studied the different translations of Rufinus and have concluded that they can be trusted within certain limits. On the whole, she says, the work gives the impression of a long paraphrase, but not of an inaccurate paraphrase. We can never be sure of having Origen's expression, but we can trust the text for his thought.[164]

The conclusions enumerated in the preceeding paragraphs were based, for the most part, on comparisons made between the Latin text of Rufinus and extant Greek texts or fragments. There are, however, very few parallel Greek fragments for the homilies translated by Rufinus.[165] This makes judgments about their reliability even more precarious. Some help in forming an opinion of what might be expected, at least, can be obtained from the statements Rufinus makes in his various prefaces to his translations and other related works. Monica Wagner, in particular, has called attention to the value of a study of Rufinus' prefaces. She thinks, based on the prefaces, that his goal was "the moral advancement of his readers and this aim determined his method." Furthermore his paraphrastic procedure and alterations of the original were "in the interests of lucidity and appropriateness."[166] Murphy is in essential agreement with that view.[167]

Winkelmann has expressed a radical disagreement with Wagner's view. He thinks the prefaces of Rufinus are primarily apologetic statements aimed at his accusers, and that as theoretical statements of his actual methodology they are

---

163 *Origène*, 150–52.
164 *Origène: Homélies sur Josué*, SC 71 (Paris: Les éditions du Cerf, 1960), 82, hereinafter cited as Jaubert, *Homélies*.
165 See below pp. 39–40 for the Greek fragments that correspond to the homilies on Genesis and Exodus.
166 *Rufinus the Translator. A Study of His Theory and Practice as Illustrated in His Version of the Apologetica of S. Gregory Nazianzen*, (Catholic University of America Press: Washington, D.C., 1945), 11. Hereinafter cited as Wagner, *Rufinus the Translator*.
167 *Rufinus of Aquileia*, 227.

imprecise and insufficient.[168] The imprecision of these statements, moreover, he thinks, is a tactical move on Rufinus' part.
He does not work in a totally honest manner, he says. Nor is it
enough to say, with Wagner, that Rufinus' method can be
explained by the fact that his primary goal was edification, for
theological and scholarly information were also important to
him.[169] Winkelmann is right, of course, that there is an apologetic purpose in the prefaces. His implicit assumption, however, can be questioned, that this negates their value for
determining what Rufinus thought he was doing and how he
perceived himself to be working. We could certainly wish that
Rufinus had been more explicit in describing his manner of
working. This does not mean, however, that we cannot trust
his truthfulness in what he says. After having studied his
prefaces and apologies it seems to me that we can obtain a
reasonably good idea of the kind of changes he made.

Rufinus undertook his translation of Origen with the assumption that heretics had tampered with the text.[170] This
assumption was based on three lines of evidence. First, he
found contradictions in Origen's treatises on the doctrines of
the Holy Spirit, on whether the Father and the Son are of one
substance, and on the resurrection of the flesh. Since so
learned and wise a man as Origen could not have contradicted
himself in this way, Rufinus reasoned, someone else had either
added to the text or changed what was originally said. Second,
Rufinus quotes from a letter of Origen addressed to some
friends at Alexandria in which Origen complains that his
adversaries corrupt and adulterate his teaching.[171] He cites one
case in which a heretic had altered his words by deletion,
addition, and alteration and then published the work under
Origen's name, and another in which a heretic had composed a
work using some things from Origen and published it as
Origen's work. Hence, Rufinus concludes, the process of the

---

168 Winkelmann, "Einige Bemerkungen," 534–35.
169 Ibid., 547.
170 *Liber de adulteratione librorum Origenis; Praef. ad Heraclium; Praef. De Princ.*
    1.3.
171 On this letter, see Nautin, *Origène*, 161–72.

corruption of Origen's texts had begun even in Origen's lifetime.

This letter of Origen to his friends in Alexandria does give some credence to Rufinus' assertion that the texts of Origen had been altered in places. It does not, however, guarantee the validity of Rufinus' criteria for recognizing such places. Rufinus thought that such alterations had occurred (1) wherever Origen contradicted himself,[172] or (2) wherever he contradicted Rufinus' own view of the orthodox faith.[173] Nor does this letter guarantee the accuracy of Rufinus' corrections. He claims to correct the doctrinally corrupted passages in Origen by what he has read in other passages of Origen.[174] Here we must admit that Rufinus knew many works of Origen now lost to us on which he might have been able to draw. We must remember also, however, that he thought the *Adamantius Dialogue* was a work of Origen and that his impression of Origen's orthodoxy may have been based on this document.

The third basis for Rufinus' assumption that Origen's texts had been altered by heretics was that this very thing had happened to the works of others. He cites the cases of Hilary, Bishop of Poitiers, Cyprian, and Damasus.[175] Since Origen had complained of the alteration of his texts in his own lifetime and it had clearly happened to others whose orthodoxy was not suspect, Rufinus concluded that it should be assumed that wherever Origen's text goes contrary to orthodox doctrine it is not the voice of Origen, but that of some heretic which is being heard.

This assumption about the state of Origen's texts had a definite influence on Rufinus' methodology in translating these texts. His methods are set forth in the various prefaces attached to his translations and in his apologies. They can be summarized as follows. (1) *He suppresses contradictory elements in Origen.*[176] By contradictions he means primarily contradictions

---

172 Rufinus, *Praef. De Princ.* 1.2.
173 Rufinus, *Praef. De Princ.* 3.
174 Rufinus, *Praef. De Princ.* 1.3.
175 *Liber de adulteratione librorum Origenis.*
176 *Praef. De Princ.* 1.3; *Apol. ad Anastasium* 7.

regarding the doctrine of the Trinity. Since Rufinus thought that Origen's genuine thought was in agreement with the orthodox faith this means, in effect, that he suppresses those elements in Origen which are not in harmony with the orthodox faith on the Trinity.[177] (2) *He has, in places, attempted to restore the authentic thought of Origen from other texts of Origen.*[178] We have already discussed the problem that his assumption that the *Adamantius Dialogue* was Origen's work poses for trusting Rufinus' restoration efforts.[179] (3) *He clarifies Origen's thought where he finds it obscure.*[180] Again, he claims to do this not by adding his own words, but only by using Origen's words from other passages where he has discussed the same subject more fully.

The remaining methods Rufinus used in his translations have no direct relation to his assumption that Origen's texts had been corrupted. (4) *He abbreviates the text of Origen.*[181] He says he omitted, for the sake of brevity, anything in Books three and four of *On First Principles* that had been discussed in Books one and two. He notes also in his preface to the *Commentary on Romans* that Heraclius, who had requested the translation, also requested that he abbreviate it. These abbreviations were prompted by the concern for size alone and have nothing to do with Origen's orthodoxy. (5) *He translates the sense into Latin, and not word for word.*[182] In this he claims, correctly, that he is following Jerome's example.[183] Jerome deviated from this method of translation only to translate Origen's *On First Principles.* He did this wishing to discredit Rufinus' version. Several modern studies have compared Rufinus' translations with the Greek texts which have survived and have shown the many ways in which he has taken liberties with his texts.[184]

---

177 *Praef. De Princ.* 1.2; *Praef. De Princ.* 3.
178 *Praef. De Princ.* 1.3.
179 See above, p. 28–29, 34.
180 *Praef. De Princ.* 1.3.
181 *Praef. De Princ.* 3; *Praef. ad Heraclium.*
182 Rufinus, *Apol.* 2.40; *Apol. ad Anastasium* 7; *Praef. ad Gaudentium.*
183 Rufinus, *Apol.* 2.40; cf. Jerome, *Ep.* 57.5.
184 See especially Wagner, *Rufinus the Translator*; Oulton, "Rufinus's Translation," 150–74; Chadwick, "Rufinus and the Tura Papyrus," 10–42; Jaubert, *Homélies*, 68–82.

Rufinus' comments about his translation of Origen's homilies on Genesis, Exodus, and Leviticus deserve special attention here. Although these homilies all lack prefaces, he refers to them in the peroration appended to his translation of Origen's *Commentary on Romans*, addressed to Heraclius.

We expended a very great effort in the other works which we translated into Latin at your urging, or more precisely, exacting the task of daily work, since we wished to fill out those things which Origen delivered extempore in the lecture room of the Church, where his purpose was not so much explanation as edification. This we did in the homilies or short speeches on Genesis and Exodus. And especially in those which he delivered in the style of public speech on the book of Leviticus have we, in fact, employed the form of explanation in translation. We have undertaken, therefore, the task of filling out what was lacking, lest questions attacked and forsaken, his common homiletical style, produce repulsion in a Latin reader. But we wrote those homilies on Joshua and the book of Judges, and the thirty-sixth, thirty-seventh, and thirty-eighth Psalms simply as we found them, and we translated them without much effort.[185]

These words immediately raise questions about how much of the text of these homilies is from Origen and how much from Rufinus. Murphy, I think, has gone too far in his statement that "Rufinus confesses to having expended considerable time and labor in his attempt to remold Origen's original sermons, filling in the lacunae and presenting the whole as a doctrinal treatise."[186] Hammond's statement, likewise, is too strong when he says Rufinus altered these homilies "from the style of a sermon to that of a commentary."[187] Neither of these men takes account of the distinction Rufinus makes between his translation of the homilies on Leviticus and those on Genesis and Exodus.[188] Rufinus' statement, "And especially (*praecipue*) in

---

185 PG 14.1291–94.
186 *Rufinus of Aquileia*, 190–91.
187 "The Last Ten Years," 394.
188 The translation of Murphy, *Rufinus of Aquileia*, 186, in fact blurs the

those . . . on the book of Leviticus . . . ," sets the extent, at least, to which he has altered these homilies apart from his alterations of those on Genesis and Exodus. Furthermore, the homilies on Genesis and Exodus, for the most part, sound like sermons when one reads them. They certainly do not read like "doctrinal treatises," nor even "commentaries." Origen's concern for edification has certainly not been eliminated from the Genesis and Exodus homilies, nor has the evidence that these were oral addresses delivered to audiences. In short, they retain the feel of sermons, delivered, to be sure, by a man with a scholarly mind, but with a pastor's heart, no less, for his audience.

On the basis of how Rufinus himself viewed his work on the homilies mentioned in the peroration to the *Commentary on Romans* we may make the following observations. He altered the homilies on Leviticus most. The homilies on Genesis and Exodus were altered less than those on Leviticus, but nevertheless, more extensively than others. Finally, he altered those homilies on Joshua, Judges, and the thirty-sixth, thirty-seventh, and thirty-eighth Psalms least of all. This does not mean that he translated these latter homilies in a word for word style. Jaubert's study of the homilies on Joshua has shown that while Rufinus has remained true to Origen's thought, his work should not be thought of as a translation, but as a free adaptation.[189]

Rufinus' statements about his translations permit us to draw the following conclusions about the reliability of his translations of Origen. First, except in those few places where Rufinus retains the Greek word in his translation,[190] it is not possible from his translation to ascertain with any confidence Origen's precise words. Second, Origen's homiletic style may

---

distinction: "This I have done for the homilies or sermons on *Genesis* and *Exodus*, and especially in those on the book of *Leviticus*. While he spoke in a hortatory manner, my translation has been done in the mode of an explanation." The last statement is made in connection with the translation of the homilies on Leviticus, not with that of all three.

189 *Homélies*, 81–82.

190 See H. Hoppe, "Griechisches bei Rufin," *Glotta* 26 (1938): 132–44, and, for an example, our Appendix, 7.

have been altered in places. Third, Rufinus may have supplied
answers to some questions Origen left unanswered. Nevertheless, one may say that, on the whole, the substance can be
regarded as representing Origen's thought. The major exception to this statement is theological statements regarding the
Trinity and the resurrection of the body. Whenever statements on these subjects agree with the doctrines of the fourth-
century Church they should be regarded with suspicion. In
regard to his other expansions, particularly those he refers to
in relation to the homilies on Genesis and Exodus, we may
assume that while Origen may not have uttered these words on
the particular occasion in question, they are, at least, in agreement with his thought. In the same peroration to the *Commentary on Romans* Rufinus complains that some say he should
put his own name on his compositions rather than Origen's
name since they contain so much of his work. To this he
replies:

> But I, who am more concerned for my conscience than my
> name, even if I seem to add some things and fill out things
> which are lacking, or abbreviate things which are long,
> nevertheless, do not think it right to steal the title of him who
> laid the foundation of the work and provided the material to
> construct the edifice.[191]

If Rufinus intended the analogy he used in that statement to
represent accurately his work on Origen's texts, it means that
while he is responsible for bringing the work into its precise
present form, it is solidly founded on Origen's work, and the
material which Rufinus has brought together comes from
Origen, though through his own Latin words and style.[192]
Chadwick, in his comparison of Rufinus' translation of the
Commentary on Romans with the Greek fragments of that com-

---

191 PG 14.1293–94.
192 Jerome, *Ep.* 33, knew of a *Commentary on Genesis* in thirteen books by
   Origen and of excerpts on Exodus and Leviticus. Rufinus could have
   drawn on these works when he "filled out" Origen's homilies on these
   books. Daniélou, *Origène*, 11, makes the same suggestion regarding these

mentary found at Tura has, perhaps, said it best: "The voice is
the voice of Origen, even though the hands are the hands of
Rufinus."[193]

The Greek Fragments of the Homilies on Genesis and Exodus.

In the homilies on Genesis, portions of Homily 2.1–2 have
been preserved in Procopius and catenae.[194] The catenae manuscripts, Baehrens points out, are in three classes: (1) the
catena on Genesis and Exodus, (2) the catena on Genesis, and
(3) the catena on the Octateuch. Louis Doutreleau has shown
that Baehrens mixed the catenae fragments with those found
in Procopius to produce one continuous text.[195] He notes,
further, that portions of this material are attributed to Didymus instead of Origen and that the attribution can be
verified in the *Commentary on Genesis* by Didymus found at
Tura.[196] Doutreleau has reedited the Genesis fragments, using
type two of the catenae manuscripts as the basic text because it
is the most complete. He prints this text of the catena fragments parallel to the fragments in Procopius and Rufinus'
translation.[197]

For the Exodus homilies there are two short catena fragments in the third class of catenae manuscripts. These fall in
Homily 8.3 and 8.4. There is also a longer fragment of Procopius containing portions of Homily 8.1,3,4.[198] Baehrens

---

homilies. Chadwick, "Rufinus and the Tura Papyrus," 25, notices evidence of this manner of working by Rufinus in the *Commentary on Romans*.
"Where Rufinus is left unsupported by the Greek," he says, "his ideas can
be vindicated as authentic Origen by parallels in other writings."
193 "Rufinus and the Tura Papyrus," 25.
194 W. Baehrens, *Überlieferung und Textgeschichte der lateinisch erhaltenen Ori-
geneshomilien zum Alten Testament*, TU 42 (Leipzig: J. C. Hinrichs'sche
Buchhandlung, 1916), 232, hereinafter cited as Baehrens, *Überlieferung*.
195 "Le fragment grec de l'homélie II d'Origène sur la Genèse," *Revue
d'histoire des textes* 5 (1975): 13, 19, hereinafter cited as Doutreleau, "Le
fragment grec."
196 Ibid., 20.
197 Ibid., 26–43.
198 Baehrens, *Überlieferung*, 233.

prints the catena fragments separate from Procopius in this homily.

A comparison of those fragments of Origen on Genesis Homily 2.1–2, as edited by Doutreleau, with Rufinus' translation of those sections shows him at work in the free style noted in our preceeding section. The following examples are not exhaustive, but demonstrate how Rufinus worked in this section and, presumably, throughout the homilies on Genesis and Exodus.

He translates the single term *schēma* with the doublet *habitum ipsum et formam*.[199] The description of the ark as *pyramoeides* is expanded into a lengthy Latin sentence. Three references to the Biblical text of Symmachus and one each to Theodotion and Aquila are omitted, as are four complete fragments of several lines each at the end of section two of the homily. In the passage discussing Marcion, some of the Greek material has been expanded, some omitted, and some re-arranged. The following is a good example of Rufinus' rhetorical expansion. The simple Greek text, "Wherefore 'the Lord God closed (the door)' behind Noah 'and so the flood occurred,' " is rendered by Rufinus: "For this reason, therefore, Scripture, although it had said about all other things, that Noah made the ark and brought in the animals and his sons and their wives, did not say of the door, that Noah closed the door of the ark, but says that 'The Lord God closed the door of the ark from without, and so the flood occurred.' "[200] There are other places, however, where Rufinus' translation is very close to the Greek, sometimes almost word for word.

The Greek fragments of the homilies on Genesis and Exodus, brief as they are, give us enough of a glimpse of Rufinus' manner of working to confirm the conclusions drawn in our preceeding section. He gives us the essence of Origen's thought, but certainly not Origen's words, at least on any regular, predictable basis. As Doutreleau has said, Origen furnishes the ideas which Rufinus rewrites in his own style.[201]

---

199 Cf. our Appendix, note 8.
200 Texts in Doutreleau, "Le fragment grec," 32–35.
201 Doutreleau, "Le fragment grec," 44.

The Latin Manuscript Tradition, Editions,
and Translations of the Homilies on Genesis and Exodus.

The definitive work on the Latin manuscript tradition of the homilies on Genesis and Exodus was done by W. A. Baehrens in 1916.[202] His research demonstrated conclusively that the seventeenth homily on Genesis present in some manuscripts was not by Origen, but was, in fact, Rufinus' own work, *De benedictionibus patriarcharum,* in fragmentary form.[203] He has also shown that the manuscripts containing the homilies on Genesis fall into eight classes and those on Exodus into seven. The classes with their major representatives and dates are listed here because some of them are referred to in footnotes in our text.[204]

A—Lugdunensis 443 s. This is the oldest manuscript, coming from the sixth or seventh century, and contains the homilies on Genesis, Exodus, and Leviticus.

B—This class is represented in the Genesis homilies by one tenth and one twelfth-century manuscript and in the Exodus homilies by two tenth and one twelfth-century manuscript. This class also contains the homilies on Leviticus, Numbers, Joshua, and Judges.

C—This class, with manuscripts from the ninth and twelfth centuries contains both sets of homilies plus those on Leviticus. It is this class also that has the seventeenth homily on Genesis.

D—Coloniensis 3 s. This is a ninth century manuscript containing the homilies on Genesis and Exodus.

E—This class is made up of manuscripts from the eleventh and twelfth-centuries containing the homilies on Genesis, Exodus, and Leviticus.

---

202 *Überlieferung,* 1–80.
203 Ibid., 1–5.
204 See Baehrens, *Überlieferung,* 10–74; *Origenes Werke: Homilien zum Hexateuch in Rufins Übersetzung,* ed. W. Baehrens, Part 1, *Die Homilien zu Genesis, Exodus und Leviticus,* GCS 29 (Leipzig: J. C. Hinrichs'sche Buchhandlung, 1920, ix–xvii, xxxvi; *Origène: Homélies sur la Genése,* ed. Louis Doutreleau, SC 7bis (Paris: Les éditions du Cerf, 1976), 17–19. Baehrens work is hereinafter cited as Baehrens; Doutreleau's as Doutreleau.

F—The manuscripts of this class come from the ninth (on Exodus) and eleventh (on Genesis) centuries.

P—Parisinus 1625 s. This is an uncial manuscript from the seventh or eighth-century containing only the homilies on Genesis. It begins in Homily 1.17 and ends in Homily 11.1 and is lacking also in Homily 7.2.

The editio princeps of Origen's homilies on the Heptateuch was done by Aldus Manutius in 1503. Baehrens thinks he may have used a manuscript which mixed class E and class B traditions. The editions of Merlin (1512), Erasmus (1536), Grinaeus (1571), and Genebrardus (1574) were all dependent on Aldus's work. The edition of Delarue (1732) marked an advance because he had some Greek fragments and some new manuscripts. Delarue's edition was printed by Oberthür (1780–94), Lommatzsch (1831), and Migne (1857). Baehrens's edition (GCS 29, 1920) was based on his extensive work on the manuscript traditions discussed above.[205] Doutreleau (SC 7bis, 1976) is the most recent editor of the homilies on Genesis. He has basically followed Baehrens, carefully noting every place where his text differs from Baehrens.[206] There has been no edition of the homilies on Exodus after that of Baehrens.

The eighth homily on Genesis was translated anonymously into English in 1565.[207] The Genesis homilies were translated into French by Doutreleau in 1944 (SC 7) and revised by him in 1976 (SC 7bis). The homilies on Exodus were translated into French by Fortier in 1947 (SC 16).[208] These seem to be all the translations of the homilies on Genesis and Exodus into modern languages.

Our translation is based on the text of Baehrens. Any changes from his text are noted in footnotes. All Biblical names of persons and places are spelled as they appear in the Douay version of the Bible, a version which in the opinion of B.

---

205 See Baehrens, *Überlieferung*, 240–42; Baehrens, xxxi–ii.
206 Doutreleau, 19.
207 Crouzel, *Bibliographie*, 94. I have not seen this translation.
208 P. Fortier, trans., *Origène: Homélies sur l'Exode*, SC 16 (Paris: Les éditions du Cerf, 1947), hereinafter cited as Fortier.

Smalley "comes closest of the English translations" to what a patristic writer read or remembered.[209] While it may certainly be questioned how much of the Latin Vulgate (the basis of the Douay version) Rufinus knew or used, many elements of the Old Latin version, according to the opinion of Bonifatius Fischer,[210] are embedded in the Latin Vulgate. Abbreviations of the books of the Scripture follow the abbreviations used in the New American Bible.

---

209 *The Becket Conflict and the Schools* (Totowa, N.J.: Rowman and Littlefield, 1973), xiv.

210 *Vetus Latina, Die Reste der altlateinischen Bibel*, vol. 1.1, *Verzeichnis der Sigel für Kirchenschriftsteller* 2nd ed. (Freiburg: Verlag Herder, 1963), 5.

HOMILIES ON GENESIS

(In Genesim homiliae)

HOMILY I

N THE BEGINNING GOD MADE HEAVEN AND EARTH.[1] What is the beginning of all things except our Lord and "Savior of all," Jesus Christ "the firstborn of every creature"?[2] In this beginning, therefore, that is, in his Word, "God made heaven and earth" as the evangelist John also says in the beginning of his Gospel: "In the beginning was the Word, and the Word was with God, and the Word was God. The same was in the beginning with God. All things were made by him and without him nothing was made."[3] Scripture is not speaking here of any temporal beginning,[4] but it says that the heaven and the earth and all things which were made were made "in the beginning," that is, in the Savior.

"And the earth was invisible and disordered and darkness was upon the abyss, and the spirit of God moved over the waters."[5] "The earth was invisible and disordered" before God said: "Let there be light," and before he divided the light from the darkness, as the order of the account shows.[6] But since in the words which follow he orders the firmament to come into existence and calls this heaven, when we come to that place the reason for the difference between heaven and the firmament will be explained there and also why the firmament was called heaven. But now the text says: "Darkness was upon the abyss."[7] What is "the abyss"? That place, of course, where "the devil

---

1 Gn 1.1.
2 1 Tm 4.10; Col 1.15.
3 Jn 1.1–3.
4 Philo *Op.* 7.26–28, too rejected a chronological meaning for "in the beginning" in Gn 1.1.
5 Gn 1.2.
6 Gn 1.3.
7 Gn 1.2.

and his angels" will be.[8] This indeed is most clearly designated also in the Gospel when it is said of the Savior: "And the demons which he was casting out were asking him that he not command them to go into the abyss."[9]

For this reason, therefore, God dissolved the darkness as the Scripture says: "And God said, 'Let there be light,' and there was light. And God saw that the light was good; and God divided between the light and the darkness. And God called the light day and he called the darkness night. And there was evening and there was morning, one day."[10]

According to the letter God calls both the light day and the darkness night. But let us see according to the spiritual meaning why it is that when God, in that beginning which we discussed above, "made heaven and earth," and said, "let there be light" and "divided between the light and the darkness and called the light day and the darkness night," and the text said that "there was evening and there was morning," it did not say: "the first day," but said, "one day." It is because there was not yet time before the world existed.[11] But time begins to exist with the following days. For the second day and the third and fourth and all the rest begin to designate time.

(2)"And God said: 'Let there be a firmament in the midst of the water and let it divide water from water.' And it was so done. And God made the firmament."[12]

Although God had already previously made heaven, now he makes the firmament. For he made heaven first, about which he says, "heaven is my throne."[13] But after that he makes

---

8 Cf. Rv 12.9, 20.3; Mt 25.41.

9 Lk 8.31.

10 Gn 1.3–5.

11 Cf. Philo *Op.* 7.26.35. L. Ginzberg, *The Legends of the Jews*, 7 vols. (Philadelphia: The Jewish Publication Society of America, 1909–38), 5.6–7 (hereinafter cited as Ginzberg, *Legends*), points out that *Genesis Rabbah* 3.7 and *Koheleth Rabbah* 3.11 contain statements indicating that time is older than the world. All references to the midrash are to H. Freedman and M. Simon, eds. *Midrash Rabbah*, 10 vols. (London: The Soncino Press, 1939). See also Cicero *N.D.* 1.21 where it is stated that the Epicureans believed that there was time before the world.

12 Gn 1.6–7.

13 Is 66.1.

the firmament, that is, the corporeal heaven. For every corporeal object is, without doubt, firm and solid; and it is this which "divides the water which is above heaven from the water which is below heaven."[14]

For since everything which God was to make would consist of spirit and body, for that reason heaven, that is, all spiritual substance upon which God rests as on a kind of throne or seat,[15] is said to be made "in the beginning" and before everything. But this heaven, that is, the firmament, is corporeal. And, therefore, that first heaven indeed, which we said is spiritual, is our mind, which is also itself spirit, that is, our spiritual man which sees and perceives God. But that corporeal heaven, which is called the firmament, is our outer man which looks at things in a corporeal way.

As, therefore, heaven is called the firmament because it divides between those waters which are above it and those which are below it, so also man, who has been placed in a body, will also himself be called heaven, that is, heavenly man,[16] in the opinion of the apostle Paul who says: "But our citizenship is in heaven,"[17] if he can divide and discern what the waters are which are higher, "above the firmament," and what those are which are below the firmament.

The very words of Scripture, therefore, contain it thus: "And God made the firmament, and divided the water which is under the firmament from the water which is above the firmament. And God called the firmament heaven. And God saw that it was good; and there was evening and there was morning, the second day."[18] Let each of you, therefore, be zealous to become a divider of that water which is above and that which is below. The purpose, of course, is that, attaining an understanding and participation in that spiritual water which is

---

14 Cf. Gn 1.7.
15 Doutreleau, 28–29, notes that the *Vetus latina* translated the Greek *thronos* by *sedes*. The doublet is introduced by Rufinus who thus follows the *Vetus latina* and yet shows the wording of the Greek text.
16 Cf. 1 Cor 15.47.
17 Phil 3.20.
18 Gn 1.7–8.

above the firmament one may draw forth "from within himself rivers of living water springing up into life eternal,"[19] removed without doubt and separated from that water which is below, that is, the water of the abyss in which darkness is said to be, in which "the prince of this world" and the adversary, "the dragon and his angels" dwell,[20] as was indicated above.

Therefore, by participation in that celestial water which is said to be above the heavens, each of the faithful becomes heavenly, that is, when he applies his mind to lofty and exalted things, thinking nothing about the earth but totally about heavenly things, "seeking the things which are above, where Christ is at the right hand of the Father."[21] For then he also will be considered worthy of that praise from God which is written here when the text says: "And God saw that it was good."[22]

And then also those things which are described in the following statements about the third day signify this same meaning. For the text says: "And God said, 'Let the water which is under heaven be gathered into one gathering, and let the dry land appear.' And it was so done."[23]

Let us labor, therefore, to gather "the water which is under heaven" and cast it from us that "the dry land," which is our deeds done in the flesh, might appear when this has been done so that, of course, "men seeing our good works may glorify our Father who is in heaven."[24] For if we have not separated from us those waters which are under heaven, that is, the sins and vices of our body, our dry land will not be able to appear nor have the courage to advance to the light. "For everyone who does evil hates the light and does not come to the light [lest his works be reproved. But he that does truth comes to the light that][25] his works may be made manifest" and appear, if "they are done in God."[26] This courage certainly will not be given

---

19 Cf. Jn 7.38, 4.14.
20 Cf. Jn 12.31; 1 Pt 5.8; Rv 12.7, 20.3.
21 Col 3.1.
22 Gn 1.8.
23 Gn 1.9.
24 Cf. Mt 5.16.
25 Conjecture of Klostermann incorporated in the text of Doutreleau.
26 Jn 3.20–21.

unless like the waters, we cast off from us and remove the vices of the body which are the materials of sins. Once this has been done our dry land will not remain "dry land" as is shown from what follows.

For the text says: "And the water which is under heaven was gathered into its gatherings and the dry land appeared. And God called the dry land earth, and the gathering together of the waters he called seas."[27] As, therefore, this dry land, after the water was removed from it, as we said above, did not continue further as "dry land," but is now named "earth," in this manner also our bodies, if this separation from them takes place, will no longer remain "dry land." They will, on the contrary, be called "earth" because they can now bear fruit for God.

Whereas indeed "in the beginning God made heaven and earth," but later made "the firmament" and "the dry land"; and "the firmament" indeed "he called heaven" giving it the name of that heaven which he had created earlier, but he called "the dry land" "earth" because he bestowed on it the capability of bearing fruits. If, therefore, anyone by his failure still remains dry and offers no fruit but "thorns and thistles,"[28] producing, as it were, fuel for the fire, in accordance with those things which he brought forth from himself, he also himself becomes "fuel for the fire."[29] But if, after the waters of the abyss, which are the thoughts of demons, have been separated from himself, he has shown himself fruitful earth by his zeal and diligence, he ought to expect similar things because he also is led by God into "a land flowing with milk and honey."[30]

(3) But let us see from the following words what those fruits are which God orders the earth, on which he himself bestowed this name, to produce. "And God saw," the text says, "that it was good, and God said: 'Let the earth bring forth vegetation producing seed according to its kind and likeness, and the fruit

---

27 Gn 1.9.
28 Cf. Gn 3.18; Heb 6.8.
29 Cf. Is 9.19.
30 Cf. Ex 3.8, 33.3; etc.

tree bearing fruit whose seed is within it according to its
likeness on the earth.' And it was so done."[31]

According to the letter, the fruits are clearly those which
"the earth," not "the dry land" produces. But again let us also
relate the meaning to ourselves. If we have already been made
"earth," if we are no longer "dry land," let us offer copious and
diverse fruits to God, that we also may be blessed by the Father
who says: "Behold the smell of my son is as the smell of a
plentiful field which the Lord has blessed,"[32] and that that
which the Apostle said might be fulfilled in us: "For the earth
that receives the rain which comes frequently upon it and
brings forth vegetation fit for those by whom it is cultivated will
receive blessings from God. But that which brings forth thorns
and briars is reprobate and very near a curse, whose end is to
be burned."[33]

(4) "And the earth brought forth green vegetation producing seed according to its kind and likeness and the fruit tree
bearing fruit containing seed producing fruit according to its
kind on the earth. And God saw that it was good. And there
was evening and there was morning, the third day."[34]

Not only does God order the earth to bring forth "green
vegetation," but also to bring forth "seed" that it can always
bear fruit. And not only does God order that there be "the fruit
tree," but also that it "produce fruit[35] containing seed according to its kind," that is, that it can always bear fruit from these
seeds which it contains.

And we, therefore, ought thus both to bear fruit and to have
seeds within ourselves, that is, to contain in our heart the seeds
of all good works and virtues, that, having these fixed in our
minds, from them now we might justly perform all the acts
which occur to us. For those are the fruits of that seed, namely

---

31 Gn 1.10–11.
32 Gn 27.27.
33 Heb 6.7–8.
34 Gn 1.12–13.
35 *Fructum* is Baehrens's conjecture. The MSS have *semen*.

our acts, which are brought forth "from the good treasure of our heart."[36]

But if, on the one hand, we hear "the word" and from the hearing "immediately" our earth produces vegetation, and this vegetation "wither" before it should come to maturity or fruit, our earth will be called "rocky."[37] But if those things which are said should press forward in our hearts with deeper roots so that they both "bear fruit" of works and contain the seeds of future works, then truly the earth of each of us will bear[38] fruit in accordance with its potential, some "a hundred fold," some "sixty," other "thirty." But also we have considered it necessary to admonish that our fruit have no "darnel," that is, no tares,[39] that it not be "beside the way,"[40] but be sown in the way itself, in that way which says, "I am the way,"[41] that the birds of heaven may not eat our fruits nor our vine. If, however, any of us should deserve to be a vine, let him beware lest he bear thorns for grapes, and for this reason "will no longer be pruned or digged" nor will "the clouds" be ordered "to rain upon it," but on the contrary it will be left "deserted" that "thorns" may overgrow it.[42]

(5) But now, after this, the firmament deserves also to be adorned with lights. For God says: "Let there be lights in the firmament of heaven, that they may give light on the earth and divide between day and night."[43]

As in that firmament which had already been called heaven God orders lights to come into existence that "they might divide between day and night," so also it can happen in us if only we also are zealous to be called and made heaven. We shall have lights in us which illuminate us, namely Christ and his

---

36 Cf. Lk 6.45.
37 Cf. Mt 13.5–9.
38 Accepting *afferet* with Doutreleau, which is the reading of ABDEF. Baehrens reads *affert* with C.
39 Probably an explanatory phrase inserted by Rufinus.
40 Cf. Lk 8.5.
41 Jn 14.6.
42 Cf. Is 5.2,6.
43 Gn 1.14.

Church. For he himself is "the light of the world"[44] who also illuminates the Church by his light. For just as the moon is said to receive light from the sun so that the night likewise can be illuminated by it, so also the Church, when the light of Christ has been received, illuminates all those who live in the night of ignorance.

But if someone progresses in this so that he is already made a "child of the day,"[45] so that "he walks honestly in the day,"[46] as "a child of the day and a child of light,"[47] this person is illuminated by Christ himself just as the day is illuminated by the sun.

(6) " 'And let them be for signs and seasons, and for days and years; and let them be for illumination in the firmament of heaven, to give light on the earth.' And it was so done."[48]

As those lights of heaven which we see have been set "for signs and seasons and days and years," that they might give light from the firmament of heaven for those who are on the earth, so also Christ, illuminating his Church, gives signs by his precepts, that one might know how, when the sign has been received, to escape "the wrath to come,"[49] lest "that day overtake him like a thief,"[50] but that rather he can reach "the acceptable year of the Lord."[51]

Christ, therefore, is "the true light which enlightens every man coming into this world."[52] From his light the Church itself also having been enlightened is made "the light of the world" enlightening those "who are in darkness,"[53] as also Christ himself testifies to his disciples saying: "You are the light of the

---

44 Cf. Jn 8.12.
45 Accepting Doutreleau's conjecture of *diei* on the basis of the context. Baehrens reads *dei* with the MSS.
46 Cf. Rom 13.13.
47 Cf. 1 Thes 5.5.
48 Gn 1.14–15.
49 Cf. 1 Thes 1.10; Mt 3.7; Lk 3.7.
50 Cf. 1 Thes 5.4.
51 Cf. Is 61.2.
52 Jn 1.9.
53 Rom 2.19.

world."[54] From this it is shown that Christ indeed is the light of the apostles, but the apostles are "the light of the world." For they, "not having spot or wrinkle or anything of this kind," are the true Church, as also the Apostle says: "That he might present it to himself a glorious Church not having spot or wrinkle or any such thing."[55]

(7) "And God made two great lights, a greater light to rule the day and a lesser light to rule the night, and the stars. And God set them in the firmament of heaven to shine upon the earth and to have authority over the day and the night and to divide between the light and the darkness. And God saw that it was good. And there was evening and there was morning, the fourth day."[56]

Just as the sun and the moon are said to be the great lights in the firmament of heaven, so also are Christ and the Church in us. But since God also placed stars in the firmament, let us see what are also stars in us, that is, in the heaven of our heart.

Moses is a star in us, which shines and enlightens us by his acts. And Abraham, Isaac, Jacob, Isaias, Jeremias, Ezechiel, David, Daniel, and all to whom the Holy Scriptures testify that they pleased God. For just as "star differs from star in glory,"[57] so also each of the saints, according to his own greatness, sheds his light upon us.

Moreover, just as the sun and the moon enlighten our bodies so also our minds are enlightened by Christ and the Church. We are enlightened in this way, however, if we are not blind in our minds. For although the sun and moon shine on those who are blind in their bodily eyes they, nevertheless, cannot receive the light. In the same way also Christ offers his light to our minds, but it will so enlighten us only if blindness of mind impede in no way. But even if this happen, those who are blind must follow Christ saying and crying out: "Have mercy

---

54 Mt 5.14.
55 Eph 5.27.
56 Gn 1.16–19.
57 Cf. 1 Cor 15.41.

on us, son of David,"[58] that also receiving sight from him they can then also be radiant in the splendor of his light.

But all who see are not equally enlightened by Christ, but individuals are enlightened according to the measure in which they are able to receive the power of the light. And just as the eyes of our body are not equally enlightened by the sun, but to the extent that one shall have ascended to higher places and contemplated its risings with a gaze from a higher vantage point, to such an extent will he perceive more of both its splendor and its heat. So also to the extent that our mind shall have approached Christ in a more exalted and lofty manner and shall have presented itself nearer the splendor of his light, to such an extent will it be made to shine more magnificently and clearly in his light as also he himself says through the prophet: " 'Draw near to me and I shall draw near to you,' says the Lord,"[59] And again he says: "I am a God who draws near, and not a God afar off."[60]

We do not, however, all come to him in the same way, but each one "according to his own proper ability."[61] For either we come to him with the crowds and he refreshes us by parables to this end only, lest we faint "in the way"[62] from many fasts, or, of course, we sit always and incessantly at his feet, being free for this alone, that we might hear "his word," not at all disturbed about "much serving," but choosing "the best part which shall not be taken away" from us.[63] And certainly those who thus approach him obtain much more of his light. But if, as the apostles, we should be moved from him in no way at all, but should always remain with him in all his tribulations, then he expounds and solves for us in secret those things which he has spoken to the crowds and enlightens us much more clearly. But if in addition someone should be such as can also ascend the mountain with him, as Peter, James, and John, he will be

---

58 Mt 9.27.
59 Cf. Zec 1.3; Jas 4.8.
60 Jer 23.23.
61 Cf. Mt 25.25.
62 Cf. Mt 15.32; Mk 8.3.
63 Cf. Lk 10.39–42.

enlightened not only by the light of Christ, but also by the voice of the Father himself.

(8) "And God said: 'Let the waters bring forth creeping creatures having life and birds flying over the earth in the firmament of heaven.' And it was so done."[64]

According to the letter "creeping creatures" and "birds" are brought forth by the waters at the command of God and we recognize by whom these things which we see have been made. But let us see how also these same things come to be in our firmament of heaven, that is, in the firmness of our mind or heart.

I think that if our mind has been enlightened by Christ, our sun, it is ordered afterwards to bring forth from these waters which are in it "creeping creatures" and "birds which fly," that is, to bring out into the open good or evil thoughts that there might be a distinction of the good thoughts from the evil, which certainly both proceed from the heart. For both good and evil thoughts are brought forth from our heart as from the waters. But by the word and precept of God let us offer both to God's view and judgment that, with his enlightenment we may be able to distinguish what is evil from the good, that is, that we may separate from ourselves those things which creep upon the earth and bear earthly cares.

But let us permit those things which are better, that is, the "birds," to fly not only "above the earth," but also "in the region of the firmament of heaven," that is, let us explore in ourselves the meaning and plan of heavenly things as well as earthly, that[65] we can also understand which of the creeping creatures in us may be harmful. If we should see "a woman to lust after her,"[66] that is a poisonous reptile in us. But if we have the disposition of continence, even if an Egyptian mistress love us deeply, we become birds and, leaving the Egyptian garments in her hands, will fly away from the indecent snare. If we should

---

64 Gn 1.20.
65 Following Doutreleau's suggestion that the text should read *id est [ut] sensum. . . , ut intelligere*, rather than *id est ut sensum. . . , intelligere.*
66 Cf. Mt 5.28.

have an inclination inciting us to steal, that is a most evil reptile. But if we have an inclination that even if we should have "two mites" we would offer these very mites out of mercy as a "gift of God,"[67] that inclination is a bird thinking nothing about earthly things, but striving for the firmament of heaven in its flights. If an inclination should come to us persuading us that we ought not bear the tortures of martyrdom, that will be a poisonous reptile. But if an inclination and thought such as this should spring up in us, that we struggle for the truth even to death, this will be a bird straining from earthly things to the things above.[68] In the same manner also we should perceive and distinguish concerning other forms of either sins or virtues, which are "creeping creatures" and which are "birds" which our waters are commanded to bring forth for separation before God.

(9) "And God made the great whales, and every creeping creature having life which the waters brought forth according to their kind, and every winged bird according to its kind."[69]

And we should observe concerning these words in the same way as those which we discussed above, that we too ought to bring forth "great whales" and "creeping creatures having life according to their kind." I think impious thoughts and abominable understandings which are against God are indicated in those great whales. All of these, nevertheless, are to be brought forth in the sight of God and placed before him that we may divide and separate the good from the evil, that the Lord might allot to each its place, as is shown from these words which follow.

(10) "And God saw that they were good, and he blessed them saying: 'Increase and multiply and fill the waters which are in the sea and let the birds be multiplied upon the earth.' And there was evening and there was morning, the fifth day."[70]

---

67 Cf. Lk 21.2.
68 Cf. Phil 3.13.
69 Gn 1.21.
70 Gn 1.21–23.

God commands "the great whales and every creeping creature having life which the waters brought forth" to remain in the sea where also "that dragon which God formed to sport with" dwells.[71] But he orders the birds to multiply upon the earth which once was "the dry land," but now already is called "earth" as we explained above.

But someone asks how the great whales and creeping creatures are interpreted as evil and the birds as good when Scripture said[72] about all together, "And God saw that they were good."[73]

Those things which are opposed to the saints are good for them because they can overcome them and when they have overcome them they become more glorious with God. Indeed when the devil requested that power be given to him against Job, the adversary, by attacking him, was the cause of double glory for Job after his victory. What is shown from the fact that he received double those things which he lost in the present is that he will, without doubt, also receive in the same manner in the heavenly places. And the Apostle says that "No one is crowned except the one who has striven lawfully."[74] And indeed, how will there be a contest if there not be one who resists? How great the beauty and splendor is of light would not be discerned unless the darkness of night intervened. Why are some praised for purity unless because others are condemned for immodesty? Why are strong men magnified unless weak and cowardly men exist? If you use what is bitter then what is sweet is rendered more praiseworthy. If you consider what is dark, the things which are bright will appear more pleasing to you. And, to put it briefly, from the consideration of evil things the glory of good things is indicated more brilliantly. For this reason, therefore, the Scripture says this about everything: "And God saw that they were good."[75]

---

71 Cf. Ps 103.26
72 Reading *est* with A and Doutreleau. Baehrens thinks *est* is "vielleicht richtig," but writes *sit* in his text.
73 Gn 1.21.
74 2 Tim 2.5.
75 Gn 1.21.

Why, nevertheless, is it not written: "And God said that they were good," instead of: "God saw that they were good"? That is, God saw the usefulness of those things and that way by which, although in themselves they are as they are, nevertheless, they could perfect good men. For this reason, therefore, he said: "Increase and multiply and fill the waters which are in the sea, and let the birds be multiplied upon the earth,"[76] that is, that the great whales indeed and the creeping creatures be in the sea, as we explained above, and the birds upon the earth.

(11) "And God said: 'Let the earth bring forth the living creature according to its kind, four-footed creatures and creeping creatures and beasts of the earth according to their kind.' And it was so done. And God made the beasts of the earth according to their kind and all the creeping creatures of the earth according to their kind. And God saw that they were good.'"[77]

There is certainly no question about the literal meaning. For they are clearly said to have been created by God, whether animals or four-footed creatures or beasts or serpents upon the earth. But it is not unprofitable to relate these words to those which we explained above in a spiritual sense.

There, for example, it is said: "Let the waters bring forth creeping creatures having life and birds flying above the earth in the region of the firmament of heaven,"[78] but here the text says: "Let the earth bring forth the living creature according to its kind, four-footed creatures, creeping creatures, and beasts of the earth according to their kind."[79] And we said that those things certainly, which are brought forth from the waters, ought to be understood as the impulses and thoughts of our mind which are brought forth from the depth of the heart. But in the present text, I think the impulses of our outer man, that is, of our carnal and earthly man, are indicated by this which is said: "Let the earth bring forth the living creature according to

---

76 Gn 1.22.
77 Gn 1.24–25.
78 Gn 1.20.
79 Gn 1.24.

its kind, four-footed creatures, creeping creatures, and beasts on the earth according to their kind."[80] In brief, the text indicated nothing winged in these things which are said about the flesh, but only "four-footed creatures, creeping creatures, and beasts of the earth." According to that, to be sure, which is said by the Apostle, that "no good dwells in my flesh"[81] and that "the wisdom of the flesh is hostile to God,"[82] those are certainly things which the earth, that is, our flesh,[83] produces, about which the Apostle again admonishes saying: "Put to death your members which are upon the earth, fornication, uncleanness, lewdness, covetousness, idolatry," etc.[84]

When, therefore, all these things which are seen came into existence by the command of God through his Word and that immense visible world was prepared (but at the same time also the allegorical figure showed what those things were which could adorn the lesser world, that is, man),[85] then at that time man himself was created according to those things which are declared subsequently.

(12) "And God said: 'Let us make man according to our image and likeness, and let him have dominion over the fish of the sea and the birds of heaven and the animals and the whole earth and everything which creeps upon the earth.' "[86]

---

80 Gn 1.24.

81 Rom 7.18.

82 Rom 8.7.

83 P bibl. univ. Giss. 17 (see below), which is assumed to be a text of Origen, gives the same interpretation to earth, the beasts, etc.: "Increase and multiply and fill the earth and have dominion over it," meaning by earth the body which encompasses him, for he comes to be from the earth. God wills that man rule the body and not be ruled by it. But only the just man, blessed by God, who has been brought into existence by him in his image and likeness, who has been infused with breath by him and thought worthy to rule the irrational elements in himself, rules this earth (*Ein Bruchstück des Origenes über Genesis 1,28*, ed. D. Glaue [Giessen: Alfred Töpelmann, 1928] 8; hereinafter cited as P bibl. univ. Giss. 17).

84 Col 3.5.

85 This comparison between the macrocosm and the microcosm was common in antiquity. Baehrens cites Aristotle *Phys.* 252b.26–27, and several passages in Philo.

86 Gn 1.26.

Consequently, in accordance with those things which we explained above, God wishes such a man as we described to have dominion over the previously mentioned beasts, birds, creeping creatures, four-footed creatures, and all the rest. We explained how these ought to be understood allegorically when we said that the water, that is, man's mind, is ordered to bring forth the spiritual sense and the earth to bring forth the carnal sense, that the mind might rule them and not they rule the mind. For God wishes that man, that great "work" of God on account of whom also the whole world has been created,[87] not only be unstained by these things which we mentioned above and free from them, but also that he might rule them. But now let us consider what sort of living being man is from these same words of Scripture.

All the rest of creation comes into being at the command of God as Scripture says: "And God said, 'Let there be a firmament.' "[88] "And God said, 'Let the water which is under heaven be gathered into one gathering and let the dry land appear.' "[89] "And God said: 'Let the earth bring forth vegetation.' "[90] So also Scripture speaks about the remaining things.

But let us see what those things are which God himself made, and in this way let us give attention to what greatness belongs to man. "In the beginning God made heaven and earth."[91] Likewise Scripture says: "And God made two great lights."[92] And now again: "Let us make man."[93] The work of God himself is attributed to these alone, but to none of the others. Only heaven and earth, the sun, moon, and stars, and now man have been made by God, but all the rest is said to be made by his command. From this, therefore, consider how

---

87 This was the Stoic view. See, for example, Epictetus *Disc.* 2.8.6–11, 10.3; Cicero *N.D.* 2.37, 133, 154–62. Origen recognizes this in *Cels.* 4.74 where he attacks Celsus' espousal of the Academic tradition that "*everything was made just as much for the irrational animals as for men*" (Chadwick, *Origen*, 243).
88 Gn 1.6.
89 Gn 1.9.
90 Gn 1.11.
91 Gn 1.1.
92 Gn 1.16.
93 Gn 1.26.

great is man's greatness, who is made equal to such great and distinguished elements, who has the honor of heaven for which reason also "the kingdom of heaven" is promised to him. And he has the honor of the earth since indeed he hopes to enter a good land and "a land of the living flowing with milk and honey."[94] He has the honor of the sun and moon having the promise of shining "as the sun in the kingdom of God."[95]

(13) I see, however, something indeed even more distinguished in the condition of man, which I do not find said elsewhere: "And God made man, according to the image of God he made him."[96] We find this attributed neither to heaven nor earth nor the sun or moon.

We do not understand, however, this man indeed whom Scripture says was made "according to the image of God" to be corporeal. For the form of the body does not contain the image of God, nor is the corporeal man said to be "made," but "formed," as is written in the words which follow. For the text says: "And God formed man," that is fashioned,[97] "from the slime of the earth."[98]

But it is our inner man, invisible, incorporeal, incorruptible, and immortal which is made "according to the image of God." For it is in such qualities as these that the image of God is more correctly understood. But if anyone suppose that this man who is made "according to the image and likeness of God" is made of flesh, he will appear to represent God himself as made of flesh and in human form. It is most clearly impious to think this about God. In brief, those carnal men who have no under-

---

94 Cf. Ex 3.8; 33.3.
95 Cf. Mt 13.43.
96 Gn 1.27. For a thorough discussion of Origen's interpretation of the significance of man being created "according to the image of God" see Crouzel, *Théologie de l'image*, 147–79. For his distinction between the image and the likeness see ibid., 217–45.
97 This insertion probably represents an addition by Rufinus to explain *plasmavit* which was borrowed from the Greek *eplasen*.
98 Gn 2.7. This distinction between "made" and "formed" and its relation to two different acts of creation is frequent in Origen. Crouzel, *Théologie de l'image*, 148, lists numerous passages in Origen where the distinction is made. For a discussion of Origen's doctrine of the two creations of man see ibid., 148–53.

standing of the meaning of divinity suppose, if they read anywhere in the Scriptures of God that "heaven is my throne, and the earth my footstool,"[99] that God has so large a body that they think he sits in heaven and stretches out his feet to the earth. But they think this because they do not have those ears which can worthily hear the words of God about God which are related by the Scripture. For the statement, "Heaven is my throne," is worthily understood of God as follows, that we might know that God rests and resides in these whose "citizenship is in heaven."[100] But in these who are still involved in earthly details, the most remote part of his providence is found, which is figuratively indicated in the mention of feet. If any perchance of this latter group lay hold of a zeal and desire to become heavenly by perfection of life and loftiness of understanding, they also become thrones of God themselves, having first been made heavenly by their warfare[101] and manner of life. These also say: "He raised us up with Christ and at the same time made us sit in the heavenly places."[102] But also those whose "treasure is in heaven"[103] can be said to be heavenly and thrones of God, since "where their treasure is, there is their heart."[104] And not only does God rest upon them, but he also dwells in them.

But if someone can become so great that he can say: "Or do you seek a proof of Christ who speaks in me?"[105] God not only dwells in this man but also walks in him. And for this reason any who are perfect, who have been made heavenly or have become of heaven, "declare the glory of God" as it says in the Psalm.[106] For this reason in brief also the apostles who were of

---

99 Is 66.1.
100 Phil 3.20.
101 Following Baehrens who reads *pro militia* with A. Doutreleau accepts *politia*, the reading of DF. He thinks Rufinus has used a doublet here for *politia* (the Latin transposition of the Greek *politeia)* of which *conversatio* is a translation. Doutreleau translates,"rendus célestes par leur conduite."
102 Eph 2.6.
103 Mt 6.20, 19.21.
104 Mt 6.21.
105 2 Cor13.3.
106 Ps 18.1.

heaven were sent to declare the glory of God and received the name of "Boanerges," "which is the sons of thunder,"[107] that by the power of thunder we might believe them truly to be heavens.

Therefore, "God made man, according to the image of God he made him."[108] We must see what that image of God is and inquire diligently in the likeness of what image man is made. For the text did not say that "God made man according to the image or likeness," but "according to the image of God he made him." Therefore, what other image of God is there according to the likeness of whose image man is made, except our Savior who is "the firstborn of every creature,"[109] about whom it is written that he is "the brightness of the eternal light and the express figure of God's substance,"[110] who also says about himself: "I am in the Father, and the Father in me," and "He who has seen me has also seen the Father"?[111] For just as one who sees an image of someone sees him whose image it is, so also one sees God through the Word of God which is the image of God. And thus what he said will be true: "He who has seen me has also seen the Father."[112]

Man, therefore, is made according to the likeness of his image and for this reason our Savior, who is the image of God, moved with compassion for man who had been made according to his likeness, seeing him, his own image having been laid aside, to have put on the image of the evil one, he himself moved with compassion, assumed the image of man and came to him, as also the Apostle attests saying: "Since he was in the form of God, he did not think it robbery to be equal with God, but emptied himself taking the form of a servant,[113] and

---

107 Mk 3.17.
108 Gn 1.27.
109 Col 1.15.
110 Heb 1.3.
111 Jn 14.10, 9.
112 Jn 14.9.
113 Baehrens, following BCF, omits "being made in the likeness of men," which is attested in ADE. He thinks it is a harmonization with the Vulgate. Doutreleau includes it in his text.

in appearance found as a man, he humbled himself even to death."[114]

All therefore, who come to him and desire to become participants in the spiritual image by their progress "are renewed daily in the inner man"[115] according to the image of him who made them, so that they can be made "similar to the body of his glory,"[116] but each one in proportion to his own powers. The apostles transformed themselves to his likeness to such an extent that he could say of them, "I go to my Father and your Father, to my God and your God."[117] For he had already petitioned the Father for his disciples that the original likeness might be restored in them when he says: "Father," grant "that just as you and I are one so also they may be one in us."[118]

Let us always, therefore, contemplate that image of God that we can be transformed to his likeness. For if man, made according to the image of God, contrary to nature by beholding the image of the devil has been made like him by sin, much more by beholding the image of God, according to whose likeness he has been made by God, he will receive that form, which was given to him by nature, through the Word and his power. And let no one, seeing his image to be more with the devil than with God, despair that he can again regain the form of the image of God, because the Savior came not "to call the just, but sinners to repentance."[119] Matthew was a publican and undoubtedly his image was like the devil, but when he comes to the image of God, our Lord and Savior, and follows that image he is transformed to the likeness of the image of God. "James, the son of Zebedee, and John his brother"[120] were fishermen and "uneducated men,"[121] who undoubtedly then bore a likeness more to the image of the

---

114 Phil 2.6–8.
115 Cf. 2 Cor 4.16.
116 Cf. Phil 3.21.
117 Jn 20.17.
118 Jn 17.21–22.
119 Cf. Lk 5.32.
120 Cf. Mt 4.21.
121 Acts 4.13.

devil, but they also, by following the image of God, are made like him, as also the other apostles. Paul was a persecutor of the very image of God; but as he was able to behold his grace and beauty, after these were seen he was remade in his likeness to such an extent that he said: "Or do you seek a proof of Christ who speaks in me?"[122]

(14) "Male and female he made them, and God blessed them saying: 'Increase and multiply and fill the earth and have dominion over it.' "[123]

It seems to be worth inquiring in this passage according to the letter how, when the woman was not yet made, the Scripture says, "Male and female he made them." Perhaps, as I think, it is because of the blessing with which he blessed them saying, "Increase and multiply and fill the earth." Anticipating what was to be, the text says, "Male and female he made them," since, indeed, man could not otherwise increase and multiply except with the female. Therefore, that there might be no doubt about his blessing that is to come, the text says, "Male and female he made them." For in this manner man, seeing the consequence of increasing and multiplying to be from the fact that the female was joined to him, could cherish a more certain hope in the divine blessing. For if the Scripture had said: "Increase and multiply and fill the earth and have dominion over it," not adding this, "Male and female he made them," doubtless he would have disbelieved the divine blessing, as also Mary said in response to that blessing which was pronounced by the angel, "How shall I know this,[124] since I know not a man?"[125]

Or perhaps, because all things which have been made by God are said to be united and joined together, as heaven and earth, as sun and moon, so, therefore, that it might be shown that man also is a work of God and has not been brought forth

---

122 2 Cor 13.3.
123 Gn 1.27–28.
124 A alone has *fiet*. Doutreleau accepts *fiet* in his text.
125 Lk 1.34.

without harmony or the appropriate conjunction, therefore, the text says in anticipation: "Male and female he made them."

These things have been said on that question, which can be raised about the literal meaning.

(15) But let us see also allegorically how man, made in the image of God, is male and female.

Our inner man consists of spirit and soul. The spirit is said to be male; the soul can be called female. If these have concord and agreement among themselves, they increase and multiply by the very accord among themselves and they produce sons, good inclinations and understandings or useful thoughts, by which they fill the earth and have dominion over it. This means they turn the inclination of the flesh, which has been subjected to themselves, to better purposes and have dominion over it, while the flesh, of course, becomes insolent in nothing against the will of the spirit. But now if the soul, which has been united with the spirit and, so to speak, joined in wedlock, turn aside at some time to bodily pleasures and turn back its inclination to the delight of the flesh and at one time indeed appear to obey the salutary warnings of the spirit, but at another time yield to carnal vices, such a soul, as if defiled by adultery of the body, is said properly neither to increase nor multiply, since indeed Scripture designates the sons of adulterers as imperfect.[126] Such a soul, to be sure, which prostrates itself totally to the inclination of the flesh and bodily desires, having forsaken conjunction with the spirit, as if turned away from God will shamelessly hear, "You have the face of a harlot; you have made yourself shameless to all."[127] She will be punished, therefore, like a harlot and her sons will be ordered to be prepared for slaughter.

(16) "And have dominion over the fish of the sea and the birds of heaven and the beasts and everything which is upon the earth and the creeping creatures which creep upon the earth."[128]

---

126 Cf. Wis 3.16.
127 Jer 3.3.
128 Gn 1.28.

These words have already been interpreted in their literal meaning, when we discussed that which God said: "Let us make man" and the rest, where he says, "And let them have dominion over the fish of the sea and the birds of heaven," etc.[129] But allegorically those things no less of which we spoke above seem to me to be indicated in the fish and birds or animals and creeping things of the earth.[130] I mean, either the things which proceed from the inclination of the soul and the thought of the heart, or those which are brought forth from bodily desires and the impulses of the flesh. The saints and all who preserve the blessing of God in themselves exercise dominion over these things guiding the total man by the will of the spirit. But on the other hand, the same things which are brought forth by the vices of the flesh and pleasures of the body hold dominion over sinners.

(17) "And God said, 'Behold I have given to you all vegetation having seed, which produces seed which is upon all the earth, and every tree which has in itself fruit-producing seed. It shall be for food for you and for all the beasts of the earth and for all the birds of heaven and for all the creeping creatures which creep upon the earth, which have in themselves a living soul.' "[131]

The historical meaning, at least, of this sentence indicates clearly that originally God permitted the use of foods from vegetation, that is, vegetables and the fruits of trees. But the opportunity of eating flesh is given to men later when a covenant was made with Noah after the flood. The reasons for

---

129 Gn 1.26.
130 Cf. P bibl. univ. Giss. 17, 8–10: "But the Scripture says that man rules not only the earth, but also the fish, the birds, the beasts, and the creeping creatures. By the fish the text indicates the desires which are secret and deep; for as the fish are in the depth, they are invisible and unseen. God wills that man rule these. And by the birds the text indicates the reason which is in us which God wills that the man in his image rule, for reason, being lightweight, flies like the birds. . . . And he says that man rules the bodily deeds, which occupy the subject matter of the beasts and creeping creatures."
131 Gn 1.29–30.

this, of course, will be explained more appropriately in their own places.

But allegorically the vegetation of the earth and its fruit which is granted to men for food can be understood of the bodily affections. For example, anger and concupiscence are offshoots of the body. The fruit of this offshoot, that is, the work, is common to us who are rational and to the beasts of the earth. For when we become angry justly, that is, for the reproach of one who is transgressing and for correction for his salvation, we eat of that fruit of the earth and the corporeal wrath with which we restrain sin, with which we restore justice, becomes our food.

And lest we appear to you to bring these things forth from our own understanding rather than from the authority of the divine Scriptures, go back to the book of Numbers and recall what Phinees the priest did when he saw a harlot of the Madianite people with an Israelite man clinging in impure embraces in the eyes of all. Filled with the wrath of divine jealousy, he drove a sword, which he had seized, through the breast of both.[132] This work was imputed to him by God for righteousness when the Lord says: "Phinees appeased my rage and it shall be imputed to him for righteousness."[133] That earthly food of anger, therefore, becomes our food when we use it rationally for righteousness.

But if anger is agitated irrationally so that it punishes the innocent, so that it rages against those who do nothing wrong, it will be the food of the beasts of the field and the serpents of the earth and the birds of heaven. For the demons also, who both feed on and promote our evil deeds, are nurtured on these foods. For Cain is a sign of this work, who deceived his innocent brother in the anger of envy.

We must think likewise also about concupiscence and the individual affections of this kind. For when "our soul longs for the living God and faints,"[134] concupiscence is our food. But

---

132 Nm 25.7–8.
133 Cf. Nm 25.11–12; Ps 105.31.
134 Cf. Ps 83.3.

when we either see another's wife to lust after her or we lust after something that belongs to a "neighbor," concupiscence becomes a beast-like food, as the lust of Achab can be an example and the deed of Jezabel concerning the vineyard of Naboth of Jezrahel.[135]

The caution of Holy Scripture certainly must be observed also in the matter of the words. Although Scripture had said of men that God said: "Behold I have given to you all the seed-bearing vegetation which is upon the earth, and every tree which is upon the earth; they shall be food for you,"[136] it did not say of the beasts that I have given all these things to them for food, but "it shall be for food for them,"[137] so that, according to the spiritual understanding which we explained, those affections are understood to have been given to man, indeed, by God, but it is announced by God that they will also be for food for the beasts of the earth. For that reason, therefore, the divine Scripture has made use of the most cautious language. It says that God says to men, indeed: "I have given you these things for food,"[138] but when it comes to the beasts, not with the import of a command, but as it were, an announcement, he says that these things will be for food also for the beasts, the birds, and the serpents.

But in accordance with the view of the apostle Paul, let us give attention to the text that we can, as he himself says, receive "the mind of Christ"[139] and know "the things that are given us from God."[140] And let us not make what has been given to us for food the food of pigs or dogs, but let us prepare such food in ourselves, by which he may think it fit that the Word and Son of God be received in the inn of our heart, who comes with his Father and wills to make his dwelling with us in the Holy Spirit whose temple we ought to be first of all by our holiness.

To him be glory forever and ever. Amen.

---

135 Cf. 3 Kgs 21.
136 Gn 1.29.
137 Gn 1.30.
138 Gn 1.29.
139 1 Cor 2.16.
140 1 Cor 2.12.

HOMILY II

S WE BEGIN TO SPEAK ABOUT THE ARK which was construct- ed by Noah at God's command, let us see first of all what is related about it literally, and, proposing the questions which many are in the habit of presenting, let us search out also their solutions from the traditions which have been handed down to us by the forefathers. When we have laid foundations of this kind, we can ascend from the historical ac- count to the mystical and allegorical understanding of the spiritual meaning and, if these contain anything secret, we can explain it as the Lord reveals knowledge of his word to us.

First, therefore, let us set forth these words which have been written. "And the Lord said to Noah," the text says, "the critical moment[1] of every man has come before me, since the earth is filled with iniquity by them; and behold, I shall destroy them and the earth. Make, therefore, yourself an ark of squared planks; you shall make nests in the ark, and you shall cover it with pitch within and without. And thus you shall make the ark: the length of the ark three hundred cubits and the breadth fifty cubits and its height thirty cubits, you shall assemble and make the ark, and you shall finish it on top to a cubit. And you shall make a door in the side of the ark. You shall make two lower decks in it and three upper decks."[2] And after a few words the text says, "And Noah did everything which the Lord God commanded him, thus he did it."[3]

In the first place, therefore, we ask what sort of appearance and form we should understand of the ark. I think, to the extent that it is manifest from these things which are described, rising with four angles from the bottom, and the same having

---

1 *Tempus* here translates *kairos* in the LXX.
2 Gn 6.13–16.
3 Gn 6.22.

been drawn together gradually all the way to the top, it has been brought together into the space of one cubit. For thus it is related that at its bases three hundred cubits are laid down in length, fifty in breadth, and thirty are raised in height, but they are brought together to a narrow peak so that its breadth and length are a cubit.[4]

But now on the inside indeed are placed those two decks, that is, comprising a double dwelling, which are called its lower decks. But the triple decks are above, as if we should say, constructed with three upper rooms. Now these separations of dwelling places appear to have been made for this reason, that the diverse kinds of animals or beasts could be separated more easily in individual rooms and whatever animals are tame and less active could be divided from the wild beasts. Those separations of dwellings, therefore, are called nests.

But the planks are said to have been squared. This was both so one piece could be fitted to the other more easily, and so the total assault of the waters might be held back when the flood overflowed, since it was protected, the joint having been coated with pitch within and without.

It has indeed been handed down to us, and not without probability, that the lower parts, which we said above were built double, which also separately are called double-decked, the upper parts which are called triple-decked excepted, were made double for this reason: since all the animals spent a whole year in the ark, and of course, it was necessary that food be provided that whole year and not only food, but also that places be prepared for wastes so that neither the animals themselves, nor especially the men, be plagued by the stench of excrement. They hand down, therefore, that the lower region itself, which is at the bottom, was given over and set aside for

---

4 This section of the homily, beginning with the question of the appearance of the ark through section 2, is preserved in Greek both in catenae and in Procopius of Gaza (see Baehrens, 23–30). In the Greek text Origen says the ark had the shape of a pyramid (*pyramoeides*). Cf. Clement *Strom.* 6.11. Philo, *QG.* 2.5, says the ark came together to a cubit, like a mound. For the subject matter of this entire homily see J. Lewis, *A Study of the Interpretation of Noah and the Flood in Jewish and Christian Literature* (Leiden: E. J. Brill, 1968).

necessities of this kind.[5] But the region above and contiguous
to this one was alloted to storing food. And indeed it seemed
necessary that animals be brought in from without for those
beasts whose nature it was to feed on flesh, that feeding on
their flesh they might be able to preserve their life for the sake
of renewing offspring, but other provisions would be stored
up for other animals, which their natural use demands.

They hand down, therefore, that the lower parts which are
called double-decked were set aside for these uses, but the
upper parts were alloted as a dwelling place for the beasts or
animals, in which the lower areas indeed were given as a
dwelling place for wild beasts and fierce beasts or serpents, but
the places contiguous to these in the upper areas were stables
for domesticated animals. But above all, the abode for men was
located at the highest point, since it is they who excel all in both
honor and reason, so that just as man, by means of his reason
and wisdom, is said to have dominion over all things which are
on the earth, so also he might be higher in place and above all
the animals which were gathered in the ark.

But they also hand down that the door which is said to have
been made in the side was at that place so that it might have the
lower areas, which the text called double-decked, below it and
the upper areas, which the text called triple-decked, may be
called upper from the location of the door and all the animals
brought in thence might be separated with the appropriate
distinction to their own places whatever they were, as we said
above.

But the protection of the door itself is no longer performed
by human methods. For how, after it is closed and there was no
human outside the ark, could the door be coated with pitch on
the outside, unless it was without doubt the work of divine
power lest the waters gain entrance by an access which a
human hand might not secure? For this reason, therefore,
Scripture, although it had said about all other things, that
Noah made the ark and brought in the animals and his sons

---

5 Among the rabbis, some said that the bottom story of the ark was for
   garbage while others reversed it and said the top floor was for garbage
   (*Genesis Rabbah* 31.11).

and their wives, did not say of the door that Noah closed the door of the ark, but Scripture says that "The Lord God closed the door of the ark from without, and so the flood occurred."[6] It should be observed, however, that after the flood Noah is not said to have opened the door, but the "window," when he sent forth "a raven to see whether the water had ceased upon the earth."[7]

But that Noah brought the food into the ark for all the animals or beasts which entered with him, hear from these words which the Lord speaks to Noah: "Take to yourself," the text says, "from all the foods which are eaten and you shall gather it to yourself, and it shall be for you and them to eat."[8] But that Noah did those things which the Lord commanded him, hear Scripture saying: "And Noah did," Scripture says, "everything which the Lord God commanded him, thus he did it."[9]

Certainly since Scripture related nothing about the places which we said were set apart for the excrement of the animals, but tradition preserves some things, it will appear opportune that silence has been maintained on this about which reason may sufficiently teach of its importance. And because it could less worthily be fitted to a spiritual meaning, rightly, therefore, Scripture, which rather fits its narratives to allegorical meanings, was silent about this.

Nevertheless, to the degree that the narrative concerns the force of the rains and the flood, no form could be given to the ark so fitting and suitable, so that, from the top, as if from a kind of roof brought to a narrow point, it might diffuse the fall of the rains, and continuing with stability four-cornered deep in the waters, the ark could neither be tipped nor sunk by the rush of the winds nor the pitching of the waves nor the restlessness of the animals which were within.

(2) But although all these things were composed with such great skill, some people present questions, and especially Ap-

---

6 Gn 7.16–17.
7 Cf. Gn 8.6,8.
8 Gn 6.21.
9 Gn 6.22.

elles, who was a disciple indeed of Marcion, but was the inventor of another heresy greater than that one which he took up from his teacher.[10] He, therefore, wishes to show that the writings of Moses contained nothing in themselves of the divine wisdom and nothing of the work of the Holy Spirit. With this intention he exaggerates sayings of this kind, and says that in no way was it possible to receive, in so brief a space, so many kinds of animals and their foods, which would be sufficient for a whole year. For when "two by two"[11] from the unclean animals, that is, two males and two females—for this is what the repeated word signifies—but "seven by seven"[12] from the clean animals, which is seven pairs, are said to have been led into the ark, how, he asks, could it happen that that space which is recorded could receive, at the least, four elephants alone? And after he opposes each species in this manner, he adds above all to these words: "It is evident, therefore, that the story is invented; but if it is, it is evident that this Scripture is not from God."

But against these words we bring to the knowledge of our audience things which we learned from men who were skilled and versed in the traditions of the Hebrews and from our old teachers. The forefathers used to say, therefore, that Moses who, as Scripture testifies about him, was "instructed in all the wisdom of the Egyptians,"[13] reckoned the number of cubits in this passage according to the art of geometry in which the Egyptians especially are skillful.[14] For with geometricians, ac-

---

10 Apelles was a second century Gnostic. He began as a disciple of Marcion at Rome, but later modified Marcion's teaching and founded his own sect. Our main source of information about him is Eusebius *H.E.* 5.13. See also Tertullian *Praes. Her.* 30, 34, and Origen *Cels.* 5.54.

11 Gn 6.19.

12 Gn 7.2.

13 Cf. Acts 7.22.

14 The Greek text of this passage (see note 4 above) says that Origen learned from one highly regarded by the Hebrews that the 300 cubits refer to what the geometricians call the second power (*dunamis*) of the square (*tetragōnou*) so that the stated dimensions should all be squared, yielding dimensions at the base of the ark of 90,000 cubits in length, 2500 in breadth, and 900 in height (Baehrens 28.16–23). A similar statement is made in Origen *Cels.* 4.41: "Should we not rather admire a construction which resembled a very large city? For when we square the measurements, the result is that it was

cording to that computation which they call the second power,[15] one cubit of a solid and square is considered as six if it is derived in general, or as three hundred if singly.[16] If this computation, at least, be observed, spaces of such great length and breadth will be discovered in the measure of this ark that they could truly receive the whole world's offspring to restore it, and the revived seedbed of all living beings. Let these things be said, as much as pertains to the historical account, against those who endeavor to impugn the Scriptures of the Old Testament as containing certain things which are impossible and irrational.[17]

(3) But now, since we have already previously prayed to him who alone can remove the veil from the reading of the Old Testament, let us attempt to inquire what spiritual edification also this magnificent construction of the ark contains.

I think, therefore, as I with my limited understanding am able to comprehend it, that that flood which nearly ended the world at that time contains a form of that end of the world which really will be. Because also the Lord himself announced saying: "For just as in the days of Noah they were buying, they were selling, they were building, they were marrying, they were giving in marriage, and the flood came and destroyed them all; so shall also the coming of the Son of man be."[18]

---

ninety thousand cubits long at the bottom, and two thousand five hundred broad" (Chadwich, *Origen*, 217).

15 *Virtus = dunamis*. See note 14 above.

16 There is nothing in the Greek corresponding to this puzzling statement. See note in Chadwick, *Origen*, 217, and Ginzberg, *Legends*, 5.176. Augustine, *Quaest. in Hept.* 1.4 (PL 34.549), knew this passage in Latin,for he says that Origen solved the problem of the size of the ark by referring to the geometric cubit. *Cubitum autem geometricum dicit tantum valere quantum nostra cubita sex valent.* He makes a similar statement about Origen stating that one geometrical cubit equals six regular cubits in *De Civ. Dei* 15.27. The rabbis alluded to the cubits in the dimensions of the ark being special Egyptian cubits (*Genesis Rabbah* 31.10).

17 Origen himself, however, often regards the literal meaning of Scripture as "impossible or irrational." He asserts in *De princ.* 4.2.9 that the word of God has inserted certain impossibilities and absurdities into both the law and history of the Old Testament as intentional stumbling blocks so that its words will not be taken literally. See below, in this same homily, 6. Cf. *Ex Hom.* 10.2 *et passim*.

18 Lk 17.26–27; Mt 24.37–39.

In this statement the Lord clearly represents that flood which preceeded and the end of the world which he says is to come as one and the same kind of flood. Therefore, just as it is said at that time to that Noah that he make an ark and bring into it along with himself not only his sons and neighbors, but also diverse kinds of animals, so also it is said by the Father in the consummation of the ages to our Noah, who alone is truly just and perfect, that he make himself an ark of squared planks and give it dimensions filled with heavenly mysteries. For this is described in the Psalm where it says: "Ask of me and I will give you the Gentiles for your inheritance and the ends of the earth for your possession."[19]

Therefore he constructs the ark and makes nests in it, that is, certain chambers in which animals of various kind are received. The prophet also speaks of these chambers: "Go, my people, into your chambers, hide yourself a while until the fury of my anger pass away."[20] This people, therefore, which is saved in the Church, is compared to all those whether men or animals which are saved in the ark.

But since neither the merit of all nor the progress in faith is one, therefore, also that ark does not offer one abode for all, but there are two lower decks and three upper decks and compartments are separated in it to show that also in the Church, although all are contained within the one faith and are washed in the one baptism, progress, however, is not one and the same for all, "but each one in his own order."[21]

These, indeed, who live by rational knowledge and are capable not only of ruling themselves but also of teaching others, since very few are found, represent the few who are saved with Noah himself and are united with him in the closest relationship, just as also our Lord, the true Noah, Christ Jesus, has few intimates, few sons and relatives, who are participants in his word and capable of his wisdom. And these are the ones who are placed in the highest position and are gathered in the uppermost part of the ark.

19 Ps 2.8.
20 Is 26.20.
21 1 Cor 15.23.

A multitude of other irrational animals or even beasts is held in the lower decks, and especially a multitude of those beasts whose fierce raging the charm of faith has not tamed. But of this group those are a little superior which, though falling short in reason, nevertheless, preserve more simplicity and innocence.

And thus by ascending through the individual levels of the dwellings, one arrives at Noah himself, whose name means rest or righteous, who is Christ Jesus.[22] For what Lamech his father says is not appropriate to the ancient Noah. For "this one," he says, "shall give us rest from the labors and the sorrows of our hands and from the earth which the Lord God cursed."[23] For how shall it be true that the ancient Noah gave rest to that Lamech or to that people who were then contained in the lands? How is there a cessation from sorrows and labor in the times of Noah? How is the curse which the Lord had placed on the earth removed when rather both the divine wrath is shown to be greater and God is reported to say, "I am sorry that I made man on the earth,"[24] and again he says, "I will destroy all flesh which is upon the earth,"[25] and the destruction of the living is given, above all, as an indication of the greatest displeasure?

But if you look to our Lord Jesus Christ of whom it is said: "Behold the lamb of God, behold him who takes away the sin of the world,"[26] and of whom it is said again: "Being made a curse for us that he might redeem us from the curse of the law,"[27] and again when Scripture says, "Come to me you who labor and are burdened and I will refresh you and you shall find rest for your souls,"[28] you will find him to be the one who truly has given rest to men and has freed the earth from the curse with which the Lord God cursed it.

---

22 See Appendix, 1.
23 Gn 5.29.
24 Cf. Gn 6.7.
25 Cf. Gn 6.7,12. Reading *delebo* with P. Baehrens prints *deleam*.
26 Jn 1.29.
27 Gal 3.13.
28 Mt 11.28–29.

Therefore, it is said to this spiritual Noah who has given rest to men and has taken away the sin of the world: "You shall make yourself an ark of squared planks."[29]

(4) Let us see, therefore, what the squared planks are. That is squared which in no way sways to and fro, but in whatever way you turn it, it stands firm with trustworthy and solid stability. Those are the planks which bear all the weight either of the animals within or the floods without. I think these are the teachers in the Church, the leaders, and zealots of the faith who both encourage the people who have been placed within the Church by a word of admonition and the grace of the teaching, and who resist, by the power of the word and the wisdom of reason, those without, whether heathens or heretics, who assail the Church and stir up floods of questions and storms of strife.

But do you wish to see that the divine Scripture understands trees to be rational? Let us review what was written by the prophet Ezechiel. "And it came to pass," Scripture says, "in the eleventh year, the third month, the first day of the month, that the word of the Lord came to me, saying: 'Son of man, speak to Pharao king of Egypt and his multitude: "To whom do you make yourself similar in your exaltation? Behold the Assyrian was like a cypress in Lebanon, with beautiful branches and thick with leaves and lofty in height. His top was among the clouds. Water nourished him, and the deep exalted him and brought all its rivers around him and it sent forth its gatherings to all the trees of the plain. Therefore his height was exalted above all the trees of the plain." ' "[30] And a little further on the text says, "The many cypresses in the paradise of God and the pines are not equal to its branches, and the fir trees were not equal to them. No tree in the paradise of God was like him, and all the trees of the paradise of God's delight were jealous of him."[31]

Do you perceive of what trees or what kind of trees the

---

29 Gn 6.14.
30 Ez 31.1–5.
31 Ez 31.8–9.

prophet speaks? How could he be describing the cypress of Lebanon to which all the trees which are in the paradise of God could not be compared? And he also adds this at the end, that all the trees which are in the paradise of God are jealous of it, showing clearly, in the spiritual sense, that the trees which are in the garden of God are to be said to be rational since he describes a certain jealousy among them against those trees which are in Lebanon.

Whence, to say this also in digression, consider if perhaps that also which is written, "Everyone who hangs on a tree is accursed of God,"[32] ought not to be so understood even as also that which is said elsewhere: "Cursed be the man who has hope in man."[33] For we ought to depend[34] on God alone and on no other, even if someone be said to proceed from the paradise of God, as also Paul says: "Even if we or an angel of heaven preach a gospel to you other than that which we have preached to you, let him be anathema."[35] But enough of this for now.

Meanwhile you have seen what the squared planks are which are arranged by the spiritual Noah as a kind of wall and defense for these who are within from the floods which come upon them from without, which planks are coated "with pitch within and without."[36] For Christ, the architect of the Church, does not wish you to be such as those "who on the outside indeed appear to men to be just, but on the inside are tombs of the dead,"[37] but he wishes you to be both holy in body without and pure in heart within, on guard on all sides and protected by the power of purity and innocence. This is what it means to be coated with pitch within and without.

(5) Next the text speaks of the length and breadth and height of the ark and numbers are proposed in these dimensions indeed which have been consecrated by great mys-

---

32 Dt 21.23.
33 Jer 17.5.
34 *Pendere*. This is the same verb that appears above in Dt 21.23.
35 Gal 1.8.
36 Gn 6.14.
37 Cf. Mt 23.27.

teries. But before we discuss the numbers, let us see what this is which Scripture calls length and breadth and height.

The Apostle, in a certain passage, when he was speaking very mystically about the mystery of the cross, says as follows: "That you might know what is the length and breadth and depth."[38] Now depth and height mean the same thing except that height appears to measure space from the lower regions to the higher, but depth begins from the higher and descends to the lower. Consequently, therefore, the spirit of God discloses figures of great mysteries through both Moses and Paul. For since Paul was preaching the mystery of the condescension of Christ, he used the term depth as if Christ comes from the upper regions to the lower. But Moses is describing the restoration of those who are recalled by Christ from the lower regions to the higher and celestial ones, from the destruction and ruin of the world, as from the violent death of a flood. For this reason Moses does not speak about depth, but height in the measure of the ark, as it were, where one ascends from the earthly and lowly regions to the heavenly and exalted ones.

Numbers also are proposed: three hundred cubits long, fifty wide, thirty high.

Three hundred is three one hundreds. Now the number one hundred is shown to be full and perfect in everything and to contain the mystery of the whole rational creation, as we read in the Gospels where it says that "a certain man having a hundred sheep, when he lost one of them, left the ninety-nine in the mountains and descended to seek that one which he had lost and when it was found he carried it back on his shoulders and placed it with those ninety-nine which had not been lost."[39] This hundred, therefore, is the number of the whole rational creation, since it does not subsist from itself but has descended

---

38 Eph 3.18. The MSS are divided on the text of this verse. Baehrens follows ABP and prints *longitudo et latitudo et profundum.* The reading of DF is accepted by Aldus Manutius: *longitudo et altitudo et profundum.* Doutreleau, with Delarue, accepts the reading of CE: *longitudo et latitudo et altitudo et profundum.* The discussion which follows the quotation seems to confirm Baehrens's choice, for it contrasts Paul's use of depth with Moses' use of height.

39 Cf. Lk 15.4–5; Mt 18.12–13.

from the Trinity and has received the length of its life, that is the grace of immortality, from the Father through the Son and the Holy Spirit. Therefore, it is stated as tripled in as much as it is this which is increased to perfection by the grace of the Trinity and which, by knowledge of the Trinity, may restore to the three hundred the one fallen by ignorance from the one hundred.

The width has the number fifty which has been consecrated as the number of forgiveness and remission.[40] For according to the law there was a remission in the fiftieth year, that is, so that if someone had sold off his property, he might receive it back; if a free man had come into slavery, he might regain his freedom; a debtor might receive remission; an exile might return to his fatherland.

Therefore Christ, the spiritual Noah, in his ark in which he frees the human race from destruction, that is, in his Church, has established in its breadth the number fifty, the number of forgiveness. For if he had not given forgiveness of sins to those who believe, the breadth of the Church would not have been spread around the world.

But the number thirty of the height contains a mystery like the number three hundred. For what a hundred multiplied by three makes there, ten multiplied by three makes here.

But the sum is reduced to one, the number of the total construction, because "there is one God the Father from whom are all things, and one Lord" and "one faith of the Church, one baptism, one body and one spirit"[41] and all things hasten to the one goal of the perfection of God.

But also if you who hear these words direct your thoughts to the Holy Scriptures in your leisure, you will discover many great events to be comprised under the number thirty or fifty. Joseph was thirty years old when he was led out of prison and received the rule of all Egypt that he might divert the calamity of an imminent famine by divine provision.[42] Jesus is reported

---

40 Cf. Clement *Strom.* 6.11.
41 1 Cor 8.6; Eph 4.5,4.
42 Cf. Gn 41.46.

to have been thirty years old when he came to baptism[43] and "saw the heavens divided and the spirit of God coming upon himself in the form of a dove,"[44] where also for the first time the mystery of the Trinity began to be disclosed. And you will discover many things like these.

But you will also find the fiftieth day a festival for the consecration of the new fruits,[45] and a fiftieth of the spoils of the Madianites is taken away for the Lord.[46] But you will find also Abraham conquering the Sodomites with three hundred men,[47] and Gideon overcomes with three hundred men who lap water with their tongue.[48]

The door, indeed, which is placed neither at the front nor above but on the side obliquely, since it is the time of divine wrath—for "the day of the Lord is a day of wrath and anger,"[49] as it is written; for although some may appear to be saved, many, nevertheless, whom their own deserts condemn, are destroyed and perish—the door is placed obliquely, that what the prophet says might be disclosed: "If you will go athwart with me, I also shall go with you with anger athwart."[50]

Next, let us see also about that which the text calls separately "two lower decks" and "three upper decks," if perhaps these words may not reveal that which the Apostle said: "In the name of Jesus every knee is bowed of those that are in heaven, on earth, and under the earth,"[51] and it be shown that what the Apostle calls under the earth is the lowest of all the decks indeed in the ark, and that next higher deck is the terrestrial region, and the three upper decks which the text mentions are, all together, the heavenly regions, but in these the merits are

---

43 Lk 3.23.
44 Mk 1.10.
45 Cf. Dt 16.
46 Cf. Nm 31.37.
47 Cf. Gn 14.14.
48 Cf. Jgs 7.6,8.
49 Cf. Zep 1.14–15.
50 Lv 26.27–28.
51 Phil 2.10.

distinguished of those who can, according to the apostle Paul, ascend "even to the third heaven."[52]

But "nests and nests" because there are many in the ark, show that there are many dwelling places with the Father.

But what other figure ought we to observe about the animals and beasts and cattle and the other diverse living beings than either the one which Isaias makes known when he says that in the kingdom of Christ the wolf is with the lamb, the panther with the kid, the lion and the ox go to pasture together and their young eat chaff together, and furthermore a small child—such, doubtless, as the Savior said: "Unless you be converted and become as this child you shall not enter the kingdom of God"[53]—will put its hand in the hole of an asp and suffer no harm?[54] Or, also that figure which Peter teaches is now already present in the Church when he relates that he had seen a vision in which all the four-footed creatures and beasts of the earth and birds of heaven were contained within one sheet of faith tied together at the four corners of the Gospels?[55]

(6) But since God orders that the ark which we are attempting to describe be constructed not only with two decks but also with three, let us also give attention to join to this twofold exposition which preceeded also a third in accordance with God's precept.

For the literal meaning which preceeded is placed first as a kind of foundation at the lower levels. This mystical interpretation was second, being higher and loftier. Let us attempt, if we can, to add a moral exposition as the third level, granting that even this text itself appears to contain a mystery not different from this very exposition we are undertaking in that it neither said "with two decks" only and was silent, nor "with three decks" alone and ceased, but when it had said "with two decks," it added also "with three decks." For "with three decks" denotes this threefold expostion.

---

52 Cf. 2 Cor 12.2.
53 Mt 18.3.
54 Cf. Is 11.6–8.
55 Cf. Acts 10.11–12.

But the historical succession cannot always be established in the divine Scriptures, but sometimes is lacking as, for example, when it is said, "Thorns will grow in the hand of a drunkard"[56] and when it is said in the temple built by Solomon, "The sound of hammer and ax was not heard in the house of God"[57] and again in Leviticus when "the leprosy of a wall and a hide and a cloth is ordered to be examined by the priests and purified."[58] Because of these things, therefore, and things like them, the ark is constructed not only "with three decks," but also "with two decks," that we might know that there is not always a triple explanation in the divine Scriptures because a literal explanation does not always follow for us, but sometimes only the mingled meaning of the double explanation.

Let us attempt, therefore, to discuss also a third exposition at the moral level.

If there is anyone who, while evils are increasing and vices are overflowing, can turn from the things which are in flux and passing away and fallen, and can hear the word of God and the heavenly precepts, this man is building an ark of salvation within his own heart and is dedicating a library, so to speak, of the divine word within himself. He is erecting faith, love, and hope as its length, breadth and height. He stretches out faith in the Trinity to the length of life and immortality. He establishes the breadth of love with the compassion of gentleness and kindness. He raises the height of hope to heavenly and exalted places. For while he walks upon the earth he has his "citizenship in heaven."[59] But he brings the sum of his acts back to one. For he knows that "all indeed run, but one receives the palm of victory,"[60] of course, being that one who was not changeable with a variety of thoughts and instability of mind.

But he does not construct this library from planks which are unhewn and rough, but from planks which have been squared

---

56 Prv 26.9.
57 Cf. 3 Kgs 6.7.
58 Cf. Lv 14.34, 13.48.
59 Cf. Phil 3.20.
60 1 Cor 9.24.

and arranged in a uniform line, that is, not from the volumes of secular authors, but from the prophetic and apostolic volumes. For these authors, who have been hewn by diverse temptations, all vices having been curtailed and excised, contain life which has been squared and set free in every part. For the authors of secular books can indeed be called "lofty trees" and "shady trees"—for Israel is accused of having fornicated "under every lofty and shady tree"[61]—because they speak indeed in a lofty manner and use flowery eloquence; they have not, however, acted as they have spoken. They cannot, therefore, be called "squared planks" because life and speech will by no means be equal in them.

If, therefore, you build an ark, if you gather a library, gather it from the words of the prophets and apostles or of those who have followed them in the right lines of faith. You shall make it "with two decks" and "with three decks." From this library learn the historical narratives; from it recognize "the great mystery" which is fulfilled in Christ and in the Church.[62] From it also learn how to correct habits, to curtail vices, to purge the soul and draw it off from every bond of captivity, setting up in it "nests and nests" of the various virtues and perfections. By all means "you shall cover it with pitch within and without,"[63] "bearing faith in your heart, offering confession with your mouth,"[64] having knowledge within, works without, advancing pure in heart within, spotless in body without.

In this ark, therefore, let us place, meanwhile, at the moral level, either that library of divine books or a faithful soul. You ought also to bring in animals of every kind not only clean but also unclean. Now we can easily say that the clean animals indeed can be understood as memory, learning, understanding, examination and discernment of those things which we read, and other things like these. But it is difficult to speak

---

61 Jer 2.20, 3.6.
62 Cf. Eph 5.32.
63 Cf. Gn 6.14.
64 Cf. Rom 10.10.

about the unclean animals which also are named "two by two."
Nevertheless we can, in such difficult passages, dare so much: I
think that concupiscence and wrath, which are in every soul,
are necessarily said to be unclean in the sense that they serve to
make man sin. But in the sense that neither succession of
posterity is renewed without concupiscence nor can any correction or discipline exist without anger, they are said to be
necessary and must be preserved.

And although these things discussed may now appear not to
be in the moral but in the natural sense, nevertheless, we have
treated for edification the ideas which could occur to us at
present.

To be sure, if someone can, at leisure, bring together
Scripture with Scripture, and compare divine Scripture, and
fit together "spiritual things with spiritual,"[65] we are not un-
mindful that he will discover in this passage many secrets of a
profound and hidden mystery which we cannot now bring
forth either because of the shortness of time or the fatigue of
the listeners.

Let us pray, however, the mercy of the omnipotent God to
make us "not only hearers of" his "word," but also "doers"[66]
and to bring upon our souls also a flood of his water and
destroy in us what he knows should be destroyed and quicken
what he knows should be quickened, through Christ our Lord
and through his Holy Spirit. To him be glory forever and ever.
Amen.[67]

---

65 Cf. 1 Cor 2.13.
66 Cf. Jas 1.22.
67 Cf. Rom 11.36.

HOMILY III
On the circumcision of Abraham

E READ IN MANY PASSAGES of the divine Scripture that God speaks to men. For this reason the Jews indeed, but also some of our people, supposed that God should be understood as a man, that is, adorned with human members and human appearance. But the philosophers despise these stories as fabulous and formed in the likeness of poetic fictions. Because of this it seems to me that I must first discuss these few matters and then come to those words which have been read.

First, therefore, let my word be to those outside the Church who arrogantly clamor around us, saying that it is not appropriate for that most exalted and invisible and incorporeal God to experience human affections. For if, they say, you give him the experience of speaking, you will, doubtless, give him also a mouth and a tongue and the other members with which the function of speaking is performed. But if this be so, one has departed from the invisible and incorporeal God. And they harass our people, joining many similar arguments to these. Therefore, if we may have the support of your prayers, we shall briefly reply to these arguments as the Lord may grant.

(2) As we profess that God is incorporeal and omnipotent and invisible, so we confess with a sure and immovable doctrine that he cares about mortal affairs and that nothing happens in heaven or earth apart from his providence. Note that we said nothing happens without his providence; not, without his will. For many things happen without his will; nothing without his providence. For providence is that by which he attends to and manages and makes provision for the things which happen. But his will is that by which he wishes something or does not wish it. But enough of these matters for

the present, for that particular discussion is too long and extensive.

In accordance with this profession, therefore, that God is the provider and manager of all things, it follows that he makes known what he wishes or what is advantageous for men. For if he should not make these things known he will not be the provider for man nor will he be believed[1] to care for mortal affairs.[2] Since, therefore, God makes known to men what he wishes them to do, in what particularly appropriate way is he to be said to make it known? Is it not by that one which is used and known by men? For if, for example, we should say that God is silent, which is believed to be appropriate to his nature, how will anything be supposed to be made known by him through silence? But now, therefore, it is said that he has spoken, that men, since they know that the will of one becomes known to another by this means, might acknowledge that those words which are delivered to them by the prophets are disclosures of God's will. The will of God is certainly not understood to be contained in these words unless he is said to have spoken them, for it is neither thought nor understood among men that the will can ever be made known through silence. But again we do not say these things to the extent, in accordance with the error of the Jews or even some of our own people who err with them, that we should think, since human frailty cannot hear of God otherwise except as the thing itself and the words are known to it, for this reason God also does these things with members similar to ours and with human appearance. This is foreign to the Church's faith.

But in this manner God is said to have spoken to man: he either inspires the heart of each of the saints or causes the sound of a voice to reach his ears. So also when he makes known that what each one says or does is known to him the Scripture says that he "has heard"; and when he makes known that we have done something unjust, it says that he "is angry"; when he censures us as ungrateful for his benefits, it says he "repents," making known indeed these things by these dis-

---

1 Accepting *credetur* in A. Baehrens has *creditur* in his text.
2 Cf. the argument in Epictetus *Disc.* 1.12.1–6.

positions which are common to men, but not performing them
by these members which belong to corporeal nature. For that
substance is simple and is composed neither of any members
nor of bodily structures and dispositions. But whatever is done
by divine powers is either cited by the name of human members or is announced by dispositions that are common and
known, so that men can understand. And in this way God is
said either to be angry or to hear or speak.

For if the human voice is defined to be air which has been
struck,[3] that is, made to reverberate by the tongue, the voice of
God can also be said to be air struck either by force or the
divine will. And thence it is that whenever there is a divine
communication it comes not to the ears of all, but to the
hearing of those to whom it is of interest, that you might know
that the sound has not been produced by the movement of a
tongue—otherwise the hearing would be common to all—but
has been governed by the control of the will from above.

However, the word of God is said to have occurred often to
the prophets and patriarchs and the rest of the holy men also
without the sound of a voice as we are copiously taught from all
the sacred volumes. In which case, to speak briefly, the mind
which has been illuminated by the spirit of God is directed to
words.

And so, whether in this way or in that which we mentioned
above, when God makes his will known he is said to have
spoken.

In this sense, therefore, let us now discuss some things from
these words which have been read.

(3) Many responses are given to Abraham by God, but they
are not all delivered to one and the same man. For some are to
Abram and some to Abraham, that is, some are expressed after
the change of name and others while he was still known by his
name given at birth. And first indeed, before the change of
name, that oracle is delivered to Abram by God which says:
"Go out from your country and from your kindred and from

---

3 This was the Stoic definition of sound (*phonē*). See the definitions of Zeno
and Diogenes quoted in C. De Vogel, *Greek Philosophy*, vol. 3 (Leiden: E. J.
Brill, 1973), 101.

your father's house," and the rest.[4] But no order is given in this about the covenant of God, no order about circumcision. For it was not possible while he was still Abram and was bearing the name of his physical birth to receive the covenant of God and the mark of circumcision. But when "he went out from his country and his kindred" then responses of a more sacred kind are delivered to him at this time. First God says to him: "You shall no longer be called Abram, but Abraham shall be your name."[5] Then at once he both received the covenant of God and accepted circumcision as a sign of faith which he could not accept while he was still in his father's house and in the relationship of flesh and while he was still called Abram. But neither himself nor his wife is called *presbyter* as long as he was in his father's house and lived with flesh and blood, but after he has departed from there he deserved to be called both *Abraham* and *presbyter*. "For they were," the text says, "both presbyters," that is, old,[6] Abraham of course and his admirable wife, "and advanced in their days."[7] How many before them lived longer in span of years, nine hundred years and more, some lived not much less until the flood, and none of these are called *presbyters*. For in Abraham it is not the old age of his body, but the maturity of his heart that is addressed by this term.

But the Lord also says to Moses: "Choose for yourself presbyters whom you yourself know to be presbyters."[8] Let us examine very carefully the word of the Lord. What does that addition appear to mean, which says: "Whom you yourself know to be presbyters"? Was it not obvious to the eyes of all that he was a presbyter, that is old, who was bearing old age in his body? Why, then, is that special inspection commanded to Moses alone, such a great prophet, that those be chosen, not whom other men knew, not whom the ignorant multitude

---

4 Gn 12.1.

5 Gn 17.5. For the distinction between Abram and Abraham discussed in this section, cf. *Origène, Sur la Pâque: Traité inédit publié d'après un papyrus de Toura*, ed. O. Guéraud and P. Nautin (Paris: Beauchesne, 1979), 164, where Origen says, "Abram does not receive the promises, but Abraham."

6 Obviously an addition by Rufinus, who has borrowed the Greek *presbyter*.

7 Cf. Gn18.11.

8 Cf. Ex 17.9; Nm 11.16.

recognized, but whom the prophet full of God should choose? For in respect to them it is not a judgment about their body nor their age, but about their mind.

Such, therefore, were those blessed presbyters Abraham and Sara.

And first of all their natural names which they received at their birth in the flesh were changed. "For when Abraham was ninety-nine years old God appeared to him and said: 'I am God. Be pleasing before me and be blameless, and I will make a covenant between me and you.' And Abraham fell on his face and worshipped God and God spoke to him saying: 'I am; behold my covenant with you, and you shall be the father of a multitude of nations, and all nations shall be blessed in you, and no longer shall your name be called Abram, but your name shall be Abraham.' "[9] And when he had given him this name immediately he added: "And I shall make my covenant between me and you and your seed after you. And this is the covenant which you shall preserve between me and you and your seed after you."[10] And after these words he adds: "And all your males shall be circumcised, and you shall circumcise the flesh of your foreskin."[11]

(4) Since, therefore, we have reached these passages I wish to inquire if the omnipotent God, who holds dominion of heaven and earth, when he wished to make a covenant with a holy man put the main point of such an important matter in this, that the foreskin of his flesh and of his future progeny should be circumcised. "For my covenant," the text says, "shall be upon your flesh."[12] Was this what "the Lord of heaven and earth"[13] was conferring in the gift of the eternal covenant on him whom alone he had chosen from all mortals?

These indeed are the only things in which the masters and teachers of the synagogue place the glory of the saints. But let them come, if they please, and let them hear how Christ's

---

9 Gn 17.1–5.
10 Gn 17.7.
11 Gn 17.10–11.
12 Gn 17.13.
13 Cf. Gn 24.3.

Church, which had said through the prophet, "But to me your friends, O God, are made sufficiently honorable,"[14] honors the friends of its bridegroom. And let them hear how much glory the Church confers on them when it reflects on their deeds.

We, therefore, instructed by the apostle Paul, say that just as many other things were made in the figure and image of future truth, so also that circumcision of flesh was bearing the form of spiritual circumcision about which it was both worthy and fitting that "the God of majesty" give precepts to mortals.[15] Hear, therefore, how Paul, "a teacher of the Gentiles in faith and truth,"[16] teaches the Church of Christ about the mystery of circumcision. "Behold," he says "the mutilation"—speaking about the Jews who are mutilated in the flesh—"for we," he says, "are the circumcision, who serve God in spirit and have no confidence in the flesh."[17] This is one opinion of Paul about circumcision. Hear also another: "For he is not a Jew who is so outwardly; nor is that circumcision which is outwardly in the flesh. But he is a Jew who is one inwardly with circumcision of the heart in the spirit, not in the letter."[18] Does it not seem more appropriate to you to speak of such a circumcision among the saints and friends of God than to speak of a pruning of the flesh?

But the novelty of the expression may perhaps deter not only the Jews, but even some of our brothers. For Paul, who introduces "circumcision of the heart," seems to assume things that are impossible. For how shall it be possible that a member be circumcised which, covered by the internal viscera, lies hidden even from the view of men?

Let us return, therefore, to the words of the prophets that, with the aid of your prayers, these matters about which we are inquiring might thence become clear. Ezechiel the prophet says: "No stranger uncircumcised in heart and uncircumcised

---

14 Ps 138.17.
15 Cf. Ps 28.3.
16 Cf. 1 Tm 2.7.
17 Phil 3.2–3.
18 Rom 2.28–29.

in flesh shall enter my sanctuary."[19] And likewise elsewhere no less the prophet, reproaching, says: "All strangers are un-circumcised in the flesh, but the sons of Israel are un-circumcised in the heart."[20] It is pointed out, therefore, that unless one has been circumcised in the heart and the flesh, "he shall not enter the sanctuary" of God.

(5) But I shall appear caught by my own proofs. For the Jew immediately constrains me with this testimony of the prophet and says: "Behold, the prophet designates both a circumcision of the flesh and heart; no place remains for allegory where both kinds of circumcision are demanded."

If you help me with your prayers, that "the Word of the living God"[21] may think fit to be present "in the opening of" our "mouth,"[22] we shall be able with him as our leader to go forth through this narrow way of inquiry to the breadth of truth. For we must refute not only the Jews in the flesh concerning circumcision of the flesh, but also some of these who appear to have taken up the name of Christ and nevertheless think circumcision of the flesh is to be received, as the Ebionites and any others who err with them in similar poverty of understanding.

Let us use, therefore, the testimonies of the Old Testament in which they freely indulge.

It is written in the prophet Jeremias: "Behold this people is uncircumcised in their ears."[23] Hear, Israel, the voice of the prophet. A great reproach is spoken to you. A great fault is thrust on you. Your accusation is brought forward: You are uncircumcised in your ears. And why, when you heard this, did you not apply the blade to your ears and cut into them? For you are reproached by God and condemned because you do not have circumcised ears. For I do not permit you to take refuge in our allegories which Paul taught. Why are you remiss

---

19 Ez 44.9.
20 Jer 9.26.
21 Cf. 1 Pt 1.23.
22 Cf. Eph 6.19.
23 Jer 6.10.

to circumcise? Cut away the ears; cut off the members which God created for the use of the senses and for the adornment of the human state, for thus you understand the divine words.

But I shall also bring forth still another passage for you which you cannot contradict. In Exodus where we have written in the codices of the Church Moses responding to the Lord and saying: "Provide, Lord another whom you will send. For I am feeble in voice and slow in tongue," you have in the Hebrew copies: "But I am uncircumcised in lips."[24] Behold you have a circumcision of lips according to your copies, which you say to be more accurate. If, therefore, according to you Moses still says that he is unworthy because he has not been circumcised in his lips, he certainly indicates this, that he would be worthier and holier who is circumcised in his lips. Therefore, apply the pruning-hook also to your lips and cut off the covering of your mouth since indeed such an understanding pleases you in the divine letters.

But if you refer circumcision of lips to allegory and say no less that circumcision of ears is allegorical and figurative, why do you not also inquire after allegory in circumcision of the foreskin?

But let us lay aside those indeed who, like idols, "have ears and do not hear and eyes and do not see."[25] But you, "O people of God, and a people chosen for an acquisition to expound the virtues of the Lord,"[26] take up the circumcision worthy of the word of God in your ears and in your lips and in your heart and in the foreskin of your flesh and in all your members together.

For let your ears be circumcised according to the word of God that they may not receive the voice of the detractor, that they may not hear the words of the slanderer and blasphemer, that they may not be open to false accusations, to a lie, to an irritaton. Let them be shut up and closed "lest they hear the judgment of blood"[27] or stand open to lewd songs and sounds

---

24 Ex 4.13,10.
25 Ps 113.14,13, 134.17,16.
26 1 Pt 2.10,9.
27 Cf. Is 33.15.

of the theater. Let them receive nothing obscene, but let them be turned away from every corrupt scene.

This is the circumcision with which the Church of Christ circumcises the ears of its infants. Those, I believe, are the ears which the Lord was seeking in his hearers when he said: "He who has ears to hear, let him hear."[28] For no one with uncircumcised and impure ears can hear the pure words of wisdom and truth.

Let us come also, if you wish, to the circumcision of lips. I think that he would be "uncircumcised in lips"[29] who has not yet ceased from silly talk, from scurrility, who disparages good men, who calumniates his neighbors, who instigates quarrels, who promotes false accusations, who sets brothers against themselves by making false statements, who utters vain words, inept words, profane words, shameless words, filthy words, injurious words, wanton words, blasphemous words, and other words which are unworthy of a Christian. But if anyone curbs his mouth from all these things and "orders his words with judgment,"[30] if he restrains verbosity, governs his tongue, keeps his words in due bounds, that man deservedly is said to be circumcised in lips. But also those "who speak iniquity on high and stretch out their tongue against heaven,"[31] as the heretics do, are to be called uncircumcised and unclean in their lips. But he is circumcised and clean who always speaks the word of God and brings forward sound doctrine fortified with evangelic and apostolic norms. In this way, therefore, also circumcicsion of lips is given in the Church of God.

(6) But now let us see how also, according to our promise, circumcision of the flesh ought to be received. There is no one who does not know that this member, in which the foreskin is seen to be, serves the natural functions of coitus and procreation. If anyone, therefore, is not troublesome in respect to impulses of this kind, nor exceeds the bounds set by the laws,

---

28 Mt 13.9.
29 Cf. Ex 6.30.
30 Ps 111.5.
31 Ps 72.8–9.

nor has known a woman other than his lawful wife, and, in the case of her also, makes use of her in the determined and lawful times for the sake of posterity alone, that man is to be said to be circumcised in the foreskin of his flesh. But that man is uncircumcised in the foreskin of his flesh who falls down in all lasciviousness and everywhere loiters for diverse and illicit caresses, and is carried along unchecked in every whirlpool of lust. But the Church of Christ, strengthened by the grace of him who has been crucified for it, abstains not only from illicit and impious beds but also from those allowed and legitimate, and flourishes like the virgin bride of Christ with pure and chaste virgins in whom true circumcision of the foreskin of the flesh has been performed and truly God's covenant and the eternal covenant is preserved in their flesh.

It remains for us to describe also circumcision of the heart. If there is anyone who burns with obscene desires and shameful passions and, to speak briefly, who "commits adultery in his heart,"[32] this man is "uncircumcised in heart."[33] But he also is "uncircumcised in heart" who holds heretical views in his mind and arranges blasphemous assertions against knowledge of Christ in his heart. But he is circumcised in heart who guards the pure faith in sincerity of conscience, about whom it can be said, "Blessed are the pure in heart, for they shall see God."[34]

But I dare in like manner to add also these things to the words of the prophets, that, in accordance with what we said above, as it is necessary to be circumcised in ears and lips and heart and the foreskin of the flesh, so perhaps also our hands need circumcision and our feet and sight and sense of smell and touch. For that the man of God might be perfect in all things,[35] all the members must be circumcised, the hands indeed from plundering, from theft, from murders, and to be extended only to the works of God. The feet must be cir-

---

32 Cf. Mt 5.28.
33 Cf. Ez 44.9.
34 Mt 5.8.
35 Cf. 2 Tm 3.17.

cumcised lest "they be swift to shed blood"[36] and lest they enter "the council of the wicked,"[37] but that they might go about only on behalf of God's commands. Let the eye also be circumcised lest it lust for things belonging to another, lest it look "to lust after a woman."[38] For that man is uncircumcised in his eyes whose gaze, lustful and curious, wanders about in respect to the figures of women. But also, if there is anyone who, whether he should eat or drink, as the Apostle prescribes, "eats and drinks to the glory of God,"[39] that man has been circumcised in his taste; but I would say that man's taste is uncircumcised, "whose God is his stomach"[40] and who is devoted to pleasantness of the palate. If someone acquires "the good odor of Christ"[41] and seeks "a sweet odor" in works of mercy, his sense of smell is circumcised. But he who goes about "anointed with the chief perfumes"[42] must be said to be uncircumcised in his sense of smell.

But also each of our members must be said to be circumcised if they are devoted to the sevice of God's commands. But if they revel beyond the laws divinely prescribed for them, they are to be reckoned uncircumcised. And I think this is what the Apostle meant: "For as you have yielded your members to serve iniquity, unto iniquity, so now yield your members to serve justice, unto sanctification."[43] For when our members served iniquity, they were not circumcised nor was the covenant of God in them. But when they began to serve "justice unto sanctification," the promise which has been made to Abraham is fulfilled in them. For then the law of God and his covenant is imprinted in them. And this is truly the "mark of faith"[44] which contains the agreement of the eternal covenant between God and man.

---

36 Cf. Is 59.7.
37 Cf. Ps 1.1.
38 Cf. Mt 5.28.
39 Cf. 1 Cor 10.31.
40 Cf. Phil 3.19.
41 Cf. 2 Cor 2.15.
42 Cf. Am 6.6, Song 4.14.
43 Rom 6.19.
44 Cf. Gn 17.11.

That is the circumcision "with stone swords" which is given to the people of God by Jesus.[45] But what is the "stone sword" and what is the "sword" with which the people of God are circumcised? Hear the Apostle saying: "For the word of God is living and effectual and sharper than any two-edged sword reaching unto the division of the soul and the spirit, of the joints also and the marrow; and is a discerner of the thoughts and intents of the heart."[46] That, therefore, is the sword with which we ought to be circumcised, about which the Lord Jesus says: "I did not come to send peace upon the earth, but the sword."[47]

Does not this circumcision seem to you to be more worthy, with which the covenant of God ought to be established. Compare, if you please, this our account with your Jewish fables and disgusting stories and see whether in those stories of yours or in these which are preached in the Church of Christ, circumcision is observed according to God's command. Do not even you yourself perceive and understand that this circumcision of the Church is honorable, holy, worthy of God; that that of yours is unseemly, detestable, disgusting, presenting a thing vulgar[48] both in condition and appearance. "And," God says to Abraham, "circumcision and my convenant shall be in your flesh."[49] If, therefore, our life has been such that, properly joined together and united in all its members so that all our movements are performed according to the laws of God, truly "the covenant of God will be in our flesh."[50]

Let these things, indeed, briefly treated by us from the Old Testament serve to confound those who trust in circumcision of the flesh; at the same time also let them serve to edify the Church of the Lord.

(7) But I come also to the New Testament in which there is a

---

45 Cf. Jos 5.2. *Jesus* is the rendering of the LXX *Iēsous*, and the Vulgate *Iosue*.
46 Heb 4.12.
47 Mt 10.34.
48 Rufinus has preserved the Greek word *kakemphaton* in his text.
49 Gn 17.13.
50 Gn 17.13.

fullness of all things, and whence I wish to show how we too can have the "covenant" of our Lord Jesus Christ "in our flesh."

For it is not sufficient that these things be said only in name and word, but they need to be fulfilled in deeds. John the apostle indeed says: "Every spirit which confesses that Jesus has come in the flesh," will he seem to confess in the spirit of God? This is not to have to covenant of God in the flesh, but in the voice. Therefore, it is said to him immediately: "You err, sir. 'The kingdom of God is not in speech, but in power.' "[52] voice. Therefore, it is said to him immediately: "You err, sir. 'The kingdom of God is not in speech, but in power.' "[52]

How, then, I ask, "will the covenant of Christ be in my flesh"? If "I shall have put to death my members which are on the earth,"[53] I have the covenant of Christ in my flesh. If "I shall always bear about the death of Jesus Christ in my body,"[54] the covenant of Christ is in my body, because "if we suffer with him we shall also reign with him."[55] If "I shall have been planted together in the likeness of his death,"[56] I show "his covenant" to be "in my flesh." For what does it profit if I should say that Jesus has come in that flesh alone which he received from Mary and I should not show also that he has come in this flesh of mine? But I show this in this manner only, if as I formerly "yielded my members to serve iniquity, unto iniquity, now I should change and yield them to serve justice unto sanctification."[57] I show the covenant of God to be in my flesh, if I shall have been able to say in accordance with Paul that "I am crucified with Christ; and I no longer live, but Christ lives in me,"[58] and if I shall have been able to say, as he said: "But I bear the marks of my Lord Jesus Christ in my body."[59] But he truly

---

51 1 Jn 4.2.
52 1 Cor 4.20.
53 Cf. Col 3.5.
54 Cf. 2 Cor 4.10.
55 2 Tm 2.12.
56 Cf. Rom 6.5.
57 Cf. Rom 6.19.
58 Gal 2.20.
59 Gal 6.17.

showed the covenant of God to be in his flesh who said: "Who shall separate us from the love of God which is in Christ Jesus? Shall tribulation, or distress, or danger, or the sword?"[60]

For if we should confess the Lord Jesus with the voice alone and not show "his covenant to be in our flesh" according to these things which we have set forth above, we ourselves also will appear to do something similar to the Jews who think they confess God with the mark of circumcision alone, but deny him with their deeds. But may the Lord grant us "to believe in the heart, to confess with the mouth,"[61] to confirm with works that the covenant of God is in our flesh, that "men seeing our good works, might magnify our Father who is in heaven"[62] through Jesus Christ our Lord, "to whom is glory forever and ever. Amen."[63]

---

60 Rom 8.35.
61 Cf. Rom 10.9–10.
62 Cf. Mt 5.16.
63 Gal 1.5.

HOMILY IV
On that which is written: "God appeared to Abraham"

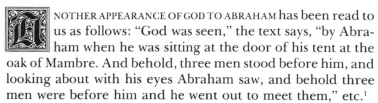NOTHER APPEARANCE OF GOD TO ABRAHAM has been read to us as follows: "God was seen," the text says, "by Abraham when he was sitting at the door of his tent at the oak of Mambre. And behold, three men stood before him, and looking about with his eyes Abraham saw, and behold three men were before him and he went out to meet them," etc.[1]

Let us compare, first of all, if you please, this appearance with that one which Lot experienced. "Three men" come to Abraham and stand "before him"; "two" come to Lot and sit "in the street."[2] See if, in the dispensation of the Holy Spirit, these events did not occur as each man deserved. For Lot was far inferior to Abraham. For if he had not been inferior, he would not have been separate from Abraham nor would Abraham have said to him, "If you go to the right, I will go to the left; if you go to the left, I will go to the right."[3] And if he had not been inferior, the land and habitation of Sodom would not have pleased him.

Three men, therefore, come to Abraham at midday; two come to Lot and in the evening.[4] For Lot could not receive the magnitude of midday light; but Abraham was capable of receiving the full brightness of the light.

Let us see now how Abraham received those who came and how Lot did, and let us compare each man's preparation of hospitality. First, however, observe that the Lord also was present with Abraham with two angels, but two angels alone proceed to Lot. And what do they say? "The Lord has sent us to

---

1 Gn 18.1–2.
2 Gn 19.1.
3 Gn 13.9.
4 Gn 19.1. Cf. Philo *QG.* 4.30.

consume the city and destroy it."[5] He, therefore, received
those who would give destruction. He did not receive him who
would save. But Abraham received both him who saves and
those who destroy.

Now let us see how each man receives his guests. "Abraham
saw," the text says, "and ran to meet them."[6] Notice that
Abraham immediately is energetic and eager in his duties. He
runs to meet them and when he had met them, "he hastens
back to the tent," the text says, "and says to his wife: 'Hasten to
the tent.' "[7] Behold in the individual matters how great is his
eagerness to receive them. He makes haste in all things; all
things are done urgently; nothing is done leisurely. Therefore,
he says to his wife Sara: "Hasten to the tent and mix three
measures of fine wheat flour and make bread upon the
hearth."[8] The Greek is *engkruphias* which indicates secret or
hidden bread. "But he ran," the text says, "to the cattle and
took a calf."[9] What kind of calf? Perhaps the first one he
encountered? Not at all, but "a good and tender" calf.[10] And
although he would hasten in all things, nevertheless he knows
that what is excellent and great should be offered to the Lord
or to angels. He took, therefore, or chose from the herd a
"good and tender" calf and delivered it to his servant. "The
servant," the text says, "hastened to slaughter it."[11] He himself
runs, his wife hastens, the servant makes haste. No one is slow
in the house of a wise man.[12] He serves, therefore, a calf and at
the same time with it bread and fine wheat flour, but also milk
and butter. The : were the courtesies of hospitality of Abraham and Sara.

Now let us see what also Lot did. He has neither fine wheat
flour nor elegant bread, but ground corn. He neither knew
how to serve three measures of fine wheat flour to his guests

---

5 Gn 19.13.
6 Gn 18.2.
7 Gn 18.6.
8 Gn 18.6.
9 Gn 18.7.
10 Cf. Gn 18.7.
11 Gn 18.7.
12 Cf. Philo *Abr.* 109.

nor could he serve them *engkruphias*, that is, hidden and mystical loaves of bread.

(2) But let us now, meanwhile, pursue what Abraham does with the three men who "stood before him."[13] Behold what sort of expression this is itself, that they come "before him," not against him. He had, to be sure, subjected himself to the will of God, therefore, God is said to stand "before him."

He serves, therefore, bread mixed "with three measures of fine wheat flour."[14] He received three men, he mixed the bread "with three measures of fine wheat flour." Everything he does is mystical, everything is filled with mystery. A calf is served; behold, another mystery. The calf itself is not tough, but "good and tender." And what is so tender, what so good as that one who "humbled himself" for us "to death" and "laid down his life" "for his friends"?[15] He is the "fatted calf"[16] which the father slaughtered to receive his repentant son. "For he so loved this world, as to give his only son"[17] for the life of this world.

Nevertheless, the wise man is not ignorant of whom he has received. He runs to three men and adores one, and speaks to the one saying "Turn aside to your servant and refresh yourself under the tree."[18]

But how does he continue again as if speaking to men: "Let water be received," the text says, "and your feet be washed"?[19]

Abraham, the father and teacher of nations, is, indeed, teaching you by these things how you ought to receive guests and that you should wash the feet of guests. Nevertheless, even this is said mysteriously. For he knew that the mysteries of the Lord were not to be completed except in the washing of feet.[20] But he was not unaware of the importance of that precept, indeed, in which the Savior says: "If any shall not receive you,

13 Cf. Gn 18.1.
14 Cf. Gn 18.6.
15 Cf. Phil 2.6; 1 Jn 3.16; Jn 15.23.
16 Cf. Lk 15.23.
17 Jn 3.16
18 Gn 18.3–4.
19 Gn 18.4.
20 Cf. Jn 13.6.

shake off even the dust which clings to your feet for a testimony to them. Truly I say to you that it shall be more tolerable
for the land of Sodom in the day of judgment than for that
city."[21] He wished, therefore, to anticipate that and to wash
their feet lest perhaps any dust should remain, which, shaken
off, could be reserved "in the day of judgment" for a testimony
of unbelief. For that reason, therefore, wise Abraham says:
"Let water be received and your feet be washed."[22]

(3) But let us now see what also is said subsequently. "But
Abraham himself," the text says, "stood by them under the
tree."[23]

We need circumcised ears for narratives of this kind. For we
ought not believe that it was of greatest concern to the Holy
Spirit to write in the books of the Law where Abraham was
standing. For what does it help me who have come to hear what
the Holy Spirit teaches the human race, if I hear that "Abraham was standing under a tree"?

But let us see what this tree is under which Abraham stood
and provided a meal for the Lord and the angels. "Under the
tree of Mambre" the text says.[24] *Mambre* in our language is
translated "vision" or "sharpness of sight."[25] Do you see what
kind of place it is where the Lord can have a meal? Abraham's
vision and sharpness of sight pleased him. For he was pure in
heart so that he could see God.[26] In such a place, therefore, and
in such a heart the Lord can have a meal with his angels. In fact,
earlier prophets were called seers.[27]

(4) What, then, does the Lord say to Abraham? " 'Where,' "
the text reads, " 'is Sara your wife?' And he said, 'Lo, she is in
the tent.' But the Lord said: 'I will certainly come to you at this
time in due season, and Sara your wife will have a son.' But
Sara, standing behind the door of the tent behind Abraham,
heard."[28]

---

21 Mk 6.11; Mt 10.15.
22 Gn 18.4.
23 Gn 18.8.
24 Gn 18.1.
25 See Appendix, 2.
26 Cf. Mt 5.8.
27 Cf. 1 Sm 9.9.
28 Gn 18.9–10.

Let the wives learn from the examples of the patriarchs, let the wives learn, I say, to follow their husbands. For not without cause is it written that "Sara was standing behind Abraham," but that it might be shown that if the husband leads the way to the Lord, the wife ought to follow. I mean that the wife ought to follow if she see her husband standing by God.

For the rest, let us ascend to a higher step of understanding and let us say that the man is the rational sense in us and the woman our flesh which, like her, has been united with a man. Therefore, let the flesh always follow the rational sense nor let it ever come into any slothfulness so that the rational sense, reduced in authority, should yield to the flesh wallowing in luxury and pleasures. Therefore, "Sara was standing behind Abraham."

But we can also perceive something mystical in this passage if we see how in Exodus "God went before them by night in a pillar of fire and by day in a pillar of a cloud" and the congregation of the Lord followed behind him.[29]

So, therefore, I understand also Sara to have followed or stood "behind Abraham."

What is said next? "And they were both," the text says, "presbyters"—that is, old—"and far advanced in their days."[30] So far as pertains to bodily age, many before them lived for more numerous years, but no one was called *presbyter*. Whence it appears that this title is ascribed to the saints, not by reason of longevity, but of maturity.

(5) What then followed the abundant and excellent meal which Abraham presented to the Lord and his angels under the tree of vision? The guests depart. "And Abraham escorted them," the text says, "and walked with them. And the Lord said: 'I shall not hide from Abraham my servant what I am about to do. But Abraham shall become a great and large nation and all the nations of the earth shall be blessed in him. For he knew that he would command his sons and they would keep the ways of the Lord, that they might do justice and

---

29 Cf. Ex 13.21.
30 Gn 18.11; Cf. Origen *Gn. Hom.* 3.3.

judgment, that the Lord might fulfill to Abraham what he made known to him.' And he said: 'The cry of Sodom and Gomorrha is filled, and their sins are very great. I have descended, therefore, to see whether their iniquities are completed as their cry which has come to me indicates; but if not, that I might know.' "[31] These are the words of the divine Scripture. Let us see, therefore, now what is fitting to be understood in them.

"I have descended," the text says, "to see."[32] When responses are delivered to Abraham, God is not said to descend, but to stand before him, as we explained above: "Three men," the text says, "stood before him."[33] But now because sinners are involved, God is said to descend. Beware lest you think of ascending and descending spatially. For this is frequently found in the sacred literature, as in the prophet Micheas: "Behold," Scripture says, "the Lord departed from his holy place and came down and will tread upon the high places of the earth."[34] Therefore, God is said to descend when he deigns to have concern for human frailty. This should be discerned especially of our Lord and savior who "thought it not robbery to be equal with God, but emptied himself, taking the form of a servant."[35] Therefore he descended. For, "No other has ascended into heaven, but he that descended from heaven, the Son of man who is in heaven."[36] For the Lord descended not only to care for us, but also to bear what things are ours. "For he took the form of a servant," and although he himself is invisible in nature, inasmuch as he is equal to the Father, nevertheless he took a visible appearance, "and was found in appearance as a man."[37]

But also when he descends he is below with some, but he ascends with others and is above. For he goes up with the

---

31 Gn 18.16–21.
32 Gn 18.21.
33 Gn 18.2.
34 Mi 1.3.
35 Phil 2.6–7.
36 Jn 3.13.
37 Phil 2.7.

chosen apostles "into a high mountain and there is trans-figured before them."[38] Therefore, he is above with those whom he teaches about the mysteries of the kingdom of heaven. But he is below with the crowds and Pharisees, whose sins he reproaches, and he is there with them where there is grass. He could not, however, be transfigured below, but ascended above with those who could follow him, and there he is transfigured.

(6) "I have descended," the text says, "therefore, to see whether their iniquities are completed as their cry which has come to me indicates; but if not, that I might know."[39] The heretics usually assail my God because of that statement, saying: "Behold, the God of the Law would not have known what was happening in Sodom unless he had descended to see and had sent those to learn."

But let us, who have been commanded to fight the battles of the Lord, sharpen "the sword of the word of God" against them and rush to meet them in battle. Let us stand in battle array "having our loins girded with truth." Let us, likewise, also "holding forth the shield of faith," intercept their poisoned darts arising from disputes and diligently hurl back at them those launched darts.[40] For such are the battles of the Lord which David and the other patriarchs fought. Let us stand against them for our brothers. "For it is better that I die"[41] than that they ravish and plunder some of my brothers and by sly verbal deception lead captive the "little children"[42] and suck-lings in Christ. But they neither will be able to do combat with the mature nor will they dare to enter the struggle. Let us, therefore, first praying to the Lord and aided by your prayers, advance against them in verbal battle.

We say, therefore, with confidence that according to the Scriptures God does not know all men. God does not know sin

---

38 Cf. Mk 9.2.
39 Gn 18.21.
40 Cf. Eph 6.14–17.
41 Cf. 1 Cor 9.15.
42 Cf. 1 Cor 3.1.

and God does not know sinners. He is ignorant of those alienated from himself. Hear the Scripture saying: "The Lord knows those who are his," and: "Let everyone depart from iniquity who calls on the name of the Lord."[43] The Lord knows his own, but he does not know the wicked and the impious. Hear the Savior saying: "Depart from me, all workers of iniquity. I have not known you."[44] And again Paul says: "If anyone among you is a prophet or spiritual, let him know that the things that I write are of the Lord. But if any man know not, he is not known."[45]

We say these things, however, not thinking anything blasphemous about God, as you do, nor ascribing ignorance to him, but thus we understand that these whose activity is considered unworthy of God are also considered to be unworthy of knowledge of God. For God does not deign to know him who has turned away from him and does not know him. And for this reason the Apostle says that "anyone who does not know is not known."

So also now, therefore, it is said of these who live in Sodom, that if indeed, on his examination, "their deeds are completed as the cry"[46] which has ascended to God, they would be considered unworthy; but if there is any conversion among them, if even ten just men might be found among them, so, at last, God would know them. And for this reason the text said: "But if not, that I might know."[47] It did not say that I might know what they are doing, but that I might know them and make them worthy of knowledge of me, if I should find some among them just, if I should find some repentant, if some such as I ought to know.

Finally, because no one besides Lot is found who would repent, no one would be converted, he alone is known, he alone is delivered from the conflagration. Neither his chil-

---

43 2 Tm 2.19; Cf. Nm 16.5.
44 Mt 7.23.
45 1 Cor 14.37–38.
46 Gn 18.21.
47 Gn 18.21.

dren, having been admonished, nor his neighbors, nor his next of kin followed him. No one wished to know the mercy of God; no one wished to take refuge in his compassion. Consequently also no one is known.

These things, indeed, have been said against those who "speak iniquity on high."[48] But let us give attention to make our acts such, our manner of life such, that we may be held worthy of knowledge of God, that he may see fit to know us, that we may be held worthy of knowledge of his son Jesus Christ and knowledge of the Holy Spirit, that we, known by the Trinity, might also deserve to know the mystery of the Trinity fully, completely, and perfectly, the Lord Jesus Christ revealing it to us. "His is the glory and sovereignty forever and ever. Amen."[49]

---

48 Cf. Ps 72.8.
49 Cf. 1 Pt 4.11.

HOMILY V
On Lot And His Daughters

HEN THE ANGELS WHO WERE SENT to destroy Sodom desired to expedite the task with which they were charged, they first had concern for their host, Lot, that, in consideration of his hospitality, they might deliver him from the destruction of the imminent fire.

Hear these words, you who close your houses to strangers; hear these words, you who avoid a guest as an enemy. Lot was living in Sodom. We do not read of other good deeds of his. The hospitality alone occurring at that time is mentioned. He escapes the flames, he escapes the conflagration for this reason alone: because he opened his house to strangers. Angels entered the hospitable house; fire entered the houses closed to strangers.

Let us therefore, see what the angels say to their host on account of his services of hospitality. "Save your life in the mountain," the text says, "lest perchance you be included."[1] Lot was indeed hospitable. And, as the Scripture has borne testimony to him, he was hidden from destruction when the angels had been hospitably received.[2] But he was not so perfect that, immediately on departing from Sodom, he could ascend the mountain; for it belongs to the perfect to say: "I have lifted up my eyes to the mountains, whence help shall come to me."[3] He, therefore, was neither such that he should perish among the inhabitants of Sodom, nor was he so great that he could dwell with Abraham in the heights. For if he had been such, Abraham would never have said to him: "If you go to the right, I will go to the left, or if you go to the left I will go to the right,"[4]

---

1 Gn 19.17.
2 Cf. Heb 13.2.
3 Ps 120.1.
4 Gn 13.9.

nor would the dwellings of Sodom have pleased him. He was, therefore, somewhere in the middle between the perfect and the doomed. And knowing that it is not appropriate with his strength to ascend the mountain, he piously and humbly excuses himself saying; "I cannot be saved on the mountain, but behold this city is small. Here I shall be saved; and is it not small?"[5] To be sure, when he entered the small city of Segor he is saved in it.[6] And after this he went up into the mountain with his daughters.[7]

For there was no possibility of ascending from Sodom into the mountain, although it is written of the land of Sodom before it was overthrown, in that time when Lot chose it as his dwelling place, that "it was as the paradise of God and as the land of Egypt."[8] And yet, to digress slightly, what similarity does there appear to be with the paradise of God and the land of Egypt that Sodom should be compared fittingly with these? Now I think it is in this way: before Sodom sinned, when it still preserved the simplicity of the unstained life, it was "as the paradise of God," but when it began to be discolored and to be darkened with the stains of sins it became "as the land of Egypt."

But since indeed the prophet says, "Your sister Sodom shall be restored to her ancient state,"[9] we inquire also whether her restoration also recovers this, that she be "as the paradise of God," or only "as the land of Egypt." I, at least, doubt, if the sins of Sodom can be diminished to such an extent and its evils purged to the point that its restoration be so great that it be compared not only to the land of Egypt, but also to the paradise of God. Those, however, who wish to establish this will press us especially from that word which appears added to this counterpromise; for the Scripture did not say "Sodom will be restored," and stop, but says: "Sodom will be restored to its ancient state."[10] And they will assert strongly that its ancient

---

5 Gn 19.19–20.
6 Cf. Gn 19.23.
7 Cf. Gn 19.30.
8 Cf. Gn 13.10.
9 Ez 16.55.
10 Ez 16.55.

state was not "as the land of Egypt," but "as the paradise of God."

(2) But let us return to Lot, who, fleeing the destruction of Sodom with his wife and daughters after he had received the command from the angels to not look back, was proceeding to Segor.[11] But his wife became negligent of the command; "she looked back"; she violated the imposed law; "she became a little statue of salt."[12] Do we think there was so much evil in this transgression, that the woman, because she looked behind her, incurred the destruction which she appeared to be fleeing by divine favor? For what great crime was it, if the concerned mind of the woman looked backward whence she was being terrified by the excessive crackling of the flames?

But because "the law is spiritual"[13] and the things which happened to the ancients "happened figuratively,"[14] let us see if perhaps Lot, who did not look back, is not the rational understanding and the manly soul, and his wife here represents the flesh. For it is the flesh which always looks to vices, which, when the soul is proceeding to salvation, looks backward and seeks after pleasures. For concerning that the Lord also said: "No man putting his hand to the plow and looking back is fit for the kingdom of God."[15] And he adds: "Remember Lot's wife."[16] But the fact that "she became a little statue of salt" appears to be an open indication of her folly. For salt represents the prudence which she lacked.

Lot, therefore, pushed on to Segor and after he had gained strength there for a while, which he could not have in Sodom, he ascended the mountain and dwelt there, as the Scripture says, "he and his two daughers with him."[17]

(3) After these things now that well-known story is related in which it is written that Lot's daughters cunningly lay with their

---

11 Cf. Gn 19.17.
12 Cf. Gn 19.26.
13 Cf. Rom 7.14.
14 Cf. 1 Cor 10.11.
15 Lk 9.62.
16 Lk 17.32.
17 Gn 19.30.

father by stealth.[18] In this matter I do not know if anyone can so excuse Lot as to free him from sin. Nor again do I think he should be so accused that he ought to become party to such serious incest. For I do not find him to have plotted against or to have violently snatched away the chastity of his daughters, but rather to have been the victim of a plot and cunningly ensnared. But on the other hand, neither would he have been ensnared by the girls, unless he could have been inebriated. Whence he seems to me to be found partly culpable and partly excusable. For indeed, he can be excused because he is free of the offense of concupiscence and pleasure and because he himself is shown neither to have wished nor to have consented to those wishing. But he is at fault because he could be trapped, because he indulged in wine too much, and this not once, but he did it a second time.

For instance, even Scripture itself seems to me to make excuse for him in a certain manner when it says: "For he did not know when he slept with them and when he arose."[19] This is not said of the daughters who intentionally and cunningly deceive their father. He, however, was so senseless from wine that he did not know that he lay with his older daughter nor with the younger.

Hear what drunkenness does. Hear what an outrage intoxication produces. Hear and beware, you who do not hold that evil to be a fault, but practice it. Drunkenness deceives him whom Sodom did not deceive. He whom the sulphurous flame did not burn is burned by the flames of women.

Lot, therefore, was deceived by cunning, not willfully. He is, therefore, somewhere between the sinners and the just, inasmuch, as he descended from the kindred of Abraham no less, but he dwelt in Sodom. For even the fact that he escaped from Sodom, as the Scripture indicates, belongs more to Abraham's honor than to Lot's merit. For as the text says: "And it came to

---

18 Cf. Gn 19.31–38.
19 Gn 19.35.

pass when God destroyed the cities of Sodom, God remembered Abraham and led Lot out of that land."[20]

(4) But I think the intention of his daughters also should be considered more carefully if perhaps they also may not deserve to receive so much fault as is supposed. For the Scripture relates that they said to one another: "Our father is old and there is no man on the earth to come in to us in the manner of the whole earth. Come and let us give our father wine to drink and let us lie with him and raise up seed of our father."[21]

As much as the Scripture says on these things about them, it seems to make excuse for them also in a certain manner. For indeed it appears that Lot's daughters had learned certain things about the end of the world, which was imminent through fire, but, as a girl, they had not learned fully and perfectly. They did not know that when the regions of Sodom had been devastated by fire much space still remained untouched in the world. They had heard that in the end of the world the earth and all the elements were to be consumed by the flame of fire. They saw the fire. They saw the sulphurous flames. They saw all things devastated. They also saw their own mother lost. They suspected that something such as they had heard of in the times of Noah had happened and that they alone with their parent had been preserved to restore human posterity.[22] They, therefore, assumed the necessity of restoring the human race and thought the beginning of the renewed age was to be given from themselves. And although their crime appeared great in lying with their father by stealth, nevertheless their impiety would have appeared more serious if, in preserving their chastity, they had, as they supposed, abolished the hope of human posterity. For this reason, therefore, they enter upon a plan with the lesser fault, in my opinion, but with the greater hope and intrinsic worth: they soothe and relax their father's grief or severity with wine. Having gone in

---

20 Gn 19.29.
21 Gn 19.31–32.
22 This was a common Jewish view. See Philo *QG*. 4.56; Josephus *Ant.* 1.205; *Genesis Rabbah* 51.8; Cf. Ginzberg, *Legends*, 5.243.

individually on individual nights, they conceive from an unknowing man; they do not repeat the deed later nor do they seek to do so.

Where is the fault of pleasure proven here; where the crime of incest? How will one be given to a vice which is not repeated in deed? I am afraid to say what I feel; I am afraid, I say, lest the incest of these women be purer than the chastity of many women. Let the married women examine themselves and seek if they approach their husbands for this reason alone, that they might receive children, and after conception desist. For those women, who appear to be proven incestuous, when they have attained conception, do not later assent to copulation with a man. But some women, for we do not censure all equally, but there are some who serve passion incessantly, like animals without any distinction, whom I would not even compare to the dumb beasts. For even the beasts themselves know, when they have conceived, not to further grant opportunity to their males. The divine Scripture also censures such when it says: "Do not become like the horse and the mule who have no understanding," and again, "They have become stallions."[23]

But, O people of God, "who love Christ in incorruption,"[24] understand the word of the Apostle in which he says: "Whether you eat or drink or whatever else you do, do all to the glory of God."[25] For his remark after eating and drinking, "whatever else you do," has designated with a modest word the immodest affairs of marriage, showing that even these acts themselves are performed to the glory of God if they are attended to with a view to posterity alone.

We have pursued, as we were able, the subject of the faults of Lot and his daughters or, on the other hand, of their excuses.

(5) But I know that some, so far as the story pertains to allegory, have referred Lot to the person of the Lord and his daughters to the two Testaments. But I do not know if anyone

---

23 Ps 31.9; Jer 5.8.
24 Cf. Eph 6.24.
25 1 Cor 10.31.

freely accepts these views who knows what the Scripture says about the Ammonites and Moabites who descend from Lot's race. For how will one be able to apply to Christ the statement that those who descend from his seed "shall not enter the church of the Lord" "to the third and fourth generation"?[26]

But we, as we are able to perceive, consider Lot to be a figure of the Law. Let not the fact that the word *law* is declined in the feminine gender in Latin appear incongruous, since it preserves the masculine gender in Greek.[27]

We consider his wife to represent the people who, after they had set out from Egypt and had been delivered from the Red Sea and the persecution of Pharao, as if from the fires of Sodom, again desiring the flesh and "pots of Egypt and onions and cucumbers,"[28] looked back and fell in the desert. Those people, too, became a memorial of concupiscence in the wilderness.[29] In regard to that first people, therefore, it was there that the Law, like Lot, lost and left his wife looking back.

Thence Lot comes and dwells in Segor about which he says: "This city is small and my life shall be saved in it; and is it not small."[30] Let us see, therefore, so far as it pertains to the Law, what "the city" is that is "small and not small." A city is so named from the manner of life of the multitude, because it orders and holds together the lives of many in one place.[31] These, therefore, who live by the Law have a small and petty manner of life as long as they understand the Law literally. For there is nothing great in observing Sabbaths and new moons and circumcision of the flesh and distinctions between foods in a fleshly manner. But if someone should begin to understand spiritually, these same observances, which in the literal sense were small and petty, in the spiritual sense are not small, but great.

---

26 Cf. Dt 23.3; Ex 34.7.
27 This is obviously a gloss by Rufinus.
28 Cf. Nm 11.5.
29 Cf. Ps 105.14.
30 Gn 19.20
31 Cf. Plato *Rep.* 369C.

After these things, therefore, Lot ascends into the mountains and there "he dwells in a cave," as the Scripture says, "he and his two daughters."[32] The Law also should be thought to have ascended, because an embellishment was added to it by the temple built by Solomon, when it became indeed "the house of God, a house of prayer."[33] Evil inhabitants, however, made it "a den of thieves."[34] Therefore, "Lot and his two daughters dwelt in a cave."[35] The prophet, evidently, describes these two daughters saying that Oolla and Ooliba are two sisters, and Oolla indeed is "Judah" and Ooliba is "Samaria."[36] The people, therefore, divided into two parts made the two daughters of the Law. Those daughters desiring carnal offspring to be preserved and the forces of earthly dominion to be fortified by an abundant posterity, depriving their father of sense and making him sleep, that is, covering and obscuring his spiritual understanding, draw only carnal understanding from him. Thence they conceive; thence they give birth to such sons as their father neither perceives nor recognizes. For that was neither the understanding nor the will of the Law to beget carnally. But the Law is deprived of its sense that such posterity might be begotten which "shall not enter the church of the Lord."[37] "For the Ammonites," Scripture says, "and Moabites shall not enter the church of the Lord unto the third and fourth generation and forever"[38] signifying that the generation of the carnal Law shall not enter the Church of Christ neither in the third generation by reason of the Trinity nor in the fourth by reason of the Gospels, nor forever unless perhaps after the present age, when "the fullness of the Gentiles should have come in and so all Israel should be saved."[39]

---

32 Gn 19.30.
33 Cf. Is 56.7.
34 Mt 21.13; Lk 19.46; Jer 7.11.
35 Gn 19.30.
36 Cf. Ez 23.4. The LXX has the identification in reverse. "Samaria was Oolla, and Jerusalem Ooliba."
37 Cf. Dt 23.3.
38 Cf. Dt 23.3; Ex 34.7.
39 Rom 11.25–26.

As we have been able, we have carved out these explanations according to the allegorical understanding of Lot and his wife and daughters. We pass no judgment on those who have been able to perceive something more sacred from this text.

(6) But above, in the moral sense, we referred Lot himself indeed to the rational understanding and the manly soul, but his wife, who looked back, we said to be the flesh given to concupiscence and pleasures. Do not, O hearer, receive these things carelessly. For you ought to watch lest perhaps even when you have fled the flames of the world and have escaped the fires of the flesh, even when you have risen above "Segor, the city" that is "small and not small,"[40] which is somewhere in the middle and is a common advance, and you have ascended to the height of knowledge, as to some mountain peak, beware lest those two daughters lie in wait for you, who do not depart from you, but follow you even when you ascend the mountain. They are vain glory and her older sister, pride. Beware lest with their embraces those daughters constrict you, deprived of sense and sleeping, while you seem neither to perceive nor know. They are called daughters because they do not come upon us from outside, but proceed from us and from a kind of innocence, as it were, of our acts. Be vigilant, therefore, as much as you can, and watch lest you beget sons from these daughters, because those who have been born from them "shall not enter the church of the Lord."[41] But if you wish to beget, beget in the spirit, since "he who sows in the spirit, of the spirit shall reap life everlasting."[42] If you wish to embrace, embrace wisdom and "say wisdom is your sister,"[43] that also Wisdom may say of you: He "who shall do the will of my Father who is in heaven, he is my brother and sister and mother."[44] Jesus Christ our Lord is this wisdom, "to whom be glory and sovereignty forever and ever. Amen."[45]

---

40 Cf. Gn 19.20.
41 Dt 23.3.
42 Gal 6.8.
43 Cf. Prv 7.4.
44 Mt 12.50.
45 1 Pt 4.11.

HOMILY VI
On Abimelech, King of the Philistines:
How he wished to take Sara in marriage

E HAVE HEARD READ FROM THE BOOK OF GENESIS the story where it is related that after the appearance of the three men, after the destruction of Sodom and the salvation of Lot either due to his hospitality or because of his kinship to Abraham, "Abraham departed thence," the text says, "to the south" and came to the king of the Philistines.[1] It is related also that he made an agreement with Sara his wife that she should not say that she was Abraham's wife, but his sister.[2] It is also said that king Abimelech took her, but God went in to Abimelech at night and said to him: "You have not touched this woman, and I have not permitted you to touch her, etc."[3] But after this Abimelech gave Sara back to her husband and at the same time rebuked Abraham for not having told him the truth. It is also related that, as a prophet, Abraham prayed for Abimelech, "and the Lord healed Abimelech and his wife and his handmaids."[4] And the omnipotent God was concerned to heal even the handmaids of Abimelech, "since he had closed up" the text says, "their wombs that they might not bear."[5] But they began to bear because of Abraham's prayer.

If anyone wishes to hear and understand these words literally he ought to gather with the Jews rather than with the Christians. But if he wishes to be a Christian and a disciple of Paul, let him hear Paul saying that "the Law is spiritual"[6] [and][7]

---

1 Gn 20.1.
2 Cf. Gn 20.2.
3 Cf. Gn 20.3,4,6.
4 Cf. Gn 20.17.
5 Cf. Gn 20.18.
6 Rom 7.14.
7 *Et* is adopted by Baehrens from Aldus Manutius and Delarue. It is lacking in the MSS.

declaring that these words are "allegorical" when the law speaks of Abraham and his wife and sons.[8] And although no one of us can by any means easily discover what kind of allegories these words should contain, nevertheless one ought to pray that "the veil might be removed" from his heart, "if there is anyone who tries to turn to the Lord,"[9]—"for the Lord is Spirit"[10]—that the Lord might remove the veil of the letter and uncover the light of the Spirit and we might be able to say that "beholding the glory of the Lord with open face we are transformed into the same image from glory to glory, as by the Spirit of the Lord."[11]

I think, therefore, that Sara, which means prince or one who governs empires, represents *aretē*, which is the virtue of the soul.[12] This virtue, then, is joined to and clings to a wise and faithful man, even as that wise man who said of wisdom: "I have desired to take her for my spouse."[13] For this reason, therefore, God says to Abraham: "In all that Sara has said to you, hearken to her voice."[14] This saying, at any rate, is not appropriate to physical marriage, since that well known statement was revealed from heaven which says to the woman of the man: "In him shall be your refuge[15] and he shall have dominion over you."[16] If, therefore, the husband is said to be lord of his wife, how is it said again to the man: "In all that Sara has said to you, hearken to her voice"?[17] If anyone, therefore, has married virtue, let him hearken to her voice in all which she shall counsel him.

Abraham, therefore, does not now wish that virtue be called his wife. For as long as virtue is called his wife, she belongs to him and can be shared with no one. And it is proper that until we reach perfection, virtue of the soul be within us and per-

---

8 Cf. Gal 4.22–24.
9 Cf. 2 Cor 3.16.
10 2 Cor 3.17.
11 2 Cor 3.18.
12 See Appendix, 3.
13 Wis 8.2.
14 Gn 21.12.
15 This rendering is based on the LXX *apostrophē*. Rufinus' text has *conversio*.
16 Gn 3.16.
17 Gn 21.12.

sonal; but when we reach perfection so that we are capable also of teaching others, let us then no longer enclose virtue within our bosom as a wife, but as a sister, let us unite her also with others who wish her. For to those who are perfect the divine word says; "Say that wisdom is your sister."[18] In this way, therefore, Abraham too said Sara was his sister. He permits, therefore, as already perfect, that anyone who wishes may have virtue.

(2) Nevertheless, Pharao too once wished to receive Sara,[19] but he did not wish with a pure heart; and virtue cannot unite except with purity of heart. For this reason, therefore, Scripture relates that "the Lord afflicted Pharao with afflictions which were grievous and most severe."[20] For virtue could not dwell with a destoyer—for this is what Pharao means in our language.[21]

But let us see what Abimelech said to the Lord. "You know, Lord," the text says, "that I have done this with a pure heart."[22] This Abimelech acts very differently from Pharao. He is not so ignorant and vile, but knows that he ought to prepare a "pure heart" for virtue. And because he wished to receive virtue with a pure heart, therfore, God heals him when Abraham prays for him. And he heals not only Abimelech, but also his handmaids.

But what is the meaning of that which Scripture adds: "And the Lord did not permit him to touch her"?[23] If Sara represents virtue and Abimelech wished to receive virtue "with a pure heart," why is it said that "the Lord did not permit him to touch her"?

Abimelech means "my father is king."[24] It seems to me, therefore, that this Abimelech represents the studious and wise men of the world, who by giving attention to philosophy, although they do not reach the complete and perfect rule of

---

18 Prv 7.4.
19 Cf. Gn 12.15.
20 Gn 12.17.
21 See Appendix, 4.
22 Cf. Gn 20.4–5.
23 Gn 20.6.
24 See Appendix, 5.

piety, nevertheless perceive that God is the father and king of
all things. Those, therefore, so far as it pertains to ethics, that is
moral philosophy, are acknowledged also to have given attention in some respects to purity of heart and to have sought the
inspiration of divine virtue with all their mind and zeal. But
"God did not permit" them "to touch" her. For this grace was
designed to be delivered to the Gentiles not by Abraham who,
although he was great was, nevertheless, a servant, but by
Christ. For this reason, therefore, although Abraham was
eager that what was said to him be fulfilled through and in
himself, that "all the nations shall be blessed in you,"[25] nevertheless the promise to him is established in Isaac, that is, in
Christ, as the Apostle says: "He did not say, And to his seeds, as
of many, but as of one, and to your seed, which is Christ."[26]

Nevertheless "the Lord heals Abimelech and his wife and
his handmaids."[27]

(3) But it does not seem to me superfluous that mention is
made not only of Abimelech's wife, but also of his handmaids,
especially in that place which says: "God healed them and they
bore children. For he had closed them that they might not
bear."[28] So far as we can perceive in such difficult passages, we
think natural philosophy can be called Abimelech's wife, but
his handmaids represent the contrivances of dialectic which
are diverse and various by virtue of the nature of the schools.

Abraham, meanwhile, desires to share the gift of divine
virtue also with the Gentiles, but it is not yet time for the grace
of God to pass over from the former people to the Gentiles. For
the Apostle also, although under another viewpont and figure,
says nevertheless: "A woman is bound to the law so long as her
husband lives; but if her husband be dead, she is loosed from
the law so that she is no longer an adulteress if she be with
another man."[29] First, therefore, the law of the letter must die

---

25 Gn 22.18.
26 Gal 3.16.
27 Cf. Gn 20.17.
28 Cf. Gn 20.17–18.
29 Rom 7.2–3.

so that, thus free at last, the soul may now marry the spirit and receive the marriage of the New Testament. Now this present time is the time of the calling of the Gentiles and of the death of the Law, in which time free souls, at last loosed from the Law of the husband, can marry a new husband, Christ.

But if you wish to be taught how the Law is dead, look and see. Where now are the sacrifices? Where now is the altar? Where is the temple? Where are the purifications? Where is the celebration of the Passover? Is not the Law dead in all these things? Or let those friends and defenders of the letter keep the letter of the Law if they can.

According to this order of the allegory, therefore, Pharao, that is an impure man and a destroyer, could not at all receive Sara, that is virtue. Later Abimelech, that is, he who was living purely and philosophically, could indeed receive her, because he was seeking "with a pure heart," but "the time had not yet come."[30] Virtue, therefore, remains with Abraham; it remains with circumcision, until the time should come that in Christ Jesus our Lord, in whom "dwells all the fullness of deity corporeally,"[31] complete and perfect virtue might pass over to the Church of the Gentiles.

At that time, therefore, both the house of Abimelech and his handmaids whom the Lord healed, will bear sons of the Church. For this is the time in which "the barren" will bear, and in which "many are the children of the desolate, more than of her who has a husband."[32] For the Lord opened the womb of the barren and made it fruitful, so that she bears a nation "all at once."[33] But also the saints cry out and say: "Lord, from fear of you we have conceived in the womb and given birth; we have produced the spirits of your salvation on the earth."[34] Whence also Paul likewise says, "My little children, of whom I am in labor again, until Christ be formed in you."[35]

---

30 Cf. Gn 20.5; Jn 7.6.
31 Cf. Col 2.9.
32 Cf. Gal 4.27; Is 54.1.
33 Cf. Is 66.8.
34 Cf. Is 26.18.
35 Gal 4.19.

Such sons, therefore, the whole Church of God produces and such it brings forth. For "he who sows in the flesh, of the flesh also shall reap corruption."[36] Now the sons of the Spirit are those about whom also the Apostle says: "The woman shall be saved through childbearing, if they continue in faith and purity."[37]

Let the Church of God, therefore, in this way understand the births, in this way receive the procreations, in this way uphold the deeds of the fathers with a fitting and honorable interpretation, in this way not disgrace the words of the Holy Spirit with foolish and Jewish fables,[38] but reckon them to be full of honor, full of virtue and usefulness. Otherwise, what edification will we receive when we read that Abraham, such a great patriarch, not only lied to king Abimelech, but also surrendered his wife's chastity to him? In what way does the wife of so great a patriarch edify us if she is supposed to have been exposed to defilements through marital indulgence? These things are what the Jews suppose, along with those who are friends of the letter, not of the spirit.

But we, "comparing spiritual things with spiritual,"[39] are made spiritual in both deed and understanding in Christ Jesus our Lord, "to whom belongs glory and sovereignty forever and ever. Amen."[40]

---

36 Gal 6.8.
37 1 Tm 2.15.
38 Cf. 1 Tm 4.7; Ti 1.14.
39 1 Cor 2.13.
40 1 Pt 4.11.

HOMILY VII
On the birth of Isaac and the fact that he is weaned

 OSES IS READ TO US IN THE CHURCH. Let us pray the Lord lest, in accordance with the Apostle's word, even with us, "when Moses is read the veil be upon" our "heart."[1] For it has been read that Abraham begot a son, Isaac, when he was a hundred years old.[2] "And Sara said: 'Who will announce to Abraham that Sara gives suck to a child?' "[3] "And then," the text says, "Abraham circumcised the child on the eighth day."[4] Abraham does not celebrate his son's birthday, but he celebrates the day of this weaning "and makes a great feast."[5]

Why? Do we think that it is the Holy Spirit's intention to write stories and to narrate how a child was weaned and a feast was made, how he played and did other childish things? Or should we understand by these things that he wishes to teach us something divine and worthy that the human race might learn from the words of God?

Isaac means "laughter" or "joy."[6] Who is it, then, who begets such a son? It is, doubtless, he who said of these whom he begot through the Gospel: "For you are my joy and crown of glorying."[7] For sons of this kind, there is a feast and great joy when they are weaned, for these who "no longer need milk, but strong meat, who by taking up their power have their senses exercised to the discerning of good or evil."[8] There is a great

---

1 Cf. 1 Cor 3.15.
2 Cf. Gn 21.5.
3 Gn 21.7.
4 Gn 21.4.
5 Cf. Gn 21.8.
6 Cf. Gn 21.6; See Appendix, 6.
7 1 Thes 2.19–20.
8 Heb 5.12,14; Cf. Philo *Som.* 2.10.

feast for such as these, when they are weaned. But a feast
cannot be offered nor joy possessed for those of whom the
Apostle says: "I gave you milk to drink, not meat; for you were
not able as yet, but neither indeed are you able still. And I
could not speak to you as to spiritual, but as to carnal, as to little
ones in Christ."[9] Let those who wish the divine Scripture to be
understood straightforwardly tell us what it means: "I could
not speak to you as to spiritual, but as to carnal, as to little ones
in Christ; I gave you milk to drink, not meat."[10] Can these
words be taken straightforwardly?

(2) But let us return, meanwhile, to those matters whence
we digressed. Abraham rejoices "and makes a great feast on
the day on which he weaned his son Isaac."[11] After this Isaac
plays, and he plays with Ismael. Sara is angry because the son
of the bondwoman plays with the son of the free woman, and
she considers that play to be a disaster. She counsels Abraham
and says: "Cast out the bondwoman and her son. For the son of
the bondwoman shall not be heir with my son Isaac."[12]

I shall not now consider how these words ought to be
understood. The Apostle discussed them in this way, saying:
"Tell me, you who have read the Law, have you not heard the
Law? For it is written that Abraham had two sons, the one by a
bondwoman and the other by a free woman. But he, indeed,
who was of the bondwoman was born according to the flesh,
but he of the free woman, was by promise. Which things are
allegorical."[13] What then? Is Isaac not "born according to the
flesh"? Did Sara not bear him? Is he not circumcised? In
regard to this very incident, that he played with Ismael, did he
not play in the flesh? This, indeed, is what is astonishing in the
Apostle's understanding, that he called things "allegorical"
which are quite obviously done in the flesh. His purpose is that
we might learn how to treat other passages, and especially
these in which the historical narrative appears to reveal noth-

---

9 1 Cor 3.2,1.
10 1 Cor 3.1–2.
11 Cf. Gn 21.8.
12 Gn 21.10.
13 Gal 4.21–24.

ing worthy of the divine Law.

Ismael, therefore, is born "according to the flesh," the son of the bondwoman. But Isaac, who was "the son of the free woman," is not born "according to the flesh," but "according to promise." And the Apostle says of these words, that "Agar engendered" a carnal people "unto bondage,"[14] but Sara, who was free, engendered a people which is not "according to the flesh," but has been called to freedom, by which "freedom Christ has made him free."[15] For Christ himself said: "If the son shall make you free, you shall be free indeed."[16]

But let us see what the Apostle adds to these words as he expounds them: "But as then he," Scripture says, "who was according to the flesh, persecuted him who was according to the spirit, so also it is now."[17] Notice how the Apostle teaches us that in all things the flesh is opposed to the spirit, whether that carnal people is opposed to this spiritual people, or even among ourselves, if someone is still carnal, he is opposed to the spiritual. For even you, if you live "according to the flesh" and direct your life "according to the flesh," are a son of Agar and for this reason are opposed to these who live "according to the spirit." Or even if we inquire in ourselves, we find that "the flesh lusts against the spirit and the spirit against the flesh and these are contrary to one another,"[18] and we find "a law in our members fighting against the law of our mind and leading us captive in the law of sin."[19] Do you see how great the battles of the flesh against the spirit are?

There is yet also another battle more violent perhaps than all these. These who understand the Law "according to the flesh" are opposed to and persecute these who perceive it "according to the spirit." Why? Because "the sensual man does not perceive the things that are of the spirit of God. For it is foolishness to him, and he cannot understand because it is

---

14 Cf. Gal 4.24.
15 Cf. Gal 5.1,13.
16 Jn 8.36.
17 Gal 4.29.
18 Cf. Gal 5.17.
19 Cf. Rom 7.23.

spiritually discerned."[20]

And if, therefore, you have in yourself "the fruit of the Spirit which is joy, love, peace, patience,"[21] you can be Isaac, "born" not "according to the flesh," but "according to promise," and you are a "son of the free woman," if only you can also say, according to Paul: "For though we walk in the flesh, we do not war according to the flesh (for the weapons of our warfare are not carnal, but mighty to God for the pulling down of fortifications) destroying thoughts and every height that exalts itself against the knowledge of God."[22] If you can be such that also that statement of the Apostle is worthily applied to you which says: "But you are not in the flesh, but in the spirit if so be the Spirit of God dwells in you,"[23] and, therefore, if you are such, you have not been "born according to the flesh," but "according to the spirit through promise," you will also be an heir of the promises, according to that which is said: "Heirs indeed of God, and joint heirs with Christ."[24] You will not be joint heirs with him who "was born according to the flesh," but joint heirs with Christ, because "even if we have known Christ according to the flesh: but now we know him so no longer."[25]

(3) And nevertheless according to those things which are written I do not see what moved Sara to order the son of the bondwoman to be expelled. He played with her son Isaac. How did he injure or harm him if he was playing? As if this ought not to be pleasing even at that age, that the son of the bondwoman played with the son of the free woman. Next, I marvel also at the Apostle who called this play a persecution, saying: "But as then he, who was according to the flesh, persecuted him who was after the spirit, so also it is now,"[26] when certainly no persecution of Ismael against Isaac is related to have been undertaken, except this play of the infant alone.

But let us see what Paul understood in this play and what

20 1 Cor 2.14.
21 Cf. Gal 5.22.
22 2 Cor 10.3–5.
23 Rom 8.9.
24 Rom 8.17.
25 2 Cor 5.16.
26 Gal 4.29.

angered Sara. Already above in our spiritual exposition we set Sara in the place of virtue. If, therefore, the flesh which Ismael, who was born according to the flesh, represents, attracts the spirit, which is Isaac, and deals with him with enticing deceitfulness, if it allures him with delights, if it mitigates him with pleasures, this kind of play of the flesh with the spirit offends Sara especially, who is virtue, and Paul judges allurements of this kind to be the most bitter persecution.

And you, therefore, O hearer of these words, do not suppose that that alone is persecution whenever you are compelled by the madness of the pagans to sacrifice to idols. But if perhaps the pleasure of the flesh allures you, if the allurement of lust sports with you, flee these things as the greatest persecution if you are a son of virtue. Indeed, for this reason the Apostle also says: "Flee fornication."[27] But also if injustice should attract you, so that, accepting "the countenance of the mighty,"[28] and because of his artful twisting you render an unjust judgment, you ought to understand that under the guise of play you suffer a seductive persecution by injustice. But you shall also consider it a persecution of the spirit by individual guises of evil, even if they are pleasant and delightful and similar to play, because in all these virtue is offended.

(4) Abraham's sons, therefore, are two, "one by a bondwoman, and the other by a free woman."[29] Each, nevertheless, is a son of Abraham, although each is not also a son of the free woman. For this reason also he who is born of the bondwoman does not become an heir, to be sure, with the son of the free woman. Nevertheless, he receives gifts and is not sent away empty. He too receives a blessing, but the "son of the free woman" receives the promise. He too becomes "a great nation,"[30] but the other becomes the people of adoption.

Spiritually, therefore, all, indeed, who come to the recognition of God through faith can be called sons of Abraham; but

---

27 1 Cor 6.18.
28 Cf. Lv 19.15.
29 Cf. Gal 4.22.
30 Cf. Gn 12.2.

among these some cling to God on the basis of love, others on the basis of dread and fear of future judgment. Whence also the apostle John says: "He who fears is not perfected in love; but perfect love casts out fear."[31] He, therefore, who "is perfected in love" is both born of Abraham and is "a son of the free woman." But he who keeps the commandments not in perfect love, but in dread of future torment and in fear of punishments is indeed also himself a son of Abraham; he too receives gifts, that is, the reward of his work (because even "he who shall give a cup of cold water only in the name of a disciple, shall not lose his reward"[32]), nevertheless he is inferior to that person who is perfected not in slavish fear, but in the freedom of love.

The Apostle also shows something similar when he says: "As long indeed as the heir is a child, he differs nothing from a servant, though he be lord of all; but is under tutors and governors until the time appointed by the father."[33] He is "a child," therefore, who is nourished "with milk" and "is unskillful in the word of justice" nor is he able to receive the "solid food" of the divine wisdom and knowledge of the Law.[34] He cannot "compare spiritual things with spiritual."[35] He cannot yet say: "But when I became a man, I put away the things of a child."[36] He "differs," therefore, "nothing from a servant."[37]

But if "leaving the word of the first principles of Christ,"[38] he be borne to perfection and "seek the things that are above, where Christ is sitting at the right hand of God, not the things that are on the earth"[39] and "look not at the things which are seen, but at the things which are not seen,"[40] nor in the divine Scriptures follow "the letter which kills," but "the spirit which

31 1 Jn 4.18.
32 Cf. Mt 10.42
33 Gal 4.1–2.
34 Cf. Heb 5.13–14.
35 Cf. 1 Cor 2.13.
36 1 Cor 13.11.
37 Cf. Gal 4.1.
38 Cf. Heb 6.1.
39 Cf. Col 3.1–2.
40 Cf. 2 Cor 4.18.

quickens,"[41] from those things he will doubtless be one who does not receive "the spirit of bondage again in fear, but the spirit of adoption, whereby they cry, Abba, Father."[42]

(5) Let us see what Abraham does meanwhile after Sara is displeased. He casts out the bondwoman and her son, but nevertheless, he gives him a bottle of water.[43] For his mother does not have a well of living water, nor could the boy draw water from a well. Isaac has wells for which he also suffers strife against the Philistines;[44] but Ismael drinks water from a bottle, but this bottle, as it is a bottle, fails, and, therefore, he is thirsty and does not find a well.

But you, who are a son "of promise as Isaac,"[45] "drink water from your own fountains, and let not the waters flow forth from your wells, but let your waters run in your streets."[46] But he "who is born according to the flesh"[47] drinks water from a bottle and the water itself fails him and he lacks in many things. The bottle of the Law is the letter, from which that carnal people drinks, and thence receives understanding. This letter frequently fails them. It cannot extricate itself; for the historical understanding is defective in many things. But the Church drinks from the evangelic and apostolic fountains which never fail, but "run in its streets,"[48] because they always abound and flow in the breadth of spiritual interpretation. The Church drinks also "from wells" when it draws and examines certain deeper things from the Law.

On account of this mystery also, I think, our Lord and Savior said to the Samaritan woman, when, as if he were speaking with Agar herself he said: "Whoever shall drink of this water shall thirst again; but he who shall drink of the water which I give him shall not thirst forever."[49] But she says to the

---

41 Cf. 2 Cor 3.6.
42 Cf. Rom 8.15.
43 Cf. Gn 21.14.
44 Cf. Gn 26.14–17.
45 Cf. Gal 4.28.
46 Cf. Prv 5.15–16.
47 Cf. Gal 4.29.
48 Cf. Prv 5.16.
49 Jn 4.13–14.

Savior: "Sir, give me this water, that I may not thirst, nor come
here to draw."[50] After this the Lord says to her: "There shall
come to be in him who believes in me a fountain of water,
springing up into life everlasting."[51]

(6) Agar, therefore, "was wandering in the wilderness" with
her child and the child was crying and Agar cast him forth
saying, "Lest I see the death of my son."[52] After this, when
already he had been abandoned as dead and had wept, the
angel of the Lord is present with him "and opened Agar's eyes,
and she saw a well of living water."[53]

How can these words be related to history? For when do we
find that Agar has closed eyes and they are later opened? Is not
the spiritual and mystical meaning in these words clearer than
light, that that people which is "according to the flesh" is
abandoned and lies in hunger and thirst, suffering "not a
famine of bread nor a thirst for water, but a thirst for the word
of God,"[54] until the eyes of the synagogue are opened? This is
what the Apostle says is a "mystery": that "blindness in part has
happened in Israel until the fulness of the Gentiles should
come in, and then all Israel should be saved."[55] That, therefore,
is the blindness in Agar who gave birth "according to the
flesh," who remains blind until "the veil of the letter be removed" by the angel of God and she see the "living water." For
now the Jews lie around the well itself, but their eyes are closed
and they cannot drink from the well of the Law and the
prophets.

But let us also beware, for frequently we also lie around the
well "of living water," that is around the divine Scriptures and
err in them. We hold the books and we read them, but we do
not touch upon the spiritual sense. And, therefore, there is
need for tears and incessant prayer that the Lord may open

---

50 Jn 4.15.
51 Jn 6.47, 4.14.
52 Cf. Gn 21.14,16.
53 Cf. Gn 21.19.
54 Cf. Am 8.11.
55 Rom 11.5.

our eyes, because even the eyes of those blind men who were sitting in Jericho would not have been opened unless they had cried out to the Lord.[56] And what am I saying? That our eyes, which are already opened, might be opened? For Jesus came to open the eyes of the blind.[57] Our eyes, therefore, are opened and the veil of the letter of the Law is removed. But I fear that we ourselves may close them again in a deeper sleep while we are not watchful in the spiritual meaning nor are we disturbed so that we dispel sleep from our eyes and contemplate things which are spiritual, that we might not err with the carnal people set around the water itself.

But rather let us be watchful and say with the prophet: "If I shall give sleep to my eyes and slumber to my eyelids, or rest to my temples, until I find a place for the Lord, a tabernacle for the God of Jacob."[58] "To him be glory and sovereignty forever and ever. Amen."[59]

---

56 Cf. Mt 20.30
57 Cf. Is 42.7.
58 Ps 131.4–5.
59 1 Pt 4.11; Rv 1.6.

HOMILY VIII
On the fact that Abraham offered his son Isaac

IVE ME YOUR ATTENTION, you who have approached God, who believe yourselves to be faithful. Consider diligently how the faith of the faithful is proved from these words which have been read to us. "And it came to pass," the text says, "after these words, God tested Abraham and said to him: 'Abraham, Abraham.' And he said: 'Here I am.' "[1] Observe each detail which has been written. For, if one knows how to dig into the depth, he will find a treasure in the details, and perhaps also, the precious jewels of the mysteries lie hidden where they are not esteemed.

This man was previously called Abram. Nowhere do we read that God called him by this name or said to him: "Abram, Abram." For God could not call him by a name that was to be abolished, but he calls him by this name which he himself gave, and not only does he call him by this name, but he also repeats it. And when he had responded: "Here I am," he says to him: "Take your dearest son Isaac, whom you love, and offer him to me. Go," the text says, "into the high land and there you shall offer him for an holocaust on one of the mountains which I shall show you."[2]

Why God gave him this particular name and called him Abraham, he himself has interpreted: "Because," the text says, "I have made you a father of many nations."[3] God gave him this promise when he had his son Ismael, but it is promised him that that promise will be fulfilled in a son who will be born of Sara. He had kindled his soul, therefore, in love for his son not only because of posterity, but also in the hope of the promises.

---

1 Gn 22.1.
2 Gn 22.2.
3 Gn 17.5.

But this son, in whom those great and marvelous promises have been made, this son, I say, on whose account his name is called Abraham, "he is ordered to offer for an holocaust to the Lord on one of the mountains."

What do you say to these things, Abraham? What kind of thoughts are stirring in your heart? A word has been uttered by God which is such as to shatter and try your faith. What do you say to these things? What are you thinking? What are you reconsidering? Are you thinking, are you turning over in your heart that, if the promise has been given to me in Isaac, but I offer him for an holocaust, it remains that that promise holds no hope? Or rather do you think of those well-known words, and say that it is impossible for him who promised to lie;[4] be that as it may, the promise shall remain?

But I, because "I am the least,"[5] am not able to examine the thoughts of such a great partriarch nor can I know what thoughts the voice of God which had proceeded to test him stirred in him, what feeling it caused, when he was ordered to slay his only son. But since "the spirit of prophets is subject to the prophets,"[6] the apostle Paul, who, I believe, was teaching by the Spirit what feeling, what plan Abraham considered, has revealed it when he says: "By faith Abraham did not hesitate, when he offered his only son, in whom he had received the promises, thinking that God is able to raise him up even from the dead."[7]

The Apostle, therefore, has reported to us the thoughts of the faithful man, that the faith in the resurrection began to be held already at that time in Isaac. Abraham, therefore, hoped for the resurrection of Isaac and believed in a future which had not yet happened. How, then, are they "sons of Abraham"[8] who do not believe what has happened in Christ, which Abraham believed was to be in Isaac? Nay rather, that I may speak more clearly, Abraham knew himself to prefigure the image of future truth; he knew the Christ was to be born from his seed,

4 Cf. Heb 6.18.
5 Cf. 1 Cor 15.9.
6 1 Cor 14.32.
7 Heb 11.17,19.
8 Cf. Jn 8.37.

who also was to be offered as a truer victim for the whole world
and was to be raised from the dead.

(2) But now meanwhile the text says, "God was testing
Abraham and says to him: 'Take your dearest son whom you
love.' "[9] For to have said "son" would not have been enough,
but "dearest" also is added. Let this too be considered. Why is
there still added also, "Whom you love"? But behold the importance of the test. The affections of a father are roused by the
dear and sweet appellations repeated frequently, that by awak-
ing memories of love the paternal right hand might be slowed
in slaying his son and the total warfare of the flesh might fight
against the faith of the soul.

"Take," therefore, the text says, "your dearest son Isaac,
whom you love."[10] Let it be, Lord, that you are reminding the
father of the son; you add also "dearest," whom you are
commanding to be slain. Let this be sufficient for the father's
torment. You add again also, "Whom you love." Let the triple
torment of the father be in this. Why is there need yet that you
bring to mind also "Isaac"? Did Abraham not know that that
dearest son of his, that one whom he loved, was called Isaac?
But why is it added at this time? That Abraham might recall
that you had said to him: "In Isaac shall your seed be called,
and that in Isaac the promises shall be yours."[11] The reminder
of the name also produces a hopelessness in the promises
which were made under this name.

But all these things happened because God was testing
Abraham.

(3) What happens after this? "Go," the text says, "into the
high land, to one of the mountains which I shall show you, and
there you shall offer him for an holocaust."[12]

Notice, in the details, how the test is augmented. "Go into
the high land." Could not Abraham with the child first be led to
that high land, and first be placed on the mountain which the
Lord had chosen, and there it be said to him that he should

---

9 Gn 22.1–2.
10 Gn 22.2.
11 Cf. Gn 21.12; Rom 9.7–8; Heb 11.18; Gal 3.16.18, 4.23.
12 Gn 22.2.

offer his son? But first it is said to him that he ought to offer his son, and then he is ordered to go "into the high land" and ascend the mountain. For what reason? That while he is walking, while he is making the journey, throughout the whole trip he might be torn to pieces with his thoughts, that hence he might be tormented by the oppressing command, hence he might be tormented by the struggling true affection for his only son. For this reason, therefore, likewise the journey and furthermore the ascent of the mountain is enjoined, that in all these things there might be a period of struggle between affection and faith, love of God and love of the flesh, the charm of things present and the expectation of things future.

He is sent, therefore, "into the high land" and the high land is not sufficient for a patriarch about to accomplish so great a work for the Lord, but he is also ordered to ascend a mountain, of course that, exalted by faith, he might abandon earthly things and ascend to things above.

(4) "Abraham arose," therefore, "in the morning and saddled his ass, and cut wood for the holocaust. And he took his son Isaac and two servants and came to the place which God had said to him, on the third day."[13]

Abraham arose in the morning (because the text adds "in the morning," perhaps it wished to show that the beginning of light shone in his heart), saddled his ass, prepared wood, took along his son. He does not deliberate, he does not reconsider, he does not take counsel with any man, but immediately he sets out on the journey.

"And he came," the text says, "to the place which the Lord had said to him, on the third day."[14] I omit now what mystery the "third day" contains. I consider the wisdom and intention of the one who tempts him. Since everything was done in the mountains, was there thus no mountain nearby, but a journey is prolonged for three days and during the whole three days the parent's heart is tormented with recurring anxieties, so that the father might consider the son in this whole lengthy period, that he might partake of food with him, that the child

13 Gn 22.3.
14 Gn 22.3.

might weigh in his father's embraces for so many nights, might cling to his breast, might lie in his bosom? Behold to what an extent the test is heaped up.

The third day, however, is always applied to mysteries. For also when the people had departed from Egypt, they offer sacrifice to God on the third day and are purified on the third day.[15] And the third day is the day of the Lord's resurrection.[16] Many other mysteries also are included within this day.

(5) "Abraham," the text says, "looking about saw the place afar off. And he said to his servants: 'Stay here with the ass, but I and the boy will go as far as yonder, and when we have worshipped, we will return to you.' "[17]

He leaves the servants. For the servants were not able to ascend with Abraham to the place of the holocaust which God had shown him. "You," therefore, the text says, "stay here, but I and the child will go and when we have worshipped, we will return to you."[18] Tell me, Abraham, are you saying to the servants in truth that you will worship and return with the child, or are you deceiving them? If you are telling the truth, then you will not make him a holocaust. If you are deceiving, it is not fitting for so great a patriarch to deceive. What disposition, therefore, does this statement indicate in you? I am speaking the truth, he says, and I offer the child as a holocaust. For for this reason I both carry wood with me, and I return to you with him. For I believe, and this is my faith, that "God is able to raise him up even from the dead."[19]

(6) After this the text says, "Abraham took the wood for the holocaust and laid it on Isaac his son, and he took the fire in his own hands and a sword, and they went off together."[20]

That Isaac himself carries on himself "the wood for the holocaust" is a figure, because Christ also "himself carried his

---

15 Cf. Ex 19.11,15,16, 24.5.
16 Cf. Mt 27.63; Mk 8.31.
17 Gn 22.4–5.
18 Gn 22.5.
19 Heb 11.19.
20 Gn 22.6.

own cross,"[21] and yet to carry "the wood for the holocaust" is the duty of a priest. He himself, therefore, becomes both victim and priest. But what is added also is related to this: "And they both went off together." For when Abraham carries the fire and knife as if to sacrifice, Isaac does not go behind him, but with him, that he might be shown to contribute equally with the priesthood itself.

What happens after this? "Isaac," the text says, "said to Abraham, his father: 'Father.'"[22] And in this moment the word of testing is uttered by the son. For how do you suppose the son to be killed struck the father's heart with this word? And although Abraham was very rigid by virtue of his faith, nevertheless he also returned an expression of affection and responded: "What is it, son?" And Isaac says, "Behold the fire and the wood. Where is the sheep for the holocaust?" Abraham responded to these words: "God himself will provide himself a sheep for the holocaust, son."[23]

Abraham's response, sufficiently accurate and cautious, moves me. I know not what he saw in his spirit,[24] for he speaks not about the present, but about the future: "God himself will provide himself a sheep."[25] He responded to his son's inquiry about present things with future things. For "the Lord himself will provide himself a sheep" in Christ, because also, "Wisdom herself has built herself a house"[26] and, "He himself humbled himself unto death."[27] And you will discover that everything you happen to read about Christ is done not by necessity, but freely.

(7) "They both proceeded, therefore, and came to the place which God had said to him."[28]

---

21 Cf. Jn 19.17.
22 Gn 22.7.
23 Gn 22.7–8.
24 Or, perhaps, "in the Spirit" (*spiritu*).
25 Gn 22.8.
26 Prv 9.1.
27 Cf. Phil 2.8.
28 Gn 22.8–9.

When Moses had come to the place which God shows him, he is not permitted to ascend, but first God says to him: "Loose the tie of the shoes from your feet."[29] None of these things are said to Abraham and Isaac, but they ascend nor do they put aside their shoes. The reason for this is perhaps that Moses although he was "great,"[30] was, nevertheless, coming from Egypt and some fetters of mortality were bound to his feet. Abraham and Isaac however, have none of these, but "they come to the place."

Abraham builds an altar; he places the wood on the altar; he binds the boy; he prepares himself for the slaying.

Many of you who hear these words are fathers in the Church of God. Do you think any one of you from the mere relating of the story acquires so much steadfastness, so much strength of soul, that when a son perhaps is lost by a death that is common and due to all, even if he be an only son, even if he be a beloved son, might bring in Abraham as an example for himself and set his magnanimity before his eyes? And indeed this greatness of soul is not required of you, that you yourself should bind your son, you yourself tie him, you yourself prepare the sword, you yourself slay your only son. All these services are not asked of you. Be constant in purpose, at least, and mind. Offer your son to God joyful, immovable in faith. Be the priest for your son's life. It is not fitting that the priest who offers to God weep.

Do you wish to see that this is required of you? In the Gospel the Lord says: "If you were the children of Abraham, you would do the works surely of Abraham."[31] Behold, this is a work of Abraham. Do the works which Abraham did, but not with sadness, "for God loves a cheerful giver."[32] But also if you should be so inclined to God, it will be said also to you: "Ascend into the high land and into the mountain which I shall show you, and there offer your son to me."[33] "Offer your son" not in

---

29 Ex 3.5.
30 Cf. Ex 11.3.
31 Cf. Jn 8.39.
32 2 Cor 9.7.
33 Gn 22.2.

the depths of the earth nor "in the vale of tears,"[34] but in the high and lofty mountains. Show that faith in God is stronger than the affections of the flesh. For Abraham loved Isaac his son, the text says, but he placed the love of God before love of the flesh and he is found not with the affection of the flesh, but "with the affection of Christ,"[35] that is with the affection of the Word of God and of the truth and wisdom.

(8) "And Abraham put forth his hand," the text says, "to take the sword and slay his son. And an angel of the Lord from heaven called him and said: 'Abraham, Abraham.' And he said: 'Here I am.' And he said: 'Do not lay your hand on the boy nor do anything to him. For now I know that you fear God.' "[36]

In this statement it is usually thrown out against us that God says that now he had learned that Abraham fears God as though he were such as not to have known previously. God knew and it was not hidden from him, since it is he "who has known all things before they come to pass."[37] But these things are written on account of you, because you too indeed have believed in God, but unless you shall fulfill "the works of faith,"[38] unless you shall be obedient to all the commands, even the more difficult ones, unless you shall offer sacrifice and show that you place neither father nor mother nor sons before God,[39] you will not know that you fear God nor will it be said of you: "Now I know that you fear God."[40]

And yet it must be considered that an angel is related to have spoken these words to Abraham and subsequently this angel is clearly shown to be the Lord. Whence I think that, just as among us men "he was found in appearance as a man,"[41] so also among angels he was found in appearance as an angel. And following his example the angels in heaven rejoice "over

---

34 Cf. Ps 83.7.
35 Cf. Phil 1.8.
36 Gn 22.10–12.
37 Dn 13.42.
38 2 Thes 1.11.
39 Cf. Mt 10.37.
40 Gn 22.12.
41 Phil 2.7.

one sinner repenting"[42] and glory in the progress of men. For they, as it were, have charge over our souls, to whom, "while we are still children we are committed," as it were, "to tutors and governors until the time appointed by the father."[43] And they, therefore, now say about the progress of each of us: "Now I know that you fear God."[44] For example, I intend to be a martyr. An angel could not say to me on this basis: "Now I know that you fear God," for an intention of the mind is known to God alone. But if I shall undertake the struggles, if I shall utter a "good confession,"[45] if I shall bear calmly all things which are inflicted, then an angel can say, as if confirming and strengthening me: "Now I know that you fear God."[46]

But grant that these words are spoken to Abraham and he is said to fear God. Why? Because he did not spare his son. But let us compare these words with those of the Apostle, where he says of God: "Who spared not his own son, but delivered him up for us all."[47] Behold God contending with men in magnificent liberality: Abraham offered God a mortal son who was not put to death; God delivered to death an immortal son for men.

What shall we say to these things? "What shall we render to the Lord for all the things that he has rendered to us?"[48] God the Father, on account of us, "spared not his own son."[49] Who of you, do you suppose, will sometime hear the voice of an angel saying: "Now I know that you fear God, because you spared not your son,"[50] or your daughter or wife, or you spared not your money or the honors of the world or the ambitions of the world, but you have despised all things and "have counted all things dung that you may gain Christ,"[51] "you have sold all

---

42 Cf. Lk 15.10.
43 Cf. Gal 4.3,2.
44 Gn 22.12.
45 1 Tm 6.12.
46 Gn 22.12.
47 Rom 8.32.
48 Ps 115.12.
49 Cf. Rom 8.32.
50 Gn 22.12.
51 Phil 3.8.

things and have given to the poor and have followed the Word of God?"[52] Who of you, do you think, will hear a word of this kind from the angels? Meanwhile Abraham hears this voice, and it is said to him: "You spared not your beloved son because of me."[53]

(9) "And looking back with his eyes," the text says, "Abraham saw, and behold a ram was held by its horns in a bush *Sabec*."[54] We said above, I think, that Isaac represented Christ. But this ram no less also seems to represent Christ. Now it is worthwhile to know how both are appropriate to Christ, both Isaac who is not slain and the ram which is slain.

Christ is "the Word of God," but "the Word was made flesh."[55] One aspect of Christ, therefore, is from above; the other is received from human nature and the womb of the virgin. Christ suffered, therefore, but in the flesh; and he endured death, but it was the flesh, of which this ram is a type, as also John said: "Behold the Lamb of God, behold him who takes away the sin of the world."[56] But the Word continued "in incorruption,"[57] which is Christ according to the spirit, of which Isaac is the image. For this reason he himself is both victim and priest. For truly according to the spirit he offers the victim to the Father, but according to the flesh he himself is offered on the altar of the cross, because, as it is said of him "Behold the Lamb of God, behold him who takes away the sin of the world,"[58] so it is said of him: "You are a priest forever according to the order of Melchisedech."[59] "A ram," therefore, "was held by its horns in a bush *Sabec*."[60]

(10) "And he took the ram," the text says, "and offered it for

---

52 Cf. Mt 19.21.
53 Gn 22.12.
54 Gn 22.13. The LXX contains the Hebrew word for thicket (*sēbak*) along with the Greek translation of the term.
55 Jn 1.14.
56 Jn 1.29.
57 Cf. 1 Cor 15.42.
58 Jn 1.29.
59 Ps 109.4.
60 Gn 22.13.

a holocaust instead of his son Isaac. And Abraham called the name of that place: *the Lord saw*."[61]

A clear way of spiritual understanding is opened for those who know how to hear these words. For everything which has been done reaches to the vision, for it is said that "the Lord saw." But the vision which "the Lord saw" is in the spirit so that you too might see these things in the spirit which are written and, just as there is nothing corporeal in God so also you might perceive nothing corporeal in all these things,[62] but you too might beget a son Isaac in the spirit, when you begin to have "the fruit of the Spirit, joy, peace."[63] Which son, however, you will at length so beget if, as it is written of Sara: "It ceased to be with Sara after the manner of women,"[64] and then she bore Isaac, so the things after the manner of women should cease also in your soul, so that you no longer have anything womanish or effeminate in your soul, but "you act manfully"[65] and manfully gird your loins. You will beget such a son if your breast is "protected with the breastplate of justice; if you are armed with the helmet of salvation and the sword of the Spirit."[66] If, therefore, the things after the manner of women cease to be in your soul, you beget joy and gladness as a son from your wife, virtue and wisdom. Now you beget joy if "you count it all joy when you fall into various temptations"[67] and you offer that joy in sacrifice to God.

For when you have approached God joyfully, he again gives back to you what you have offered and says to you: "You will see me again, and your heart shall rejoice, and no man shall

---

61 Gn 22.13–14.
62 It should be noted that this statement leaves no place for a literal interpretation of the account. It has been asserted by modern scholars that Rufinus tended to alter Origen's statements which rejected the literal interpretation of the Bible (see Hansen, *Tradition*, 44, who cites also Butterworth's Introduction to his translation of *De Principiis*). No such tendency is apparent here.
63 Cf. Gal 5.22.
64 Cf. Gn 18.11.
65 Cf. Dt 31.6.
66 Cf. Eph 6.14,17.
67 Cf. Jas 1.2.

take your joy from you."[68] So, therefore, what you have offered to God you shall receive back multiplied. Something like this, although in another figure, is related in the Gospels when in a parable someone is said to have received a pound that he might engage in business, and the master of the house demanded the money. But if you have caused five to be multiplied to ten, they themselves are given to you, they are granted to you. For hear what Scripture says: "Take his pound and give it to him who has ten pounds."[69]

So, therefore, we appear at least to engage in business for the Lord, but the profits of the business go to us. And we appear to offer victims to the Lord, but the things we offer are given back to us. For God needs nothing, but he wishes us to be rich, he desires our progress through each individual thing.

This figure is shown to us also in these things which happened to Job. For he too, although he was rich, lost everything because of God. But he bore well the struggles with patience and was magnanimous in everything which he suffered and said: "The Lord gave, the Lord has taken away; as it has pleased the Lord so is it done. Blessed be the name of the Lord."[70] Because of this, behold what finally is written about him: "He received back twice as much," Scripture says, "as he had lost."[71]

Do you see what it means to lose something for God? It means to receive it back multiplied. But the Gospels promise you something even more, "a hundred-fold" is offered you, besides also "life eternal"[72] in Christ Jesus our Lord "to whom belongs glory and sovereignty forever and ever. Amen."[73]

---

68 Jn 16.22, 17.
69 Lk 19.24.
70 Jb 1.21.
71 Jb 42.10.
72 Cf. Mt 19.29.
73 1 Pt 4.11; Rv 1.6.

HOMILY IX
On the promises made to Abraham the second time

HE FURTHER WE PROGRESS IN READING, the greater grows the accumulation of mysteries for us. And just as if someone should embark on the sea borne by a small boat, as long as he is near land he has little fear. But, when he has advanced little by little into the deep and has begun either to be lifted on high by the swelling waves or brought down to the depths by the same gaping waves then truly great fear and terror permeate his mind because he has entrusted a small craft to such immense waves. So also we seem to have suffered, who, small in merits and slight in ability, dare to enter so vast a sea of mysteries. But if by your prayers the Lord should see fit to give us a favorable breeze of his Holy Spirit we shall enter the port of salvation with a favorable passage of the word.

Let us see now, therefore, what the words are which have been read to us. "And the angel of the Lord," the text says, "called to Abraham a second time from heaven saying: 'By my own self have I sworn,' says the Lord, 'because you have done this thing¹ and have not spared your beloved son because of me, I shall certainly bless you and multiply you, and your seed shall be as the stars of heaven in multitude and as the sand of the sea which cannot be numbered,' " etc.² These words require a concerned and attentive hearer.

For this part of the statement is new: "And the angel of the Lord called to Abraham a second time from heaven."³ But what the text adds is not new. For "I shall certainly bless you" has already been said earlier, and "I shall certainly multiply you" has been promised earlier, and "your seed shall be as the

1 *Verbum.* The LXX has rhēma, which can mean either "word" or "thing."
2 Gn 22.15–17.
3 Gn 22.15.

stars of heaven and as the sand of the sea" also had been announced previously.[4] What, therefore, is there now in addition which is declared a second time from heaven? What new word is added to the old promises? What additional reward is given in that which the text says: "Because you have done this thing,"[5] that is because you have offered your son, because you have not spared your only son? I see nothing additional. The same things are repeated which were previously promised. Will, it therefore, seem superfluous to go over the same things again and again? On the contrary, it is necessary. For all things which happen happen in mysteries.

One promise would have sufficed if Abraham had lived only "according to the flesh" and had been the father of one people whom he begot "according to the flesh."[6] But now, to show, in the first place, that he is to be the father of those who are circumcised "according to the flesh," the promise which should affect the people of circumcision is given to him at the time of his circumcision. In the second place, because he was to be the father also of those who "are of faith"[7] and who come to the inheritance through the passion of Christ, the promise which should apply to that people which is saved by the passion and resurrection of Christ is renewed at the time, no less, of the passion of Isaac.

The same things indeed appear to be repeated, but they are widely different. For those things which are said first and apply to the previous people, are said on the earth. For thus the Scripture says: "And he brought him forth"—from the tent, of course,—"and said to him: 'Look at the stars of heaven. Can they be numbered in their multitude?'" And he adds: "So shall your seed be."[8] But when the promise is repeated the second time, the text designates that it is said to him "from heaven."[9] The first promise is given from the earth, the second "from

---

4 Gn 22.17; Cf. 12.2; 13.16.
5 Gn 22.16.
6 Cf. Gal 4.29.
7 Cf. Gal 3.9.
8 Gn 15.5.
9 Cf. Gn 22.15.

heaven." Does not this clearly seem to represent that which the Apostle says: "The first man was of the earth, earthly; the second man from heaven, heavenly."[10] This latter promise, therefore, which applies to the faithful people is "from heaven," the former from the earth.

In the former promise there was only the statement; here an oath is interposed, which the holy Apostle writing to the Hebrews interprets in this way, saying: "God, meaning to show the heirs of the promise the immutability of his counsel, interposed an oath."[11] And again, Scripture says: "Men swear by one greater than themselves."[12] "But God, because he had no one greater by whom he might swear,"[13] " 'I swear by myself,' said the Lord."[14] It was not that necessity forced God to swear (for who would exact the oath from him?), but as the apostle Paul has interpreted it, that by this he might point out to his worshippers "the immutability of his counsel."[15] So also elsewhere it is said by the prophet: "The Lord has sworn nor will he repent: You are a priest forever according to the order of Melchisedech."[16]

At that time in the first promise there is no reason stated why the promise is given, only that he brought him forth and "showed him," Scripture says, "the stars of heaven, and said: 'So shall your seed be.' "[17] But now he adds the reason on account of which he confirms with an oath the promise which will be steadfast. For he says: "Because you have done this thing and have not spared your son."[18] He shows, therefore, that because of the offering or passion of the son the promise is steadfast. This clearly points out that the promise remains

---

10 1 Cor 15.47.
11 Heb 6.17.
12 Heb 6.16.
13 Heb 6.13.
14 Gn 22.16.
15 Cf. Heb 6.17.
16 Ps 109.4.
17 Cf. Gn 15.15.
18 Gn 22.16.

steadfast because of the passion of Christ for the people of the gentiles "who are of the faith of Abraham."[19]

And are the second words firmer than the first in this passage alone? You will discover secret mysteries in many passages of this kind. Moses shattered and threw aside the first tablets of the Law in the letter. He received the second Law in the spirit and the second words are firmer than the first. Again, the very same man, when he had included all the Law in four books, writes Deuteronomy which is called a second Law. Ismael is first, Isaac second, and a similar kind of preference is reserved for the second. You will also find this suggested likewise in Esau and Jacob, in Ephraim and Manasses and in a thousand others.

(2) Let us return now to ourselves and treat the moral subject in every detail.

The Apostle says, as we have already related above: "The first man was of the earth, earthly, the second man from heaven, heavenly. Such as is the earthly, such also are the earthly; and such as is the heavenly, such also are they that are heavenly. As we have borne the image of the earthly, let us bear also the image of the heavenly."[20] You see what he is showing, that if you remain in that which is first, which is of the earth, you will be rejected, unless you change yourself, unless you have been converted, unless, having been made "heavenly," you have received "the image of the heavenly."[21] This is the same thing he also says elsewhere: "Stripping yourselves of the old man with his deeds, and putting on the new, who has been created according to God."[22] He writes that very thing also in another place: "Behold the old things are passed away, all things are made new."[23]

For this reason, therefore, God renews his promises to show you that you also ought to be renewed. He does not continue in

---

19 Cf. Rom 4.16.
20 1 Cor 15.47–49.
21 1 Cor 15.49.
22 Col 3.9–10.
23 2 Cor 5.17.

the old, lest you also continue as "the old man";[24] this is said
"from heaven," that you also might receive "the image of the
heavenly."[25] For what will it profit you if God should renew the
promises and you should not be renewed? If he should speak
from heaven and you should hear from earth? What does it
profit you if God binds himself with an oath and you should
pass over these things as if hearing a common story?

Why do you not consider that because of you God embraces
even those things which seem less fitted to his nature? God is
said to swear, that you, when you hear, might be struck with
fear and begin to tremble, and, overwhelmed with terror,
might inquire what it is that is so great that God is said to swear
for it. These things come about, therefore, that you might
become attentive and disturbed, and, hearing that a promise is
prepared for you in heaven, might be watchful and seek to
know how you may be worthy of the divine promises.

Nevertheless the Apostle interprets this passage also,
saying: "To Abraham God promised and to his seed. He did
not say, 'And to his seeds' as of many; but as of one, 'And to
your seed', which is Christ."[26] It is said, therefore, of Christ: "I
shall certainly multiply your seed, and they shall be as the stars
of heaven in multitude and as the sand which is by the sea
shore."[27] What man now needs an explanation to know how the
seed of Christ is multiplied, who sees the preaching of the
Gospel extended from the ends of the earth "to the ends of the
earth,"[28] and who sees that there is now almost no place which
has not received the seed of the word? For indeed this also was
prefigured in the beginnings of the world when God said to
Adam: "Increase and multiply."[29] Which same thing also the
Apostle says "is said in Christ and in the Church."[30]

But in reference to what the text said: "As the stars of

---

24 Cf. Rom 6.6.
25 Cf. 1 Cor 15.49.
26 Gal 3.16.
27 Gn 22.17.
28 Cf. Rom 10.18.
29 Gn 1.28.
30 Eph 5.32.

heaven in multitude," and what it added: "and innumerable as the sand which is by the sea shore,"[31] perhaps indeed someone may say that the figure of the heavenly number fits the Christian people; the figure of the sand of the sea, the Jew. But I think rather this, that each example can be applied to each people. For there were also in the former people many just men and prophets with whom the example of the stars of heaven is deservedly compared; and among our people there are many who "mind earthly things"[32] and whose foolishness "is heavier than the sand of the sea,"[33] among whom especially, I think, the crowds of heretics are to be considered. But lest we indeed be negligent; for as long as anyone of us does not lay aside "the image of the earthly" and put on "the image of the heavenly,"[34] he is compared to the earthly examples.

Whence also the Apostle, as I think, moved by these things fashions the image of the resurrection in heavenly and earthly bodies, saying: "One is the glory of the heavenly, and another of the earthly. And star differs from star in glory; so also shall be the resurrection of the dead."[35] But the Lord also reminds him who knows how to hear of this same thing when he says: "That your light might shine before men, and men, seeing your good works, might glorify your Father who is in heaven."[36]

(3) But if you wish to learn more clearly in the words of Scripture that Christ is the seed of Abraham and the son of Abraham, hear how it is written in the Gospel: "The book," it says, "of the generation of Jesus Christ, the son of David, the son of Abraham."[37] In this, therefore, is fulfilled also that word regarding which Scripture says: "Your seed shall take possession of the cities of their enemies for an inheritance."[38] How

---

31 Gn 22.17.
32 Cf. Phil 3.19.
33 Jb 6.3.
34 Cf. 1 Cor 15.49.
35 1 Cor 15.40–42.
36 Mt 5.16.
37 Mt 1.1.
38 Gn 22.17.

has Christ taken possession of "the cities of his enemies for an inheritance?" Doubtless in this way, that "the sound" of the apostles "has gone forth into all the earth," and "their words into the whole world."[39] Whence also those angels have been roused to wrath who held each individual nation under their authority. "For when the Most High divided the nations according to the number of the angels of God, then Jacob became his portion and Israel the lot of his inheritance."[40] For Christ, to whom the Father had said: "Ask of me and I will give you the nations for your inheritance and the utmost parts of the earth for your possession,"[41] expelling those very angels from the authority and domination which they had among the nations, provoked them to wrath. And for this reason Scripture says: "The kings of the earth stood up, and the princes met together, against the Lord and against his Christ."[42] Therefore they resist us also and stir up struggles and strife against us. Hence also the Apostle of Christ: "Our struggle is not against flesh and blood, but against principalities and powers and rulers of this world."[43] For this reason, therefore, we must be watchful and act carefully, because "our adversary, as a roaring lion, goes about seeking whom he may devour."[44] Unless we shall resist him "strong in faith,"[45] he shall again recall us into captivity. If this should happen to us, we will make thankless the work of him who "fastened to his cross principalities and powers, confidently triumphing over them in himself"[46] and who came "to set at liberty the captives."[47]

But rather, following faith in Christ "who has triumphed over them,"[48] let us break their bonds asunder with which we have been bound by their power. The bonds, indeed, with

---

39 Cf. Ps 18.5; Rom 10.18.
40 Dt 32.8–9.
41 Ps 2.8.
42 Ps 2.2.
43 Eph 6.12.
44 1 Pt 5.8.
45 Cf. 1 Pt 5.9.
46 Col 2.14–15.
47 Lk 4.18.
48 Col 2.15.

which they bind us are our passions and vices with which we are bound until "we crucify our flesh with the vices and concupiscences"[49] and so at last "break their bonds asunder and cast away their yoke from us."[50]

The seed of Abraham, therefore, that is, the seed of the word, which is the preaching of the Gospel and faith in Christ, has occupied "the cities of their enemies."[51]

But I say: Has the Lord used iniquity to snatch the nations from the power of his enemies and recall them to faith in him and to his dominion? By no means. For "Israel" was once "the Lord's portion,"[52] but they made Israel turn from her God in sin,[53] and because of their sins God said to them: "Behold you have been separated by your sins and because of your sins you have been scattered under the whole heaven."[54] But again he says to them:" 'If your dispersion should be from one end of heaven to the other, thence I will gather you,' says the Lord."[55] Because, therefore, "the princes of this world"[56] had first invaded "the Lord's portion," "the good shepherd"[57] had, necessarily, the ninety and nine having been left on the heights,[58] to descend to the lands[59] and seek the one sheep which was lost and when it was found and carried back on his shoulders, to recall it to the sheepfold of perfection on high.

---

49 Cf. Gal 5.24.
50 Ps 2.3.
51 Cf. Gn 22.17.
52 Cf. Sir 17.17 (LXX); Dt 32.9.
53 *peccare. . . a Deo suo.*
54 Neh 1.8.
55 Neh 1.9; Cf. Dt 30.4.
56 Cf. Jn 16.11.
57 Jn 10.11.
58 Cf. Mt 18.12; Lk 15.4–5.
59 *Terras.* Perhaps "worlds." Might the plural be a hint of Origen's belief that there are numerous worlds through which the soul must pass in its ascent back to God (See *De Princ.* 2.3.1,5)? He seems not, however, (at least as Rufinus has preserved the text in *De Princ.* 2.3.5) to have thought that Christ came to any world other than the present one. Or, does the plural point to the various nations controlled by the angels which have been discussed in this section? The singular *terram* is supported only by FP. Both Baehrens and Doutreleau print the plural in their texts, though the latter translates it with the singular *terre* (p. 251).

But what does it profit me, if the seed of Abraham, "which is Christ"[60] should possess "the cities of his enemies for an inheritance,"[61] and should not possess my city? If in my city, that is in my soul, which is "the city of the great king,"[62] neither his laws nor his ordinances should be observed? What does it profit me, that he has subjected the whole world and possesses the cities of his enemies if he should not also conquer his enemies in me, if he should not destroy "the law which is in my members fighting against the law of my mind and which leads me captive in the law of sin?"[63]

So, therefore, let each one of us do what is necessary that Christ may also conquer the enemies in his soul and in his body, and, subjecting and triumphing over them, may possess the city even of his soul. For in this way we are made to belong to his portion, the better portion, which is "as the stars of heaven in glory,"[64] that also we might be able to receive the blessing of Abraham through Christ our Lord, "to whom belongs glory and sovereignty for ever and ever. Amen."[65]

---

60 Cf. Gal 3.16.
61 Cf. Gn 22.17.
62 Cf. Ps 47.3; Mt 5.35.
63 Cf. Rom 7.23.
64 Cf. 1 Cor 15.41.
65 1 Pt 4.11; Rv 1.6.

HOMILY X

On Rebecca, when she went out to draw water and Abraham's servant met her

SAAC, SCRIPTURE SAYS, "GREW"[1] and became strong, that is, Abraham's joy grew as he looked not at those things "which are seen, but at the things which are not seen."[2] For Abraham did not rejoice about present things nor about the riches of the world and the activities of the age. But do you wish to hear why Abraham rejoiced? Hear the Lord saying to the Jews: "Abraham your father desired to see my day, and he saw it and was glad."[3] In this way, therefore, "Isaac grew";[4] that vision of Abraham, in which he saw the day of Christ, and the hope which is in Christ were increasing his joys. And would that you too might be made Isaac and be a joy to your mother the Church!

But I fear that the Church is still bearing sons in sadness and sorrow. Or does it not cause her sadness and sorrow when you do not gather to hear the word of God? And scarcely on feast days do you proceed to the Church, and you do this not so much from a desire for the word as from a fondness for the festival and to obtain, in a certain manner, common relaxation.

What then shall I do, to whom the dispensation of the word is committed?[5] Although I am "an unprofitable servant,"[6] I have, nevertheless, received from the Lord "to distribute the measure of wheat to the master's servants."[7] But behold what the word of the Lord adds: "to distribute the measure of wheat

1 Cf. Gn 21.8.
2 Cf. 2 Cor 4.18.
3 Jn 8.56.
4 Cf. Gn 21.8.
5 Cf. 1 Cor 9.17.
6 Cf. Lk 17.10.
7 Cf. Lk 12.42.

in due season."[8] What, then, shall I do? Where or when shall I find your due season? You spend most of this time, no rather almost all of it in mundane occupations; you pass some of it in the marketplace, some in business; one has time for the country, another for lawsuits, and no one or very few have time to hear the word of God.

But why do I reproach you about occupations? Why do I complain about absences? Even when you are present and placed in the Church you are not attentive, but you waste your time on common everyday stories; you turn your backs to the word of God or to the divine readings. I fear that the Lord may say to you also that which is said through the prophet: "They turned their backs to me and not their faces."[9]

What, then, shall I do, to whom the ministry of the word is entrusted? The words which have been read are mystical. They must be explained in allegorical secrets. Can I throw "the pearls"[10] of the word of God to your deaf and averted ears? The Apostle did not do so. For see what he says: "You who read the Law," he says, "do not hear the Law. For Abraham had two sons," etc.,[11] to which he adds: "Which things are allegorical."[12] Did he open the secrets of the Law to those who neither read nor hear the Law? But he said to those who read the Law: "You do not hear the Law."[13] How, then, shall I be able to open and make known the mysteries and allegories of the Law, which we are taught by the Apostle, to these for whom both the hearing and the reading of the Law are unknown?

Perhaps I seem rather harsh to you, but I cannot "white-wash" a falling "wall."[14] For I fear that which is written: "O my

---

8 Lk 12.42.
9 Cf. Jer 39.33 (LXX).
10 Cf. Mt 7.6.
11 Gal 4.21–22. The quotation of Gal 4.21, as preserved here, conflates the reading of the Vulgate and that of the Greek text. The Vulgate reads: *legem non legistis*. The Greek text has: *ton nomon ouk akouete*. Both verbs play an important role in the exposition which follows. The verse is quoted in the same form in *Gn. Hom.* 7.2 (except that the verbs are perfect instead of present tense), but no comments are made there regarding either clause.
12 Gal 4.24.
13 Gal 4.21.
14 Cf. Ez 13.10.

people, those who bless you lead you away and confuse the paths of your feet."[15] "I admonish you as my dearest children."[16] I marvel if the way of Christ has not yet become known to you; if you have not heard this indeed, that it is not "wide and broad," but "the way which leads to life is straight and narrow." And you, therefore, "Enter in at the narrow gate."[17] Leave breadth to the perishing. "The night is passed, and the day is at hand."[18] "Walk as children of light."[19] "The time is short; it remains that they also who have be as if they had not, and they that use this world as if they used it not."[20]

The Apostle orders that we pray "without ceasing."[21] How do you, who do not convene for prayers, fulfill "without ceasing" what you always omit? But the Lord also orders: "Watch and pray lest you enter into temptation."[22] But if those who watch and pray and always cling to the word of God have, nevertheless, by no means escaped temptation, what do these do who come to Church only on festive days? "If the just man scarcely be saved, where shall the sinner and the ungodly appear?"[23]

It troubles me to say anything from these words which have been read. For even the Apostle says of words of this kind that they are "hard to be uttered intelligibly, because you," he says, "have become weak to hear."[24]

(2) Let us consider, nevertheless, this which has now been read to us. "Rebecca," the text says, "came with the daughters of the city to draw water from the well."[25]

Rebecca came to the wells daily; she drew water daily. And because she spent time at the wells daily, therefore, she could

---

15 Is 3.12.
16 1 Cor 4.14.
17 Cf. Mt 7.13–14.
18 Rom 13.12.
19 Eph 5.8.
20 1 Cor 7.29,31.
21 Cf. 1 Thes 5.17.
22 Mk 14.38; Mt 26.41.
23 1 Pt 4.18.
24 Heb 5.11.
25 Cf. Gn 24.15–16.

be found by Abraham's servant and be united in marriage with
Isaac.

Do you think these are tales and that the Holy Spirit tells
stories in Scriptures? This is instruction for souls and spiritual
teaching which instructs and teaches you to come daily to the
wells of the Scriptures, to the waters of the Holy Spirit, and
always to draw water and carry home a full vessel just as also
holy Rebecca used to do. She could not otherwise have been
joined to so great a patriarch as Isaac, who "was born by
promise."[26] It is only by drawing water and by drawing so much
that she could give a drink not only to those who are at home,
but also to Abraham's servant, and not only to the servant, but
also she had such an abundance of water which she drew from
the wells that she could also water the camels "until," the text
says, "they stopped drinking."[27]

All these things which are written are mysteries. Christ
wishes to espouse you also to himself, for he speaks to you
through the prophets saying: "I will espouse you to me forever
and I will espouse you to me in faith and in mercy, and you
shall know the Lord."[28] Because, therefore, he wishes to espouse you to himself he dispatches that servant to you in
advance. That servant is the prophetic word. Unless you have
received it first, you cannot be married to Christ.

Know, however, that no one untrained and inexperienced
receives the prophetic word, but he who knows how to draw
water from the depth of the well and who knows how to draw
in such quantity that it may be sufficient also for these who
appear irrational and perverse, whom the camels represent,
that he also may be able to say, "I am a debtor to the wise and to
the unwise."[29]

Indeed, that servant had said thus in his heart: "Whoever of
these virgins who come to the water," the text says, "shall say to
me: 'Drink, and I will water your camels,' the same shall be the

---

26 Gal 4.23.
27 Gn 24.22.
28 Hos 2.19–20.
29 Rom 1.14.

bride of my master."[30] So, therefore, Rebecca, which means "patience,"[31] when she saw the servant and contemplated the prophetic word "puts the water jar down" from her shoulder.[32] For she puts down the exalted arrogance of Greek eloquence and, stooping down to the lowly and simple prophetic word, says: "Drink, and I will water your camels."[33]

(3) But you say perhaps, if the servant represents the prophetic word, how is he given a drink by Rebecca, to whom he rather ought to give a drink?

Consider, therefore, whether it may be as follows. Although, on the one hand, the Lord Jesus himself is "the bread of life,"[34] and he himself feeds the hungry souls, on the other hand, he admits that he hungers when he says: "I was hungry and you gave me to eat."[35] Again, on the one hand although he himself is "the living water"[36] and gives drink to all who thirst, on the other hand, he himself says to the Samaritan woman, "Give me to drink."[37] So also, although the prophetic word itself gives drink to the thirsting, it is nevertheless, said to be given a drink by these when it receives the exercises and vigilances of the zealous. A soul such as this, then, which does all things patiently, which is so eager and is undergirded with so much learning, which has been accustomed to draw streams of knowledge from the depths, can itself be united in marriage with Christ.

Unless, therefore, you come daily to the wells, unless you daily draw water, not only will you not be able to give a drink to others, but you yourself also will suffer "a thirst for the word of God."[38] Hear also the Lord saying in the Gospels: "Let him who thirsts come and drink."[39] But, as I see it, "you neither hunger

---

30 Gn 24.14.
31 See Appendix, 7.
32 Cf. Gn 24.18.
33 Gn 24.14.
34 Cf. Jn 6.35,48.
35 Mt 25.35.
36 Cf. Jn 7.38.
37 Jn 4.7.
38 Cf. Am 8.11.
39 Jn 7.37.

nor thirst after justice,"[40] and how will you be able to say, "As the hart pants after the fountains of water, so my soul pants after you, O God. My soul has thirsted after the living God; when shall I come and appear before his presence?"[41]

I entreat you who are always present in this place where the word is preached,[42] listen patiently while we admonish a little the negligent and idle. Have patience, because our sermon is about Rebecca, that is, about patience. And we must patiently castigate a little those who neglect the assemblage and shun hearing the word of God, who do not desire "the bread of life"[43] nor "living water,"[44] who do not depart from the camp nor proceed from their "houses of clay"[45] that they might gather manna for themselves,[46] who do not come to the rock, that they may drink "from the spiritual rock. For the rock is Christ,"[47] as the Apostle said. Have a little patience, I say, for our sermon is to the negligent and those "who are sick." "For those in sound health need not the physician, but they who are sick."[48]

Tell me, you who come to Church only on festal days, are the other days not festal days? Are they not the Lord's days? It belongs to the Jews to observe religious ceremonies on fixed and infrequent days. And for this reason God says to them: "I cannot bear your new moons and sabbaths and great day. My soul hates the fast day and festivals and your feast days."[49] God

---

40 Cf. Mt 5.6.
41 Ps 41.2–3.
42 *Auditorio verbi*. Doutreleau (265) translates: "ce lieu où l'on écoute la parole." The reference here, as throughout this homily, is to the daily (cf. the preceding paragraph where he emphasizes coming *daily* to the wells, etc.) services of preaching as opposed to those sevices in which the sacraments were celebrated. Nautin, *Homélies sur Jérémie*, 1.100–112, uses this homily as one of the major sources showing the existence of daily assemblies devoted to the word in the time of Origen. The phrase, *auditorium verbi*, may suggest that there was a special room where such services were held.
43 Cf. Jn 6.35,48.
44 Cf. Jn 7.38.
45 Cf. Jb 4.19.
46 Cf. Ex 16.13f.
47 Cf. 1 Cor 10.4.
48 Lk 5.31.
49 Is 1.13–14.

hates, therefore, those who think that the festal day of the Lord is on one day.

Christians eat the flesh of the lamb every day, that is they consume daily the flesh of the word. "For Christ our pasch is sacrificed."[50] And because the law of the Pasch is such that it is eaten in the evening,[51] for this reason the Lord suffered in the evening of the world that you may always eat of the flesh of the Word, because you are always in the evening until the morning come.[52] And if in this evening you shall be anxious and "in weeping and fasting"[53] and shall lead your life in every labor of justice, you also shall be able to say: "In the evening weeping shall have place and in the morning gladness."[54] For you shall rejoice in the morning, that is in the world to come, if in this world you have gathered "the fruit of justice"[55] in weeping and labor.

Come, therefore, and let us drink, while there is time, from "the well of vision" where Isaac "walks" and where he proceeds to his spiritual exercise.[56]

Observe how many things take place at waters, so that you too may be invited to come daily to the waters of the word of God and stand by its wells, as also Rebecca used to do, of whom the Scripture says: "The virgin was very beautiful; a virgin, a man had not known her."[57]

And this virgin, the text says, "went out late to draw water."[58]

(4) This is not written of her in vain. Nevertheless the meaning of the statement disturbs me: "She was a virgin; a virgin, a man had not known her."[59] It is, indeed, as if a virgin

---

50 1 Cor 5.7.
51 Cf. Ex 12.8–10, 16; 8.12–13.
52 Cf. Origen *Ex. Hom.* 7.8.
53 Cf. Jb 2.12.
54 Ps 29.6.
55 Cf. Jas 3.18; Phil 1.11.
56 Cf. Gn 24.62–63. I take *procedit ad exercitium* to have reference to the statement in Gn 24.63 that Isaac went out into the field to meditate (*adoleschēsai*).
57 Gn 24.16.
58 Cf. Gn 24.15,11.
59 Gn 24.16.

were something other than one whom a man has not touched. And what does the addition seem to mean in reference to a virgin that it should be said, "A man had not known her"? Is there, indeed, another virgin whom a man has touched?

I have often said already that in these stories history is not being narrated, but mysteries are interwoven. I think, therefore, that something such as this is indicated in this story.

Just as Christ is said to be the husband of the soul, to whom the soul is married when it comes to faith, so also, contrary to this, he who also is called "an enemy" when "he oversows tares among the wheat"[60] is called the husband to whom the soul is married when it turns away to faithlessness. It is not sufficient, therefore, for the soul to be pure in body; it is necessary also that this most wicked man "has not known it." For it can happen that someone may possess virginity in body, and knowing that most wicked man, the devil, and receiving darts of concupiscence from him in the heart destroy the purity of the soul. Because, therefore, Rebecca was a virgin "holy in body and spirit,"[61] for this reason the Scripture doubles her praise and says: "She was a virgin; a man had not known her."[62]

"In the evening," therefore, she came to the waters.[63] We have already spoken above about evening. But behold the prudence of the servant. He does not wish to take a bride for his master, Isaac, unless he find a virgin becoming and beautiful in appearance, and not only a virgin, but one whom a man has not touched, and except one whom he should discover drawing water. He does not wish to betroth another to his master.

He does not give her jewelry unless she be such a person. He does not give "earrings;" he does not give "bracelets."[64] She remains simple, unlearned, unadorned. Do we suppose that Rebecca's father, a rich man, did not have bracelets and ear-

---

60 Cf. Mt 13.25.
61 1 Cor 7.34.
62 Cf. Gn 24.16.
63 Cf. Gn 24.11.
64 Cf. Gn 24.22.

rings which he might place on his daughter? Was he so negligent or greedy that he would not give jewelry to his daughter?
But Rebecca does not wish to be adorned with Bathuel's gold.
The jewelry of a barbarous and ignorant man is not worthy of
her. She needs jewels of the house of Abraham because
patience is adorned from the house of the wise man.

Rebecca's ears, therefore, could not receive their beauty,
unless Abraham's servant come and himself adorn them; nor
could her hands receive jewelry except that which Isaac sent.
For she wishes to receive golden words in her ears and to have
golden deeds in her hands. But she could not previously
receive or deserve these things unless she had come to the wells
to draw water. How will you, who do not wish to come to the
waters, who do not wish to receive the golden words of the
prophets in your ears, be able to be adorned with instruction,
adorned with deeds, adorned with character?

(5) But to pass over many things—for now is not the time for
a thorough consideration of the text, but the time for edifying
the Church of God and for challenging very sluggish and
inactive hearers with the examples of the saints and mystical
explanations—Rebecca followed the servant and comes to
Isaac. The Church followed the prophetic word, to be sure,
and comes to Christ. Where does she find him? "Walking," the
text says, "at the well of the oath."[65] On no occasion is one
withdrawn from wells; on no occasion does one stand apart
from waters. Rebecca is found "at a well."[66] Rebecca in turn
finds Isaac "at a well."[67] There she gazed upon his countenance
for the first time. There "she dismounted from the camels."[68]
There she sees Isaac who was pointed out to her by the servant.

Do you think these are the only words related about wells?
Jacob also goes to a well and finds Rachel there. There Rachel
becomes known to him as "good in her eyes and beautiful in

---

65 Cf. Gn 24.62.
66 Gn 24.16.
67 Gn 24.62.
68 Cf. Gn 24.64.

appearance."[69] But also Moses finds Sephora, the daughter of Raguel, at a well.[70]

Are you not yet moved to understand that these words are spoken spiritually? Or do you think that it always happens by chance that the patriarchs go to wells and obtain their marriages at waters? He who thinks in this way is "a sensual man" and "does not perceive these things which are of the spirit of God."[71] But let him who wishes remain in these understandings, let him remain "a sensual man." I, following Paul the apostle, say that these things are "allegories"[72] and I say that the marriages of the saints are the union of the soul with the word of God: "For he who joins himself to the Lord is one spirit."[73]

But it is certain that this union of the soul with the word cannot come about otherwise than through instruction in the divine books, which are figuratively called wells. If anyone should come to these and draw from these waters, that is by meditating on these words should perceive the deeper sense and meaning, he will find a marriage worthy of God; for his soul is united with God.

She also "dismounts from the camels,"[74] that is she departs from vices, she casts off the irrational senses and is united with Isaac. For it is worthy that Isaac pass "from virtue to virtue."[75] He who is the son of virtue, that is of Sara, is now united and joined with patience, which is Rebecca. And this is to pass "from virtue to virtue"[76] and "from faith to faith."[77]

But let us come also to the Gospels. Let us see where the Lord himself seeks rest when he was "wearied from the journey." "He came," Scripture says, "to the well and sat upon it."[78]

---

69 Cf. Gn 29.17.
70 Cf. Ex 2.15f.
71 Cf. 1 Cor 2.14.
72 Cf. Gal 4.24.
73 1 Cor 6.17.
74 Cf. Gn 24.64.
75 Cf. Ps 83.8.
76 Cf. Ps 83.8.
77 Cf. Rom 1.17.
78 Cf. Jn 4.6.

You see that everywhere the mysteries are in agreement. You see the patterns of the New and Old Testament to be harmonious. There one comes to the wells and the waters that brides may be found; and the Church is united to Christ in the bath of water.

You see how great a heap of mysteries presses upon us. We cannot treat all the things which present themselves. These things at least ought to stimulate you to listen, to assemble. Even if we hurry over some things for the sake of brevity, you yourself even, when you read the text again and inquire into it, may dispel the mystery and discover (certainly if you shall continue in the examination of these matters) that the Word of God, finding you also at the waters, may take you up and unite you with himself, that you may be made "one spirit"[79] with him in Christ Jesus our Lord. "To him belongs glory and sovereignty forever and ever. Amen."[80]

---

79 Cf. 1 Cor 6.17.
80 Cf. 1 Pt 4.11; Rv 1.6.

HOMILY XI
On the fact that Abraham took Cetura as a wife and that Isaac dwelt at the well of vision

HE HOLY APOSTLE ALWAYS OFFERS US OPPORTUNITIES for spiritual understanding and shows the zealous signs by which one may recognize in all things that "the Law is spiritual."[1] Though few, these signs are, nevertheless, necessary.

He says, discussing Abraham and Sara in a certain passage: "Not weakened in faith," Scripture says, "he considered his own body dead, since he was almost a hundred years old, and Sara's womb dead."[2] This man, therefore, whom Paul says to have been dead in his body at the age of one hundred and to have begotten Isaac more by the power of his faith than by the fertility of his body, Scripture now relates has taken a wife named Cetura and has begotten more sons from her when he seems to have been about one hundred thirty-seven years old.[3] For Sara his wife is recorded to have been ten years younger than he. Since Sara died in her one-hundred and twenty-seventh year, it shows that Abraham was more than one hundred thirty-seven years old when he took Cetura as his wife.

What then? Are we to suppose that inducements of the flesh have flourished in so great a partriarch at that time? And shall he who is said to have been dead long ago in his natural impulses now be supposed to have been revived for passion? Or, as we have already often said, do the marriages of the patriarchs indicate something mystical and sacred, as also he suggests who said of wisdom: "I decided to take her as my wife"?[4]

---

1 Cf. Rom 7.14.
2 Rom 4.19.
3 Cf. Gn 25.1f.
4 Cf. Wis 8.9.

Perhaps, therefore, already at that time Abraham also thought something like this and, although he was wise, for this very reason, nevertheless, he knew that there is no end of wisdom nor does old age impose a limit on learning. For when can that man who has been accustomed to share a marriage in that manner in which we indicated above, that is, who is accustomed to have virtue in marriage, cease from such a union? For indeed the death of Sara is to be understood as the consummation of virtue. But a man of consummate and perfect virtue ought always to be engaged in some learning. The divine language calls this learning his wife.

For this reason I think that the unmarried man and the sterile man is subject to a curse in the Law, for it says: "Cursed is he who has not left seed in Israel."[5] But if these words be supposed to be spoken about physical seed, all the virgins of the Church will appear to be placed under a curse. And what do I say about the virgins of the Church? John himself, than whom "no one among those born of women was greater,"[6] and many other saints left no physical seed, since indeed they are not even reported to have married. But it is certain that they left behind spiritual seed and spiritual sons and that each one had wisdom as a wife, as also Paul begot sons through the Gospel.[7]

Abraham, therefore, as an old man with a body already dead took Cetura as his wife. I think it better, in accordance with the reason which we set forth above, that a wife is taken then, when the body is dead, when the members have been put to death.[8] For there is a greater capacity for wisdom in our sense when "the mortification of Christ is borne about in our" mortal "bodies."[9]

Indeed *Cetura*, whom Abraham, now an old man, obtains in marriage, means *thymiama*[10] which is incense or a good odor.[11] He also, in fact, was saying, just as Paul said, "We are the

---

5 Cf. Dt 7.14; 25.5–10.
6 Cf. Mt 11.11.
7 Cf. 1 Cor 4.15.
8 Cf. Col 3.5.
9 Cf. 2 Cor 4.10.
10 Rufinus preserves the Greek term in his text.
11 See Appendix, 8.

good odor of Christ."[12] But let us see how someone becomes "the good odor of Christ." Sin is a foul affair. In fact, sinners are compared to pigs who wallow in sins as in foul dung.[13] And David, as a repentant sinner, says: "My sores have putrified and are abscessed."[14]

(2) If there is, therefore, anyone of you in whom there is now no odor of sin, but an odor of justice, the sweetness of mercy, if anyone, by praying "without ceasing"[15] always offers incense to the Lord and says, "Let my prayer be directed as incense in your sight, the lifting up of my hands as evening sacrifice,"[16] this man has married Cetura.

In this way, therefore, I think the marriages of the elders are interpreted more fittingly; in this way the unions entered by the patriarchs in their now final and weakened age are understood nobly; in this way I hold the necessary begetting of children should be reckoned. For young men are not so well fitted as old men for such marriages and for offspring of this kind. For to the extent that someone is feeble in the flesh, to such an extent will he be stronger in virtue of the soul and more fit for the embraces of wisdom. So also that just man Elcana in the Scriptures is reported to have had two wives at the same time, one of whom was called Phenenna, the other Anna, that is, "conversion" and "grace."[17] And first, indeed, he is said to have had sons by Phenenna, that is, of conversion, and later by Anna, that is, of grace.[18]

And indeed the Scripture designates the progress of the saints figuratively by marriages. Whence also you can, if you wish, be a husband of marriages of this kind. For example, if you freely practice hospitality, you will appear to have taken her as your wife. If you shall add to this care of the poor, you will appear to have obtained a second wife. But if you should

---

12 2 Cor 2.15.
13 Cf. Mt 8.30
14 Cf. Ps 37.6.
15 Cf. 1 Thes 5.17.
16 Ps 140.2
17 See Appendix, 9 and 10.
18 Cf. 1 Sm 1.1ff.

also join patience to yourself and gentleness and the other virtues, you will appear to have taken as many wives as the virtues you enjoy.

Thence it is, therefore, that Scripture recounts that some of the patriarchs had many wives at the same time, that others took other wives when previous wives had died.[19] The purpose of this is to indicate figuratively that some can exercise many virtues at the same time; others cannot begin those which follow before they have brought the former virtues to perfection. Accordingly, Solomon is reported to have had many wives at the same time,[20] to whom the Lord had said: "There was no wise man like you before you and there will not be after you."[21] Because, therefore, the Lord had given him an abundance of prudence, "like the sand of the sea,"[22] that he might judge his people "in wisdom,"[23] for this reason he could exercise many virtues at the same time.

However, beyond this which we are taught from the Law of God, if we also are in touch with some of these instructions which appear to be on the outside in the world—for example, as the knowledge of literature or the theory of grammar, as geometry or mathematics or even the discipline of dialectic— and we bring over to our purposes all these things which have been sought from without and we approve them in the declaration of our law, then we will appear to have taken in marriage either foreign wives or even "concubines."[24] And if, from marriages of this kind, by disputing, by discussing, by refuting those who contradict, we shall be able to convert some to the faith, and if, overcoming them with their own reasonings and skills, we shall persuade them to receive the true philosophy of Christ and the true piety of God, then we shall appear to have begotten sons from dialectic or rhetoric as if from some foreign wife or concubine.

---

19 Cf. Gn 16.3; 25.1.
20 Cf. Song 6.7.
21 Cf. 2 Chr 1.2; 3 Kgs 3.13.
22 Cf. Gn 22.17.
23 Cf. 2 Chr 1.11.
24 Cf. Song 6.7.

Old age, therefore, excludes no one from such marriages or from begetting sons of this kind. On the contrary rather this pure offspring is more suited to mature age. So also now, aged Abraham even as Scripture says, "old and full of days,"[25] takes Cetura as his wife.

But indeed, we should not fail to notice from these things which are reported by the literal meaning, what generations and of what sort they are, which are propagated from Cetura.

For if we remember these things we will be able to recognize more easily those things which are said about the diverse nations in the Scriptures. For example, as when it is said that Moses took as his wife the daughter of Jethro, priest of Madian, this Madian is found to be a son of Cetura and Abraham.[26] We know, therefore, that Moses' wife is from the seed of Abraham and was not a foreigner. But also when it is written: "the queen of Cedar,"[27] it should be known no less that also Cedar descends from the very stock of Cetura and Abraham.[28] But you will also find similar things in the generations of Ismael. If you consider these diligently, you will detect more accounts in them which escape others' notice. But meanwhile, putting these matters back for another time, let us hasten to those things which have been read to us in the following verses.

(3) "And it happened," the text says, "after Abraham died, the Lord blessed Isaac his son and he dwelt at the well of vision."[29]

What more can we say about the death of Abraham than what the word of the Lord in the Gospels contains, saying: "Concerning the resurrection of the dead, have you not read how he says in the bush: 'the God of Abraham, and the God of Isaac, and the God of Jacob'? Now he is not God of the dead, but of the living. For all those are living."[30] Let us also, there-

---

25 Cf. Gn 24.1.
26 Cf. Gn 25.2.
27 Cf. Jer 49.28.
28 Cf. Gn 25.13. Our texts of Gn 25.12–13 say that Cedar was a descendant of Abraham and Agar.
29 Gn 25.11.
30 Mk 12.26–27.

fore, choose this kind of death, as also the Apostle says, that "we may die to sin, but live to God."[31] For indeed the death of Abraham should be understood to be such, which death has amplified his bosom so much that all the saints who come from the four parts of the earth "may be borne by the angels into the bosom of Abraham."[32] But let us see now how, after his death, "the Lord blessed Isaac his son"[33] and what that blessing is.

"The Lord blessed Isaac," the text says, "and he dwelt at the well of vision."[34] This is the whole blessing with which the Lord blessed Isaac: that he might dwell "at the well of vision." That is a great blessing for those who understand it. Would that the Lord might give this blessing to me too, that I might deserve to dwell "at the well of vision."

What kind of man can know and understand what the vision is "which Isaias the son of Amos saw"?[35] What kind of man can know what Nahum's vision is?[36] What kind of man can understand what that vision contains which Jacob saw in Bethel when he was departing into Mesopotamia, when he said: "This is the house of the Lord and the gate of heaven"?[37] And if anyone can know and understand each individual vision or the things which are in the Law or in the prophets, that man dwells "at the well of vision."

But also consider this more carefully, that Isaac deserved to receive such a great blessing from the Lord that he might dwell "at the well of vision." But when shall we sufficiently deserve to pass by, perhaps, "the well of vision"? He deserved to remain and dwell in the vision; we, what little we have been illuminated by the mercy of God, can scarcely perceive or surmise of a single vision.

If, however, I shall have been able to perceive some one meaning of the visions of God, I shall appear to have spent one

---

31 Cf. Rom 6.10.
32 Cf. Lk 16.22.
33 Gn 25.11.
34 Gn 25.11.
35 Cf. Is 1.1.
36 Cf. Na 1.1f.
37 Gn 28.17.

day "at the well of vision." But if I shall have been able to touch not only something according to the letter, but also according to the spirit, I shall appear to have spent two days "at the well of vision." But if also I shall have touched the moral point, I shall have spent three days. Or certainly even if I shall not have been able to understand everything, if I am, nevertheless, busily engaged in the divine Scriptures and "I meditate on the Law of God day and night"[38] and at no time at all do I desist inquiring, discussing, investigating, and certainly, what is greatest, praying God and asking for understanding from him who "teaches man knowledge,"[39] I shall appear to dwell "at the well of vision."

But if I should be negligent and be neither occupied at home in the word of God nor frequently enter the church to hear the word, as I see some among you, who only come to the church on festive days, those who are of this sort do not dwell "by the well of vision." But I fear that perhaps those who are negligent, even when they come to the church, may neither drink from the well of water nor be refreshed, but they may devote themselves to the occupations and thoughts of their heart which they bring with them and may depart thirsty no less from the wells of the Scriptures.

You, therefore, hasten and act sufficiently that that blessing of the Lord may come to you, that you may be able to dwell "at the well of vision," that the Lord may open your eyes and you may see "the well of vision," and may receive from it "living water,"[40] which may become in you "a fountain of water springing up into eternal life."[41] But if anyone rarely comes to church, rarely draws from the fountains of the Scriptures, and dismisses what he hears at once when he departs and is occupied with other affairs, this man does not dwell "at the well of vision."

Do you want me to show you who it is who never withdraws

---

38 Cf. Ps 1.2.
39 Cf. Ps 93.10.
40 Cf. Gn 26.19.
41 Cf. Jn 4.14.

from the well of vision? It is the apostle Paul who said: "But we all with open face behold the glory of the Lord."[42]

You too, therefore, if you shall always search the prophetic visions, if you always inquire, always desire to learn, if you meditate on these things, if you remain in them, you too receive a blessing from the Lord and dwell "at the well of vision." For the Lord Jesus will appear to you also "in the way" and will open the Scriptures to you so that you may say: "Was not our heart burning within us when he opened to us the Scriptures?"[43] But he appears to these who think about him and meditate on him and live "in his law day and night."[44] "To him be glory and sovereignty forever and ever. Amen."[45]

---

42 Cf. 2 Cor 3.18.
43 Lk 24.32.
44 Cf. Ps 1.2.
45 Cf. 1 Pt 4.11; Rv 1.6.

HOMILY XII
On Rebecca's pregnancy and giving birth

E SHOULD PRAY THE FATHER OF THE WORD during each individual reading "when Moses is read,"[1] that he might fulfill even in us that which is written in the Psalms: "Open my eyes and I will consider the wondrous things of your Law."[2] For unless he himself opens our eyes, how shall we be able to see these great mysteries which are fashioned in the patriarchs, which are pictured now in terms of wells, now in marriages, now in births, now even in barrenness?

For the present text reports that "Isaac asked for Rebecca his wife, because she was barren; and God heard him and she conceived. "And the children," the text says, "leaped in her womb."[3]

First of all consider why it is that many holy women in the Scriptures are related to have been barren, as Sara herself, and lo now Rebecca.[4] But also Rachel, Israel's beloved, was barren.[5] Anna also, the mother of Samuel, is recorded to have been barren.[6] But also in the Gospels Elizabeth is related to have been barren.[7] But in all these instances this term is used because after sterility they all gave birth to a holy person.

So, therefore, also this present Rebecca is said to have been barren but "Isaac prayed," the text says, "the Lord for her, and he heard him and she conceived. And the children leaped in her womb."[8] Behold, what did this barrenness conceive? The

---

1 2 Cor 3.15.
2 Ps 118.18.
3 Gn 25.21–22.
4 Cf. Gn 11.30.
5 Cf. Gn 29.31.
6 Cf. 1 Sm 1.2.
7 Cf. Lk 1.7.
8 Gn 25.21–22.

sons of the barren woman leap before they are born. And she who had despaired of offspring bears nations and peoples in her womb. For thus the text says: "Rebecca departed to inquire of the Lord, and the Lord said to her: 'Two nations are in your womb, and two peoples are divided out of your womb.' "[9]

It would be tedious if we wished now to examine the leaping of the children while they still remained in the womb. It would be tedious if we should mention the interpretations and enigmas which the Apostle wrote about these matters, what mysteries, what reasons they contain; why it is said of them, "before the children are born or do anything good or evil in this world":[10] "One people shall overcome the other and the elder shall serve the younger";[11] why, before they proceeded from their mother's womb, it is said by the prophet: "I have loved Jacob, but have hated Esau."[12] These matters surpass both my ability to speak and your ability to hear.

(2) Now, meanwhile, let us see what the statement means: "Rebecca departed to inquire of the Lord."[13] "She departed." Where did she go? Did she depart from that place where the Lord was not to that place where he was? This, indeed, appears to be indicated when it is said: "She departed to inquire of the Lord." Is not the Lord everywhere? Did he not say himself: "I fill heaven and earth, says the Lord?"[14] Where, then, did Rebecca go?

I think that she did not depart from one place to another, but she passed over from one life to another, from one deed to another, from good things to better; she proceeded from profitable things to more profitable; she hastened from holy things to holier. For it is absurd if we suppose Rebecca who had been educated in the house of wise Abraham by her most learned husband Isaac, to have been so ignorant and uninstructed that she thought the Lord was enclosed within some

---

9 Gn 25.22–23.
10 Cf. Rom 9.11.
11 Gn 25.23.
12 Mal 1.2–3; Rom 9.13.
13 Gn 25.22.
14 Jer 23.24.

place, and she might go there to inquire what the leaping of the children in her womb might mean.

But do you wish to see that this has become customary with the saints, so that when they have seen that anything is shown them by God, they say that they either depart or pass over?

When Moses had seen the bush burning and not being consumed he was astonished at the sight and said: "I will cross over and see this sight."[15] He certainly also did not mean that he was about to cross over some earthly space, nor to ascend mountains nor to descend the steep sides of valleys. The vision was near him, in his countenance and in his eyes. But he says: "I will cross over,"[16] that he might show that he, reminded forcefully by the heavenly vision, ought to ascend to a higher life and cross over to better things than those in which he was.

So, therefore, also now it is related of Rebecca: "She departed to inquire of the Lord."[17] As we have said, she should be considered to have departed not by the steps of her feet, but by the advances of her mind.

You also, therefore, will be said to have departed "to inquire of the Lord" if you have begun to contemplate not those things "which are seen, but those which are not seen,"[18] that is, not carnal but spiritual things, not present but future things.

If you should tear yourself away from your old manner of life and from the fellowship of those with whom you have lived shamefully and notoriously, but should associate yourself with honorable and religious actions, when you shall have been searched for among companions of shamefulness and shall never have been found in crowds of the guilty, it will be said also of you: "He departed to inquire of the Lord."[19]

So, therefore, the saints depart not from one place to another, but from one life to another, from beginning instructions to more advanced instructions.

(3) Therefore the Lord said to her: "Two nations are in your

---

15 Ex 3.3.
16 Ex 3.3.
17 Gn 25.22.
18 Cf. 2 Cor 4.18.
19 Gn 25.22.

womb, and two peoples shall be divided out of your womb. And one people shall overcome the other, and the elder shall serve the younger."[20]

How "one people has risen above the other," that is, the Church over the Synagogue, and how "the elder serves the younger" is known even to the Jews themselves although they do not believe. I think it is superfluous, therefore, to speak about these things which are well known and very commonplace to everyone. Let us add this, if it is agreeable, which can edify and instruct each of us who hear these words.

I think that this can be said also of us as individuals, that "two nations and two peoples are within you." For there is both a people of virtues within us and there is no less a people of vices within us. "For from our heart proceed evil thoughts, adulteries, thefts, false testimonies,"[21] but also "deceits, contentions, heresies, jealousies, revelings and such like."[22] Do you see how great a people of evils is within us? But if we should deserve to utter that word of the saints: "From fear of you, Lord, we have conceived in the womb and have brought forth; we have wrought the spirit of your salvation on the earth,"[23] then also another people, begotten in the spirit, is found within us. For "the fruit of the spirit is love, joy, peace, patience, goodness, gentleness, temperance, purity" and such like.[24]

You see another people which is also itself within us. But this one is less, that one greater. For there are always more evil than good people and vices are more numerous than virtues. But if we should be such as Rebecca and should deserve to conceive from Isaac, that is, from the word of God, "one people shall overcome the other and the elder shall serve the younger"[25] even in us, for the flesh shall serve the spirit and vices shall yield to virtues.

"And her days were fulfilled," the text says, "that she should

---

20 Gn 25.23.
21 Mt 15.19.
22 Gal 5.20–21.
23 Is 26.18 (LXX).
24 Gal 5.22–23.
25 Cf. Gn 25.23.

give birth, and there were twins in her womb."[26] This statement, that is, "her days were fulfilled that she should give
birth," is almost never written except of holy women. For this is
said of this Rebecca and of Elizabeth the mother of John[27] and
of Mary the mother of our Lord Jesus Christ.[28] Whence a birth
of this kind seems to me to show something extraordinary and
beyond other human beings. The fulfillment of the days seems
to indicate the birth of perfect offspring.

(4) "And the firstborn son came forth," the text says, "red
and hairy all over like a skin. And he named him Esau. And
after that his brother came forth and his hand had clasped
Esau's heel; and he called his name Jacob."[29]

Another Scripture relates of these things that "in the womb
Jacob supplanted his brother,"[30] and the proof of this is that his
hand had clasped his brother Esau's heel.

This Esau proceeded from his mother's womb "hairy all
over like a skin," [31] but Jacob was smooth and simple. Whence
also Jacob received his name from wrestling or supplanting,[32]
but Esau—as those who interpret Hebrew names say—
received his name either from redness or from earth, that is,
"red" or "earthly" or, as it seemed to others, his name appears
to mean "something made."[33]

But what those prerogatives of birth are, why either the one
"supplanted his brother" and was born smooth and simple,
although certainly, as the Apostle says, both sons were conceived "from our one father, Isaac,"[34] or why the other was
born "hairy all over" and shaggy and, so to speak, enwrapped
in the squalor of sin and vileness is not mine to discuss. For if I
shall wish to dig deeply and open the hidden veins "of living

---

26 Gn 25.24.
27 Cf. Lk 1.57.
28 Cf. Lk 2.16.
29 Gn 25.25–26.
30 Hos 12.3.
31 Cf. Gn 25.27.
32 See Appendix, 11.
33 See Appendix, 12.
34 Cf. Rom 9.10.

water,"[35] immediately the Philistines will be present and will strive with me. They will stir up disputes and malicious charges against me and will begin to refill my wells with their earth and mud. For certainly if those Philistines would permit and I wished to approach my Lord, my most patient Lord, who says: "I do not reject him who comes to me,"[36] if I wished to approach and, as the disciples said to him: "Lord, who has sinned, this man or his parents that he should be born blind?"[37] and I wished to ask him and say: "Lord, who has sinned," this Esau or his parents, that he should be born thus "hairy all over" and shaggy, that he should be supplanted by his brother in the womb? But if I shall wish to ask the word of God of these things and inquire, immediately the Philistines stir up quarrels and malicious charges against me. And for this reason, leaving this well and calling it "enmity," let us dig another.[38]

(5) And after these things the text says, "Isaac sowed barley and found a hundredfold. And the Lord blessed him and the man was magnified and by his progress he became greater until he became very great."[39]

Why is it that Isaac "sowed barley" and not wheat, and is blessed because he sows "barley," and is magnified "until he becomes great"? It appears, therefore, that he was not yet great, but after "he sowed barley" and gathered "a hundredfold," then "he became very great."

Barley is the food especially of beasts or of peasants. For it is a harsher species and would seem to prick one who touches it as if with some kind of points. Isaac is the word of God. This word sows barley in the Law, but wheat in the Gospels. He provides the one food for the perfect and spiritual, the other for the inexperienced and natural, because it is written: "Men and beasts you will preserve, O Lord."[40] Isaac, therefore, the word of the Law, sows barley and yet in that very barley he

---

35 Gn 26.19.
36 Jn 6.37.
37 Jn 9.2.
38 Cf. Gn 26.21–22.
39 Gn 26.12–13.
40 Ps 35.7.

finds "fruit a hundredfold."[41] For even in the Law you find martyrs, in whose "fruit" is "a hundredfold."

But also our Lord, the Isaac of the Gospels, said certain things which were more perfect to the apostles, but to the crowds he said things which were plain and common.[42] But do you wish to see that even he presents barley to beginners? It is written in the Gospels that he fed the crowds a second time.[43] But those whom he feeds the first time, that is the beginners, he feeds "with barley loaves."[44] But later, when they had progressed by this time in the word and teaching, he presents them loaves of wheat.

But after this the text says, "The Lord blessed Isaac and he became very great."[45]

Issac was insignificant in the Law, but with the passing of time he becomes great. He becomes great, with the passing of time, in the prophets. For while he is in the Law alone he is not yet great, since indeed it too is covered with a veil. He grows, therefore, now in the prophets; but when he has arrived at this point that also he may cast aside the veil, then he will be "very great." When the letter of the Law has begun to be separated like the chaff of its barley and it has appeared that "the Law is spiritual,"[46] then Isaac will be magnified and will become "very great."

For notice that also the Lord in the Gospels breaks a few loaves, and notice how many thousand people he refreshes "and how many baskets" of leftovers remain.[47] While the loaves are whole, no one is filled, no one is refreshed, nor do the loaves themselves appear to be increased. Consider, therefore, now how we break a few loaves: we take up a few words from the divine Scriptures and how many thousand men are filled. But unless those loaves have been broken, unless they have

---

41 Cf. Mt 13.8.
42 Cf. Mt 13.34f.
43 Cf. Mt 15.32f.
44 Cf. Jn 6.9; Mt 14.19f.
45 Gn 26.12.
46 Cf. Rom 7.14.
47 Cf. Mt 14.19f, 15.36f, 16.9.

been crumbled into pieces by the disciples, that is, unless the letter has been discussed and broken in little pieces, its meaning cannot reach everyone. But when we have begun to investigate and discuss each single matter, then the crowds indeed will assimilate as much as they shall be able. But what they shall not have been able should be gathered and preserved, "lest anything be lost."[48]

We also, therefore, preserve whatever the "crowds" cannot receive and gather it into baskets and hampers.[49] For a little earlier, when we had broken the bread about Jacob and Esau, how many fragments remained from that bread? Let us see what fragments we have diligently collected lest they be lost, and what we are preserving in baskets until the Lord command what also should become of them.

But now, as much as possible, let us either eat of the bread or draw water from the wells. Let us attempt to do also that which wisdom admonishes saying: "Drink the waters of your own springs and wells, and let your spring be your own."[50]

Therefore, you also attempt, O hearer, to have your own well and your own spring, so that you too, when you take up a book of the Scriptures, may begin even from your own understanding to bring forth some meaning, and in accordance with those things which you have learned in the church, you too attempt to drink from the fountain of your own abilities. You have the nature of "living water" within you.[51] There are within you perennial veins and streams flowing with rational understanding, if only they have not been filled with earth and rubbish. But get busy to dig out your earth and to clean out the filth, that is, to remove the idleness of your natural ability and to cast out the inactivity of your heart. For hear what the Scripture says: "Prick the eye and it will bring forth a tear; prick the heart and it brings forth understanding."[52]

---

48 Cf. Jn 6.12.
49 The text specifies *cophinis* (wicker baskets) and *sportis* (baskets used by fishermen) from the Gospel accounts (Cf. Mt 14.20 and 15.37).
50 Cf. Prv 5.15,18.
51 Cf. Gn 26.19.
52 Sir 22.19.

You too, therefore, cleanse your natural ability that sometime also you may drink from your own springs[53] and may
draw "living water" from your wells.[54] For if you have received
the word of God in yourself, if you have accepted "the living
water" from Jesus and have accepted it faithfully, "a fountain
of water springing up into life eternal"[55] will arise in you, in
Jesus Christ himself, our Lord, "to whom be glory and sovereignty forever and ever. Amen."[56]

---

53 Cf. Prv 5.15.
54 Cf. Gn 26.19.
55 Cf. Jn 4.14.
56 Cf. 1 Pt 4.11; Rv 1.6.

HOMILY XIII

On the wells which Isaac dug and which were filled by the Philistines

E ARE ALWAYS ENCOUNTERING THE HABITUAL WORKS of the patriarchs regarding wells. For behold the Scripture relates that Isaac, after "the Lord blessed him and he was greatly magnified,"[1] undertook a great work. And he began, the text says, to dig wells, "wells which his servants had dug in the time of his father Abraham, but the Philistines had stopped them up and filled them with earth."[2] First, therefore, "he dwelt at the well of vision,"[3] and having been illuminated by the well of vision, he undertakes to open other wells, and not first new wells, but those which his father Abraham had dug.

And when he had dug the first well, "the Philistines," the text says, "were envious of him."[4] But he was not deterred by their envy nor did he yield to their jealousy, but the text says, "he again dug the wells which the servants of his father Abraham had dug and the Philistines had stopped up after the death of his father Abraham; and he gave them names in accordance with the names which his father had given them."[5] He dug therefore, those wells which his father had dug and which had been filled with earth by the malice of the Philistines. He dug also other new wells "in the valley of Gerara," not indeed himself, but his servants, "and he found there," the text says, "a well of living water. But the shepherds of Gerara quarreled with Isaac's shepherds saying the water was theirs. And he called the name of the well *Injustice*. For they dealt

---

1 Cf. Gn 26.12–13.
2 Gn 26.15.
3 Gn 26.11.
4 Gn 26.14.
5 Gn 26.18.

unjustly with him."[6] But Isaac withdraws from their malice and "again dug another well, and for it no less," the text says, "they quarreled, and he called its name *Enmity*. And he withdrew from there and dug again another well and they did not quarrel about it; and he called its name *Breadth* saying that now God has given us room and has increased us on the earth."[7]

Well does the holy Apostle say in a certain passage when considering the magnitude of mysteries: "And for these things who is sufficient?"[8] In a similar way—nay rather dissimilar by far, to the extent that we are by far inferior to him—we also, seeing such great depth in the mysteries of the wells, say: "And for these things who is sufficient?" For who is able worthily to explain either the mysteries of such great wells or of those things which are related to have been done for the wells, unless we invoke the Father of the living Word and he himself should deign to put the word in our mouth so that we may be able to draw a little "living water"[9] for you who thirst from those wells which are so copious and numerous?

(2) There are, therefore, wells which the servants of Abraham dug, but the Philistines had filled these with earth. Isaac, therefore, undertakes first to clear these wells. The Philistines hate water; they love earth. Isaac loves water; he is always seeking wells; he cleans old wells, he opens new ones.

Consider our Isaac, who "has been offered as a sacrifice for us"[10] coming into the valley of Gerara which means wall or hedge,[11] coming, I say, that "he might destroy the middle wall of hedge, the enmities, in his flesh,"[12] coming to remove the wall which is between us and the heavenly virtues, that he might make "both one"[13] and carry back to the mountains[14] "on

---

6 Gn 26.19–20.
7 Gn 26.21–22.
8 2 Cor 2.16.
9 Cf. Gn 26.19.
10 Cf. Eph 5.2.
11 See Appendix, 13.
12 Cf. Eph 2.14.
13 Cf. Eph 2.14.
14 Cf. Mt 18.12.

his shoulders" the lamb which had strayed and restore it to the other "ninety-nine which had not strayed."[15]

This Isaac, therefore, our Savior, when he has come into that valley of Gerara, first of all wishes to dig those wells which the servants of his father had dug; he wishes to renew the wells of the Law, of course, and the prophets, which Philistines had filled with earth.

Who are those who fill the wells with earth? Those, doubtless, who put an earthly and fleshly interpretation on the Law and close up the spiritual and mystical interpretation so that neither do they themselves drink nor do they permit others to drink.

Hear our Isaac, the Lord Jesus, saying in the Gospels: "Woe to you, Scribes and Pharisees, since you have taken away the key of knowledge and you yourselves have not entered nor have you permitted those who wish to enter."[16] Those, therefore, are the ones who have filled with earth the wells "which the servants of Abraham had dug"; those who teach the Law carnally and defile the waters of the Holy Spirit; who hold the wells for this purpose, not that they might bring forth water, but that they might put earth in them. Isaac, therefore, undertakes to dig these wells. And let us see how he digs them.

When the servants of Isaac, who are the apostles of our Lord, were passing through grain fields on the Sabbath, Scripture says, "they plucked the ears and ate, rubbing them in their hands."[17] At that time, therefore, those who had filled his father's wells with earth said to him: "Behold your disciples are doing that which is not lawful on the sabbath days."[18] In order to dig out their earthly understanding, he says to them: "Have you not read what David did when he was hungry, and those who were with him, how he went in to Abiathar the priest and ate the loaves of proposition, he and his servants, which it was not lawful to eat but for the priests only?"[19] And he adds to

---

15 Cf. Lk 15.5–6.
16 Mt 23.13; Cf. Lk 11.52.
17 Cf. Lk 6.1.
18 Mt 12.2.
19 Mt 12.3–4.

these words: "If you knew what this means: 'I desire mercy and
not sacrifice,' you would certainly never have condemned the
innocent."[20] But what do those men reply to these words? They
quarreled with his servants and say: "This man is not of God
who does not keep the Sabbath."[21] In this way, therefore, Isaac
dug the wells "which the servants of his father had dug."

Moses, who had dug the well of the Law, was a servant of his
Father; David and Solomon and the prophets were servants of
his Father, and whoever those are who had written the books
of the Old Testament which the earthy and squalid understanding of the Jews had filled. When Isaac wished to cleanse
this understanding and show that whatever "the Law and
prophets"[22] have said, they have said about himself, the Philistines quarreled with him. But he parts from them, for he
cannot be with these who do not wish to have water in the wells,
but earth; and he says to them: "Behold your house is left to
you desolate."[23]

Isaac, therefore, digs also new wells, nay rather Isaac's
servants dig them. Isaac's servants are Matthew, Mark, Luke,
John; his servants are Peter, James, Jude; the apostle Paul is his
servant. These all dig the wells of the New Testament. But
those, who "mind earthly things"[24] nor permit new things to be
established nor old things to be cleansed, also quarrel for these
wells. They oppose the Gospel wells; they resist the apostolic
wells. And since they oppose in all things, since they quarrel in
all things, it is said to them: "Since you have made yourselves
unworthy of God's grace, henceforth now we go to the Gentiles."[25]

(3) After these things, then, Isaac dug a third well and
"called the name of that place *Breadth* saying: Now the Lord
has given us room and has increased us on the earth."[26]

For truly now Isaac is given room and his name is increased

20 Mt 12.7; Hos 6.6.
21 Jn 9.16.
22 Cf. Mt 7.12; Jn 5.46.
23 Mt 23.38.
24 Cf. Phil 3.19.
25 Cf. Acts 13.46, 18.6.
26 Gn 26.22.

on all the earth since he has fulfilled for us the knowledge of the Trinity. For then "God was known" only "in Judea"[27] and his name was named in Israel, but now "their sound has gone forth into all the earth, and their words into the ends of the world."[28] For the servants of Isaac going throughout the whole world have dug wells and have shown "the living water"[29] to all, "baptizing all the nations in the name of the Father and of the Son and of the Holy Spirit."[30] For "the earth is the Lord's and the fullness thereof."[31]

But also each of us who serves the word of God digs wells and seeks "living water," from which he may renew his hearers. If, therefore, I too shall begin to discuss the words of the ancients and to seek in them a spiritual meaning, if I shall have attempted to remove the veil of the Law and to show that the things which have been written are "allegorical,"[32] I am, indeed, digging wells. But immediately the friends of the letter will stir up malicious charges against me and will lie in ambush for me. They will contrive hostilities immediately and persecutions, denying that the truth can stand except upon earth.

But if we are servants of Isaac, let us love "wells of living water" and springs. Let us withdraw from those who are contentious and contrive malicious charges and leave them in the earth which they love. But let us never cease digging "wells of living water." And by discussing now indeed things that are old, and again things that are new let us become like that scribe in the Gospel, of whom the Lord said: "He brings forth from his treasures new things and old."[33]

But also if anyone who has a secular education should now hear me preaching, he is perhaps saying: "The things you are saying belong to us, and is the learning of our science. This very eloquence with which you discuss and teach is ours." And, like some Philistine, he stirs up quarrels with me saying: "You

27 Cf. Ps 75.2.
28 Ps 18.5.
29 Cf. Gn 26.19.
30 Cf. Mt 28.19.
31 Ps 23.1.
32 Cf. Gal 4.24.
33 Mt 13.52.

dug a well in my soil." And he will seem right to himself to lay claim to those things which are of his own land.

But I shall respond to these things that all the earth has waters, but he who is a Philistine and "minds earthly things"[34] does not know how to find water in all the earth. He does not know how to find rational understanding and the image of God in every soul. He does not know how to discover that there can be faith, piety, and religion in everything. What does it benefit you to have learning and not know how to use it? What do you benefit to have a word and not know how to speak?

This is particularly the work of the servants of Isaac, who dig "wells of living water" in every land, that is they proclaim "the word of God" to every soul and find fruit. Indeed do you wish to see how many wells one servant of Isaac dug in the land of foreigners? Behold Paul, who "replenished the Gospel of God from Jerusalem round about as far as to Illyricum."[35] But for each of those wells he suffered the persecutions of the Philistines. Hear him saying himself: "How many things happened to me at Iconium, at Lystra,"[36] how many at Ephesus?[37] How many times was he beaten; how many times was he stoned;[38] how many times did he fight with beasts? But he endured until he might go out to "the breadth,"[39] that is until he might establish Churches in the breadth of the whole earth.

So, therefore, the wells which Abraham dug, that is the Scriptures of the Old Testament, have been filled with earth by the Philistines, or evil teachers, Scribes and Pharisees, or even hostile powers; and their veins have been stopped up lest they provide a drink for these who are of Abraham. For that people cannot drink from the Scriptures, but suffers a "thirst for the word of God,"[40] until Isaac should come and open them that his servants may drink. Thanks, therefore, to Christ, the son of Abraham—of whom it is written: "The book of the generation

---

34 Cf. Phil 3.19.
35 Cf. Rom 15.19.
36 2 Tm 3.11.
37 Cf. 1 Cor 15.32.
38 Cf. 2 Cor 11.25.
39 Cf. 2 Sm 22.20; Ps 17.20.
40 Cf. Am 8.11.

of Jesus Christ, the son of David, the son of Abraham"[41]—who
has come and opened the wells for us. For he opened them for
those men who said: "Was not our heart burning in us when he
opened to us the Scriptures?"[42] He opened, therefore, these
wells and "called them," the text says, "as his father Abraham
had called them."[43] For he did not change the names of the
wells.

And it is astonishing that Moses is called Moses even among
us and each of the prophets is addressed by his own name. For
Christ did not change the names in them, but the understanding. And he changes it there that now later we might not
pay attention "to Jewish fables"[44] and "endless genealogies,"[45]
because "they turn their hearing away from the truth indeed,
but are turned to fables."[46]

He opened, therefore, the wells and taught us, that we
might not seek God in some one place, but might know that
"sacrifice is offered to his name in every land."[47] For it is now
that time "when the true worshippers worship the Father"
neither in Jerusalem nor on mount Garizim, "but in spirit and
truth."[48] God, therefore, dwells neither in a place nor in a land,
but he dwells in the heart. And if you are seeking the place of
God, a pure heart is his place. For he says that he will dwell in
this place when he says through the prophet: " 'I will dwell in
them and walk in them; and they shall be my people and I will
be their God,' says the Lord."[49]

Consider, therefore, that perhaps even in the soul of each of
us there is "a well of living water," there is a kind of heavenly
perception and latent image of God, and the Philistines, that is
hostile powers, have filled this well with earth. With what kind
of earth? With carnal perceptions and earthly thoughts, and

---

41 Mt 1.1.
42 Lk 24.32.
43 Gn 26.18.
44 Cf. Ti 1.14.
45 Cf. 1 Tm 1.4.
46 Cf. 2 Tm 4.4.
47 Cf. Mal 1.11.
48 Cf. Jn 4.20–23.
49 2 Cor 6.16; Lv 26.12.

for that reason "we have borne the image of the earthly."[50] At
that time, therefore, when we were bearing "the image of the
earthly," the Philistines filled our wells. But now, since our
Isaac has come, let us receive his advent and dig our wells. Let
us cast the earth from them. Let us purge them from all filth
and from all muddy and earthly thoughts and let us discover in
them that "living water" which the Lord mentions: "He who
believes in me, from within him shall flow rivers of living
water."[51] Behold how great the Lord's liberality is: the Philistines filled our wells and hindered our small and trifling veins
of water, and in place of these, springs and rivers are restored
to us.

(4) If, therefore, also you hearing these words today should
faithfully perceive what is said, Isaac would work also in you,
he would cleanse your hearts from earthly perceptions. And
seeing these mysteries which are so great to be lying hidden in
the divine Scriptures, you progress in understanding, you
progress in spiritual perceptions. You yourselves will also
begin to be teachers, and "rivers of living water" will proceed
from you.[52] For the word of God is present and this now is his
work, that he might remove the earth from the soul of each of
you and open your spring. For he is within you and does not
come from without, just as "also the kingdom of God is within
you."[53]

And that woman who had lost a drachma did not find it on
the outside, but in her house, after "she lit a lamp and cleaned
her house" from dirt and filth which the sloth and dullness of a
long time had heaped up, and then she found the drachma.[54]
And, therefore, if you should light a lamp, if you should devote
your attention to the illumination of the Holy Spirit and "see
the light in his light,"[55] you will discover a drachma within you.
For the image of the heavenly king has been placed within you.

---

50 Cf. 1 Cor 15.49.
51 Jn 7.38.
52 Cf. Jn 7.38.
53 Cf. Lk 17.21.
54 Cf. Lk 15.8.
55 Cf. Ps 35.10.

For when God made man in the beginning, "he made him according to his own image and likeness";[56] and he did not place this image on the outside, but within him. This image could not be seen in you as long as your house was dirty with filth and filled with rubbish. That spring of knowledge was lying within you, but it could not flow because the Philistines had filled it with earth and had made in it "the image of the earthly."[57] But you bore indeed at that time "the image of the earthly," but now since these things have been heard, having been cleansed from that whole earthly mass and weight by the Word of God, make the "image of the heavenly"[58] shine brightly in you.

This, then, is the image about which the Father said to the son: "Let us make men according to our image and likeness."[59] The son of God is the painter of this image. And because he is such a great painter his image can be obscured by negligence; it cannot be destroyed by malice. For the image of God always remains, even if you yourself draw "the image of the earthly" over it in yourself.

You yourself paint that picture in yourself. For when lust has darkened you, you have brought in one earthly color. But if you also burn with covetousness you have blended in also another color. And also when rage makes you bloodred you add no less also a third color. Another shade of red is added also of pride and another of impiety. And so by each individual kind of malice, like various colors which have been brought together, you yourself paint in yourself this "image of the earthly" which God did not make in you. For that reason, therefore, we should entreat him who says through the prophet: "Behold I blot out your iniquities as a cloud, and your sins as a mist."[60] And when he has blotted out all those colors in you which have been taken up from the reddish hues of malice, then that image which was created by God shines brightly in

---

56 Cf. Gn 1.26, 5.1.
57 Cf. 1 Cor 15.49.
58 Cf. 1 Cor 15.49.
59 Gn 1.26.
60 Is 44.22.

you. You see, therefore, how the divine scriptures bring in forms and figures by which the soul may be instructed to the knowledge or cleansing of itself.

Do you wish to see still even another form of this image? There are certain documents which God writes; certain documents which we ourselves write. We write documents of sin. Hear the Apostle saying: "Blotting out the handwriting in the decrees that was against us, which was contrary to us, he has taken it out of the way, fastening it to his cross."[61] That which he calls handwriting was the bond of our sins. For each of us in these things which he commits is made a debtor and writes the documents of his sins. For also in the judgment of God which Daniel describes as having sat, he mentions "the books which were opened,"[62] without doubt the books which contained the sins of men. We ourselves, therefore, write these documents for ourselves by those things which we commit. For that which is said in the Gospel of "the unjust steward" is also an image of this matter.[63] He says to each debtor, "take your bill and sit down and write eighty," and the other things which are related.[64] You see, therefore, that it is said to each man: "Take your bill." Whence it is evident that ours are documents of sin, but God writes documents of justice. For thus the Apostle says: "For you are an epistle written not with ink, but with the Spirit of the living God; not in tables of stone, but in the fleshly tables of the heart."[65] You have, therefore, in yourself documents of God and documents of the Holy Spirit. But if you transgress, you yourself write in yourself the handwriting of sin. But notice that at any time when you have approached the cross of Christ and the grace of baptism, your handwriting is affixed to the cross and blotted out in the fountain of baptism. Do not rewrite later what has been blotted out nor repair what has been destroyed. Preserve only the documents of God in yourself. Let only the Scripture of the Holy Spirit remain in you.

---

61 Col 2.14.
62 Cf. Dn 7.10.
63 Cf. Lk 16.8.
64 Lk 16.7.
65 2 Cor 3.2–3.

But let us return to Isaac and let us dig with him "wells of living water." Even if the Philistines resist, even if they quarrel, nevertheless let us persist in digging wells with him, that it may also be said to us: "Drink water out of your own vessels and out of your own wells."[66] And let us dig so much that the waters of the well overflow into our "streets"[67] so that our knowledge of the Scriptures suffices not only for us, but we may also teach others and instruct others, that men may drink, and cattle may drink. Let the wise hear. Let all the simple hear. For the teacher of the Church is "debtor to the wise and to the unwise."[68] He ought to give a drink to men and to cattle, because the prophet also says: "Men and beasts you will preserve, O Lord."[69] The Lord Jesus Christ himself, our Savior illuminates us and cleanses our hearts, "to whom be glory and sovereignty forever and ever. Amen."[70]

---

66 Prv 5.15.
67 Prv 5.16.
68 Rom 1.14.
69 Ps 35.7.
70 Cf. 1 Pt 4.11; Rv 1.6.

HOMILY XIV

On the fact that the Lord appeared to Isaac at the well of the oath, and on the covenant which he made with Abimelech

T IS WRITTEN IN THE PROPHET speaking in the person of the Lord: "I have used similitudes by the ministries of the prophets."[1] What this statement means is this: although our Lord Jesus Christ is one in his substance and is nothing other than the son of God, nevertheless he is represented as various and diverse in the figures and images of the Scriptures.[2]

For example, as I recall we have explained in what precedes that Christ himself was Isaac, in type, when he was offered as a holocaust. Nevertheless, the ram also represented him. I say furthermore that he is exhibited also in the angel who spoke to Abraham and says to him: "Lay not your hand on the boy."[3] For he says to him: "Because you have done this thing, I will certainly bless you."[4]

He is said to be the sheep or the lamb which is sacrificed in the Passover,[5] and he is designated as the shepherd of the sheep.[6] He is also described, no less, as the high priest who offers the sacrifice.[7] As the Word of God he is called the bridegroom,[8] and as wisdom he is in turn called the bride as also the prophet says in his person: "He has placed a crown on me as a groom and as a bride he has adorned me with jewelry,"[9]

---

1 Hos 12.10.
2 This is a basic tenet of Origen's Christology. See Koch, 62–78; cf. Origen *Ex. Hom.* 7.8.
3 Gn 22.12.
4 Gn 22.16–17.
5 Cf. 1 Cor 5.7.
6 Cf. Jn 10.11,14; Heb 13.20.
7 Cf. Heb 5.1–10.
8 Cf. Mt 9.15.
9 Is 61.10.

and many other things which would take too long to pursue at the present.

As, therefore, the Lord himself accommodates his form in correspondence to the place and time and certain individual conditions, so also the saints, who prefigured him, should be believed to have represented types of mysteries in correspondence to places and times and conditions, as also we see now to be the case in Isaac, of whom we have heard it read: "He went up," the text says, "from there to the well of the oath, and the Lord appeared to him that night and said: I am the God of Abraham your father; fear not. For I am with you and I will bless you and multiply your seed because of Abraham your father."[10]

The apostle Paul set forth two figures of this Isaac to us. One, about which he said that Ismael indeed, the son of Agar, represented the people according to the flesh, but Isaac the people who are of faith.[11] The other, about which he said: "He did not say, and to his seeds, as of many, but to his seed, as of one, which is Christ."[12] Isaac, therefore, represents both the people and Christ. Now it is certain that Christ is spoken of as the Word of God not only in the Gospels, but also in the Law and prophets. But in the Law he teaches beginners; in the Gospels he teaches the perfect. And Isaac, therefore, represents now the Word which is in the Law or the prophets.

(2) "Isaac, therefore, went up to the well of the oath and the Lord appeared to him."[13]

We have also already said previously that the embellishment of the temple and of those divine services which were performed therein was an ascent of the Law.[14] The increase of the prophets also can be called an ascent of the Law. And for this reason perhaps Isaac is said to have gone up to the well of the oath and there the Lord is said to have appeared to him. For

---

10 Gn 26.23–24.
11 Cf. Gal 4.22.
12 Gal 3.16.
13 Gn 26.23–24.
14 Cf. *Gn. Hom.* 5.5.

through the prophets "the Lord has sworn and he will not repent, that he is a priest forever according to the order of Melchisedech."[15] God appeared to him, therefore, "at the well of the oath" confirming the fulfillment of the promises made to him.

"And Isaac built there an altar and called on the name of the Lord and pitched his tent there. And Isaac's servants dug a well there."[16] Isaac builds indeed an altar even now in the Law and pitches his tent, but in the Gospels he does not pitch a tent, but builds a house and establishes a foundation. For hear Wisdom saying of the Church: "Wisdom," Scripture says, "has built herself a house and has set up seven columns."[17] Hear Paul also saying about this: "For no man can lay a foundation but that which is laid, which is Christ Jesus."[18]

Where, therefore, there is a tent, even if it should be pitched, it is, doubtless, to be folded up. But where there are foundations and a house is built "upon a rock," that house is never destroyed, "for it has been founded on a rock."[19] Nevertheless Isaac digs a well there too nor does he ever cease digging wells until "the fountain of living water"[20] arises and "the stream of the river makes the city of God joyful."[21]

(3) But also "Abimelech" (that man who had formerly honored Abraham) "comes" now with his friends "from Gerara" to Isaac. "And Isaac says to them: 'Why have you come to me? For you hated me and thrust me out from you.' They responded to these words: 'We certainly saw,' " the text says, "that the Lord is with you and we said: 'Let there be an oath between us and you and let us establish a covenant with you, lest you do evil with us,' " etc.[22]

This Abimelech, as I see it, does not always have peace with

---

15 Cf. Ps 109.4.
16 Gn 26.25.
17 Prv 9.1.
18 1 Cor 3.11.
19 Cf. Mt 7.24f.
20 Cf. Gn 26.19.
21 Cf. Ps 45.5.
22 Cf. Gn 26.26–29.

Isaac, but sometimes he disagrees, at other times he seeks peace. If you remember how, in what preceeds,[23] we said of Abimelech that he represents the learned and wise of the world, who have comprehended many things even of the truth through the learning of philosophy, you can understand how he can be neither always in dissension nor always at peace with Isaac who represents the Word of God in the Law. For philosophy is neither opposed to everything in the Law of God nor in harmony with everything.

For many of the philosophers write that there is one God who has created all things.[24] In this they agree with the Law of God. Some also have added this, that God both made and rules all things by his Word and it is the Word of God by which all things are directed. In this they write in harmony not only with the Law, but with the Gospels. Indeed almost the total philosophy which is called moral and natural holds the same views we do. But it disagrees with us when it says matter is coeternal with God.[25] It disagrees when it denies that God is concerned about mortal things but that his providence is confined beyond the spaces of the lunar sphere.[26] They disagree with us when they appraise the lives of those being born by the courses of the stars. They disagree when they say this world is permanent and is to have no end. But there are also many other things in which they either disagree with us or are in harmony.

And, therefore, in accordance with this figure, Abimelech is sometimes described as being at peace with Isaac and sometimes as disagreeing.

But also I do not think that this was of idle concern to the Holy Spirit, who writes these things, to relate that two others

---

23 Cf. Origen *Gn. Hom.* 6.2.
24 For a discussion of this and the following paragraphs, see Henri Crouzel, *Origène et la philosophie* (Aubier, 1962), 19–25. Cf. Cicero, N.D. 1.2–5 for a general discussion of the views of ancient philosophers on the gods.
25 Origen identifies this view with the Gnostics in *De Princ.* 1.3.3, as does also Tertullian *Adv. Marc.* 1.15.
26 This appears to be a reference to Epicurus' view of the blessed, tranquil life of the gods in the intermundane spaces. See Cicero, N.D. 1.18,45; Lucretius, *De rerum natura* 2.646–651; 3.18–24 *et passim.*

came with Abimelech, that is "Ochozath his kinsman and
Phicol the leader of his army."[27]

Now *Ochozath* means "containing"[28] and *Phicol* "the mouth
of all,"[29] but *Abimelech* himself means "my father is king."[30]
These three, in my opinion, figuratively represent all philosophy, which is divided into three parts among them: logic, phys-
ics, ethics, that is, rational, natural, moral. The rational is that
which acknowledges God to be father of all, that is, Abimelech.
The natural is that which is fixed and contains all things, as
depending on the forces of nature itself, which Ochozath,
which means "containing," professes to be. The moral is that
which is in the mouth of all and pertains to all and is situated in
the mouth of all because of the likeness of the common precepts. That Phicol, which means "the mouth of all," signifies
this.

All these, therefore, come to the Law of God in the learning
of instructions of this kind and say: "We certainly saw that the
Lord is with you and we said: 'Let there be an oath between us
and you and let us establish a covenant with you, lest you do evil
with us, but as we have not cursed you, so also you are blessed
by the Lord.' "[31]

Those three, who seek peace from the Word of God and
desire to anticipate his fellowship with a covenant, can indeed
represent the magi who come from parts of the East learned in
the books of their fathers and in the instruction of their
ancestors and say: "We certainly saw"[32] "the one born king,"[33]
"and we have seen that God is with him,"[34] "and we have come
to worship him."[35]

But also if there is anyone who has been instructed in
learning of this kind, seeing that "God was in Christ recon-

---

27 Cf. Gn 26.26.
28 See Appendix, 14.
29 See Appendix, 15.
30 See Appendix, 16.
31 Gn 26.28–29.
32 Cf. Gn 26.28.
33 Mt 2.2.
34 Gn 26.28.
35 Mt 2.2.

ciling the world to himself,"[36] and who has admired the majesty
of his works, let him say: "We certainly saw that the Lord is with
you, and we said, 'Let there be an oath between us.' "[37] For
approaching the Law of God he says necessarily: "I have sworn
and am determined that I shall keep your commandments."[38]

(4) But what do they seek? "Lest you do," they say, "evil with
us; but as we have not cursed you, so also you, are blessed by
the Lord."[39] They seem to me to request remission of sins by
these words, lest they receive evil. They are asking for a
blessing, not retribution. For notice what follows.

"And Isaac made them," the text says, "a great feast; and
they ate and drank."[40] For it is certain that he who serves the
word "is debtor to the wise and the unwise."[41] Because, therefore, he is producing a feast for the wise, for this reason it is
said that "he made" not a small, but "a great feast."

And you, if you should not still be "a little child" and in need
of "milk," but should bring your "senses exercised"[42] and
should come more capable to an understanding of the word of
God after very much instruction has been set before you, there
will also be "a great feast" for you. The "vegetables" of the
weak[43] will not be prepared for you as food nor will you be
nourished with milk with which "little children" are nourished,
but the servant of the word will make a "great feast" for you.
He will speak to you the "wisdom" which is offered "among the
perfect." He will offer you the "wisdom of God hidden in a
mystery, which none of the princes of this world knew."[44] He
will reveal Christ to you in this respect, that in him "all the
treasures of wisdom are hidden."[45]

He makes you, therefore, "a great feast" and he himself eats

---

36 Cf. 2 Cor 5.19.
37 Gn 26.28.
38 Ps 118.106.
39 Gn 26.29.
40 Gn 26.30.
41 Cf. Rom 1.14.
42 Cf. Heb 5.12–14.
43 Cf. Rom 14.2.
44 Cf. 1 Cor 2.6–8.
45 Cf. Col 2.3.

with you if he should not find you to be such that he should say to you: "I could not speak to you as to spiritual, but as to carnal, as to little ones in Christ."[46]

He says this to the Corinthians, to which he also adds: "For when there are contentions and dissensions among you, are you not carnal and walk according to man?"[47] Paul did not "make a great feast" for these, in so far that when he was with them and was in need, he was a burden to no one nor did he eat bread gratis from anyone, but laboring night and day, his own hands served himself and all who were with him.[48] The Corinthians, therefore, were so far from having a "great feast" that the preacher of the word of God could have not even the least or a little feast with them.

But there is a great feast for those who know how to hear more perfectly, who bring their "senses" instructed and "exercised"[49] for hearing the word of God. Isaac eats with them, and not only does he eat, but also rising with an oath, he promises peace with them for the future.

Let us also pray, therefore, to undertake to hear the word of God with such a mind, with such a faith that he may see fit to make us "a great feast." For "Wisdom has slain her victims, mixed her wine in the mixing bowl, and sent her servants"[50] who all bring as many as they find to her feast.

It is so great a feast, that having entered wisdom's feast let us not again bring with us garments of foolishness, neither wrapped with the clothing of infidelity nor darkened with the stains of sin, but in simplicity and purity of heart let us embrace the word and serve the divine Wisdom which is Christ Jesus our Lord, "to whom be glory and sovereignty forever and ever. Amen."[51]

---

46 1 Cor 3.1–2.
47 1 Cor 3.3.
48 Cf. 1 Cor 4.12; 2 Thes 3.8.
49 Cf. Heb 5.14.
50 Prv 9.1–3.
51 Cf. 1 Pt 4.11; Rv 1.6.

HOMILY XV

On that which is written: "And they went up out of Egypt
and came into the land of Chanaan to their father Jacob,
and they told him saying, 'Joseph your son is living and has
dominion over all the land of Egypt.' "[1]

E SHOULD OBSERVE IN READING THE HOLY SCRIPTURES how
"to go up" and "to go down" are employed in each individual passage. For if we were to give diligent consideration, we would discover that almost never is anyone said to
have gone down to an holy place nor is anyone related to have
gone up to a blameworthy place. These observations show that
the divine Scripture was not composed, as it seems to most, in
illiterate and uncultivated language, but was adapted in accordance with the discipline of divine instruction. Nor is Scripture
devoted so much to historical narratives as to things and ideas
which are mystical.

You will find it written, therefore, that those who are born
of the seed of Abraham have gone down into Egypt and again
that the sons of Israel have gone up out of Egypt. Indeed
Scripture speaks thus also of Abraham himself: "But Abraham
went up out of Egypt into the desert, he and his wife and all
that was his, and Lot with him."[2] Then afterwards it is said also
of Isaac: "The Lord appeared to him and said to him: 'Go not
down into Egypt.' "[3] But also the Ismaelites who were carrying
thymiamata[4] and resin and oil of myrrh, who also themselves
came from the seed of Abraham, are said to go down into
Egypt with whom also Joseph is said to have gone down into
Egypt.[5] But also after these words Scripture says: "Jacob,

---

1 Gn 45.25–26.
2 Gn 13.1.
3 Gn 26.2.
4 Rufinus has the Greek word in his text. It means "incense."
5 Cf. Gn 37.25f.

203

seeing that there is traffic in grain in Egypt, said to his sons:
'Why are you idle? Behold I hear that there is grain in Egypt;
go down there and buy food for us, that we may live and not
die.' "[6] And a little later, Scripture says: "The brothers of
Joseph went down into Egypt to purchase grain."[7]

To be sure, when Simeon had been detained in Egypt and
his nine brothers were released and returned to their father, it
is not written that they went up out of Egypt, but "loading the
grain on their asses," Scripture says, "they departed."[8] For they
would not properly be said to go up whose brother was held
bound in Egypt, with whom they too, anxious in mind and
soul, were afflicted, bound, as it were, by certain bonds of love.
But when their brother has been received and Joseph has been
recognized, but also after Benjamin has been presented to
their eyes, when they return with joy, then it is said that: "They
went up out of Egypt and came into the land of Chanaan to
their father Jacob."[9] It is at that time when they also say to their
father: "Joseph, your son, is living and has dominion over all
the land of Egypt."[10] For by necessity those who announce that
Joseph is living and holds dominion over all Egypt are said to
go up from the lowest and humble places to steep and lofty
ones.

Meanwhile these are the things we have been able to think
of at present about going up and going down. All who are
studious can have opportunities from these words to collect
more proofs from the Holy Scriptures for an assertion of this
kind.

(2) Let us see, by all means, how we ought to hear about that
which is written, that "Joseph your son is living."[11]

I do not understand these words to have been said in the
usual sense. For if, for example, we should assume that he
could have been overcome with lust and sinned with his mas-

---

6 Gn 42.1–2.
7 Gn 42.3.
8 Cf. Gn 42.26.
9 Gn 45.25.
10 Gn 45.26.
11 Gn 45.26.

ter's wife,[12] I do not think that this would have been announced about him by the patriarchs to his father Jacob: "Your son Joseph is living."[13] For if he had done this, without doubt he would not be living. For "the soul that sins, the same shall die."[14]

But Susanna also teaches the same things when she says: "I am straitened on every side. for if I do this thing—that is, if I sin—it is death to me; and if I do it not, I shall not escape your hands."[15] Notice, therefore, that she too understood that there is death in sin.

But also the judgment revealed by God to the first man contains the same things when he says: "But on the day that you shall eat of it you shall die the death."[16] For as soon as he has transgressed the commandment, he is dead. For the soul which has sinned is dead, and the serpent which said, "You shall not die the death,"[17] is shown to have deceived him.

And these words have been about that which was said by the sons of Israel to Jacob: "Your son Joseph is living."[18]

Words similar to these are related also in what follows, when Scripture says: "And the spirit of Jacob their father was revived. And Israel said: "It is a great thing for me if Joseph my son is still living."[19]

What Latin expresses by saying: "his spirit was revived," is written in Greek *anezōpyrēsen*. This means not so much to revive as to rekindle, so to speak, and reignite. This expression is usually used when, perhaps in some material, the fire fails to the point that it appears to be extinguished; and if perhaps it be renewed when kindling has been added, it is said to have been rekindled. Or if the light of a lamp should reach the point that it be thought to have gone out, if perhaps it be revived when oil has been poured in, although the expression is less

---

12 Cf. Gn 39.7f.
13 Gn 45.26.
14 Ez 18.4.
15 Dn 13.22 (LXX: Susanna 22).
16 Gn 2.17.
17 Gn 3.4.
18 Gn 45.26.
19 Gn 45.27–28.

refined, the lamp is said to have been rekindled. One will speak similarly also of a torch or other lights of this kind.

This expression seems to indicate something like this also in Jacob. As long as he was far from Joseph and received no information about his life, his spirit had failed in him, as it were, and the light which was in him had been darkened, as the kindling already failed. But when those who reported to him about Joseph's life came, that is those who said that "the life was the light of men,"[20] he rekindles his spirit in himself, and the brightness of the true light is renewed in him.

(3) But because occasionally the divine fire can be extinguished even in the saints and faithful, hear the apostle Paul warning these who were worthy to receive gifts of the Spirit and grace, and saying: "Extinguish not the Spirit."[21] The Scripture says of Jacob, therefore: "And Jacob rekindled his spirit and Israel said: 'It is a great thing for me if my son Joseph is still living,' "[22] as if he has experienced something like that which Paul warned against and has renewed himself through those words which had been spoken to him about Joseph's life.

But this also should be noticed, that he who "rekindled his spirit," meaning , of course, that spirit which seemed almost extinguished, is said to be Jacob. But he who says: "It is a great thing for me if my son Joseph is living,"[23] as if he understands and sees that the life which is in the spiritual Joseph is great, is no longer called Jacob, but Israel, as it were, he who sees in his mind the true life which is Christ, the true God.[24]

But he is excited not only about the fact that he has heard that "Joseph his son is living," but also especially about that which has been announced to him that it is Joseph who holds "dominion over all Egypt."[25] For the fact that he has reduced Egypt to his rule is truly great to him. For to tread on lust, to flee luxury, and to suppress and curb all the pleasures of the

20 Jn 1.4.
21 1 Thes 5.19.
22 Gn 45.27–28.
23 Gn 45.28.
24 See Appendix, 17.
25 Gn 45.26.

body, this is what it means to have "dominion over all Egypt." And this is what is considered great and held in admiration by Israel.

But if there is someone who should subject at least some vices of the body, but yield to others and be subject to them, it is not said correctly of him that he holds "dominion over the whole land of Egypt," but, for example, he will appear to hold dominion over one, perhaps, or two, or three cities. But Joseph, whom no bodily lust ruled, was prince and Lord "of all Egypt."

Therefore no longer Jacob, but Israel, whose spirit has been rekindled, says: "It is a great thing for me if Joseph my son is living. I will go and see him before I die."[26]

But not even this is to be neglected idly, that the text says not the soul, but the spirit as its better part, was revived or rekindled. For indeed the brightness of the light which was in him, even if it was not completely extinguished then when his sons showed him Joseph's robe stained with the blood of a kid, and he could be deceived by their lie so that "he tore his garments and put sackcloth on his loins and mourned his son nor did he wish at all to be consoled," but said: "I go down to my son into the nether world, mourning,"[27] even if then, as we said, the light in him had not been completely extinguished, nevertheless it had been darkened in the greatest degree because he could be deceived, because he could tear his garments, because he could mourn by mistake, because he could call on death, because he desired to go down into the nether world, mourning. On account of these things, therefore, he now revives and "rekindles his spirit," because it followed logically that hearing the truth would rekindle and restore the light which the deceit of a lie had obscured in him.

(4) But because we said that it is Jacob who "rekindled his spirit," but it is Israel who says: "It is a great thing for me if my son Joseph is still living,"[28] you too who hear these words, can discover the difference of this name by beginning from that

26 Gn 45.28.
27 Gn 37.31–35.
28 Gn 45.28.

passage where it is written: "He said to him: 'Your name shall no longer be called Jacob, but Israel, because you have prevailed with God and have become mighty with men,' "[29] and running through all the Scripture.

For example, as when Scripture says: "Tell me your name,"[30] here he who does not know the name is not said to be Israel, but Jacob. But where Scripture says, "They do not eat the sinew which was benumbed in the broad area of the thigh"[31] of the patriarch, they are not said to be the sons of Jacob, but the sons of Israel. But he who "looked and saw Esau coming and with him four hundred men," and "seven times honored"[32] the fornicator and profane man and him who "sold his birthright"[33] for one meal is not said to be Israel, but Jacob. But also when he offers him gifts and says: "If I have found favor before you, receive these gifts at my hands, because I have seen your face as one who sees the face of God,"[34] this was not Israel, but Jacob. And when he heard that Dina his daughter was defiled, "and Jacob held his peace until his sons should come,"[35] he is not said to be Israel. But you too, as I said, will discover similar things if you are observant.

In the present text, therefore, not Jacob, but Israel says: "It is a great thing for me if my son Joseph is still living."[36] But also when he comes to the well of the oath and "offers a victim to the God of his father Isaac,"[37] he is not called Jacob, but Israel. But if you should ask why God speaking to him in a vision at night does not say, "Israel, Israel," but "Jacob, Jacob," it is perhaps for this reason, that it was night and he deserved to hear the voice of God still by means of a vision and not yet openly.[38] And when he enters Egypt, he is not said to be Israel, but Jacob "and

---

29 Gn 32.28.
30 Gn 32.29.
31 Gn 32.32.
32 Cf. Gn 33.1–3.
33 Cf. Gn 25.33; Heb 12.6.
34 Gn 33.10.
35 Cf. Gn 34.5.
36 Gn 45.28.
37 Cf. Gn 46.1.
38 Cf. Gn 46.2.

his sons with him."[39] And when he stands "before Pharao" to bless him,[40] he is not called Israel, but Jacob; for Pharao could not receive the blessing of Israel. And it is Jacob, not Israel, who says to Pharao that "the days of his life are few and evil."[41] That, certainly, Israel would never say. But after these things it is said not of Jacob, but of Israel: "He called his son Joseph and says to him: 'If I have found favor in your sight, put your hand under my thigh, and you shall show me this kindness and truth.' "[42] And he who worshipped upon the top of Joseph's rod was not Jacob, but Israel.[43] Then afterwards when he blesses Joseph's sons he is called Israel. And when he calls his sons together, he says: "Gather together that I may tell what shall befall you in the last days. Gather yourselves together, sons of Jacob, and hearken to Israel your father."[44]

But perhaps you may ask, why they are said to be "the sons of Jacob" who gather together, but it is said to be "Israel" who blesses them. Consider whether perhaps this is indicated, that they had not yet advanced to the point that they could be placed on an equality with the merits of Israel. And, for this reason, they are called "sons of Jacob" as inferior, but he is called "Israel," who was already perfect and conscious of future things gives blessings.

Clearly the statement that "the embalmers" of Egypt embalmed not Jacob, but Israel,[45] will appear to be a major problem. But I think that in this, that the saints have died with the impious and been embalmed, the error may be exposed of those by whom Israel is said to be embalmed, because all understanding of good things and all keenness of heavenly understanding was odious to them. We have related these things about the difference between Jacob and Israel to the extent that it has been possible to attain at the present.

---

39 Cf. Gn 46.6.
40 Cf. Gn 47.7.
41 Cf. Gn 47.9.
42 Gn 47.29.
43 Gn 47.31 (LXX); Cf. Heb 11.21.
44 Gn 49.1–2.
45 Cf. Gn 50.2 (LXX).

(5) It appears fitting indeed after these things, to contemplate and look into what God says to Israel himself through the vision and how he sends him to Egypt strengthening and encouraging him as if he were setting out to some struggles.

For he says: "Fear not to descend into Egypt,"[46] this is to say: You shall contend "against principalities and powers and against the rulers of this world of this darkness,"[47]—which is figuratively called Egypt—fear not, be not afraid. But if also you wish to know the reason that you ought not fear, hear my promise: "For I will make a great nation of you there, and I will go down with you into Egypt, and I will recall you from there in the end."[48]

He, therefore, with whom God shall go down into the struggles, is not afraid "to go down into Egypt"; he is not afraid to approach the struggles of this world and the battles with resisting demons. For hear the apostle Paul saying, "I have labored more," he says, "than all those, yet not I, but the grace of God with me."[49] But also when dissension had been stirred up against him in Jerusalem, and he performed a most brilliant struggle for the word and preaching of the Lord, the Lord stood by him and said the same things which now are said to Israel: "Fear not, Paul," Scripture says, "for as you have testified of me in Jerusalem, so must you bear witness also at Rome."[50]

But I think a still greater mystery lies hidden in this passage. For this statement disturbs me: "I will make a great nation of you, and I will go down with you into Egypt, and I will recall you from there in the end."[51] Who is it who is made "into a great nation" in Egypt and is recalled "in the end"? To the extent that it pertains to that Jacob of whom one supposes it to be said, it will not appear true. For he was not recalled from Egypt "in the end," since he died in Egypt. But it will be absurd if

---

46 Gn 46.3.
47 Cf. Eph 6.12.
48 Gn 46.3–4.
49 1 Cor 15.10.
50 Acts 23.11.
51 Gn 46.3–4.

someone says Jacob was recalled by God in that his body was carried back. But if it be accepted, it will not be true that "God is not the God of the dead, but of the living."[52] It is not proper, therefore, that these words be understood of a dead body, but that they apply to the living and vigorous.

Let us consider, therefore, whether there may be depicted in this statement a figure of the Lord who descends into this world and is made "into a great nation," that is, the Church of the Gentiles, and after all things were completed, returned to the Father. Or, whether it is a figure of "the first-formed man"[53] who descends to the struggles of this world after he was cast out of the delights of paradise. The struggle with the serpent was set before him when it is said: "You shall watch for his head and he shall watch for your heel,"[54] and again, when it is said to the woman: "I will put enmity between you and him, and between your seed and his seed."[55]

Nevertheless, God does not desert those placed in this struggle, but is always with them. He is pleased with Abel; he reproaches Cain;[56] he is present with Enoch, when he is invoked;[57] he commands Noah to construct an ark of salvation in the flood;[58] he leads Abraham "from the house of his father" and "from his kinsmen";[59] he blesses Isaac and Jacob;[60] he leads the sons of Israel out of Egypt.[61] He writes the Law of the letter through Moses; he completes what was lacking through the prophets. This is what it means to be with them in Egypt.

But regarding the statement: "I will recall you from there in

---

52 Mt 22.32.
53 Wis 7.1.
54 Cf. Gn 3.15.
55 Gn 3.15. In each citation of Gn 3.15 here Origen has changed the address-ee. Both statements are addressed to the serpent in Gn. Doutreleau, 367, appears to be correct when he asserts that Origen has accommodated the citation to his own purpose.
56 Cf. Gn 4.4,10–12.
57 Cf. Gn 5.22.
58 Cf. Gn 6.14.
59 Cf. Gn 12.1.
60 Cf. Gn 25.11, 32.27,29.
61 Cf. Ex 14.

the end,"[62] I think this means, as we said above, that at the end of the ages his only begotten Son descended even into the nether regions[63] for the salvation of the world and recalled "the first-formed man"[64] from there. For what he said to the thief, "This day you shall be with me in paradise,"[65] understand not to have been said to him alone, but also to all the saints for whom he had descended into the nether regions. In this man, therefore, more truly than in Jacob the words "I will recall you from there in the end," will be fulfilled.

(6) But each of us also, in the same manner and in the same way, enters Egypt and struggles and, if he be worthy that God should always remain with him, he will make him "into a great nation." For the number of virtues and the multitude of righteousness in which all the saints are said to be multiplied and to increase is a great nation.

That which is said is also fulfilled in the saint: "I will recall you from there in the end."[66] For the end is considered to be the perfection of things and the consummation of virtues. Indeed for this reason also another saint said: "Recall me not in the midst of my days."[67] And again the Scripture bestows testimony on the great patriarch Abraham since "Abraham died full of days."[68] This statement, therefore, "I will recall you from there in the end," is as if he had said: Since "you have fought a good fight, you have kept the faith, you have finished the course,"[69] I will now recall you from this world to the future blessing, to the perfection of eternal life, to "the crown of justice which the Lord will give in the end of the ages to all who love him."[70]

(7) But let us see how also the statement after that should be understood: "And Joseph shall put his hands upon your

---

62 Gn 46.4.
63 Cf. Eph 4.9.
64 Cf. Wis 7.1.
65 Lk 23.43.
66 Gn 46.4.
67 Ps 101.25.
68 Gn 25.8.
69 Cf. 2 Tm 4.7.
70 Cf. 2 Tm 4.8; Jas 1.12.

eyes."[71] I think many mysteries indeed of secret understanding are hidden within the veil of this statement. It belongs to another time to approach and touch upon these mysteries. Now, meanwhile, it will not appear to be said without reason, since it has appeared also to some of our predecessors that a certain prophecy seemed to be designated in this statement: since, indeed, that Jeroboam who made two golden calves that he might seduce the people to worship them,[72] was from the tribe of Joseph, and by this he blinded and closed the eyes of Israel, as if his hands were placed on them, lest they see their impiety, of which it is said: "Because of the impiety of Jacob are all these things, and because of the sin of the house of Israel. But what is the impiety of Jacob? Is it not Samaria?"[73]

But if someone perhaps asserts that those things which are said by God about a future form of piety ought not be turned to a censurable function, we will say that just as the true Joseph, our Lord and Savior, put his physical hand on the eyes of the blind man and restored his sight which he had lost, so also he put his spiritual hands on the eyes of the Law, which had been blinded by the corporeal understanding of the Scribes and Pharisees, and he restored sight to them, that to these to whom the Lord has opened the Scriptures[74] spiritual vision and understanding might appear in the Law.

And would that the Lord Jesus might put "his hands on" our "eyes" too, that we too might begin to look not at those things "which are seen, but at the things which are not seen."[75] And would that he might open for us those eyes which contemplate not present things, but future, and might reveal to us the aspect of the heart by which God is seen in spirit, through the Lord Jesus Christ himself, to whom belongs "glory and power forever and ever. Amen."[76]

---

71 Gn 46.4.
72 3 Kgs 12.28.
73 Cf. Mi 1.5.
74 Cf. Lk 24.32.
75 2 Cor 4.18.
76 Rv 5.13.

HOMILY XVI

On that which has been written: "And Joseph acquired all the land of Egypt for Pharao; for the Egyptians sold their land to Pharao because the famine prevailed over them. And the land became Pharao's, and he reduced the people to slavery to himself from one end of Egypt to the other."[1]

CCORDING TO THE TRUSTWORTHINESS OF SCRIPTURE, no Egyptian was free. For "Pharao reduced the people to slavery to himself " nor did he leave anyone free within the borders of the Egyptians, but freedom was taken away in all the land of Egypt. And perhaps for this reason it is written: "I am the Lord your God who brought you out of the land of Egypt, out of the house of bondage."[2] Egypt, therefore, became the house of bondage and, what is more unfortunate, of voluntary bondage.

For although it is related of the Hebrews that they were reduced to bondage, and that, freedom having been snatched away, they bore the yoke of tyranny, nevertheless they are said to have been brought to this state "violently." For it is written: "The Egyptians abhorred the children of Israel and with might the Egyptians violently oppressed the sons of Israel and afflicted their life with hard works in mud and brick, and with all the works which were in the plains, in all of which they reduced them to bondage by force."[3] Notice carefully, therefore, how the Hebrews are recorded to have been reduced to bondage "violently." There was a natural freedom in them which was not wrenched away from them easily or by some deception, but by force.

But Pharao easily reduced the Egyptian people to bondage

---

1 Gn 47.20–21.
2 Ex 20.2.
3 Ex 1.12–14.

214

to himself, nor is it written that he did this by force. For the Egyptians are prone to a degenerate life and quickly sink to every slavery of the vices. Look at the origin of the race and you will discover that their father Cham, who had laughed at his father's nakedness,[4] deserved a judgment of this kind, that his son Chanaan should be a servant to his brothers,[5] in which case the condition of bondage would prove the wickedness of his conduct. Not without merit, therefore, does the discolored posterity imitate the ignobility of the race.

But the Hebrews, even if they be reduced to bondage, even if they suffer tyranny from the Egyptians, suffer "violently" and by necessity. For this reason, therefore, they are freed "from the house of bondage" and recalled to the original freedom which they had lost against their will. For it is even provided for in the divine laws that if perhaps someone buy a Hebrew servant, he may not possess him in perpetual bondage, but he may serve him for six years but in the seventh year he may depart free.[6] Nothing like this is proposed concerning the Egyptians. Nowhere does the divine Law entertain concern for Egyptian freedom, because they had lost it willingly. It leaves them to the eternal yoke of their condition and to perpetual bondage.

(2) If, therefore, we understand these words spiritually, what the bondage of the Egyptians is, we recognize that to serve the Egyptians is nothing other than to become submissive to carnal vices and to be subjected to demons. At any rate, no necessity coming from without forces anyone into this state. Rather, the sluggishness of the soul and the lust and pleasure of the body overcome each one. The soul, by its own carelessness, subjects itself to this. But he who bears a concern for the freedom of the soul and improves the dignity of his mind with thought pertaining to heaven, belongs to the children of Israel. Although he may be "violently" oppressed for a time, nevertheless he does not lose his freedom forever. For our

---

4 Cf. Gn 9.22.
5 Cf. Gn 9.25.
6 Cf. Ex 21.2.

Savior also, discussing freedom and bondage in the Gospel, speaks thus: "Everyone," he says, "who sins, is a servant of sin."[7] And again he says: "If you continue in my word you shall know the truth and the truth shall make you free."[8]

But if someone perhaps should say to us: "How then is all the land delivered into the possession of Pharao by Joseph, and all that bondage which we explained above to have been received from the condition of sin, said to be administered for Pharao by a holy man?"—we can respond to these words that the statement itself of Scripture excuses the administration of the holy man when it says that the Egyptians sold themselves and their possessions.[9] Blame, therefore, is not reflected on the administrator when things befitting the merits of the recipients are provided.

For you will discover that Paul also did something like this when he delivered to Satan, "that he might learn not to blaspheme,"[10] that man who made himself unworthy of the fellowship of the saints by the hideousness of his actions. In which case, at least, no one has said that Paul, who cast a man out of the Church and delivered him to Satan, acted harshly. But without doubt, the blame is referred to him who by his actions deserved that there be no place in the Church for him, but deserved to be joined to the fellowship of Satan. So, therefore, also Joseph, when he had discerned none of the Hebrew freedom, none of the Israelite nobility in the Egyptians associated the suitable servitude with the suitable tyranny.

I say even something more. You will discover also in the divine dispensations something like this to have taken place in that which Moses says: "When the Most High divided the nations and distinguished the boundaries of the nations, he established them according to the number of the angels of God, and Jacob became the Lord's portion, and Israel the lot of his inheritance."[11] You see, therefore, that the reign of angels

---

7 Jn 8.34.
8 Jn 8.31–32.
9 Cf. Gn 47.20.
10 Cf. 1 Cor 5.5; 1 Tm 1.20.
11 Dt 32.8–9.

was established deservedly for each nation, but the people of Israel became "the Lord's portion."

(3) After this there follows: "The Egyptians sold," the text says, "their land to Pharao, for the famine prevailed over them."[12]

It seems to me that censure of the Egyptians is contained also in this statement. For you would not easily find it written of the Hebrews that "the famine prevailed over them." For although it is written that "the famine prevailed over the land,"[13] nevertheless, it is not written that famine prevailed over Jacob or his sons, as it is said of the Egyptians, that "the famine prevailed over them." For although famine should come also to the just, nevertheless it does not prevail over them. For which reason also the just glory in famine, as Paul is found to rejoice cheerfully in sufferings of this kind when he says: "In hunger and thirst, in cold and nakedness."[14] What therefore is an exercise of virtue for the just, is a penalty of sin for the unjust.

For it is written also in the times of Abraham that, "there came a famine in the country, and Abraham went down to Egypt to dwell there, since the famine prevailed in the land."[15] And certainly if, as some think, the text of the divine Scripture was composed carelessly and awkwardly, it could have said that Abraham went down to Egypt to dwell there because the famine prevailed over him. But observe how great a distinction the divine word uses, how great a caution it employs. When it speaks of the saints it says the famine had prevailed "over the land"; when it speaks of the unjust it says they were held by the famine. Famine, therefore, prevailed over neither Abraham nor Jacob nor their sons. But also if it should prevail it is said to prevail "over the land." And in the times of Isaac no less it is written: "A famine came in the land, besides that former famine which came in the times of Abraham."[16] But the famine

---

12 Gn 47.20.
13 Cf. Gn 43.1.
14 Cf. 2 Cor 11.27.
15 Gn 12.10.
16 Gn 26.1.

was unable to prevail over Isaac to such an extent that the Lord says to him: "Do not go down into Egypt, but dwell in the land which I shall show you, and dwell in it and I will be with you."[17]

In accordance with this observation, in my opinion, long after that time the prophet said: "I have been young and now am old and I have not seen the just forsaken, nor his seed seeking bread."[18] And elsewhere: The Lord will not strike down the just soul with famine."[19] From all these texts it is declared that the earth indeed can suffer famine and those who "mind earthly things."[20] But they can never be oppressed by the fasting of famine whose is that bread that "they should do the will of the Father who is in heaven,"[21] and whose soul that "bread which comes down from heaven"[22] nourishes.

For this reason, therefore, the divine Scripture carefully does not say that those were held by famine who it knew possessed knowledge of God and to whom the food of the heavenly wisdom was offered. But also in the third book of Kings you will find that there is a similar caution observed about the report of a famine, where, when the famine had prevailed over the land Elias says to Ahab: "As the Lord God of the powers lives, the God of Israel, in whose sight I stand, there shall not be dew nor rain upon the land in these years, except by the word of my mouth."[23] After these words the Lord commands that the ravens feed the prophet and that he drink water from the stream Carith.[24] And again in Sarephta he orders a Sidonian widow to feed the prophet.[25] She did not have food for more than one day. By sharing it, it became unfailing and the exhausted food abounded in many ways. For

---

17 Gn 26.2–3.
18 Ps 36.25.
19 Prv 10.3.
20 Cf. Phil 3.19.
21 Cf. Mt 7.21.
22 Cf. Jn 6.51,59.
23 3 Kgs 17.1.
24 3 Kgs 17.3–4.
25 3 Kgs 17.9.

according to the word of the Lord, "the pot of meal" and "flask of oil" did not fail for feeding the prophet.[26]

You will also find similar things in the times of Eliseus too, when the son of Jader, king of Syria, came up against Samaria," and besieged it. "And there was a great famine in Samaria," Scripture says, "for so long that an ass's head became worth fifty shekels of silver and a quarter of pigeon dung five pieces of silver."[27] But suddenly an amazing change occurs through the word of the prophet who says: "Hear the word of the Lord. Thus says the Lord: 'Thus tomorrow, at this hour a measure of the finest wheat flour shall be one shekel and two measures of barley shall be one shekel, in the gates of Samaria.' "[28]

Notice, therefore, what is inferred from all these texts: when famine prevails over a land, not only does it not prevail over the just, but rather through them, a remedy is brought to the threatened destruction.

(4) Since you see, therefore, that an observation of this kind is preserved correctly in almost all the texts of Holy Scripture, change these words to their figurative and allegorical meaning, which we are taught by the words of the prophets themselves no less. For one of the twelve prophets proclaims clearly and mainfestly in a simple statement that a spiritual famine is intended, when he says: "Behold the days come, says the Lord, and I will send forth a famine on the land, not a famine of bread nor thirst for water, but a famine for hearing the word of the Lord."[29]

Do you see what the famine is which prevails over sinners? Do you see what the famine is which prevails over the land? For they who are of the earth and "mind earthly things"[30] and cannot "perceive what things are of the spirit of God,"[31] suffer "a famine of the word of God." They do not hear the commands

---

26 Cf. 3 Kgs 17.14.
27 4 Kgs 6.25.
28 4 Kgs 7.1.
29 Am 8.11.
30 Cf. Phil 3.19.
31 Cf. 1 Cor 2.14.

of the Law; they do not know the reproaches of the prophets; they are ignorant of the apostolic consolations; they do not experience the medicine of the Gospel. And for this reason it is said rightly of them: "Famine prevailed over the land."[32]

But for the just and "those who meditate on the Law" of the Lord "day and night,"[33] "wisdom prepares her table, she kills her victims, she mixes her wine in the mixing bowl, and calls with a loud voice,"[34] not that all may come, not that the abounding, not that the rich nor that the wise of this world may turn aside to her, but "if there are those," Scripture says, "who are weak in understanding, let them come to me."[35] That is, if there are those who are "lowly in heart," who have learned from Christ "to be meek and lowly in heart"[36] (which elsewhere is called "poor in spirit),"[37] but rich in faith, these gather at the feasts of wisdom and, refreshed by her banquets, they drive out the famine which "prevails over the land."

You also take heed, therefore, lest perhaps you be found an Egyptian and famine should prevail over you, lest perhaps occupied with the affairs of the world, or bound by the bonds of avarice or enfeebled by the extravagance of luxury you become estranged from wisdom's foods which are always served in the Churches of God. For if you turn aside your hearing from these words which are either read in church or discussed, without doubt you will suffer "a famine of the word of God."[38] But if you descend from the stock of Abraham and preserve the nobility of the race of Israel, the Law always feeds you, the prophets feed you, and the apostles offer you a rich banquet. The Gospels will invite you to recline also in the bosoms of Abraham and Isaac and Jacob "in the kingdom of the Father,"[39] that there you may eat "from the tree of life"[40]

---

32 Gn 43.1.
33 Cf. Ps 1.2.
34 Cf. Prv 9.2–3.
35 Cf. Prv 9.4; Mt 11.25,28.
36 Cf. Mt 11.29.
37 Cf. Mt 5.3; Jas 2.5.
38 Cf. Am 8.11.
39 Cf. Mt 8.11.
40 Cf. Rv 2.7.

and drink wine from "the true vine,"[41] "the new wine with Christ in the kingdom of his Father."[42] For "the children of the bridegroom, as long as the bridegroom is with them"[43] cannot abstain from these foods nor suffer famine.

(5) It is related, to be sure, in what follows that the land of the Egyptian priests was not reduced to bondage to Pharao and that they did not sell themselves with the other Egyptians, but that moreover they received either grain or gifts not from Joseph, but from Pharao himself. And "for this reason," as if more familiar than the others, "they did not sell their land" to Pharao.[44] But by this they are shown to be more wicked than the others, who for too much familiarity between themselves and Pharao receive no change, but continue in the evil possession. And as the Lord says to these who have advanced in faith and holiness: "I no longer call you servants, but friends"[45] so also Pharao says to these, as it were, who have ascended to the highest step of wickedness and to the priesthood of perdition: "I no longer call you servants, but friends."

Indeed do you wish to know what the difference is between the priests of God and the priests of Pharao? Pharao grants lands to his priests. The Lord, on the other hand, does not grant his priests a portion in the land, but says to them: "I am your portion."[46] You, therefore, who read these words, observe all the priests of the Lord and notice what difference there is between the priests, lest perhaps they who have a portion in the land and have time for earthly cares and pursuits may appear not so much to be priests of the Lord as priests of Pharao. For it is Pharao who wishes his priests to have possessions of lands and to work at the cultivation of the soil not of the soul, to give attention to the fields, and not to the Law. But let us hear what Christ our Lord admonishes his priests: "He who has not

---

41 Cf. Jn 15.1.
42 Cf. Mt 26.29.
43 Cf. Lk 5.34; Mt 9.15.
44 Cf. Gn 47.22.
45 Cf. Jn 15.15.
46 Cf. Nm 18.20.

renounced all he possesses," he says, "cannot be my disciple."[47]

I tremble when I speak these words. For I myself am my own, I say, my own accuser first of all. I utter my own condemnations. For Christ denies that that man whom he has seen possessing anything and that man who "renounces" not "all which he possesses" is his disciple. And what do we do? How do we, who not only do not renounce these things which we possess, but also wish to acquire those things which we never had before we came to Christ, either read these words ourselves or explain them to people? For since conscience rebukes us, are we able to hide and not bring forth the words which are written? I do not wish to be guilty of a double crime. I admit, and I admit openly to the people who are listening, that these things are written, although I know that I have not yet fulfilled them. But warned from this, let us, at least, hasten to fulfill them, let us hasten to pass over from the priests of Pharao, who have an earthly possession, to the priests of the Lord who have no portion in the earth, whose "portion" is "the Lord."[48]

For such also was he who said: "As needy, yet enriching many, as having nothing, and possessing all things."[49] It is Paul who glories in such things.

Do you wish to hear what also Peter himself pronounces about himself? Hear him with John equally professing and saying: "Gold and silver I do not have, but what I have, I give you. In the name of Jesus Christ, arise and walk."[50] Do you see the riches of Christ's priests? Do you see the greatness and nature of the gifts they bestow when they have nothing? Earthly possession cannot bestow those riches.

(6) We have compared priests with priests. Now, if you please, let us compare also the Egyptian people with the Israelite people.

For it is said subsequently that after the famine and bondage the Egyptian people should offer a fifth part to Pharao.[51]

---

47 Lk 14.33.
48 Cf. Nm 18.20; Ps 118.57.
49 2 Cor 6.10.
50 Acts 3.6.
51 Cf. Gn 47.24.

But on the contrary the Israelite people offer tithes to the priests. Behold also in this that the divine Scripture is suported by remarkable reasonableness. See the Egyptian people weighing out contributions with the number five; for the five senses in the body are designated, which carnal people serve; for the Egyptians always submit to things visible and corporal. But on the other hand the Israelite people honor ten, the number of perfection; for they received the ten words of the Law, and, held together by the power of the Decalogue, they entered upon, by the bestowing, divine mysteries unknown to this world. But also in the New Testament likewise ten is venerable as both the fruit of the spirit is explained to sprout forth in ten virtues,[52] and the faithful servant offers his lord ten pounds in profits from his business dealings and receives authority over ten cities.[53]

But because there is one author of all things and Christ alone is the fountain and "beginning," therefore also the people present tithes, indeed, to the ministers and priests, but they offer their firstborn to "the firstborn of every creature,"[54] and their firstfruits to the "beginning" of all things, of whom it is written: "Who is the beginning,[55] the firstborn of every creature."[56]

Behold, therefore, from all these things the difference between the Egyptian people and the people of Israel and the difference between the priests of Pharao and the priests of the Lord, and, examining yourself, consider to which people you belong and the priesthood of which order you hold. If you still serve the carnal senses, if you still pay tax with the number five and look to those things which are "visible" and "temporal" and do not look to those things which are "invisible" and "eternal,"[57] know that you are of the Egyptian people. But if you always have before your eyes the Decalogue of the Law

---

52 Cf. Gal 5.22.
53 Cf. Lk 19.16–17.
54 Cf. Col 1.15.
55 Col 1.18.
56 Col 1.15.
57 Cf. 2 Cor 4.18.

and the decade of the New Testament, which we explained above, and from these you offer tithes, and in faith you sacrifice the firstborn of your senses "to the firstborn from the dead,"[58] and you bring back your firstfruits to the "beginning" of all things, "you are a true Israelite in whom there is no guile."[59]

But also if the priests of the Lord should examine themselves and be free from all earthly activities and from mundane possession, they can truly say to the Lord: "Behold we have left all things and have followed you,"[60] and they can hear from him: "You who have followed me, in the regeneration of all things, when the son of man shall come in his kingdom, you also shall sit on twelve thrones judging the twelve tribes of Israel."[61]

(7) Let us see what Moses says after these words: "And Israel dwelt," the text says, "in Egypt, in the land of Gessen."[62] Now *Gessen* means "proximity" or "nearness".[63] By this it is shown that although Israel dwells in Egypt it is, nevertheless, not far from God, but is close to him and near, as he himself also says: "I will go down with you into Egypt, and I will be with you."[64]

And, therefore, even if we appear to have gone down into Egypt, even if placed in the flesh we undergo the battles and struggles of this world, even if we dwell among those who are subject to Pharao, nevertheless, if we are near God, if we live in meditation on his commandments and inquire diligently after "his precept and judgments"[65]—for this is what it means to be always near God, to think the things which are of God, "to seek the things which are of God"[66]—God also will always be with us, through Christ Jesus our Lord, "to whom belongs glory forever and ever. Amen."[67]

---

58 Col 1.18.
59 Cf. Jn 1.47.
60 Mt 19.27.
61 Mt 19.28.
62 Gn 47.27.
63 See Appendix, 18.
64 Gn 46.4, 26,3.
65 Cf. Dt 12.1.
66 Cf. Phil 2.21.
67 Cf. Gal 1.5.

HOMILIES ON EXODUS

(In Exodum homiliae)

HOMILY I

I THINK EACH WORD OF DIVINE SCRIPTURE is like a seed whose nature is to multiply diffusely, reborn into an ear of corn or whatever its species be, when it has been cast into the earth. Its increase is proportionate to the diligent labor of the skillful farmer or the fertility of the earth.[1] So, therefore, it is brought to pass that, by diligent cultivation, a little "mustard seed," for example, "which is least of all, may be made greater than all herbs and become a tree so that the birds of heaven come and dwell in its branches."[2] So it is also with this word which now has been read to us from the divine books. Although when first approached it seems small and insignificant, if it find a skillful and diligent farmer, as it begins to be cultivated and handled with spiritual skill, it grows into a tree and puts forth branches and foliage. "The debaters and orators of this world" can come to it.[3] Like "birds of heaven" on light wings pursuing lofty and difficult thoughts with a pompous array of words alone, and captives to arguments, they wish "to dwell in those branches"[4] in which there is no eloquent language but a rule for living.

What then shall we do about these things which have been read to us? If the Lord deign to grant me the discipline of spiritual agriculture, if he grant the skill of cultivating a field, one word from these which have been read could be scattered far and wide to such an extent that—if your capacity to listen would permit—scarcely would a day suffice for us to treat it. We shall attempt, nevertheless, as we are able, to discuss some things even if it is not possible for us to treat everything nor for

---

1 Cf. Origen *Phil.* 10.2 (*Hom. Jer.* 39); Clement *Paed.* 1.11.
2 Mt 13.31–32.
3 1 Cor 1.20; Cf. Dio Chrysostom 12.1–5.
4 Mt 13.32.

you to hear all things. For I also think that it is important to recognize that there is knowledge of these words beyond our power. Let us see, therefore, what the text of Exodus says at the beginning, and, as briefly as possible, let us follow it so far as it edifies the hearers. May you help with your prayers, that the Word of God may be present with us and deign himself to be the leader of our discourse.

(2) "These," its says, "are the names of the sons of Israel who entered Egypt with Jacob, their father (each one entered with his whole house): Ruben, Simeon, Levi, Juda," and the other patriarchs. "Joseph, however, was in Egypt. All the souls of Jacob's house were seventy-five."[5] I think what the prophet says is similar to this mystery, if anyone is able to perceive it: "My people descended into Egypt to dwell there and were carried off into Assyria by force."[6] If anyone, therefore, can compare these texts with one another, he can also understand from these texts what has been discussed by our predecessors or even our contemporaries, and also at times by us: what "Egypt" is into which the people of God descended, not so much for dwelling as for cultivating; who, moreover, the "Assyrians" are who, asserting force, carried them off. Consequently, he will perceive what is the number and order of the patriarchs, or what are designated as their houses and households which are said to have "entered Egypt with Jacob their father." For the text says, "Ruben with his whole house and Levi with his whole house," and also all the others. "Joseph, however, was in Egypt" and took a wife from Egypt. And though he was in Egypt, nevertheless, he is considered in the number of the patriarchs.

Anyone, therefore, can perhaps, "by comparing spiritual things with spiritual things"[7] and putting old things together with new and new with old, perceive the mystery of Egypt and the descent of the patriarchs into it, if he can investigate those words spiritually and follow the thought of the Apostle when

---

5 Ex 1.1–5.
6 Is 52.4.
7 1 Cor 2.13.

he distinguishes and separates Israel and says that there is a certain "Israel according to the flesh"[8] which doubtlessly suggests that there is another Israel according to the spirit. The Lord's statement also points this out to anyone who considers it carefully. When he says of a certain person, "Behold a true Israelite in whom there is no guile,"[9] he also gives it to be understood that some are true Israelites, others, without doubt, are not true. But the careful student will also observe the differences between the tribes, that he may conjecture what excellence was seen in the tribe of Levi because the priests and ministers of the Lord are chosen from it; what eminence also the Lord perceived in the tribe of Juda, because kings and princes are taken from it and, what is greatest of all, because also our Lord and Savior was born from it according to the flesh.[10] I do not know if privileges of this kind are to be ascribed to the merits of those from whose stock they derive their name or origin, that is, to Juda himself or Levi or each of those who gave his name to a tribe. That which John writes in the Apocalypse about the people who believed in Christ moves me to this application. For John says, "From the tribe of Ruben twelve thousand" and "from the tribe of Simeon twelve thousand" and likewise twelve thousand from each tribe whom all together, he says, were "one hundred forty-four thousand," who had not defiled themselves with women, but had remained virgins.[11] It certainly cannot be an absurd suggestion that this can be applied to those Jewish tribes, Simeon, Levi, and the others which derived their descent from Jacob.

I, at least, dare not advance farther by inquiring to which fathers, therefore, that number of virgins, so equal, so whole, so well arranged that no one is counted superior or inferior to another, is to be ascribed. It is with some risk that I proceed even to this point. The Apostle, however, makes some suggestions for those who are able to see farther, when he says: "For

---

8 1 Cor 10.18.
9 Jn 1.47.
10 Cf. Heb 7.14.
11 Rv 7.4–8, 14.4. Cf. Origen *Comm. Jn.* 1.1–2.

which reason I bow my knees to the Father of our Lord Jesus
Christ, from whom all paternity in the heavens and earth is
named."[12] And indeed, the meaning concerning earthly paternity does not appear to be difficult, for the fathers of tribes or
houses to whom the succession of posterity is ascribed are
called[13] collectively "all paternity." But what it means in
heaven; how or in what manner there are fathers; or for what
heavenly posterities "paternity" is mentioned, he alone knows
whose "is the heaven of heaven, and who gave the earth to the
sons of men."[14]

(3) The fathers, therefore, descended into Egypt, "Ruben,
Simeon, Levi, each with all his house."[15] How might someone
also explain that "they entered Egypt with their whole house"?
The text says in addition, "And all the souls that entered with
Jacob were seventy-five."[16] Here now the prophetic word, by
mentioning "souls," almost disclosed the mystery which it had
everywhere concealed. It reveals that it says these things not
about bodies, but about souls. Nevertheless it still has its own
veil. It is usually believed that "souls" mean men.

"Seventy-five souls descended into Egypt with Jacob."[17]
Those are the souls which Jacob begot. I do not think that any
man can beget a soul unless, perhaps, he be someone like that
man who said, "For although you have many thousand teachers in Christ, you have not many fathers. For in Christ Jesus I
begot you through the Gospel."[18] Such are those men who
beget and give birth to souls, as he says elsewhere, "My little
children, with whom I am in labor again, until Christ be
formed in you."[19] For others either do not wish to have the
trouble of this kind of begetting or are not able. In short, what
did Adam himself say at the beginning? "This is now bone of

12 Eph 3.14–15.
13 Read *appellantur* with BCF.
14 Ps 113.24.
15 Ex 1.2.
16 Ex 1.5.
17 Ex 1.5.
18 1 Cor 4.15.
19 Gal 4.19.

my bones and flesh of my flesh."[20] He does not add, however, "and soul of my soul." But I wish that you would tell me, Adam, if you recognized "bone of" your "bones" and perceived "flesh of" your "flesh," why you did not understand also that a soul had proceeded from your soul. For if you handed on all things which were in you, why did you not mention the soul, which is the best part of the whole man, with the other things? But he appears to indicate to those who understand that he acknowledges that the things which are of the earth are his own, but does not dare call his own what he knows are not of the earth when he says, "Bone of my bones and flesh of my flesh."[21] But also Laban likewise, when he says to Jacob, "You are my bone and my flesh,"[22] does not appear to dare call his own anything more than what he recognizes to be of earthly blood relationship. There is to be sure, another kinship of souls which is either associated with Jacob descending into Egypt or is ascribed to the other patriarchs and saints under the enumeration of mystical posterity. But I do not know how a very violent surge of waves carries us off into the deep. Sailing in the vicinity of land we arranged to maintain our course and, as it were, to graze the edge of the shore. Let us return, therefore, to those things which are added subsequently.

(4) "Joseph," the text says, "died and all his brothers and all that generation. But the sons of Israel increased and were multiplied and were extended into a great multitude and became very strong, for the land multiplied them."[23] While Joseph was living it is not reported that the sons of Israel were multiplied nor is anything at all mentioned about increases and multitudes in these times. I, believing in the words of my Lord Jesus Christ, do not think that one "iota or one point" in the Law and prophets is void of mysteries, nor do I think "any of these things can pass away until all things come about."[24] But

---

20 Gn 2.23.
21 Gn 2.23.
22 Gn 29.14.
23 Ex 1.6–7.
24 Mt 5.18.

since our ability is small, let us attack those things now in which we may advance more safely.

The sons of Israel were very few before our Joseph died, who was sold for thirty pieces of silver by Juda one of his brothers. But when he tasted death for all,[25] by which "he destroyed him who had the rule of death, that is the devil,"[26] the people of faith were multiplied "and the sons of Israel were extended and the land multiplied them and they increased exceedingly beyond measure."[27] For unless, as he said, "a grain of wheat had fallen into the earth and died,"[28] the Church would certainly not have produced this huge harvest of the whole earth. Therefore after "the grain fell into the earth and died," this whole crop of the faithful arose from it "and the sons of Israel were multiplied and became very strong."[29] For "the voice" of the apostles "went out into all the earth and their words to the ends of the earth"[30] and through them, as it is written, "the word of the Lord increased and was multiplied."[31] This has reference to a very great mystical meaning. But let us not omit the moral aspect in these words also for it edifies the souls of the hearers.

If, therefore, Joseph die in you also, that is, if you assume the dying of Christ in your body and you make your members dead to sin, then "the sons of Israel are multiplied" in you.[32] The "sons of Israel" are interpreted as good and spiritual senses. If, therefore, the senses of the flesh are put to death, the senses of the spirit increase, and while the vices in you are dying daily, the number of virtues is being increased. But also the "land multiplies" you in good works, which are accomplished through the body. But if you want me to show you from the Scriptures who it is whom the land multiplied, con-

---

25 Cf. Heb 2.9.
26 Heb 2.14.
27 Ex 1.7.
28 Jn 12.24.
29 Ex 1.7.
30 Ps 18.5.
31 Acts 12.24.
32 Ex 1.7.

sider the apostle Paul as he says: "But if to live in the flesh, this is to me the fruit of labor, and what I shall choose I do not know. For I am straitened between two, having a desire to be dissolved and to be with Christ, for this is much better; but to remain in the flesh is more needful for you."[33] Do you see how the "land multiplied" this man? For while he remains in the land, that is in his flesh, he is multiplied by founding Churches; he is multiplied by acquiring a people for God and by preaching the gospel of God "from Jerusalem all the way round to Illyricum."[34] But let us see what is added subsequently.

(5) "But another king arose in Egypt," the text says, "who did not know Joseph. And he said to his people, 'Behold, the race of the sons of Israel is a great multitude and is stronger than us.'"[35] First of all I wish to investigate who the king is in Egypt who knows Joseph and who he is who does not know him. For while he who knew Joseph reigned, the sons of Israel are not reported to have been afflicted nor exhausted "by mud and brick." Nor is it reported that their males were killed and their females kept alive. But when he who did not know Joseph arose and began to reign, then all these things are reported to have happened. Let us see, therefore, who that king is.

If the Lord guides us, and our understanding illuminated by the Lord always remembers Christ, as Paul writes to Timothy, "Remember that Christ Jesus has arisen from the dead,"[36] as long as it remembers these things in Egypt, that is in our flesh, our spirit holds the kingdom with justice and does not exhaust the sons of Israel, whom we said above to be the rational senses or virtues of the soul, "by mud and brick,"[37] nor does it weaken them with earthly cares and troubles. But if our understanding should lose the memory of these things, if it should turn away from God, if it should become ignorant of Christ, then the wisdom of the flesh which is hostile to God[38]

---

33 Phil 1.22–24.
34 Cf. Rom 15.19.
35 Ex 1.8–9.
36 2 Tm 2.8.
37 Ex 1.14.
38 Cf. Rom 8.7.

succeeds to the royal power and addresses its own people, bodily pleasures. When the leaders of the vices have been called together for consultation, deliberation is undertaken against the sons of Israel. They discuss how the sons of Israel may be distressed, how they may be oppressed. Their goal is to afflict the sons of Israel "by mud and bricks"; to expose the males and raise the females; to build the cities of Egypt and "fortified cities."[39]

These words were not written to instruct us in history, nor must we think that the divine books narrate the acts of the Egyptians. What has been written "has been written for our instruction and admonition."[40] Its purpose is that you, who hear these words, who perhaps have already received the grace of baptism and have been numbered among the sons of Israel and received God as king in yourself and later you wish to turn away and do the works of the world, to do deeds of the earth and muddy services, may know and recognize that "another king has arisen in you who knows not Joseph,"[41] a king of Egypt, and that he is compelling you to his works and is making you labor in bricks and mud for himself. It is he who leads you by whips and blows to wordly works with magistrates and supervisors put over you that you may build cities for him. It is he who makes you run about through the world to disturb the elements of sea and earth for lust. It is this king of Egypt who makes you agitate the forum with lawsuits and weary your neighbors with altercations for a little piece of land, to say nothing about lying in ambush for chastity, to deceive inno-cence, to commit foul things at home, cruel things abroad, shameful things within your conscience. When, therefore, you see yourself acting in these ways, know that you are a soldier for the king of Egypt, which is to be led by the spirit of this world.

But if also something even more profound is to be under-stood from this, that "king who knew not Joseph" can be seen

39 Cf. Ex 1.10–16.
40 1 Cor 10.11.
41 Ex 1.8.

to be the devil. He is "that fool who has said in his heart: 'there is no God.'"[42] He addresses his people, the apostate angels, and says, "Behold the race of the sons of Israel"—meaning these, of course, who can see God with their minds—"is a great multitude and is stronger than us. Come, therefore, let us restrain them, lest perhaps they increase and, when war shall befall us, these also side with our adversaries and, overcoming us, they shall depart from our land."[43] But whence does the devil perceive this? Whence does he understand that Israel is a great nation and stronger than his own people, unless from the fact that he has often met them in combat; has often struggled with them and has often been overcome? For he also knows that Jacob himself wrestled and, with the help of an angel, held his opponent and prevailed with God.[44] I do not doubt that he also was aware of the struggles of other saints and had often borne spiritual struggles and hence says, "The race of the sons of Israel is very great and is stronger than us."[45] But also his fear that some day "war befall" them and the sons of Israel "side with" his "adversaries" and when they have been conquered, depart from his land indicates to me that he perceived beforehand what had been disclosed from time to time about the advent of Christ by the holy patriarchs or prophets, and hence knows that war threatens himself. He perceives that he will come "who despoils his principalities and powers and with confidence conquers them and fastens them to the wood of his cross."[46] Therefore, when his whole race has been called together, he desires to restrain and limit in men the rational sense, which now is figuratively called Israel. Therefore, "he sets taskmasters over them,"[47] to compel them to learn works of the flesh, as also it says in the Psalms: "And they were mingled among the heathens, and learned their works."[48] He teaches

---

42 Ps 13.1.
43 Ex 1.10–11.
44 Cf. Gn 32.25–30.
45 Ex 1.9.
46 Cf. Col 2.14–15.
47 Ex 1.11.
48 Ps 105.35.

them also to build cities for Pharao, "Phithom," which in our
language means "mouth of rebellion" or "mouth of the abyss,"
"and Ramesses" which is translated as "the commotion of a
moth," "and On, that is Heliopolis" which is called "city of the
sun."[49]

Do you see what sort of cities Pharao commands to be built
for himself! "Rebelling mouth," it says, for the mouth rebels
when it speaks a lie and when it rebels from truth and proof.
For he "was a liar from the beginning"[50] and, therefore, wishes
such cities to be built for himself. Or also, mouth of the abyss,
because his place is the abyss of ruin and destruction. And
another of his cities is the commotion of a moth. For all who
follow him gather their treasures there where "the moth destroys and thieves dig through and steal."[51] But they also build
the city of the sun for him with a false name because "he
changes himself as an angel of light."[52] By these means, therefore, he hinders, by these means he seizes the minds which
were made to see God.

But he foresees that war threatens himself and he perceives
that the swift destruction of his people is near. Therefore he
says, "The race of Israel is stronger than us."[53] Would that he
might also say this about us; that he might feel that we are
stronger than himself! How will he be able to feel this? If, when
he hurls evil thoughts at me and very bad desires, I should not
receive them, but repel his "fiery darts with the shield of
faith."[54] If, in all things which he suggests to my mind, I,
mindful of Christ my Lord, should say: "Go behind me, Satan.
For it is written, 'You shall adore the Lord your God, and shall
serve only him.'"[55] If, therefore, we should do these things with
all faith and conscience, he says of us also, "The race of Israel is

---

49 See Appendix, 19, 20, and 21.
50 Cf. Jn 8.44.
51 Cf. Mt 6.19.
52 Cf. 2 Cor 11.14.
53 Ex 1.9.
54 Cf. Eph 6.16.
55 Mt 4.10.

great and is stronger than us."[56]

But also in this which he says, "Lest perhaps war befall us and these also side with our adversaries,"[57] he foresees from the words of the prophets that war will come to himself and that he will be left by the sons of Israel and that they will side with his adversary and be added to the Lord. For this is what the prophet Jeremiah predicted about him: "As the partridge has cried out, she has gathered a brood not her own, so is he who has made his wealth unjustly; in the midst of his days his wealth shall leave him and in his last days he shall be a fool."[58] He understands, therefore, that "the partridge has gathered a brood not her own" has been said of himself and that these whom "he has gathered unjustly will leave him in the midst of his days" and follow their Lord and creator Christ Jesus who has begotten them. "He has gathered," however, "those whom he did not beget." And, therefore, "he shall be left a fool in his last days" when "the whole creation" which now "groans" by virtue of his tyranny[59] takes refuge with "its maker" and parent. And he is indignant at this and says: Lest conquering us they depart from our land."[60] He does not want us to leave his land, but wants us always to "bear the image of the earthly."[61] For if we take refuge with his opponent, that is with him who prepared the kingdom of heaven for us, we must leave "the image of the earthly" and receive "the image of the heavenly."[62] For that reason, therefore, Pharao appoints "taskmasters" to teach us their skills, to make us contrivers of malice, to tutor us in evils. And because those masters and teachers of malice whom Pharao put over us are many, and there is a huge multitude of that kind of supervisors, all of whom drive, command, and extort earthly works, therefore, when the Lord Jesus comes, he makes others masters and teachers. They fight against Pharao's taskmasters and subdue all their "prin-

---

56 Ex 1.9.
57 Ex 1.10.
58 Jer 17.11.
59 Cf. Rom 8.22.
60 Ex 1.11.
61 1 Cor 15.49.
62 Cf. 1 Cor 15.49.

cipalities and powers and virtues."[63] They defend the sons of
Israel from the taskmasters' violence and teach us the works of
Israel. They teach us again to see God with the mind, to leave
the works of Pharao, to depart from the land of Egypt, to cast
aside Egyptian and barbarian customs. They teach us to lay
aside the whole "old man with his deeds" and "to put on the
new, who has been created in accordance with God,"[64] always to
be renewed from day to day according to the image of him who
made us,[65] Christ Jesus our Lord, "to whom belongs glory and
sovereignty forever and ever. Amen."[66]

63 Cf. Eph 1.20–22.
64 Cf. Eph 4.22–24.
65 Cf. Col 3.10; 2 Cor 4.16.
66 1 Pt 4.11.

HOMILY II
On the midwives and the birth of Moses

HAT "KING WHO KNEW NOT JOSEPH"[1] devises many things a-
gainst the people of God and is always seeking new
methods of harming them. But at this time his shrewd-
ness goes beyond measure, when by the service of the midwives, by whose skill life usually is preserved, he tries to destroy
the offspring of the race. What does the text say? "And the
king of the Egyptians spoke to the Hebrew midwives, one of
whom was named Sephora and the other Phua, and said,
'When you shall serve as midwives to the Hebrew women and
they shall be near birth, if it be a male child, kill it; if a female,
preserve it.' "[2] But the following statement adds: "But the
midwives feared God and did not do as the king of Egypt had
commanded them, and they preserved the male children."[3]

If what is written were to be taken to relate historical facts,
the statement in Scripture that "the midwives did not do as the
king of Egypt commanded them,"[4] would seem impossible of
being correct. For we find no evidence that the midwives did
not preserve the lives of the females whom the king of Egypt
ordered preserved. For thus he said, "If it is a male child, kill it;
if a female, preserve it."[5] And if "the midwives did not do as the
king of Egypt had commanded,"[6] they should, certainly, as
they were preserving the male children against the command
of the kind, so have killed the females, that this also might be
against the command of the king. For to have preserved the

---

1 Ex 1.8.
2 Ex 1.15–16.
3 Ex 1.17.
4 Ex 1.17.
5 Ex 1.16.
6 Ex 1.17.

lives of the females is to have acted according to the Pharao's command. These words, however, are for those who are friends of the letter and do not think that the Law is spiritual and is to be understood spiritually.[7] But we, who have learned that all things which are written are written not to relate ancient history, but for our discipline and use,[8] understand that these things which are said also happen now not only in this world, which is figuratively called Egypt, but in each of us also.

Let us inquire, therefore, why the king of Egypt, who is "the prince of this world,"[9] does not wish the male children to be preserved and wishes the females preserved. If you remember, we have often pointed out in our discussions that the flesh and the passions of the flesh are designated by the females, but the man is the rational sense and the intellectual spirit.[10] Pharao, king and prince of Egypt, therefore, hates the rational sense which is able to understand heavenly things, to perceive God, and "to seek the things which are above."[11] He desires this sense to be killed and destroyed. He desires, however, that whatever things are of the flesh live. And what pertains to bodily matter he desires not only to live, but also to be increased and cultivated. For he wants everyone to understand fleshly things, desire temporal things, and seek "the things which are on the earth."[12] He wants no one to "lift his eyes to heaven,"[13] no one to inquire whence he has come here, no one to remember the fatherland of paradise.[14]

When, therefore, you see men living in pleasures and delights, wallowing in luxury, devoting themselves to feasts,

---

7 Cf. Rom 7.14.
8 Cf. 1 Cor 10.11.
9 Cf. Jn 16.11.
10 Cf. Philo *L.A.* 3.3.243; *QE.* 1.8.
11 Col 3.1.
12 Cf. Col 3.1–2.
13 Cf. Lk 18.13.
14 Origen (See *De Princ.* 1.4.1, 2.8.3–4, 2.9.1–2,6) believed that all souls existed originally as pure souls in the presence of God before their existence in bodies in this earthly life. His Platonism is obvious in this doctrine (See Plato *Phdr.* 246 B–D).

wine, banquets, beds, and shamelessness, you may be sure that
the king of Egypt is killing the males and preserving the
females. But if you should see some extraordinary person,
"one in a thousand," who turns to God, raises his eyes upwards,
seeks the things which are enduring and eternal, contemplates
not those things "which are seen, but which are not seen,"[15]
hates pleasures, loves chastity, flees wantonness and cultivates
virtue, Pharao desires to kill that person as if he were a male, a
man. He persecutes him; he pursues him; he fights against him
with a thousand devices. He hates such people. He does not
permit them to live in Egypt. This is why God's servants and all
who seek God are held in disrespect and contempt in this
world. This is why they are exposed to abuses, filled with
reproaches, hatreds and persecutions are stirred up against
them. It is because Pharao, who loves females, hates them; he
hates males of this kind. He even attempts to corrupt the
midwives and to accomplish what he desires by them. Their
names are also indicated to us by the providence of the Holy
Spirit who wished these things to be written. "Sephora," the
text says was "one," which is translated as "sparrow," and
"Phua" which we can call either "blushing" or "modest."[16] By
these women, therefore, Pharao seeks to kill the males and to
preserve only the females.

(2) But what does Scripture say? "The midwives feared God
and did not do as the king of Egypt commanded them."[17]

Some before us have said that those midwives represent
rational understanding. For the midwives are as inter-
mediaries and assist the males being born as well as the females. That common understanding of rational knowledge,
therefore, falls to nearly every mind, instructs all, assists all.
Should one be a masculine soul and wish to seek heavenly
things and follow divine things, he will come better prepared
for an understanding of divine things as if attended and
assisted by understanding of that kind. For one midwife is like

---

15 Cf. 2 Cor 4.18.
16 Cf. Ex 1.15. See Appendix, 22 and 23.
17 Ex 1.17.

a sparrow who teaches lofty things and calls forth souls to fly to
the heights on rational wings of instruction. The other, who is
blushing or modest, is moral. She regulates morals, teaches
modesty, and institutes integrity.[18]

It seems to me, however, since Scripture says of these
women, "Because they feared God, they did not carry out the
command of the king of Egypt,"[19] that the two midwives serve
as a figure of the two testaments. "Sephora," which is translated as sparrow, can be applied to the Law which "is
spiritual."[20] But "Phua," who is blushing or modest, indicates
the Gospels which are red with the blood of Christ and glow
reddish through the whole world by the blood of his passion.
The souls, therefore, which are born in the Church are attended by these testaments as if by midwives, because the
entire antidote of instruction is conferred on them from the
reading of the Scriptures.

Pharao, nevertheless, attempts to kill the males of the
Church by means of these testaments when he suggests heretical meanings and perverted teachings in the divine Scriptures
to those who study. But God's foundation stands immovable.
For "the midwives fear God,"[21] that is they teach the fear of
God, because "the fear of the Lord is the beginning of wisdom."[22] In fact, I think also that clause which follows where the
text says, "Because the midwives feared God, they made
houses for themselves,"[23] is applied more suitably in this way.
This statement can make no sense according to the letter. For
what is the relationship that the text should say, "Because the
midwives feared God, they made houses for themselves"?[24] It is
as if a house is built because God is feared. If this be taken as it
stands written, not only does it appear to lack logic, but also to

---

18 This entire paragraph probably represents Origen's report of how his
   predecessors had interpreted this verse. His own interpretation follows in
   the next paragraph, which begins, *mihi tamen . . . videntur.*
19 Ex 1.17.
20 Cf. Rom 7.14.
21 Ex 1.17.
22 Ps 110.10.
23 Ex 1.21.
24 Ex 1.21.

be inane. But if you should see how the Scriptures of the Old and New Testaments, teaching the fear of God, make the houses of the Church and fill the whole earth with houses of prayer, then what is written will appear to have been written rationally.

So, therefore, because those midwives fear God and teach the fear of God, they do not carry out the command of the king of Egypt, but keep the males alive. It is not said, however, that they obeyed the command of the king to keep the females alive. I confidently dare to say in accordance with the sense of Scripture that those midwives do not keep the females alive. For vices are not taught in the Churches nor wantonness proclaimed nor sins nourished—this is what Pharao wishes when he orders the females to be kept alive—but virtue alone is cultivated and it alone is nourished.

But let us apply these words also to ourselves. If you too fear God, you do not carry out the command of the king of Egypt. For he commands you to live in pleasure, to love the present world, to desire present things.[25] If you fear God and perform the office of midwife for your own soul, if you desire to confer salvation on it, you do not do these things. You keep alive the male which is in you. You attend and assist your inner man[26] and seek eternal life for him by good actions and understandings.

(3) But after this, when Pharao saw that he could not kill the Israelite males by the midwives, "he commanded all the people saying, 'Throw every male child which has been born to the Hebrews into the river and keep every female alive.' "[27] Notice that "the prince of this world"[28] orders his people to seize our infants and cast them into the river. He orders that his people continually lie in wait for the first sign of the birth of our infants and as soon as they touch the breasts of the church, force entry, ravage, pursue, and overwhelm with the waves

---

25 Cf. 1 Jn 2.15–16.
26 Cf. 2 Cor 4.16.
27 Ex 1.22.
28 Jn 16.11.

and billows of this age. "Take heed what you hear."[29] The wisdom of God says through Solomon, "Understand intelligently what is set before you."[30] Behold what threatens you as soon as you have been born, nay rather reborn. This is what you read in the Gospel, that Jesus, as soon as he ascended from baptism, "was led by the Spirit into the desert to be tempted by the devil."[31] This is also, therefore, what Pharao ordered his people in this passage: to attack, to snatch away, to drown the Hebrew baby boys as soon as they were born. This is also, perhaps, what is said by the prophet: "For the waters are come in even to my soul. I stick fast in the mire of the deep and there is no sure standing."[32]

But for this reason Christ has overcome and conquered, that he might open the way for you to conquer. For this reason he conquered while fasting,[33] that you also might know that "the race of demons of this kind" is to be conquered "by fasts and prayers."[34] For this reason he despised "all the kingdoms of the world" which were offered to him "and their glory,"[35] that you also, despising the glory of the world, might be able to conquer the tempter.

The Egyptians, therefore, to whom Pharao gave orders, keep only the female children alive. They hate the males, for they hate virtues. They rear only vices and pleasures. And now, therefore, if any male happen to be born to the Hebrews, the Egyptians are lying in wait that they may immediately persecute and kill him, unless the Hebrews beware, unless they watch and hide the male offspring. In fact, Scripture reports that "a woman from the tribe of Levi who bore a male child and saw him to be a fine child hid him three months."[36] Consider if this is not admonished for our sake, lest we perform our good

---

29 Mk 4.24.
30 Prv 23.1.
31 Mt 4.1.
32 Ps 68.2–3.
33 Cf. Mt 4.2.
34 Cf. Mk 9.29.
35 Mt 4.8.
36 Ex 2.1–2.

deeds in public, "lest we do our righteousness before men,"[37] but rather that "after the door has been shut we might pray to our Father in secret,"[38] and that "the left hand might not know what our right hand does."[39] For unless our good deed be in secret, it will be plundered by the Egyptians, it will be attacked, it will be thrown into the river, it will be submerged by waves and floods. If, therefore, I give alms because it is a work of God, I beget a male child. But if I should do it that it may be noted by men and I should seek praise from men and shall not have concealed it, my alsmgiving is snatched away by the Egyptians and is plunged into the river and I, with so much labor and zeal, have begotten a male child for the Egyptians. Do not think, therefore, O people of God who hear this, as we have now often said, that stories of the forefathers are read to you. Think rather that you are being taught through these stories that you may learn the right order of life, moral teachings, the struggles of faith in virtue.

(4) When, therefore, those of the tribe of Levi "saw that it was a fine child, they hid him three months. And when they were not able to hide him any longer, his mother," the text says, "took a basket and smeared it with bitumen and placed the child in it and put it in the marsh along the river. And his sister watched from a distance to see what would happen to him. Now Pharao's daughter descended to bathe in the river and heard the child crying. She sent and took him up. And Pharao's daughter said, "This is one of the Hebrew children."[40] What follows relates how his sister said that she would call the boy's mother to nurse him. "And Pharao's daughter said to her, 'Keep this child for me and nurse him for me, and I will pay you.' And when she had nursed him and he grew stronger, she brought him to Pharao's daughter and he became her son. And she called his name Moses, saying, 'I took you up from the water.' "[41] Each of these statements is filled with great mysteries

---

37 Cf. Mt 6.1.
38 Cf. Mt 6.6.
39 Cf. Mt 6.3.
40 Ex 2.1–6.
41 Ex 2.9–10.

and demands much time. If we were to spend a whole day on this passage it would scarcely be sufficient. Nevertheless, we must briefly touch on some things for the edification of the Church.

I think Pharao's daughter can be regarded as the Church which is gathered from the Gentiles. Although she has an impious and hostile father, nevertheless, the prophet says to her, "Hear, O daughter, and behold and incline your ear. Forget your people and the house of your father because the king has desired your beauty."[42] This, therefore, is the daughter who leaves her father's house and comes to the waters to be washed from the sins which she had contracted in her father's house. And then immediately she experiences "deeply felt compassion"[43] and pities the child.

This Church, therefore, coming from the Gentiles finds Moses in the marsh lying cast off by his own people and exposed, and gives him out to be reared. He is reared by his own family and spends his childhood there. When, however, "he has grown stronger,"[44] he is brought to her and adopted as a son. We have already frequently argued in many places that the Law is referred to as Moses. The Church, therefore, coming to the waters of baptism, also took up the Law. The Law, however, had been enclosed in "a basket" and smeared with pitch and "bitumen."[45] The "basket" is a kind of covering woven together from twigs or papyrus or even formed from the bark of trees. The infant placed within this basket was seen exposed. The Law, therefore, was lying helpless enclosed in coverings of this kind, besmeared with pitch and bitumen. It was dirty and enclosed in cheap and offensive meanings of the Jews until the Church should come from the Gentiles and take it up from the muddy and marshy places and appropriate it to itself within courts of wisdom and royal houses. This Law, however, spends its childhood with its own people. With those who are not able to understand it spiritually it is little, an infant,

---

42 Ps 44.11.
43 Cf. Col 3.12.
44 Ex 2.10.
45 Cf. Ex 2.3.

and has milk as its food. But when Moses comes to the Church, when he enters the house of the Church, he grows stronger and more robust. For when the veil of the letter is removed "perfect and solid food"[46] is discovered in its text.

Why is it, nevertheless, that she who both gave birth to and raised the Law also receives wages from the daughter of Pharao for rearing it? What is it that the Synagogue receives from the Church? I think that can be understood from the words of the same Moses: "I will provoke you to envy against a non-nation; I will stir you up to anger against a foolish nation."[47] The Synagogue, therefore, receives this as a wage from the Church: that it might not further worship idols. For seeing the Gentiles converted to God so that they no longer know idols, so that they worship no one except the one God, the Synagogue feels shame farther now to worship idols. The Synagogue, therefore, receives this benefit from the Church because it is seen to have reared the little Law for it.

But let us also take up the Law of God to ourselves when we come to the waters even if we had Pharao as father, even if "the prince of this world"[48] begot us in evil works. Let not its cheap and obscure cover of the letter be despised by us. Let us give up what is small and milky. Let us take up what is perfect and robust and let us set these up within the royal dwellings of our heart. Let us have Moses large and strong. Let us think nothing small, nothing lowly about him, but let him be totally magnificent, totally distinguished, totally elegant. For whatever is spiritual, whatever of elevated understanding is great in every respect. And let us pray our Lord Jesus Christ that he himself might reveal and show us in what manner Moses is great and elevated.[49] For he himself "reveals" it to whom he wishes "by the Holy Spirit."[50] "To him belong glory and sovereignty forever and ever. Amen."[51]

---

46 Cf. Heb 5.12–14.
47 Dt 32.21.
48 Jn 16.11.
49 Cf. Ex 11.3.
50 Cf. 1 Cor 2.10.
51 Cf. 1 Pt 4.11.

HOMILY III
On that which is written: "I am feeble in speech and slow in tongue."[1]

HILE MOSES WAS IN EGYPT and "was educated in all the wisdom of the Egyptians," he was not "feeble in speech" nor "slow in tongue" nor did he profess to be ineloquent.[2] For, so far as concerned the Egyptians, his speech was sonorous and his eloquence incomparable. But when he began to hear the voice of God and recognize divine communications, then he perceived his own voice to be meager and feeble and he understands his own tongue to be slow and impeded. When he began to recognize that true Word which "was in the beginning with God,"[3] then he announces that he is mute. But let us use an analogy that what we are saying may be more easily understood. If a rational man be compared to the dumb animals, although he may be ignorant and unlearned, he will appear eloquent in comparison to those who are devoid of both reason and speech. But if he be compared to learned and eloquent men who are most excellent in all wisdom, he will appear ineloquent and dumb. But if someone should contemplate the divine Word himself and look at the divine wisdom itself, however learned and wise he be, he will confess that he is a dumb animal in comparison with God to a much greater extent than the cattle are in comparison with us. The blessed David was doubtless contemplating this and weighing himself in the balance of the divine wisdom when he said, "I became like a beast of burden before you."[4] It is in this sense,

1 Ex 4.10.
2 Cf. Acts 7.22; Ex 4.10.
3 Jn 1.1. Philo, *Mos.* 1.83, says that Moses declared that he was feeble in speech and slow in tongue, "especially after he heard God speaking, for he considered human eloquence in comparison with God's to be dumbness."
4 Ps 72.22.

therefore, that Moses also, the greatest of the prophets, says to God in the present text that he is "feeble in speech" and "slow in tongue" and that he is not eloquent.[5] For all men, in comparison to the divine Word must be considered not only ineloquent, but also dumb.

(2) Divine dignity, therefore, recompenses him because he advanced into self-understanding where lies the greatest portion of wisdom. Hear how rich and magnificent were his gifts. "I," the text says, "will open your mouth and instruct you what you must say."[6] Blessed are those whose mouth God opens that they might speak. God opens the prophets' mouth and fills it with his eloquence, just as he says in the present text: "I will open your mouth and instruct you what you must say."[7] But God also says through David, "Open your mouth wide and I will fill it."[8] Paul likewise says, "That speech might be given to me in the opening of my mouth."[9] God, therefore, opens the mouth of those who speak the words of God.

I fear, however, that, on the contrary, there are some whose mouth the devil opens. For it is certain that the devil has opened the mouth of the man who speaks falsehood to speak falsehood. The devil has opened the mouth of the man who speaks false testimony. He has opened the mouth of those who bring forth scurrility, foulness, and other things of this kind from their mouth. I fear that also the devil opens the mouth "of the whisperers and disparagers,"[10] and also of those who "bring forth idle words for which an account must be given in the day of judgment."[11] Now indeed who doubts that the devil opens the mouth of those who "speak iniquity against the Most High,"[12] "who deny that my Lord Jesus Christ has come in the

---

5 Ex 4.10.
6 Ex 4.12.
7 Ex 4.12.
8 Ps 80.11.
9 Eph 6.19.
10 Cf. Rom 1.29–30.
11 Cf. Mt 12.36.
12 Ps 72.8.

flesh,"[13] or "who blaspheme the Holy Spirit" for whom "there will be forgiveness neither in the present nor in the future age"?[14]

Do you wish that I show you from the Scriptures how the devil opens the mouth of men of this kind who speak against Christ? Note what has been written about Judas, how it is reported that "Satan entered him,"[15] and that "the devil put it in his heart to betray Him."[16] He, therefore, having received the money, opened his mouth that "he might confer with the leaders and the Pharisees, how he might betray him."[17] Whence it seems to me to be no small gift to perceive the mouth which the devil opens. Such a mouth and words are not discerned without the gift of the Holy Spirit. Therefore, in the distributions of spiritual gifts, it is also added that "discernment of spirits" is given to certain people.[18] It is a spiritual gift, therefore, by which the spirit is discerned, as the Apostle says elsewhere, "Test the spirits, if they are from God."[19]

But as God opens the mouth of the saints, so, I think, God also may open the ears of the saints to hear the divine words. For thus Isaias the prophet says: "The Lord will open my ear that I may know when the word must be spoken."[20] So also the Lord opens eyes, as "the Lord opened Agar's eyes and she saw a well of living water."[21] But also Eliseus the prophet says: " 'Open, O Lord, the eyes of the servant that he may see that there are more with us than with the enemy.' And the Lord opened the eyes of the servant and behold, the whole mountain was full of horses and chariots and heavenly helpers."[22] For "the angel of the Lord encircles those who fear him and will deliver them."[23]

---

13 Cf. 2 Jn 7.
14 Cf. Lk 12.10.; Mt 12.32.
15 Jn 13.27.
16 Cf. Jn 13.2.
17 Cf. Lk 22.4.
18 Cf. 1 Cor 12.10.
19 Cf. 1 Jn 4.1.
20 Cf. Is 50.4–5.
21 Gn 21.19.
22 Cf. 4 Kgs 6.16–17.
23 Ps 33.8.

As we said, therefore, God opens the mouth, the ears and the eyes, that we may either speak, or discern or hear what words are of God. But I also take this which the prophet says to be meaningful: "The instruction of the Lord has opened my ear."[24] This, I take it, pertains to us, that is commonly to the whole Church of God. For if we live in the instruction of the Lord, "the instruction of the Lord" opens our "ear" also. But the ear which is opened by the instruction of the Lord is not always opened, but is sometimes opened, sometimes closed. Hear the lawgiver saying, "Do not receive a vain report."[25] If ever, therefore, vain things are said, if ever things are brought forth which are empty, improper, shameful, profane, wicked, he who knows "the instruction of the Lord," closes his ears and turns away from listening and says: "I, however, as one deaf, did not hear, and I was as one dumb who has not opened his mouth."[26] But if what is said is useful for the soul, if it is a word from God, if it teaches morals, if it invites virtues, if it restrains vices, the ears ought to stand open to teachings of this kind, and not only the ears, but also the heart and mind and every entrance of the soul should be thrown open to such a report.

The Law, nevertheless, has used great moderation in stating the precept, "You shall not receive a vain report."[27] It did not say, "You shall not hear a vain report," but "You shall not receive such." We frequently hear vain words. What Marcion says is vain. What Valentinus says is vain. All who speak against the creator God speak vain words. Nevertheless, we frequently listen to those words so that we can respond to them lest they secretly snatch away by their embellished speech some of the simple who are also our brothers. Therefore, we hear these words, but we do not receive them. For they are spoken by that mouth which the devil has opened. And, therefore, we should pray that the Lord may think it proper to open our mouth that we might be able to refute those who contradict us and to close the mouth which the devil opens. We have said these things

---

24 Is 50.5.
25 Ex 23.1.
26 Ps 37.14.
27 Ex 23.1.

about the statement: "I will open your mouth and instruct you what you must say."[28]

It is promised not only to Moses, however, that his mouth will be opened by the Lord, but also to Aaron. For it is said of him also, "I will open your mouth and his mouth, and I will instruct you what you shall do."[29] For Aaron also "went to meet" Moses and he departed from Egypt. Where, however, did he go to meet him; to what sort of place? For it is of interest where he whose mouth is to be opened by God "meets" Moses. "He went to meet him," it says, "on the mountain of God."[30] Do you see that his mouth is opened deservedly who can "go to meet Moses "on the mountain of God"? Peter, James, and John ascended the mountain of God that they might be worthy to see Jesus transfigured and that they might see Moses and Elias with him in glory. And you, therefore, unless you ascend the "mountain of God" and "go to meet" Moses there, that is unless you ascend the lofty understanding of the Law, unless you mount up to the peak of spiritual understanding, your mouth has not been opened by the Lord. If you stand in the lowly place of the letter and connect the text of the story with Jewish narratives, you have not gone to meet Moses "on the mountain of God," nor has God "opened your mouth" nor "instructed you in what you must say."[31] Unless, therefore, "Aaron had gone to meet Moses on the mountain,"[32] unless he had seen his sublime and elevated mind, unless he had perceived his lofty understanding, never would Moses have spoken the words of God to him nor delivered to him the power of signs and wonders nor have decreed him a participant in such a great mystery.

(3) But since it would take too long to speak about the individual things one after another, let us see what "Moses and Aaron" said "when they went in" to Pharao. "Thus says the Lord, 'Send my people out that they may serve me in the

---

28 Ex 4.12.
29 Ex 4.15.
30 Ex 4.27.
31 Cf. Ex 4.12.
32 Ex 4.27.

wilderness.' "[33] Moses does not wish the people to serve God while they are in Egypt, but to go out into the desert and serve the Lord there. This means, without doubt, that as long as anyone remains in the gloomy activities of the world and lives in the darkness of daily business he cannot "serve the Lord," for he is not able "to serve two Lords." He cannot "serve the Lord and mammon."[34] Therefore, we must go forth from Egypt. We must leave the world behind if we wish "to serve the Lord." I mean, however, that we must leave the world behind not in space, but in the soul; not by setting out on a journey, but by advancing in faith. Hear John saying these same things: "Little children, do not love the world nor those things which are in the world, since everything which is in the world is the desire of the flesh and the desire of the eyes."[35]

And what, however, does Moses say? Let us see how or to what extent he orders us to set out from Egypt. "We will go," he says, "a journey of three days into the wilderness and there we will sacrifice to the Lord our God."[36] What is the "journey of three days" which we are to go, that going out from Egypt we can arrive at the place in which we ought to sacrifice? I understand "way" to refer to him who said, "I am the way, the truth, and the life."[37] We are to go this way for three days. For he who "has confessed with his mouth the Lord Jesus and believed in his heart that God raised him from the dead" on the third day, "will be saved."[38] This, therefore, is "the way of three days" by which one arrives at the place in which the "sacrifice of praise"[39] is sacrificed and offered to the Lord. What we have said pertains to the mystical meaning.

But if we also require a place for the moral meaning which is very useful for us, we travel a "journey of three days" from Egypt if we thus preserve ourselves from all filth of soul, body,

---

33 Ex 5.1.
34 Cf. Lk 16.13; Mt 6.24.
35 1 Jn 2.15–16.
36 Ex 3.18.
37 Jn 14.6.
38 Cf. Rom 10.9.
39 Cf. Ps 49.14.

and spirit, that, as the Apostle said, "our spirit and soul and body may be kept whole in the day of Jesus Christ."[40] We travel a "journey of three days" from Egypt if, ceasing from worldy things we turn our rational, natural, moral wisdom to the divine laws. We travel a "journey of three days" from Egypt if, purifying our words, deeds, or thoughts—for these are the three things by which men can sin—we would be made "pure in heart" so that we could "see God."[41]

Do you wish to see, however, that this is what the Holy Spirit indicates in the Scriptures? When this Pharao, who is the prince of Egypt, sees that he is strongly pressed to send the people of God out, he wishes to effect by this inferior place that "they not go farther away," that they not travel the full three days. He says, "Go not far away."[42] He does not wish the people of God to be far from himself. He wishes them to sin, if not in deed, certainly in word: to fail, if not in word, certainly in thought. He does not want them to travel a full three days from himself. He wishes to have one day at least in us as his own. In some he has two days, in others he possesses the full three days. But blessed are those who withdraw a whole three days from him and he possesses no day in them as his own.

Do not suppose, therefore, that Moses led the people out of Egypt only at that time. Even now Moses, whom we have with us—"for we have Moses and the prophets"[43]—that is, the Law of God, wishes to lead you out of Egypt. If you would hear it, it wishes to make you "far" from Pharao. If only you would hear the Law of God and understand it spiritually, it desires to deliver you from the work of mud and chaff. It does not wish you to remain in the acitivities of the flesh and darkness, but to go out to the wilderness, to come to the place free from the confusions and disturbances of the world, to come to the rest of silence. For "words of wisdom are learned in silence and rest."[44] When you come to this place of rest, therefore, you will be able

---

40 1 Thes 5.23.
41 Cf. Mt 5.8.
42 Ex 8.24.
43 Cf. Lk 16.29.
44 Cf. Eccl 9.17.

"to sacrifice to the Lord" there. You will be able to know the Law of God and the virtue of the divine voice there. For that reason, therefore, Moses desires to bring you out of the midst of vacillating daily business and from the midst of noisy people. For that reason he desires you to depart from Egypt, that is from the darkness of ignorance that you might hear the Law of God and receive the light of knowledge.

But Pharao resists. "The ruler of this darkness"[45] does not wish you to relax; he does not wish you to be dragged away from his darkness and to be led to the light of knowledge. And hear what he says, "Who is he whose voice I shall heed? I do not know the Lord, and I will not send Israel out."[46] Do you hear what "the prince of this world" responds?[47] He says he does not know God. Do you see what crude pride does? Pride controls him as long as "he does not share in human sufferings and is not scourged with men."[48] A little later you will see how much he advances by scourgings, how much better he is made having been chastised. He who now says, "I do not know the Lord,"[49] will say later, when he shall have felt the force of the whip, "Pray to the Lord for me."[50] And not only this, but he will also admit with is own magicians as witnesses that "it is the finger of God"[51] in the power of the signs. Let no one, therefore, be so ignorant of divine discipline that he thinks the divine scourgings to be destruction or believes the chastenings of the Lord to be penal annihilation. Behold even Pharao, a most hard man; nevertheless, he profits when he has been scourged. He does not know the Lord before the scourgings; after being scourged he asks that Moses pray to the Lord for him. He has advanced by punishments to recognize why he deserves punishment. Therefore, he said, "I do not know the Lord and I am not sending Israel out."[52] But notice how, having been scourged,

---

45 Cf. Eph 6.12.
46 Ex 5.2.
47 Cf. Jn 16.11.
48 Cf. Ps 72.5.
49 Ex 5.2.
50 Ex 8.8.
51 Cf. Ex 8.19, where the magicians say this to Pharao.
52 Ex 5.2.

he corrects this statement in the Gospels. For it is written that
the demons cried out to the Lord and said, "Why have you
come to torment us before the time? We know who you are.
You are the Son of the living God."[53] When they have experienced torments they know the Lord. Before the scourgings he
says: "I do not know the Lord and I am not sending Israel
out."[54] But he will send Israel out and not only will he send
them out, but he himself will urge them to depart. For there is
no "fellowship between light and darkness," no "sharing between faith and unbelief."[55]

But what does he add further to his responses? "Why," he
says, "O Moses and Aaron do you turn my people aside from
their work? Each of you go off to your work."[56] While the
people are with him and work in "mud" and "brick," while they
are occupied in "chaff," he does not think them perverted, but
to be travelling the right way. But if the people say, I wish to go
"a way of three days" and "serve the Lord,"[57] he says they are
perverted by Moses and Aaron.

This indeed "was said to the ancients."[58] But even today, if
Moses and Aaron, that is the prophetic and priestly word, stir a
soul to the service of God, invite it to depart from the world, to
renounce all things which it possesses, to give attention to the
divine Law and to follow the word of God, immediately you
will hear it said by those who are of one mind with Pharao and
his friends: "See how men are seduced and perverted. Like
youths, they do not work, they do not serve as soldiers, they do
not do anything which profits them. They abandon necessary
and useful things and follow silliness and leisure. Is this what
serving God means? They do not wish to work and they seek
opportunities for idle leisure." These were Pharao's words at
that time, and now his friends and close associates say these
things.

---

53 Cf. Mt 8.29; Mk 1.24; Lk 4.34; Mt 16.16.
54 Ex 5.2.
55 Cf. 2 Cor 6.14–15.
56 Ex 5.4.
57 Cf. Ex 3.18.
58 Cf. Mt 5.24.

Pharao does not limit himself to words; scourgings also \
follow. He orders that the Hebrew scribes be beaten, that chaff
not be given, that work be exacted. This is what the fathers
endured. The people of God who are in the Church also often
suffer in a manner similar to them. For you will find, if you
consider those who have delivered themselves anew "to the
prince of this world,"[59] that they act with prosperous results,
that all things, as they themselves think, turn out favorably for
them. Often, however, not even these small and lowly things of
human sustenance prosper for the servants of God. I consider
such things to be the chaff which is handed out by Pharao. It
often turns out, therefore, that those who fear God lack even
this sustenance which is cheap and similar to chaff. They also
often endure the persecutions of tyrants and bear tortures and
fierce torments so that some, wearied, say to Pharao, "Why do
you afflict your people?"[60] For some, overcome by the scourgings, fall away from the faith and confess that they are the
people of Pharao. "For not all who are of Israel are Israelites;
nor because they are seed are they all also sons."[61] Those,
therefore, who are doubtful and wearied by the tribulations
also speak against Moses and Aaron and say, "From the day
which you went in to Pharao and went out, you made our odor
detestable before him."[62] They speak the truth, although perhaps they do not know what they say, just as Caiphas, when he
said, "It is expedient for you that one die for the people," was
speaking the truth, but did not know what he was saying.[63] For,
as the Apostle says, "We are a good odor of Christ," but he
adds, "To some an odor of life to life, but to others an odor of
death to death."[64] So also the prophetic word is "a sweet odor"
to those who believe, but to the doubting and unbelieving and
those who confess that they are Pharao's people, it becomes a
detestable odor.

---

59 Cf. Jn 16.11.
60 Cf. Ex 5.22 where Moses says this to God.
61 Rom 9.6–7.
62 Cf. Ex 5.23,21.
63 Jn 11.50.
64 2 Cor 2.15–16.

But Moses himself also says to the Lord, "Ever since I have spoken with Pharao, he has afflicted your people."[65] It is certain that before the word of God is heard, before the divine preaching is known, there is no trouble, there is no temptation, because war does not begin unless the trumpet sounds. But where the trumpet of preaching gives the signal for war, there affliction follows; there every troublesome fight arises. The people of God are afflicted from the moment that Moses and Aaron began to speak to Pharao. From the moment the word of God has been brought into your soul a struggle is necessarily stirred up within you between virtues and vices. Before the word which reproves comes, the vices within you continue in peaceful existence, but when the word of God begins to make a division between each, then a great disturbance arises and war without treaty is born. "For when can there be agreement between justice and injustice," immodesty and moderation, a lie and the truth?[66] And, therefore, let us not be greatly disturbed if our "odor" seems detestable to Pharao, for virtue is an abomination to vices.

Nay rather as it says later that Moses stood "before Pharao," let us also stand "against Pharao" and let us neither bow nor bend, but let us stand "having girded our loins with the truth and having shod our feet with the preparation of the Gospel of peace."[67] For thus the Apostle exhorts us saying, "Stand, therefore, and do not again submit to the yoke of slavery."[68] And again he says, "In which we stand, and we glory in the hope of the glory of God."[69] We stand confidently, however, if we pray to the Lord that "he set our feet upon the rock,"[70] lest that happen to us which the same prophet says: "But my feet were nearly shaken, and my steps nearly slackened."[71] Therefore, let us stand "before Pharao," that is, let us resist him in the

---

65 Cf. Ex 5.23.
66 Cf. 2 Cor 6.14.
67 Eph 6.14–15.
68 Gal 5.1.
69 Cf. Rom 5.2.
70 Cf. Ps 39.3.
71 Ps 72.2.

struggle as also the apostle Peter says, "Whom resist ye strong in the faith."[72] But Paul also says no less: "Stand in the faith and act like a man."[73] For if we stand strongly, that also which Paul prays for the disciples consequently happens. "God will swiftly grind Satan under your feet."[74] For the longer we stand firmly and staunchly the weaker and feebler Pharao will be. If, however, we begin to be either feeble or doubtful, he will become stronger and firmer against us. And truly that of which Moses gave a figure is fulfilled in us. For when Moses "lifted his hands" Amalec was conquered. But if "he cast" them "down" as though weary and put down weak arms, "Amalec would become strong."[75] So, therefore, let us also lift our arms in the power of the cross of Christ and "let us raise holy hands" in prayer "in every place without anger and dispute"[76] that we might deserve the Lord's help. For the apostle James also urges this same thing, saying, "Resist the devil and he will flee from you."[77] Therefore, let us go in full confidence that not only "may he flee from us," but also "Satan may be ground under our feet," as also Pharao was drowned in the sea and destroyed in the deep abyss. If, however, we withdraw from the Egypt of vices we will pass over the floods of the world as on a solid road through Jesus Christ our Lord, "to whom belong glory and sovereignty for ever and ever. Amen."[78]

---

72 1 Pt 5.9.
73 1 Cor 16.13.
74 Rom 16.20.
75 Cf. Ex 17.11.
76 Cf. 2 Tm 2.8.
77 Jas 4.7.
78 Cf. 1 Pt 4.11.

HOMILY IV
On the ten plagues with which Egypt was smitten

E HAVE JUST HEARD A MOST FAMOUS STORY READ. The story should be known in the whole world because of its importance. It relates that Egypt, along with Pharao the king, was chastened with great scourgings of signs and prodigies that they might restore to their natural freedom the Hebrew people whom, born from free parents, they had violently reduced to slavery. But the story of the events is so connected that if you should diligently examine the individual parts you would discover more things to which your mind clings than things which can be dismissed. And because it would take a long time to set forth the individual statements in the order of the Scripture, we will survey briefly the contents of the whole story.

As the first sign, therefore, "Aaron threw down his rod and it became a snake."[1] The assembled enchanters and magicians of the Egyptians "likewise made" snakes from their rods.[2] But the snake which had been made from Aaron's rod devoured the snakes of the Egyptians. What ought to have amazed Pharao and made belief easy had the opposite effect. For the Scripture says, "Pharao's heart was hardened and he did not listen to them."[3] Now here indeed the text says, "Pharao's heart was hardened." The same thing is written also in the first plague no less, where water is turned into blood.[4] It is the same also in the second plague when frogs appear in abundance;[5] in

---

1 Cf. Ex 7.10.
2 Cf. Ex 7.11.
3 Ex 7.13. Cf. *Phil*. 27 for Origen's discussion elsewhere of the hardening of Pharoah's heart.
4 Cf. Ex 7.22.
5 Cf. Ex 8.11.

the third when mosquitos attack;[6] in the fourth also when flies
are brought forth;[7] and in the fifth when "the hand of the Lord
is upon the cattle" of the Egyptians.[8] But in the sixth, when
Moses "took up ashes from the furnace and sprinkled them
and there came sores and feverish boils on men and four-
footed animals and the magicians were no longer able to stand
in the presence of Moses,"[9] it is not said that Pharao's heart was
hardened. Something more terrible is added. It is written that
"the Lord hardened Pharao's heart and he did not listen to
them as the Lord ordained."[10] Again in the seventh plague,
when hail and fire devastate all Egypt, "the heart of Pharao is
hardened," but not by the Lord.[11] But in the eighth, when
locusts are brought forth, "the Lord" is said "to harden
Pharao's heart."[12] Also in the ninth, when "the whole land of
Egypt experiences darkness that can be felt,"[13] "the Lord" is
said "to harden Pharao's heart."[14] Finally, also when the Hebrew people had left after the firstborn of the Egyptians were
killed, much further in the story it is said: "And the Lord
hardened the heart of Pharao king of Egypt and the heart of
his servants, and he followed after the sons of Israel."[15] But also
when Moses is sent from the land of Madian to Egypt and is
commanded "to do all the prodigies which the Lord placed in
his hand"[16] it is added: "You shall do those things in the

---

6 Cf. Ex 8.15.

7 Cf. Ex.8.28.

8 Cf. Ex 9.7.

9 Cf. Ex 9.10–11. "Feverish boils": *vessicae ferventes* translating the LXX
phlyktides anazeousai "boils breaking out." Elsewhere in this homily it appears as *vessicae cum fervore* (3, 4, 6). In section 6, where they are interpreted,
he treats the phrase as if it were "boils and fevers," breaking this plague
down into sores, boils, and fevers.

10 Ex 9.12. Murmelstein,108, calls attention to the fact that the Agada also
notes this difference and takes it to signify an intensification. He cites
Exodus Rabbah 11.6 and 13.3.

11 Ex 9.35.

12 Ex 10.20.

13 Cf. Ex 10.21–22.

14 Ex 10.27.

15 Ex 14.8.

16 Cf. Ex 4.21.

presence of Pharao. I, however, am hardening Pharao's heart and he will not send the people out."[17] This was the first time the Lord said, "I am hardening Pharao's heart." A second time, when the leaders of Israel have been enumerated, a little later it adds that the Lord said, "I am hardening Pharao's heart, and I am multiplying my signs."[18]

(2) But if we believe these writings to be divine and written by the Holy Spirit, I do not think that we should regard the divine Spirit so lowly as to suppose that that distinction was made by chance in so great a work as this, and that at one time God is said "to have hardened Pharao's heart," at another it is said to be hardened not by God, but, as it were, voluntarily. I admit, to be sure, that I am not fit or able in such differences to pry into the secrets of divine wisdom. I see, however, the apostle Paul, who because of the Spirit of God dwelling in himself dared to say confidently, "But God has given us a revelation through his Spirit. For the Spirit searches all things even the deep things of God."[19] I see this man as one who understands the difference between, "Pharao's heart was hardened," and, "The Lord hardened Pharao's heart." He says elsewhere, "Or do you despise the riches of his goodness and patience and longsuffering, not knowing that the patience of God leads you to repentance? But by your hard and impenitent heart you are treasuring up for yourself wrath in the day of wrath and revelation of God's just judgment."[20] In this passage he condemns, without doubt, him who was hardened voluntarily. But elsewhere as if proposing a certain question on this subject, he says, "Therefore he is merciful to whom he wishes and hardens whom he wishes. Therefore you say to me: Why then does he still complain? For who will resist his will?" And he also adds to these words, "O man, who are you, who reply against God?"[21] I believe, in these words, he is responding

---

17 Cf. Ex 4.21.
18 Ex 7.3.
19 1 Cor 2.10.
20 Rom 2.4–5.
21 Rom 9.18–20.

to the question about the man who is said to be hardened by the Lord not so much by providing the solution of the question as by relying on apostolic authority. Because of the incapacity of his hearers he does not judge it fitting to entrust the secrets of solutions of this kind "to paper and ink,"[22] as he says also in another place about certain words, that he "had heard" certain things "which men are not permitted to speak."[23] Whence also the severity of the noble teacher in what follows deters the man who, curious, immerses himself in very secret questions not so much for the reward of studies as in the desire of knowing, when he says, "O man, who are you who reply against God? Does the thing formed say to him who formed it: Why did you make me thus?" etc.[24] Therefore let it be sufficient also for us only to have observed and examined these things and to have shown our hearers how many things in the divine Law have been submerged in deep mysteries before which we ought to pray: "From the depths I have cried to you, Lord."[25]

(3) But I also think that remark must be considered when Aaron is said to inflict some blows on Pharao or Egypt, and Moses inflicted some blows, and the Lord himself. For in the first plague, when "he turns the waters to blood," Aaron is said to have lifted his rod and struck the water.[26] The same is true also in the second, when he struck the waters and "brought forth frogs,"[27] and in the third when "he stretched out the rod with his hand and struck the dust of the earth and the mosquitoes were made."[28] Aaron was the instrument in these three blows. But in the fourth, the Lord is said to have acted so that "the flies came" and filled "the houses of Pharao."[29] Also in the fifth, when "the cattle of the Egyptians are destroyed," the

---

22 Cf. 2 Jn 2.
23 Cf. 2 Cor 12.4.
24 Rom 9.20.
25 Ps 129.1.
26 Cf. Ex 7.20. The Agada also comments on the different authors of the various plagues. See *Exodus Rabbah* 9.10; 10.4, 6, 7, and *Tanhuma Waera* 14 (Murmelstein, 109).
27 Cf. Ex 8.2.
28 Cf. Ex 8.13.
29 Cf. Ex 8.20.

Lord, no less, is said to have done "this deed."[30] But in the sixth,
Moses "scatters ashes from the furnace and there come ulcers
and feverish boils on men and cattle."[31] Also in the seventh,
"Moses lifts his hand to heaven" and there is "thunder and hail,
and fire dashes about upon the earth."[32] In the eighth also the
same Moses stretches out his hand to heaven "and the Lord
brings in a wind all day and all night" and it brings the locusts.[33]
Also in the ninth the same "Moses," no less, "stretches out his
hand to heaven and there is darkness and gloom upon all the
land of Egypt."[34] But in the tenth, the goal and the completion
of the whole work is accomplished by the Lord. For thus it is
written: "It happened, however, about midnight and the Lord
struck every firstborn in the land of Egypt, from the firstborn
of Pharao who was seated on the throne, to the firstborn of the
captive who was in the pit, and every firstborn of the cattle."[35]

(4) There is also another difference which we have observed
in these words. In the first plague, when the water flows into
blood, Moses is not yet told to go to Pharao, but he is told, "Go
to meet him at the bank of the river, when he goes forth to the
water."[36] but in the second plague, after the first had been
firmly and faithfully inflicted by these men it is said to Moses,
"Go in to Pharao," and having entered he says: "Thus says the
Lord," and the rest.[37] But now in the third, when the mosquitoes are brought in, the magicians who previously had
shown resistance ceased, confessing that "this is the finger of
God."[38] In the fourth also Moses is ordered "to watch early and
to confront Pharao as he goes forth to the water when the
houses of the Egyptians are filled with flies."[39] In the fifth, no
less, when the cattle of the Egyptians are destroyed, Moses is

---

30 Cf. Ex 9.6.
31 Cf. Ex 9.10.
32 Cf. Ex 9.23.
33 Cf. Ex 10.13.
34 Cf. Ex 10.22.
35 Ex 12.29.
36 Cf. Ex 7.15.
37 Ex 7.26 (8.1). Numbers in parentheses indicate Vulgate enumeration.
38 Cf. Ex 8.15 (19).
39 Cf. Ex 8.16 (20).

ordered "to go into Pharao."[40] In the sixth Pharao is completely spurned and it is not said that Moses or Aaron went in to Pharao because "there were ulcers and feverish boils even upon the magicians of Egypt and they were not able to resist Moses."[41] In the seventh, when he brings forth hail, fire, and thunder, Moses is commanded "to watch very early and to confront Pharao."[42] In the eighth, when the locusts are brought forth, he is ordered "to go in" to Him.[43] In the ninth Pharao is again spurned and Moses is commanded "to stretch out his hands to heaven that there might be darkness in the whole land of Egypt, a darkness that could be felt."[44] He does not go in, but he is summoned to Pharao.[45] Likewise also in the tenth plague when the firstborn are destroyed and the people are assembled to depart with haste from Egypt.

There are also many other remarks in which individually disclosures of divine wisdom can be seen. You will find that in the first plague, when the waters are turned into blood, Pharao is not persuaded nor does he yield to the divine blows. But in the second it appears that he is softened a little for "he called Moses and Aaron and said to them, 'Pray to the Lord for me and let him remove the frogs from me and my people, and I will send the people out.'"[46] In the third plague the magicians yield and say to Pharao, "this is the finger of God."[47] In the fourth, after being afflicted by flies, Pharao says: "Go, sacrifice to your God, but you shall not go too far. Pray, therefore, to the Lord for me."[48] In the fifth, when he is struck by the death of the cattle, not only does he not yield, but he is also hardened even more. He does likewise also in the sixth during the plague of the sores. But in the seventh plague, when he is desolated by

---

40 Cf. Ex 9.1.
41 Cf. Ex 9.10–11.
42 Cf. Ex 9.13.
43 Cf. Ex 10.1.
44 Cf. Ex 10.21.
45 Cf. Ex 10.24.
46 Cf. Ex 8.4 (8).
47 Ex 8.15 (19).
48 Ex 8.21,24 (25,28).

hail and fire, "Pharao sent," it says, "and called Moses and
Aaron and said to them: 'I have sinned this time also; the Lord
is just. I and my people, however, are wicked. Therefore, pray
to the Lord for me.'"[49] In the eighth, when he is burdened with
locusts, the text says, "And Pharao hastened and called Moses
and Aaron saying, I have sinned before the Lord your God and
against you. Take care of my sin this time also and pray to the
Lord your God."[50] In the ninth when he is covered with
darkness the text says, "Pharao called Moses and Aaron saying,
'Go, serve the Lord your God.'"[51] But now in the tenth plague,
when the firstborn of men and cattle are destroyed, the text
says, "Pharao called Moses and Aaron in the night and said to
them: 'Arise and go out from my people, both you and the sons
of Israel. Go, serve the Lord your God, as you say; take along
both your sheep and cattle and go, as you have said. But bless
me also.' And the Egyptians urged the people to depart from
the land of Egypt as quickly as possible. For they were saying,
'We shall all die.'"[52]

(5) Who is that man whom God fills with that spirit with
which he filled Moses and Aaron when they performed these
prodigies and signs, that, illuminated by the same spirit, he
may be able to discuss what they did? For I do not think these
various and diverse remarkable things are otherwise explained
unless they are discussed in that same spirit by which they were
done, for the apostle Paul also says, "Let the spirit of the
prophets be subject to the prophets."[53] The words of the
prophets, therefore, are not said to be "subject" to just anyone
to be explained, but "to the prophets." But since the same
blessed Apostle orders us to become imitators of this grace,
that is of the prophetic gift, although it is "imperfect"[54] and in

---

49 Ex 9.27–28.
50 Ex 10.16–17.
51 Ex 10.24.
52 Ex 12.31–33.
53 1 Cor 14.32. See *The Oration and Panegyric Addressed to Origen,* 15, for a
   similar statement about interpreting the prophets by one of Origen's
   students.
54 Cf. 1 Cor 13.9.

our power, saying: "But be zealous for the better gifts, but rather that you may prophesy,"[55] let us also attempt to assume a zeal for the good gifts and, if we have any, to prove it, but to await the fullness of the gift from the Lord. For this reason the Lord says through the prophet: "Open your mouth, and I will fill it."[56] For that reason another Scripture says, "Prick the eye and it produces a tear; prick the heart and it produces understanding."[57] Lest therefore, from despair, we deliver ourselves to silence which by no means edifies the Church of God, let us resume briefly to speak about what things we are able and in what measure we are able.

(6) As far as I can perceive, I think that this Moses, who comes to Egypt and brings the rod with which he punishes and strikes Egypt with the ten plagues, is the Law of God which was given to this world that it might reprove and correct it with the ten plagues, that is the ten commandments which are contained in the Decalogue. But the rod by which all these things are done, by which Egypt is subjugated and Pharao overcome, is the cross of Christ by which this world is conquered and the "ruler of this world"[58] with the principalities and powers are led in triumph.[59] The significance of the fact that the rod, having been cast forth, becomes a dragon or serpent, and devours the serpents of the Egyptian magicians who "had done likewise,"[60] is indicated in the statement in the Gospel which shows that the serpent represents wisdom or prudence: "Be wise as serpents," Scripture says;[61] and elsewhere, "The serpent was wiser than all animals and beasts which were in paradise."[62] Therefore, the cross of Christ whose preaching appeared as "foolishness,"[63] this cross which Moses, that is the Law, con-

---

55 Cf. 1 Cor 14.1, 12.31.
56 Ps 80.11.
57 Cf. Sir 22.19.
58 Cf. Jn 16.11.
59 Cf. Col 2.15.
60 Cf. Ex 7.10–12.
61 Mt 10.16.
62 Gn 3.1.
63 Cf. 1 Cor 1.18.

tains, as the Lord said: "For he wrote about me,"[64] this cross, I
say, of which Moses wrote, after it was cast forth in the earth,
that is once it came to be believed in by men, was changed into
wisdom and such a great wisdom that it devoured all the
wisdom of the Egyptians, that is of this world. For consider
how "God made the wisdom of this world foolish"[65] after he
manifested "Christ, who was crucified, to be the power of God
and wisdom of God"[66] and now the whole world has been
caught by him who said, "I catch the wise in their own craftiness."[67]

The fact that the waters of the river are turned into blood is
suitably enough applied. First, it is appropriate that that river
to which they had delivered the children of the Hebrews in
cruel slaughter should give back a drink of blood to the authors
of evil and that they should have to drink the blood of a
polluted stream which they had defiled by murderous slaughter. Thereafter, that nothing might be lacking from the allegorical laws, the water is turned into blood and its own blood is
given to Egypt to drink. The waters of Egypt are the erring and
slippery teachings of the philosophers. Since those teachings
deceived some who were deficient in understanding and children in knowledge, when the cross of Christ shows the light of
truth to this world, those teachings have to pay the penalty for
the death of the children and the guilt of blood. For thus also
the Lord himself says, "All the blood which has been poured
out on the earth from the blood of Abel the just even to the
blood of Zacharias will be required from this generation."[68]

I think the songs of the poets are indicated figuratively by
the second plague in which frogs are produced. The poets with
a certain empty and puffed up melody introduced deceptive
stories to this world as if by the sounds and songs of frogs. For
that animal is useless except that it produces an inferior harsh

---

64 Jn 5.46.
65 Cf. 1 Cor 1.21.
66 Cf. 1 Cor 1.23–24.
67 1 Cor 3.19.
68 Cf. Mt 23.35–36.

sound. After this the mosquitoes are produced. This animal, indeed, is suspended by wings while flying through the air, but it is so fine and small that it escapes the sight unless one looks closely. Nevertheless, when it sits on the body, it bores with the sharpest sting so that what one cannot see flying he feels stinging. This kind of animal, therefore, I think most fittingly to be compared to the art of dialectic which bores souls with minute and subtle stinging words and circumvents so shrewdly that the one who has been deceived neither sees nor understands the deception. In the fourth place, I would compare the fly to the sect of Cynics who, in addition to the other depravities of their deception, proclaim pleasure and lust as the highest good.

Since, therefore, the world was first deceived by these individual things, when the word and Law of God come, they reprove the world with reproaches of this kind that it might learn the nature of its errors from the natures of the penalties. But Egypt is struck in the fifth place by the death of animals or cattle. In this the madness and foolishness of mortals are reproved who, for example, gave worship to irrational cattle and the designation of god to figures not only of men, but also of cattle, impressed in wood and stone. They reverence Jove Hammon in the ram and Anubis in the dog. They worship Apis in the bull and other animals which Egypt admires as portents of the gods. Consequently, they see miserable suffering in these animals in which they believed there was a divinity to worship. After this sores and feverish boils are produced in the sixth plague. It seems to me that in the sores deceitful and festering malice is reproved; in the boils, swelling and inflated pride; in the fevers, the insanity of anger and madness. To such an extent are the sufferings in the world governed by the forms of their own errors.

(7) But after these blows "sounds" come from above, the text says, of thunder no doubt, "and hail and fire dashing about in the hail."[69] Behold the measure of the divine reproof. It does not strike silently, but makes sounds and sends teaching

---

69 Ex 9.23.

from heaven by which the chastised man can recognize his fault. And it sends hail by which the still tender immature vices are laid waste. And it sends fire knowing that there are "thorns and thistles" which that fire ought to eat up, of which the Lord says, "I came to cast fire on the earth."[70] The incentives of pleasure and passion are consumed by this fire. The locusts are mentioned in the eighth place. I think that the fickleness of the human race which is always disagreeing and differing with itself is checked by this kind of plague. For although the locusts do not have a king, as Scripture says, "He marches the well-ordered army in one line";[71] but men, although they have been made rational by God, have been able neither to rule themselves orderly nor to endure patiently the control of God as king. The ninth plague is darkness either that the blindness of their mind might be reproved or that they might understand that the reasons of the divine dispensation and providence are most obscure. For "God made darkness his hiding place."[72] Those desiring audaciously and rashly to examine this darkness and appropriating for themselves one thing from another have fallen headlong into the "darkness" of errors which is dense and capable of being touched. Finally the death of the firstborn is mentioned. There is, perhaps, in this something beyond our understanding which appears to have been committed by the Egyptians against "the church of the first born which is enrolled in heaven."[73] Whence also the destroying angel is sent to this task, who spares only those who are found to have each doorpost marked with the blood of the lamb. Meanwhile the firstborn of the Egyptians are destroyed. We would say that they are either "the principalities and powers" and "leaders of this world of darkness" whom Christ is said "to have exposed to public ridicule" in his coming, that is to have led captives "and triumphed over them in the wood of the cross";[74] or they are the authors and inventors of the false

---

70 Lk 12.49.
71 Prv 30.27.
72 Ps 17.12.
73 Cf. Heb 12.23.
74 Cf. Col 2.15; Eph 6.12.

religions which were in this world which the truth of Christ extinguished and destroyed with their authors. These things pertain to the mystical meaning.

(8) But now if we are also to discuss the moral nature, we will say that any soul in this world, while it lives in errors and ignorance of the truth is in Egypt. If the Law of God begins to approach this soul it turns the waters into blood for it, that is, it changes the fluid and slippery life of youth to the blood of the Old or New Testament. Then it draws out of the soul the vain and empty talkativeness and complaining against the providence of God which is like the noise of frogs. It also purifies its evil thoughts and scatters the stinging mosquitoes which are like the power of craftiness to sting. It also removes the bites of the passions which are like the stings of the fly and destroys the foolishness and brutish understanding in the soul, by which "man when he was in honor, did not understand, but has been compared to stupid beasts, and made like to them."[75] And in respect to the sores on the cattle, the Law censured the soul's swelling arrogance and extinguished the heat of madness in it. After this, moreover, it employs the sounds of "the sons of thunder,"[76] that is the teachings of the Gospels and apostles. But it also attends to the chastening of hail, that it might restrain the luxury of pleasure. At the same time it also employs the fire of penance, that the soul also might say: "Was not our heart burning within us?"[77] Nor does the Law of God take away the example of the locusts from the soul by which all its restless and disturbed motions are devoured and eaten up, whereby it too learns what the Apostle teaches: "That all its activities be according to order."[78] But when the soul has been sufficiently restrained for morals and constrained to make its life more faultless, when it has perceived the author of the blows and has now begun to confess that "it is the finger of God"[79] and it has acquired some understanding, then espe-

---

75 Ps 48.21.
76 Cf. Mk 3.17.
77 Lk 24.32.
78 Cf. 1 Cor 14.40.
79 Cf. Ex 8.19.

cially the soul sees the darkness of its own conduct, then it perceives the gloom of its own errors. And when the soul has reached this point, then it will deserve that the firstborn of the Egyptians in it be destroyed.

I think something like the following can be understood in this. Every soul when it has arrived at fullness of life and, as it were, a kind of natural law in it has begun to defend its own rights, without doubt, produces first movements according to the desire of the flesh which a soul incited by lust or anger sets in motion. Whence the prophet says something about Christ alone which, as it were, is peculiar and not shared with other men: "He will eat butter and honey before he does or speaks wicked things, he will choose the good, since before he knows good or evil as a child," he resists evil that he might choose what is good.[80] But another prophet, speaking about himself, said, "Do not remember the transgressions of my youth and ignorance."[81] Because, therefore, those first movements of the soul, brought forth according to the flesh, rush into sin, they shall justly be represented, in the moral sense, as the firstborn of the Egyptians which are destroyed, so far as conversion directs a more perfect course for the rest of life. So, therefore, the firstborn of the Egyptians are understood to be destroyed in the soul which the divine Law restrains and corrects after taking it up from its errors, unless after all these things the soul continues in unfaithfulness and does not wish to be joined to the Israelite people that it might go out from the depth and go forth unimpaired, but remains in iniquity and descends "like lead in the most vehement water."[82] For iniquity, according to the vision of Zacharias the prophet, sits upon a talent of lead. Therefore, he who remains in iniquity is said to be submerged in the depth "like lead."

In certain things above we have observed clearly some prodigies executed by Aaron, some by Moses, but others by the Lord himself. These distinctions can be understood to show us

80 Cf. Is 7.15–16.
81 Ps 24.7.
82 Cf. Zec 5.6–7.

in what things we are to be purified by the sacrifices of the priests and the supplications of the high priests which the person of Aaron represents; in what things we are to be corrected by knowledge of the divine Law, as the office of Moses represents. But in others, which doubtless are more difficult, we are in need of the power of the Lord himself.

(9) But do not think that we observed in vain that Moses at first does not go in to Pharao but goes to him when he goes out to the waters, but later goes in to him, and after this does not go in, but approaches Pharao after he has been summoned. I think this means that whether our struggle against Pharao is about the word of God and the exercise of religion or, whether we attempt to snatch from his power the souls besieged by him and have to struggle with reasoning, we ought not immediately at the first appearance to go in to the ultimate subjects of inquiry, but we must go to meet the adversary and go to meet him at his waters, for his waters are the pagan philosophers. At first, therefore, we must go there to meet them to argue with those who are willing, that we might show them and teach them that they have erred. After this we must go in also to the deeper subjects of the struggle. For the Lord also says, "Unless one first bind the strong man, he cannot enter his house and plunder his vessels."[83] First, therefore, we must bind "the strong man." He must be bound with the bonds of questions and thus we must go in to plunder "his vessels," and to free the souls which he had possessed by deceptive fraud. When we have done this often and have opposed him—we have stood, moreover, as the Apostle says: "Stand therefore, having your loins girded with truth,"[84] and again, "Stand in the Lord and act like a man"[85]—when, therefore, we have opposed him in this manner, that ancient and crafty contriver will pretend that he is conquered and will pretend to yield, if perhaps by this he may make us more neglectful in the struggle. But he will also feign repentance and will pray that we depart, but that we not

---

83 Cf. Mt 12.29.
84 Eph 6.14.
85 Cf. Phil 4.1; 1 Cor 16.13.

depart far. He wants us near himself in some degree; he wishes for his own ends that we not depart far. But unless we withdraw far from him and cross the sea and say, "As far as east is from west, he has removed our iniquities from us,"[86] we cannot be saved. For this reason let us pray the mercy of the Lord that he snatch us also from the land of Egypt, from the power of darkness and "submerge" Pharao with his army "like lead in the most vehement water."[87] Let us, however, when we have been freed, "sing" a hymn "to the Lord" with joy and exultation, "for he is glorious and honorable,"[88] because "honor and glory" are his "forever and ever. Amen."[89]

---

86 Ps 102.12.
87 Cf. Ex 15.10.
88 Cf. Ex 15.1.
89 Cf. Rom 16.27.

HOMILY V
On the departure of the children of Israel

HE APOSTLE PAUL, "TEACHER OF THE GENTILES in faith and truth"[1] taught the Church which he gathered from the Gentiles how it ought to interpret the books of the Law. These books were received from others and were formerly unknown to the Gentiles and were very strange. He feared that the Church, receiving foreign instructions and not knowing the principle of the instructions, would be in a state of confusion about the foreign document. For that reason he gives some examples of interpretation that we also might note similar things in other passages, lest we believe that by imitation of the text and document of the Jews we be made disciples. He wishes, therefore, to distinguish disciples of Christ from disciples of the Synagogue by the way they understand the Law. The Jews, by misunderstanding it, rejected Christ. We, by understanding the Law spiritually, show that it was justly given for the instruction of the Church.[2]

The Jews, therefore, understand only this, that "the children of Israel departed" from Egypt and their first departure was "from Ramesse" and they departed from there and came "to Socoth,"[3] and "they departed from Socoth" and came "to Etham" at Epauleus next to the sea.[4] Then, next, they understand that there the cloud preceded them[5] and the "rock" from which they drank water followed;[6] and furthermore,

---

1 Cf. 1 Tm 2.7.
2 J. Kelly, *Early Christian Doctrines* (New York: Harper and Row, 1960), 32, notes that it was universally believed in the early church "that the Jewish Scriptures did not belong to the Jews but to the Christians."
3 Cf. Ex 12.37.
4 Cf. Ex 13.20; 14.2.
5 Cf. Ex 13.21.
6 Cf. Ex 17.6.

they crossed the Red Sea and came into the desert of Sina.[7]

Let us see, however, what sort of rule of interpretation the apostle Paul taught us about these matters. Writing to the Corinthians he says in a certain passage, "For we know that our fathers were all under the cloud, and all were baptized in Moses in the cloud and in the sea, and all ate the same spiritual food, and all drank the same spiritual drink. And they drank of the spiritual rock which followed them, and the rock was Christ."[8] Do you see how much Paul's teaching differs from the literal meaning? What the Jews supposed to be a crossing of the sea, Paul calls a baptism; what they supposed to be a cloud, Paul asserts is the Holy Spirit. He wishes that to be understood in a similar manner to this which the Lord taught in the Gospels, "Unless a man be born again of water and the Holy Spirit, he cannot enter the kingdom of heaven."[9] And again, the manna which the Jews supposed to be food for the stomach and the satiation of the appetite, Paul calls "spiritual food."[10] And not only Paul, but the Lord also says on the same subject in the Gospel: "Your fathers ate manna in the desert and died. He, however, who eats the bread which I give him will not die forever."[11] And after this he says, "I am the bread which came down from heaven."[12] Then again Paul declares plainly of "the rock which followed them," "the rock was Christ."[13]

What then are we to do who received such instructions about interpretation from Paul, a teacher of the Church? Does it not seem right that we apply this kind of rule which was delivered to us in a similar way in other passages? Or as some wish, forsaking these things which such a great Apostle taught, should we turn again to "Jewish fables?"[14] It seems to me that if I differ from Paul in these matters I aid the enemies of Christ,

---

7 Cf. Ex 14.22; 16.1.
8 1 Cor 10.1–4.
9 Jn 3.5.
10 1 Cor 10.3.
11 Cf. Jn 6.49–50.
12 Jn 6.51.
13 1 Cor 10.4.
14 Ti 1.14.

and this is what the prophet says, "Woe to him who causes his neighbor to drink by foul subversion!"[15] Let us cultivate, therefore, the seeds of spiritual understanding received from the blessed apostle Paul, in so far as the Lord shall see fit to illuminate us by your prayers.

(2) The children of Israel "departed," the text says, "from Ramesse and came to Socoth. And they departed from Socoth and came to Etham."[16] If there is anyone who is about to depart from Egypt, if there is anyone who desires to forsake the dark deeds of this world and the darkness of errors, he must first of all depart "from Ramesse." *Ramesse* means "the commotion of a moth."[17] Depart from Ramesse, therefore, if you wish to come to this place that the Lord may be your leader and preceed you "in the column of the cloud"[18] and "the rock" may follow you,[19] which offers you "spiritual food" and "spiritual drink" no less. Nor should you store treasure "there where the moth destroys and thieves dig through and steal."[20] This is what the Lord says clearly in the Gospels: "If you wish to be perfect, sell all your possessions and give to the poor, and you will have treasure in heaven; and come, follow me."[21] This, therefore, is to depart "from Ramesse"[22] and to follow Christ. Let us see, however, what the campsites may be to which one goes "from Ramesse"

"They came," the text says, "to Socoth." The etymologists teach that *Socoth* is understood as "tents" among the Hebrews.[23] When, therefore, leaving Egypt, you have dispelled the moths of all corruption from yourself and have cast aside the inducements of vices, you will dwell in tents. For we dwell in tents of which "we do not wish to be unclothed but to be further

---

15 Cf. Hb 2.15.
16 Cf. Ex 12.37; 13.20.
17 See Appendix, 24.
18 Cf. Ex 13.21.
19 1 Cor 10.3–4.
20 Mt 6.20.
21 Mt 19.21.
22 Cf. Ex 12.37.
23 See Appendix, 25.

clothed."[24] Dwelling in tents, however, indicates that he who hastens to God is free and has no impediments. But departure is urged lest there be a stopping in this place. The camp must also be moved "from Socoth." One must hasten to go "to Etham."

Etham, they say, is translated in our language as "signs for them,"[25] and rightly so, for here you will hear it said: "God was preceeding them by day in a column of cloud and by night in a column of fire."[26] You do not find this done at Ramesse nor at Socoth, which is called the second encampment for those departing. It is the third encampment in which divine signs occur. Recollect what was read above when Moses said to Pharao, "We will go a journey of three days in the wilderness and sacrifice to the Lord our God."[27] This was the three days to which Moses was hastening and Pharao was opposing, for he said, "You shall not go far."[28] Pharao would not permit the children of Israel to reach the place of signs; he would not permit them to advance so far that they could enjoy fully the mysteries of the third day. Hear what the prophet says: "God will revive us after two days, and on the third day we will arise and live in his sight."[29] The first day is the passion of the Savior for us. The second is the day on which he descended into hell. The third day is the day of resurrection.[30] Therefore, on the third day "God went before them, by day in a column of cloud, by night in a column of fire."[31] But if according to what we said above, the Apostle teaches us rightly that the mysteries of baptism are contained in these words,[32] it is necessary that "those who are baptized in Christ are baptized in his death and are buried with him," also arise from the dead with him on the

---

24 2 Cor 5.4.
25 See Appendix, 26.
26 Ex 13.21.
27 Ex 5.3; Cf. Origen *Ex. Hom.* 3.3.
28 Ex 8,28 (LXX 8,24).
29 Hos 6.2.
30 Cf. Mt 16.21; Origen, *Gn. Hom.* 8.4.
31 Cf. Ex 13.21.
32 Cf. 1 Cor 10.2.

third day[33] whom also, according to what the Apostle says, "He raised up together with him and at the same time made them sit in the heavenly places."[34] When, therefore, you shall have undertaken the mystery of the third day, God will begin to lead you and will himself show you the way of salvation.

(3) But let us see what is said to Moses after this, what way he is ordered to choose. "Turn from Etham," the text says, "and travel between Epauleus and Magdal, which is opposite Beelsephon."[35] These are interpreted as follows. *Epauleus* means "winding ascent"; *Magdal* "tower"; and *Beelsephon* "ascent of a watchtower" or "having a watch-tower."[36] Perhaps you used to think that the way which God shows would be level and easy and certainly would involve no difficulty or labor. It is an ascent and a winding ascent. For it is not a downhill way on which one strives toward virtue, but it is ascended and it is ascended with great difficulty. Hear also the Lord saying in the Gosepl how "straight and narrow is the way which leads to life."[37] See, therefore, to what extent the Gospel agrees with the Law. In the Law the way of virtue is shown to be a winding ascent; in the Gospels it is said that "the way which leads to life is straight and narrow." Cannot even the blind see clearly that one and the same Spirit wrote the Law and the Gospels? The way, therefore, which they march along is a winding ascent and the "ascent of a watchtower" or "having a watchtower." The ascent pertains to action; the watchtower to faith. It shows, therefore, that in both actions and faith there is much difficulty and labor. There are many temptations, many stumbling blocks for those who wish to do God's work. Next, you may find many winding things in the faith, many questions, many objections of heretics, many contradictions of the unfaithful. This, therefore, is the way to be pursued by those who follow God. But there is also a tower in this way. What is this tower? Surely it is that one about which the Lord says in the Gospel, "Who of

---

33 Cf. Rom 6.3–4.
34 Eph 2.6.
35 Cf. Ex 14.2.
36 See Appendix, 27, 28, and 29.
37 Mt 7.14.

you wishing to build a tower will not first sit down and reckon the cost if he has wherewith to complete it?"[38] That tower, therefore, is the high and lofty seat of virtues.

But hear what Pharao says when he sees these things: "They are going astray."[39] In Pharao's opinion, he who follows God is said to go astray, because, as we said, the way of wisdom is winding, having many turns, many difficulties, many bendings. For when you confess one God and in the same confession assert the one God is Father, Son, and Holy Spirit, how winding, how difficult, how inextricable this appears to be to the unbelievers! Then, when you say "the Lord of majesty"[40] and Son of Man "who descended from heaven"[41] was crucified, how winding these things appear and how difficult! He who hears this, if he does not hear with faith, says they are going astray; but you, be immovable and have no doubt about faith of this kind knowing that God shows you this way of faith. For he himself said, "Depart from Etham and set up camp between Epauleus and Magdal opposite Beelsephon."[42] Therefore, as you flee Egypt you come to these places; you come to these ascents of works and faith; you come to the edifice of the tower; you come also to the sea and the waves rush upon you. For the way of life is not pursued without the waves of temptations, as also the Apostle says, "All who wish to live piously in Christ will suffer persecution."[43] But Job also, no less, declares, "Our life upon earth is a temptation."[44] This, therefore, is what it means to have come to the sea.

(4) But if in following Moses, that is the Law of God, you go this way, the Egyptian follows and pursues you. But see what happens. "The angel of the Lord," the text says, "which was preceeding the camp of Israel arose and went behind them. And the column of cloud rose from before them and stood

---

38 Lk 14.28.
39 Cf. Ex 14.3.
40 Cf. Ps 28,3.
41 Cf. Jn 6.33.
42 Ex 14.2.
43 2 Tm 3.12.
44 Jb 7.1.

behind them, and went between the camp of the Egyptians and the camp of the Israelites."[45] This "column of cloud" becomes a wall for the people of God; it places obscurity and darkness before the Egyptians. For the column of fire is not brought over to the Egyptians that they might see light, but they remain in darkness because "they loved darkness rather than light."[46] And, therefore, if you should depart from the Egyptians and flee the power of demons, see what great helps are prepared for you from heaven, see what great helpers you would enjoy. This help is sufficient that you may remain strong in the faith, that the cavalry of the Egyptians and the fear of the four-horse chariots may not terrify you,[47] that you may not cry out against Moses, the Law of God, and say as some of those said, "Were there not enough graves in Egypt? Have you thus brought us out that we might die in this wilderness? It were better for us to serve the Egyptians than to die in this wilderness."[48] These are the words of a soul growing weak in temptation.

But who is so blessed, who so dispatches the weight of temptations that no uncertainty creeps up on his mind? Look at that great foundation of the Church, its most solid rock upon which Christ founded the Church.[49] What does the Lord say? "Why did you doubt, O you of little faith?"[50] But nevertheless, because they say, "It were better for us to serve the Egyptians than to die in the wilderness,"[51] these are the words of temptation and frailness. But it is false. It is far better "to die in the wilderness" than "to serve the Egyptians." For he who dies in the wilderness, for the very reason that he has been separated from the Egyptians and has departed from "the rulers of darkness"[52] and from the power of Satan, has a certain perfection even if he was not able to arrive at completion. For it

---

45 Ex 14.19–20.
46 Jn 3.19.
47 Cf. Ex 14.9.
48 Ex 14.11–12.
49 Cf. Mt 6.18.
50 Mt 14.31.
51 Ex 14.12.
52 Eph 6.12.

is better for one seeking the perfect life to die on the way than not to set out to seek perfection. On this basis they also appear to be mistaken who, while they expound the excessively steep way of virtue and enumerate its many difficulties, dangers, and falls, decide not to enter it or begin. But it is much better that I even die in this way, if thus it is necessary, than to be killed remaining among the Egyptians and buried by salty and bitter waves.

But meanwhile Moses cries out to the Lord. How does he cry out? No sound of his cry is heard and yet God says to him. "Why do you cry out to me?"[53] I should like to know how the saints cry out to God without a sound. The Apostle teaches, "God has given the spirit of his Son in our hearts crying: 'Abba, Father!' "[54] And he adds, "The Spirit himself intercedes for us with indescribable groans." And again, "he who searches the heart knows what the Spirit desires because he pleads for the saints according to God."[55] So, therefore, when the Holy Spirit intercedes with God the cry of the saints is heard through silence.

(5) And what happens next? Moses is ordered to strike the sea with a rod that it might part and withdraw for the people of God who are entering the sea[56] and the compliance of the elements might serve the divine will. And when the waters, which they feared, became a "wall on the right and left"[57] for the servants of God, they were not destructive, but protective. The water, therefore, is driven into a heap and the restrained wave is curved on itself. The liquid regains solidity and the bottom of the sea becomes dry as dust. Notice the goodness of God the Creator. If you obey his will, if you follow his Law, he compels the elements themselves to serve you even against their own nature.

I have heard a tradition from the ancients that in that parting of the sea individual divisions of the waters were made

---

53 Ex 14.15.
54 Gal 4.6.
55 Rom 8.27.
56 Cf. Ex 14.21–22,26.
57 Cf. Ex 14.29.

for each individual tribe of the sons of Israel and a special way was opened in the sea for each tribe[58] and I have proven it from that which is written in the Psalms: "He who divided the Red Sea into divisions."[59] This teaches that many divisions were made, not one. The following, no less, seems to enumerate a special entrance for each tribe: "There is Benjamin the younger in amazement, the princes of Juda their leaders, the princes of Zabulon, the princes of Nepthali."[60] I thought that the careful student should not be silent about these things observed by the ancients in the divine Scriptures.

What then are we taught by these words? We already mentioned above what the Apostle's understanding is in these matters. He calls this "baptism in Moses consummated in the cloud and in the sea,"[61] that you also who are baptized in Christ,[62] in water and the Holy Spirit, might know that the Egyptians are following you and wish to recall you to their service. They are "the rulers of this world," of course, and "the spiritual evils" which you previously served.[63] These attempt to follow, but you descend into the water and come out unim-

---

58 Origen is probably dependent on Rabbinic tradition here. Eusebius, *In Psalm.* 77.13 PG 23.913), says the Hebrews say the sea was divided into twelve sections according to the number of the twelve tribes. C. Kraeling, *The Synagogue, The Excavations at Dura-Europos* (New Haven: Yale, 1956), 84–85, states that in the scene depicting the crossing of the Red Sea in the synagogue at Dura-Europos there is "a group of lavender bands, probably twelve in number, that trace a fairly regular course across the gray background on either side of Moses." He thinks these strips should most probably be taken to represent the Haggadic concept that the sea was divided into twelve paths. He notes the Targum pseudo-Jonathan on Ex 14.21, *Genesis Rabbah* 84.5,8, *Deuteronomy Rabbah* 9.10, and *Mekilta ad Ex.* 14.16. E. Goodenough, *Jewish Symbols in the Greco-Roman Period*, vol 10 (New York: Pantheon Books, 1964), 128, calls attention to "a new Red Sea fresco in Rome" which he thinks confirms the interpretation of the strips as paths in the sea. Theodoret, *Quaest. 25 in Exod.* (PG 80.256 B, C), may have Origen in mind when he says, "Some say the sea was divided into twelve divisions and each tribe crossed individually, and they think the blessed David said this: 'The one who divided the Red Sea into divisions.' "
59 Ps 135.13.
60 Ps 67.28.
61 Cf. 1 Cor 10.2.
62 Cf. Rom 6.3.
63 Cf. Eph 6.12.

paired, the filth of sins having been washed away. You ascend "a new man"[64] prepared to "sing a new song."[65] But the Egyptians who follow you are drowned in the abyss even if they appear to ask Jesus that he not send them into the abyss.[66]

But we can also apply these words another way. If you flee Egypt, if you leave behind the darkness of ignorance and follow Moses, the Law of God, should the sea hinder you and the waves of contradictions rush against you, strike the opposing waves with the rod of Moses, that is the word of the Law and by vigilance in the Scriptures open a way for yourself by disputing with the adversaries. Immediately the waves will yield and the floods which surmounted will give place to the conquerors. And when these who a little earlier were resisting have been rendered immovable with admiration, astonishment, and amazement, you will travel the right way of faith with legitimate lines of reasoning and will advance so much in the word of doctrine that your hearers, whom you instructed with the rod of the Law, themselves now rise up against the Egyptians like a flood of the sea and not only attack them but also overcome and destroy them. For he who does not do "the works of darkness"[67] destroys the Egyptian; he who lives not carnally but spiritually destroys the Egyptian; he who either casts out of his heart all sordid and impure thoughts or does not receive them at all destroys the Egyptian, as also the Apostle says, "Taking up the shield of faith that we may be able to extinguish all the fiery darts of the evil one."[68] In this way, therefore, we can "see" even today "the Egyptians dead and lying on the shore,"[69] their four-horse chariots and cavalry drowned. We can even see Pharao himself drowned if we live by such great faith that "God may quickly grind Satan under our feet"[70] by Jesus Christ our Lord, "to whom belongs glory and sovereignty forever and ever. Amen."[71]

---

64 Cf. Eph 2.15; 4.24.
65 Cf. Is 42.10.
66 Cf. Lk 8.31.
67 Cf. Rom 13.12.
68 Eph 6.16.
69 Cf. Ex 14.30.
70 Cf. Rom 16–20.
71 Cf. 1 Pt 4.11.

HOMILY VI
On the song which Moses sang with the people and Miriam with the women

E READ IN THE DIVINE SCRIPTURES that many songs indeed were composed. Yet of all of these, this song is first which the people of God sang after the victory when the Egyptians and Pharao were drowned. It is the custom of the saints to offer a hymn of thanks to God when an adversary is conquered, as men who know the victory came about not by their own power but by the grace of God. When they sing the hymn, however, they also take tambourines in their hands just as it is related of Mary the sister of Moses and Aaron.[1] And therefore, if you cross the Red Sea, if you see the Egyptians drowned and Pharao destroyed and cast headlong into the depth of the abyss, you can sing a hymn to God; you can utter a sound of praise and say, "Let us sing to the Lord, for he has been glorified magnificently; he cast forth horse and rider into the sea."[2] You will say these things better and more fittingly, however, if you have a tambourine in your hand, that is if "you have crucified your flesh with its vices and concupiscences,"[3] and if "you have put to death your members which are upon the earth."[4]

Let us see, however, what the text says. "Let us sing to the Lord for he has been glorified magnificently."[5] As if "he has been glorified" were not sufficient, it adds, "He has been glorified magnificently." So far as I can conjecture, it seems to me that it is one thing to be glorified, another to be glorified magnificently. For my Lord Jesus Christ, when he received

---

1 Cf. Ex 15.20.
2 Ex 15.1.
3 Gal 5.24.
4 Col 3.5.
5 Ex 15.1.

flesh from the virgin for our salvation, was glorified indeed, because "he came to seek what was lost."[6] He was not, however, "glorified magnificently."[7] For it is said of him: "We saw him and he did not have form nor beauty. His face was undistinguished among the sons of men."[8] He was glorified both when he came to the cross and when he suffered death. Do you wish to know that he was glorified? He himself said, "Father the hour has come. Glorify your son, that your son might glorify you."[9] Even the suffering of the cross, therefore, was glory for him, but this glory was not magnificent, but humble. For it is said of him, "He humbled himself unto death, even to the death of the cross."[10] The prophet also had predicted this: "Let us condemn him to a most shameful death."[11] But Isaias also says of him. "In lowliness his judgment was removed."[12] In all these things, therefore, the Lord was glorified, but, so to speak, "he was glorified" in a lowly manner, not "magnificently." But because "it was necessary that the Christ suffer these things and thus enter into his glory,"[13] "when he comes in the glory of the Father and his holy angels,"[14] "when he comes in his majesty"[15] "to judge the earth,"[16] when he also "shall destroy" the true Pharao, that is, the devil, "with the spirit of his mouth,"[17] when, therefore, he shall brightly shine "in the majesty of his Father"[18] and after the coming of lowliness he shall show us the second coming in glory, then the Lord is not

---

6 Mt 18.11.
7 Ex 15.1. De Lange, *Origen and the Jews*, 110 notes that "Origen often, in his commentaries and homilies, seizes on an apparently superfluous word or a peculiarity of grammar and uses it as a starting-point for his exposition."
8 Is 53.2–3.
9 Jn 17.1.
10 Phil 2.8.
11 Wis 2.20.
12 Is 53.8.
13 Lk 24.26.
14 Lk 9.26.
15 Cf. Mt 25.31.
16 Cf. Ps 95.13, 97.9; Mt 25.31f.
17 Cf. 2 Thes 2.8.
18 Mk 8.38.

only glorified, but he is also "glorified magnificently," when "all honor the Son as they honor the Father."[19]

(2) "He cast forth horse and rider into the sea; he became my helper and protector in salvation."[20] The men who pursue us are horses, and, so to speak, all who have been born in the flesh are figuratively horses. But these have their own riders. There are horses whom the Lord mounts and they go around all the earth, of whom it is said, "And your cavalry is salvation."[21] There are horses, however, who have the devil and his angels as riders. Judas was a horse, but as long as he had the Lord as his rider he was part of the cavalry of salvation. Having been sent with the other apostles indeed, he gave health to the sick and wholeness to the weak.[22] But when he surrendered himself to the devil—for "after the morsel, Satan entered him"[23]—Satan became his rider and when he was guided by his reins he began to ride against our Lord and Savior. All, therefore, who persecute the saints are neighing horses, but they have evil angels as riders by whom they are guided and, therefore, are wild. If, then, you ever see your persecutor raging very much, know that he is being urged on by a demon as his rider and, therefore, is fierce and cruel.

The Lord, therefore, "cast forth horse and rider into the sea and became my salvation. This is my God and I will honor him; the God of my father and I will exalt him."[24] This, therefore, is also "my God" and the God "of my father." Our father who made and begot us is Christ. He himself says, "I go to my father and your father, to my God and your God."[25] If, therefore, I know that God is "my God" I shall glorify him. But if I also know that he is "God of my father," Christ, I will exalt him, for it is a higher understanding, how Christ, that he might bind

---

19 Jn 5.23.
20 Ex 15.1–2.
21 Hb 3.8.
22 Cf. Mt 10.1.
23 Jn 13.27.
24 Ex 15.1–2.
25 Jn 20.17.

together and defend the truth of the one God says that he whom he calls father by nature is his God.

"The Lord who destroys wars, the Lord is his name."[26] I do not wish you to think that "the Lord destroys" only visible battles. He also "destroys" those battles which we have "not against flesh and blood, but against principalities and powers and against the rulers of the darkness of this world."[27] For "the Lord is his name" and there is no creature of which he is not Lord.

(3) "He cast into the sea the four-horse chariots of Pharao and his army; he drowned in the Red Sea the chosen riders, the captains."[28] Pharao, as most powerful in evil and master of the kingdom of wickedness, leads "the four-horse chariots." It is not sufficient for him to mount one horse. He drives several at the same time; he compels several to be tortured at the same time by the blows of his whip. Know that all whom you see who are most disgraceful in luxury, most fierce in cruelty, most offensive in avarice, most shameful in impiety, are from the four-horse chariots of Pharao. He sits on them; he harnesses them to his chariot; he is borne by them. He flies and guides them with slackened reins through open plains of evils. Others are "chosen riders," chosen without doubt for evil. But we have already spoken above of the riders. Let us now see who "the captains" are.

The "captains" seem to me to be mentioned because men can sin in three ways: they sin either in deed, in speech, or in thought. Therefore, those who beset these three ways of sinning in us are called individually "captains." They keep watch constantly and act in crafty devices, that one might elicit an evil word from a miserable man, or another might twist out a sinful work, or the other might snatch an evil thought. In fact, where the seed of the word of God falls and perishes is also described

---

26 Ex 15.3.
27 Eph 6.12.
28 Ex 15.4. "Captains" translates *ternos statores* (*tristatas* LXX). Origen may have thought that this term meant that there were three men in each chariot. See below where he says the term suggests the three ways in which men sin. Cf. Gregory of Nyssa, *De vita Moysis*, p. 71 (ed. H. Musurillo).

as a threefold place. One is said to be "beside the road" which is trodden under foot by men; another "in thorns"; another in "rocky soil." And on the contrary "the good ground" is said to bring forth threefold fruit either "a hundredfold" or "sixty" or "thirty."[29] For the way of doing good is also threefold, for nothing good is done except by deed or thought or word. The Apostle also points to this same thing when he says: "He who builds upon this foundation gold, silver, precious stones," thereby indicating a threefold way of good. Nevertheless he subjoins also the threefold way of evil when he says, "wood, hay, straw."[30] Those "captains" therefore, are evil angels from Pharao's army who stand in ways of this kind watching each of us to lead us into sin by these ways. The Lord will drown these "captains" in the Red Sea and deliver them to fiery turbulence on the day of judgment and cover them in the sea of punishments if you, following God, have removed yourself from their power.

(4)   "They sank in the depth like a stone."[31] Why "did they sink in the depth like a stone?" Because they were not the kind of "stones from which sons of Abraham could be raised up,"[32] but the kind which love the depth and desire the liquid element, that is, who seize the bitter and fluid desire of present things. Whence it is said of these: "They sank like lead in very deep water."[33] They are serious sinners. For iniquity also is shown "to sit upon a talent of lead," as Zacharias the prophet says: "I saw a woman sitting upon a talent of lead, and I said, 'Who is this'? And he answered, 'Iniquity.' "[34] Hence it is, therefore, that the unjust "sank in the depth, like lead in very deep water."[35]

The saints, however, do not sink, but walk upon the waters, because they are light and are not weighed down with the

29 Cf. Mt 13.4–8.
30 1 Cor 3.12.
31 Ex 15.5.
32 Cf. Mt 3.9.
33 Ex 15.10.
34 Cf. Zec 5.7.
35 Cf. Ex 15.5,10.

weight of sin. Indeed our Lord and Savior "walked upon the waters,"[36] for it is he who truly did not know sin.[37] His disciple Peter also "walked," although he was somewhat anxious,[38] for he was not so great and of the same quality as the one who has no lead at all mixed in himself. He had some, though very little. For this reason the Lord says to him, "O you of little faith, why did you doubt?"[39] He who is saved, therefore, is saved through fire so that if he has, by chance, any lead mixed in himself, the fire may melt it away and separate it, that all may be made good gold because "the gold of that land" which the saints are to have is said "to be good."[40] And "just as a furnace tests gold,"[41] so temptation tests just men. All, therefore, must come to the fire; all must come to the melting furnace, "for the Lord sits and melts down and purifies the sons of Juda."[42] But when one comes to that place, if he brings many good works and very little iniquity, that little is separated by fire "like lead" and is purified and the whole is left pure gold. And if someone brings more lead to that place, more is burned away, so that he is diminished to a greater extent, so that even if there is very little gold, it may be left purified nevertheless. But if someone should come to that place totally lead, this which has been written will happen to him: He will sink "in the depth like lead in very deep water."[43] But it would take too long to explain everything in order. It is sufficient to glance over a few things.

(5) "Who," the text says, "is like you among the gods, O Lord? Who is like you, glorious among the holy ones, marvelous in majesty, doing prodigies?"[44] The words "Who is like you among the gods?" do not compare God to the images of the Gentiles nor to the demons, who falsely appropriate the

---

36 Cf. Mt 14.25.
37 Cf. 2 Cor 5.21.
38 Cf. Mt 14.29–30.
39 Mt 14.31.
40 Cf. Dn 2.12.
41 Cf. Prv 27.3.
42 Cf. Mal 3.3.
43 Cf. Ex 15.5,10.
44 Ex 15.11. See Murmelstein, 109–11, for ways this verse was interpreted in Jewish literature.

name of gods to themselves, but mean those gods who by grace and participation in God are called gods. Scripture also speaks elsewhere of these gods: "I said, 'You are gods,' "[45] and again, "God has stood in the congregation of the gods."[46] But although these are susceptible of God and appear to be given this name by grace, nevertheless no one is found like God in either power or nature. And although the apostle John says, "Little children we do not yet know what we shall be; but if he has been revealed to us"—speaking about the Lord, of course,—"we shall be like him,"[47] nevertheless this likeness is applied not to nature but to beauty.[48] For example, it is as if we should say that a painting is a likeness of him whose image is expressed in the painting. So far as the appearance pertains to beauty, it is said to be similar; so far as it pertains to substance, it is very dissimilar. For the painting is a figure of the flesh and the beauty of a living body. It is an artifice of colors and wax placed on tablets lacking sensation. No one, therefore, "among the gods is like the Lord," for no one is invisible, no one incorporeal, no one immutable, no one without beginning and end, no one creator of all, except the Father with the Son and the Holy Spirit.

(6) "You stretched out your right hand; the earth devoured them."[49] The earth devours the impious today too. Or do you not think that he is devoured by the earth who always thinks about the earth,[50] who always has earthly business, who speaks of the earth, sues because of the earth, desires the earth, and places all his hope in the earth? Is he not devoured by the earth who does not look to heaven, who does not think about

---

45 Ps 81.6. This is one of two verses (the other is Jn 10.34–35), Crouzel notes, that Origen uses as the Scriptural basis for his view that men and angels are transformed into gods by participation in God. He is very careful, however, to maintain, as he does in the discussion following the verse here, that these other beings can be divine only by participation and grace, never by nature (See Crouzel, *Théologie de l'image*, 163–65; Cf. Origen *Ex. Hom.* 8.2).
46 Ps 81.1.
47 1 Jn 3.2. Cf. Origen *De Princ.* 3.6.1.
48 *Gratiam.*
49 Ex 15.12.
50 Cf. Phil 3.19.

future things, who does not fear the judgment of God nor desire his blessed promises, but always thinks about present things and longs for earthly things? When you see such a man, say, "The earth has devoured him." But also if you see someone given to wantonness of the flesh and pleasures of the body in whom the soul has no value, but the lust of the flesh possesses the whole man, say also of this man, "The earth has devoured him."

It bothers me yet because the text says, "You stretched out your right hand and the earth devoured them,"[51] as if the fact that "the Lord stretched out his right hand" was the cause that they were devoured by the earth. If you consider how the Lord, exalted on the cross, "stretched out his hands all day to an unbelieving and contradicting people,"[52] and how his death overthrew a faithless people for their admitted crime, who cried out, "Crucify, crucify him,"[53] you will discover clearly how "he stretched out his right hand and the earth devoured them."

One need not, however, despair completely. For it is possible that if, by chance, he who has been devoured recover his senses he can again be vomited forth like Jonas.[54] But I also think that at some time the earth retained in the innermost parts of its depths all of us who were devoured, and for this reason our Lord descended not only to the earth but also to the "lower parts of the earth."[55] And there he found us devoured and "sitting under the shadow of death."[56] And leading us hence, he does not now prepare a place on earth for us, lest we be devoured again, but a place in the kingdom of the heavens.

(7) "You have led in your righteousness this your people whom you freed. You have comforted them by your strength in your holy rest."[57] The Lord "led out in righteousness" his

51 Ex 15.12.
52 Cf. Is 65.2.
53 Lk 23.21.
54 Cf. Jn 2.11.
55 Cf. Eph 4.9.
56 Cf. Lk 1.79.
57 Ex 15.13.

people "whom he freed by the laver of regeneration."[58] He also comforted them by the consolation of the Holy Spirit in "his strength and in his rest."[59] For the hope of future rewards provides rest for those who labor, as the hope of a crown soothes the pain of injuries for those entered in an athletic contest.

(8) "The nations heard and were angered; grief seized the inhabitants of Philisthiim. Then the leaders of Edom and the princes of the Moabites hastened; trembling seized them. All the inhabitants of Chanaan wasted away."[60] As far as the record shows it is clear that no one from these nations was present when the miracles occured. How then will "the Moabites" and "Edom" and the other nations which are listed appear frightened with trembling, or "to have hastened" as the text says, or "the Philistines to have been angered"? But if we go back to the spiritual meaning you will find that "the Philistines," that is people who fall, and "Edom," which means earthly,[61] are in a state of confusion and the princes of all of these run about and are terrified, gripped by distress when they see their kingdoms which are in the lower realm penetrated by him "who descended into the lower parts of the earth,"[62] that he might snatch away those whom death possessed. For this reason "fear and trembling seized" them because they sensed "the greatness of his arm."[63] For this reason also "all the inhabitants of Chanaan," who are interpreted to mean mutable and changeable, "wasted away,"[64] when they see their kingdoms troubled, "the strong man bound and his vessels plundered."[65] Therefore, "let fear and trembling come upon them at the greatness of his arm."[66] What do the demons fear? At what do they tremble?

---

58 Cf. Ti 3.5.
59 Cf. Ex 15.13.
60 Ex 15.14–15.
61 See Appendix, 30 and 31.
62 Cf. Eph 4.9.
63 Cf. Ex 15.16, 15.
64 Ex 15.15. See Appendix, 32.
65 Cf. Mt 12.29.
66 Ex 15.16.

Without doubt, the cross of Christ in which "they have been conquered, in which their principalities and powers have been stripped."[67] Therefore, "fear and trembling shall fall upon them," when they see the sign of the cross faithfully fixed on us and "the greatness of his arm" which the Lord spread out on the cross as Scripture says, "All day I spread out my hands to a people who do not believe and who speak against me."[68] They will not, therefore, otherwise fear you, nor "will dread of you come upon them" unless they see the cross of Christ in you, unless you also can say, "But let me not glory except in the cross of my Lord Jesus Christ, by which the world has been crucified to me and I to the world."[69]

(9) "Let them become like stone until your people pass over Lord, until this your people whom you acquired pass over."[70] "To become as stone" is, by nature, not to be stone, for one becomes only what one was not originally. We say this because of those who say that Pharao or the Egyptians had an evil nature and were not brought into this state by freedom of the will, as well as for those who reproach the creator God as harsh because he turns men into stones.[71] Let these, therefore, before they blaspheme, consider most attentively what is written. For the text did not say, "Let them become as stone," and then become silent. It establishes a time and determines a measure of the condemnation. For the text says, "Until your people pass over," by which, of course, it indicates that after the people pass over they would not be "as stones." I think something prophetic is latent in this. For I see that the people who were before us became hard and unbelieving "as stone," but not to the extent that they should remain by nature among stones, but "until this people pass over, the people whom you acquired." For "partial blindness has seized Israel"—that Israel according to the flesh—"until the fullness of the Gentiles

---

67 Cf. Col 2.15.
68 Is 65.2.
69 Gal 6.14.
70 Ex 15.16.
71 The reference is to the Valentinians and Marcionites respectively.

should come in."[72] For when "the fullness of the Gentiles has come in" then also "all Israel," who by the hardness of unbelief had become "like stone," "will be saved."[73] And do you wish to see how "they will be saved"? "God is able," Scripture says, "to raise up sons of Abraham from these stones."[74] They remain stones now, therefore, "until your people pass over Lord, this your people whom you acquired."[75]

But if the Lord himself is creator of all things, we must consider in what manner he is said "to have acquired" what is without doubt his own. It is said also in another song in Deuteronomy: "Is not he himself your God who made you and created you and acquired you?"[76] For each one appears to acquire that which was not his own. Indeed on this basis the heretics also say of the Savior that he "acquired" those who were not his; for with the price which was paid he purchased men whom the creator had made. And it is certain, they say, that everyone buys that which is not his own; indeed the Apostle says, "You have been bought with a price."[77] But hear what the prophet says, "You have been sold for your sins and for your iniquities I sent your mother away."[78] You see, therefore, that we are all creatures of God. But each one is sold for his own sins and, for his iniquities, parts from his own creator. We, therefore, belong to God in so far as we have been created by him. But we have become slaves of the devil in so far as we have been sold for our sins. Christ came, however, and "bought us back"[79] when we were serving that lord to whom we sold ourselves by sinning. And so he appears to have recovered as his own those whom he created; to have acquired as people belonging to another indeed those who had sought another lord for themselves by sinning.

---

72 Rom 11.25.
73 Rom 11.25–26.
74 Mt 3.9.
75 Cf. Ex 15.16.
76 Dt 32.6.
77 1 Cor 7.23.
78 Is 50.1.
79 Cf. Gal 3.13.

But perhaps Christ, who gave his own blood as the price for us, is rightly said to have bought us back. But what sort of price did the devil, too, pay that he might purchase us? Pay attention then. Murder is the money of the devil; for "he is a murderer from the beginning."[80] You have committed murder; you have received the devil's money. Adultery is the money of the devil for "the image and superscription"[81] of the devil is on it. You have committed adultery; you have received a coin from the devil. Theft, false testimony, greediness, violence, all these are the devil's property and treasure for such money proceeds from his mint. With this money, therefore, he buys those whom he buys and makes all of those his slaves who have received however insignificant a coin from his property of this kind. But I fear that the devil is secretly purchasing even some of these who are in the Church, some of these who are present, while we do not know it. I fear that he also may present this money which we enumerated above to some of us and make those his own again, and again write for them documents of slavery and bond sureties of sin and mingle those whom he made his slaves for the price of sin with the servants of God. For he is accustomed, because he is "the enemy," "to mix tares with the wheat."[82] Nevertheless, if someone, perhaps having been deceived by the devil, accepts money of this kind, he is not totally hopeless. For "the Lord is merciful and full of pity"[83] and "does not wish the death" of his creation, but wishes "that it might be converted and live."[84] By repenting, by weeping, by making amends, let him destroy what has been committed. For the prophet says, "When you have turned and mourned, you will be saved."[85] We have proceeded far afield while wishing to explain how God is said "to acquire" what is his own and Christ is said "to buy back with his precious blood"[86] those whom the devil bought with the cheap wages of sin.

---

80 Jn 8.44.
81 Mt 22.20.
82 Cf. Mt 13.25–28.
83 Ps 110.4.
84 Cf. Ez 33.11.
85 Cf. Is 45.22.
86 Cf. 1 Pt 1.19.

(10) "Bring them in and plant them on the mountain of your inheritance."[87] God does not want to plant us in Egypt nor in low and humble places, but he wishes to plant those whom he plants "on the mountain of" his "inheritance." Then besides, do not the words, "Bring them in and plant them," seem to you to speak of children who are brought to schools, who are brought to learning, who are brought to all instruction? Understand, therefore, by these words, if you have "ears to hear," how God plants, lest perhaps when you hear that he "brings in" and "plants" you think that he puts fig trees in the earth or other slips of this kind. Hear also elsewhere how God plants. The prophet says, "You brought over a vine from Egypt; you drove out nations and planted it. You made a passable way before it; you planted its roots and it filled the earth. Its shade covered the mountains and its branches the cedars of God."[88]

Do you perceive now how God plants and where he plants? He does not plant in the valleys, but on the mountains in high and lofty places. He does not wish to place again in lowly places those whom he led out of Egypt, whom he led from the world to faith, but he wishes their mode of life to be uplifted. He wishes us to dwell in the mountains, but also in these very mountains no less does he not wish us to crawl all over the ground, nor does he wish further that his vine have its fruit cast down to the ground, but he wishes its shoots to be led upwards, to be placed aloft. He wishes that there be vine branches and vine branches not in just any lowly trees, but in the loftiest and highest cedars of God. I think the "cedars of God" are the prophets and apostles. If we are joined to them as the vine which "God brought over from Egypt" and our shoots are spread along their branches and, resting on them, we become like vine branches bound to one another by bonds of love, we shall doubtless produce very much fruit. For "every tree which does not produce fruit is cut down and cast into the fire."[89]

---

87 Ex 15.17.
88 Cf. Ps 79.9–11.
89 Lk 3.10.

(11) "Into your prepared habitation, which you prepared, Lord."[90] Behold the goodness of the merciful Lord. He does not wish to bring you into labor; he does not wish that you make yourself a dwelling; he brings you out to "an habitation" already "prepared." Hear the Lord saying in the Gospel: "Others have labored and you have entered into their labor."[91]

(12) "The sanctuary, Lord, which your hands have prepared."[92] The tabernacle of God or the temple is said to be a "sanctuary" from the fact that he sanctifies those who approach. This, it says, was "not made by the hand of man," but by the hand of God.[93] Why? Because God both plants and builds you. He becomes vinedresser and builder lest you lack anything. Hear also Paul say, "You are God's field, God's building."[94] What then is that "sanctuary" which has "not been made by the hand of man," but prepared by the hands of God? Hear Wisdom saying, "She has built a house for herself."[95] I think, however, that this is understood more correctly of the Lord's incarnation. For "it was not made by the hand of men," that is the temple of flesh is not built in the virgin by human work, but, as Daniel had prophesied, "A stone cut without hands separated and became a great mountain."[96] That is the "sanctuary" of the flesh which was taken up and "cut" from the mountain of human nature and the substance of flesh "without hands," that is, apart from the work of men.

(13) "Lord, you who rule from age to age and beyond."[97] As often as "from age to age" is said a length of time is indicated but there is some end. And if Scripture says "into another age," certainly something longer is indicated, but an end is set. And as often as "the ages of the ages" is mentioned some termination is indicated, although perhaps unknown to us, never-

---

90 Ex 15.17.
91 Jn 4.38.
92 Ex 15.17.
93 Cf. Hb 9.24.
94 1 Cor 3.9.
95 Prv 9.1.
96 Dn 2.34–35.
97 Ex 15.18.

theless established by God. But Scripture adds in this passage: "and beyond." No sense of any termination or end remains. For at whatever time you might think there could be an end, the word of the prophet always says to you: "and beyond," as if it should speak to you and say, "Do you think the Lord will reign into the age of the age?": "and beyond." Do you think he will reign "into the ages of the ages?": "and beyond." And whatever you say about the duration of his reign the prophet always says to you: "and beyond."

(14) "For Pharao's cavalry with his four-horse chariots and riders entered the sea and the Lord brought the water of the sea upon them. The sons of Israel, however, walked on dry ground in the midst of the sea."[98] And if you are a "son of Israel" you can walk "on dry ground in the midst of the sea." If you should be "in the midst of a crooked and perverse people, holding the word of life like the light of the sun for glory,"[99] it can happen that marching in the midst of sinners the liquid of sin may not pour over you; it can happen that no wave of lust sprinkle you as you pass through this world, that no surge of desire strike you. He who is an Egyptian, however, and follows Pharao is drowned in the flood of vices. But for him who follows Christ and walks as he walked, the "waters" become a "wall on the right hand and on the left."[100] But he himself goes the middle way "on dry ground." "He does not turn aside to the right hand nor to the left"[101] until he goes forth to freedom and sings a hymn of victory to the Lord saying: "I will sing to the Lord for he has been glorified magnificently,"[102] through Jesus Christ our Lord, "to whom belongs glory and sovereignty forever and ever. Amen."[103]

---

98 Ex 15.19.
99 Cf. Phil 2.15–16.
100 Cf. Ex 14.22.
101 Cf. Dt 17.20.
102 Ex 15.1.
103 Cf. 1 Pt 4.11.

HOMILY VII
On the bitterness of the water of Mara

FTER THE CROSSING OF THE RED SEA and the secrets of the magnificent mystery, after dances and tambourines, after triumphant hymns, they come to Mara. The water of Mara, however, was bitter and the people could not drink it. Why, then, after marvels so numerous and so magnificent are the people of God led to bitter waters and the danger of thirst? For the text says, "And the sons of Israel came to Mara and were not able to drink the water of Mara because it was bitter. For this reason the name of that place was called bitterness"[1] But what is added after this? "Moses," the text says, "called to the Lord and the Lord showed him a tree and he threw it into the water and the water became sweet. And there," the text says, "the Lord established ordinances and precepts for him."[2] There, where there was bitterness; there, where there was thirst, and what is worse, thirst in the presence of an abundance of water; there "God established ordinances and judgments for them."[3] Was there not another place more worthy, more fit, more fruitful, than that place of bitterness?

In addition, the statement, "The Lord showed him a tree, and he threw it into the water, and the water became sweet,"[4] is very strange. Why should God show Moses a tree which he should throw into the water to make it sweet? It is as if God had not been able to make the water sweet without the tree. Or did Moses not know about the tree, that God should show it to him? But we must see what beauty the inner meaning holds in these words.

---

1 Ex 15.23.
2 Ex 15.25.
3 Ex 15.25.
4 Ex 15.25.

I think that the Law, if it be undertaken according to the letter, is sufficiently bitter and is itself Mara. For what is so bitter as for a child to receive the wound of circumcision on the eighth day and tender infancy suffer the hardness of the iron? A cup of this kind of Law is extremely bitter, so bitter in fact that the people of God—not that people who were baptized "in Moses in the sea and in the cloud,"[5] but that people who were baptized "in spirit" and "in water"[6]—cannot drink from that water. But indeed they cannot taste the bitterness of circumcision nor are they able to endure the bitterness of victims or the observance of the Sabbath. But if "God shows a tree" which is thrown into this bitterness so that the "water" of the Law becomes "sweet," they can drink from it. Solomon teaches us what that "tree" is which "the Lord showed," when he says that wisdom "is a tree of life for all who embrace it."[7] If, therefore, the tree of the wisdom of Christ has been thrown into the Law and has shown us how circumcision ought to be understood, how the Sabbath and the law of leprosy are to be observed, what sort of distinction should be held between clean and unclean, then the water of Mara is made sweet and the bitterness of the letter of the Law is changed into the sweetness of spiritual understanding and then the people of God can drink.

If these things are not interpreted spiritually the people who have forsaken idols and taken refuge in God immediately avoid the Law and cannot drink if they hear it giving instructions about sacrifices. They feel this to be bitter and harsh. For "if he again build up these things which he destroyed he makes himself a transgressor."[8] In this bitterness of Mara, therefore, that is in that letter of the Law, "the Lord established ordinances and judgments."[9] Does this not seem to you to say that God established the treasures of his wisdom and knowledge in

---

5 1 Cor 10.2.
6 Cf. Mt 3.11; Jn 3.5.
7 Prv 3.18.
8 Cf. Gal 2.18.
9 Cf. Ex 15.25.

the letter of the Law as in some small vessel? This is, then, the meaning of the statement, "And there God established ordinances and judgments for them."[10] This was also what the Apostle was saying: "But we have this treasure in earthen vessels, that the excellency may be of the power of God, and not of us."[11] That, therefore, this water of Mara might be drunk, "God shows a tree" which is thrown into it that he who drinks may not die nor taste the bitterness. Whence it is established that if anyone without "the tree of life,"[12] that is without the mystery of the cross, without faith in Christ, without spiritual understanding should wish to drink from the letter of the Law, he will die from too much bitterness. Because the apostle Paul knew this he said, "The letter kills."[13] This openly states that the water of Mara kills if it is drunk unchanged and not made sweet.

(2) But what does the text add to these words? After "God established ordinances and judgments for them," it says, "And there he tested them saying, 'If you will certainly hear the voice of the Lord your God and do what plainly pleases him and hear his precepts and keep them, I will not bring on you all the sickness which I brought on the Egyptians. For I am the Lord who heals you.' "[14] It seems good to me to set forth the purpose for which the "ordinances and judgments" and testimonies of the Law have been given: "That he might test them," the text says, "if they would hear the voice of the Lord and keep what they were commanded." But to what extent does it have the earlier people in view? What were they commanded that was good and perfect while they were murmuring and contradicting? For a little later they are even turned back to idols and having forgotten the benefits and marvels performed by God they set up the head of a calf. For this reason, therefore,

---

10 Ex 15.25.
11 Cf. 2 Cor 4.7.
12 Cf. Prv 3.18.
13 2 Cor 3.6.
14 Ex 15,25–26.

precepts are given to them by which they are tested. Hence it is that also through the prophet Ezechiel the Lord says to them, "I gave you precepts and ordinances which were not good, by which you will not live."[15] For when they were tested in the precepts of the Lord they were not found faithful. Therefore "the commandment that was ordained to life, the same was found to be unto death for them,"[16] because one and the same commandment, if it is observed, produces life; if it is not observed, death. For this reason, therefore, the commandments which produce death for those who do not observe them are called "commandments which are not good by which they do not live."[17] But because he has mixed the tree of the cross of Christ with them and they have become sweet and are observed, having been spiritually understood, those same commandments are called "commandments of life," as also it says elsewhere: "Hear, O Israel, the commandments of life."[18]

But let us see what it is which is promised if they should be observed. "If," the Lord says, "you observe my precepts I will not bring on you all the sicknesses which I brought on the Egyptians."[19] What does he appear to say? That if someone should observe the commandments he would not suffer sickness, that is, he would neither have a fever nor suffer other pains of the body? I do not think that these are what are promised to those observing the divine commandments. Elsewhere Job, that man who was so just and observant of all piety, who was filled with the "worst sores from his head to his feet,"[20] serves as an indication to us. Those, therefore, who keep the commandments are not said to be free from these infirmities, but they will not have those infirmities which the Egyptians have, for the world is figuratively called Egypt. The Egyptian sickness, therefore, is "to love the world and those things which

---

15 Ez 20.25.
16 Cf. Rom 7.10.
17 Ez 20.25.
18 Bar 3.9.
19 Ex 15.26.
20 Cf. Jb 2.7.

are in the world."[21] The Egyptian sickness is "to observe days and months and times,"[22] to seek for signs, to cling to the courses of the stars. The Egyptian sickness is zealously to serve the luxury of the flesh, to give attention to pleasures, to devote one's self to delights. He, therefore, who has kept the commandments has been free from these infirmities and sicknesses.

(3) After this the text says that "they came to Elim and there were twelve springs of water and seventy palm trees there."[23] Do you suppose there is no reason why the people were not previously led "to Elim" where "there were twelve springs of water" in which there was no bitterness but rather exceptional pleasantness from the density of the palms, but first were led to the salty and bitter waters and come to the springs only after the bitter waters have been made sweet by the tree which was shown by the Lord? If we follow only the simple record of facts, it does not edify us much to know to what place they came first and to what place second. But if we pry into the mystery lying hidden in these matters we discover the order of faith. For first people are led to the letter of the Law. They cannot withdraw from this while they remain in its bitterness. But when the Law has been made sweet by "the tree of life"[24] and has begun to be understood spiritually, then they pass over from the Old Testament to the New and come to the twelve apostolic springs. "Seventy palm trees" will be found there also. For not only did the twelve apostles preach the faith of Christ, but also seventy others who were sent to preach the word of God are mentioned through whom the world might recognize the palms of Christ's victory. It is, therefore, not sufficient for the people of God to drink the water of Mara, even though it has been made sweet, even though all the bitterness of the letter has been cast out "by the tree of life" and the mystery of the cross. The old document alone is not sufficient for drinking.

---

21 Cf. 1 Jn 2.15.
22 Cf. Gal 4.9–10.
23 Ex 15.27.
24 Cf. Prv 3.18.

They must come also to the New Testament from which they are given a drink without hesitation and without any difficulty. The Jews even now are at Mara. Even now they attend to the bitter waters, for "God" has not yet "shown" them "the tree" by which their waters might become sweet. For the prophet predicted to them, "Unless you believe, you will not understand."[25]

(4) After these things it is written, "In the second month after they set forth from Egypt, on the fifteenth day of the month, the people murmured against Moses saying, 'Would that we had died in the land of Egypt when we sat over kettles of flesh and ate bread to satiety, since you led us into this wilderness to kill the whole congregation with famine.'"[26] Granted, the sin of the people, that they murmured and were ungrateful for the divine benefits when they received the heavenly manna, is pointed out for the correction of the readers. But why is the day also recorded on which "the people murmured"? The text says, "In the second month on the fifteenth day of the month." Certainly it was not written without reason. Recall what was said about the laws of the Passover and you will discover there that this is the time which is established to celebrate the second Passover for those who were "impure in soul" or occupied with foreign business.[27] Those, therefore, who were not "impure in soul" or not "on a long journey," celebrated the Passover "on the fourteenth day of the first month." Those, however, who "were on a long journey and were impure" celebrate a second Passover at this time, at which time also the manna descended from heaven. The manna did not descend on the day on which the first Passover occurred but at this time on which the second Passover occurred.

Let us now see, therefore, what order of mystery these words contain. The first Passover belongs to the first people; the second Passover is ours. For we were "impure in soul,"[28]

25 Is 7.9.
26 Ex 16.1–3.
27 Cf. Nm 9.9–11.
28 Cf. Nm 9.10.

who "used to worship wood and stone"[29] and "not knowing
God we used to serve those things which, by nature, were not
gods."[30] We also were those who "were on a long journey,"[31] of
whom the Apostle says that we were "strangers and foreigners
to the testaments of God, not having hope and without God in
this world."[32] Nevertheless the manna from heaven was not
given on that day on which the first Passover was celebrated,
but on that day on which the second was celebrated. For "the
bread which descended from heaven"[33] did not come to those
who celebrated the first celebration, but to us who received the
second. "For our Passover, Christ, has been sacrificed,"[34] who
"descended" to us as the true "bread from heaven."[35]

But nevertheless let us see what it is which is shown to have
happened on this day. "On the fifteenth day of the second
month," the text says, "the people murmured and said that it
would have been better for us to die in Egypt when we sat over
kettles of flesh."[36] O ungrateful people! They who saw the
Egyptians destroyed desire Egypt! They who saw the flesh of
the Egyptians given to the fish of the sea and the birds of the
sky again seek the flesh of Egypt! They raise, therefore, a
murmur against Moses, nay rather against God. But this is
pardoned the first time, and a second time, and perhaps a
third. But if they persist and do not desist, hear what next
ensues for the people who murmur.

The Apostle revealed in his writings what is also related in
the book of Numbers: "Nor should you murmur as some of
those murmured and died from the snakes."[37] The poisonous
bite of snakes destroyed the murmuring people in the wilderness. Let us who hear these words beware, I mean us for whom

---

29 Ez 20.32.
30 Gal 4.8.
31 Cf. Nm 9.10.
32 Eph 2.12.
33 Cf. Jn 6.51.
34 1 Cor 5.7.
35 Cf. Jn 6.51.
36 Cf. Ex 16.1–3.
37 1 Cor 10.9-10.

these things were written, "For they happened for correction
for those; they have been written, however, for us on whom the
end of the ages has come."[38] If we do not desist murmuring, if
we do not cease from our complaints which we frequently have
against God, let us take heed lest we incur a similar kind of
offense. For we lift up a murmuring against God when we
complain about the inclemency of the sky, about the un-
fruitfulness of the produce, about the scarcity of rains, about
the prosperity of some and the lack of prosperity of others.
These things are forgiven at their beginnings, but they are
seriously punished in those who do not desist. For snakes are
sent against them, that is, they are delivered to unclean spirits
and poisonous demons, which destroy them with secret and
hidden bites and kill by thoughts which are internal and
enclosed in the inner parts of the heart. But I beseech you, may
the examples of correction which were set before us be useful;
may their punishments be our correction. For God says, "I
have heard the murmuring of the sons of Israel."[39] Do you see
that our murmuring does not escape God's notice. He hears all
things and the fact that he does not immediately punish means
he awaits the repentance of our conversion.

(5) But what was read after these words. "The Lord said to
Moses, 'Behold I will rain bread from heaven for you, and the
people will go out and collect it daily, that I may put them to the
test, if they will walk in my Law or not. And it shall be on the
sixth day, they shall prepare whatever they bring in, and it shall
be double whatever they bring in daily.' "[40] I, at least, wish first
to have a word about this Scripture with the Jews to whom "the
words of God" are said to be "entrusted."[41] What do they take it
to mean when it says, "For six consecutive days you shall
gather. On the sixth day, however, you shall gather double"?[42]
It appears that that day which is placed before the Sabbath is

---

38 Cf. 1 Cor 10.11.
39 Ex 16.12.
40 Ex 16.4–5.
41 Cf. Rom 3.2.
42 Cf. Ex 16.26,5.

called the sixth day, which we call the Day of Preparation. The
Sabbath, however, is the seventh day.[43]

I ask, therefore, on what day the heavenly manna began to
be given, and I wish to compare our Lord's Day with the
Sabbath of the Jews. For from the divine Scriptures it appears
that manna was first given on earth on the Lord's Day. For if, as
Scripture says, it was gathered for six consecutive days, but on
the seventh day, which is the Sabbath, it was stopped, without
doubt it began on the first day which is the Lord's Day. But if it
is plain from the divine Scriptures that on the Lord's Day God
rained manna and on the Sabbath he did not, let the Jews
understand that already at that time our Lord's Day was
preferred to the Jewish Sabbath. Even then it was revealed that
on their own Sabbath no grace of God descended to them from
the sky; no bread of heaven, which is the word of God, came to
them. For a prophet also says elsewhere: "The sons of Israel
will sit for many days without a king, without a prince, without
a prophet, without a victim, without a sacrifice, without a
priest."[44] On our Lord's Day, however, the Lord always rains
manna from the sky.

But even today I say that the Lord rains manna from the
sky. For those words which have been read to us, and the words
which descended from God which have been recited to us are
from heaven. Manna from the sky, therefore, is always given to
us who received such manna. Those unfortunate people
grieve and sigh and say they are miserable because they are not
worthy to receive the manna as their fathers received it. They
never eat manna. They cannot eat it because it is "small like the
seed of the coriander and white like frost."[45] For they perceive
nothing in the word of God which is "small," nothing subtle,
nothing spiritual, but everything is fat, everything is thick "for
the heart of that people has been made thick."[46] But the
interpretation of the name also signifies this same thing, for

---

43 Murmelstein, 112, points out that Origen's methodology here is Agadic.
44 Hos 3.4.
45 Cf. Ex 16.14,31.
46 Is 6.10.
47 See Appendix, 33.

manna means, "What is this?"[47] See if the force itself of the name does not provoke you to learning so that when you hear the Law of God read you always inquire and ask and say to the teachers, "What is this?" For this is what manna means. Therefore, if you wish to eat manna, that is if you desire to receive the word of God, know that it "is small and very subtle like the seed of the coriander." It is partially vegetable by which it can nourish and recreate the weak, for "he who is weak eats vegetables."[48] It is also partially hard and, therefore, is "as frost." It is also very white and sweet. For what is whiter, what more splendid than divine instruction? What is sweeter or what more delightful than the words of the Lord which are "beyond honey and the honeycomb?"[49]

But what does Scripture mean when it says, "That on the sixth day a double amount might be gathered" to store up enough also for the Sabbath? We ought not, as we understand, pass this by idly and carelessly. The sixth day is this life in which we now are ("For in six days God made this world"[50]). On this day, therefore, we ought to put back and store away as much as will suffice also for the day to come. For if you acquire any good work here, if you store away any justice, mercy, and piety, this will be food for you in the world to come. Do we not thus read in the Gospel that he who acquired ten talents here received ten cities there; and he who acquired four received four cities? This is also what the Apostle says in another figure: "What a man sows, this he also reaps."[51] What then are we doing who love to store away that which is destroyed and does not remain and endure into tomorrow? "The rich of this world"[52] store away those things which are destroyed in this world, nay rather with the world. If, however, anyone stores away good works, those remain until tomorrow.

(6) For thus it is also written that those who were unfaithful "saved some manna, and worms came forth in abundance

---

48 Rom 14.2.
49 Cf. Ps 18.11.
50 Cf. Ex 20.11.
51 Gal 6.7.
52 Cf. 1 Tm 6.17.

from it and it rotted."⁵³ That, however, which was stored away the day before the Sabbath was not destroyed nor did "worms come forth in abundance in it," but it remained whole. If, therefore, you store up treasure for this present life only and for love of the world, immediately "worms come forth in abundance." How "do worms come forth in abundance"? Hear what the judgment of the prophet is about sinners and these who love the present world: "Their worm," he says, "will not die and their fire will not be extinguished."⁵⁴ Those are worms which avarice generates; those are worms which the blind desire for riches generates in these who have money and seeing their brothers in need "shut their hearts from them."⁵⁵ For that reason the Apsotle also says, "Warn the rich of this world not to be high minded nor to hope in the uncertainty of riches, but let them be rich in good deeds, let them give freely, let them share and treasure up for themselves true life."⁵⁶ But someone says, "If you say that the word of God is manna, how does it produce worms?" The worms in us come from no other source than from the word of God. For he himself says, "If I had not come and spoken to them they would not have sin."⁵⁷ If anyone, therefore, sins after the word of God has been received, the word itself becomes a worm in him which always pricks his conscience and gnaws at the hidden things of his heart.

(7) But what more does the divine word teach us? "And in the evening," the text says, "You will know that I am the Lord, moreover in the morning you will see the majesty of the Lord."⁵⁸ I wish that the Jews would tell me how the Lord is known "in the evening," and how his majesty is seen "in the morning." Where was the Lord known "in the evening" and his majesty seen "in the morning"? Answer us, you who are instructed from infancy to old age "always learning and never

---

53 Cf. Ex 16.20.
54 Is 66.24.
55 Cf. 1 Jn 3.17.
56 Cf. 1 Tm 6.17–19.
57 Jn 15.22.
58 Cf. Ex 16.6–7.

coming to a knowledge of the truth."[59] Why do you not understand that these words are spoken prophetically? But if you
wish to understand these words, you cannot, except through
the Gospel. For there you will find it written that "on the
evening of the Sabbath which is dawning on the first day of the
week, Mary Magdalene and Mary the mother of James came to
the sepulcher and found the stone rolled away from the tomb"
after an earthquake had occurred.[60] They found the tombs
burst asunder and the centurion and the guards who had been
stationed to guard the tomb "saying, 'Truly this was the son of
God.'"[61] The Lord, therefore, was recognized to be the Lord by
these things in the evening; he was recognized in the power of
the resurrection. But how was his glory seen "in the morning"?
When the other women came "on the first day of the week very
early in the morning,"[62] they found angels in great splendor
sitting at the sepulcher and saying, "He is not here. He arose
from the dead. Come and see the place in which he was placed,
and go, tell his disciples that he is risen and preceeds you into
Galilee."[63] Therefore, the "majesty of the Lord" was seen "in
the morning" when the resurrection was announced by the
angels.

(8) It is added, however, in the words which follow: "In the
evening you will eat flesh and in the morning you will be filled
with bread."[64] I would like to know in what sort of order the
Jews take the sayings of the prophet. For what logic will appear
so that either "in the evening" they might eat meat without
bread or "in the morning" they might eat bread without
anything else? What do you make known from this of the
divine gift or the moderation of the heavenly grace? Is this
what you call "knowing" God, that they eat flesh in the evening
without bread? And do you say the "majesty" of God appears if
again they eat bread without flesh? But save those things for

59 Cf. 2 Tm 3.7.
60 Cf. Mt 28.1 and parallels.
61 Mt 27.54.
62 Mk 16.2f.
63 Mt 28.6–7.
64 Ex 16.12.

yourselves and those who acquiesce in you and think that God can be known in quails. We, however, for whom at the end of the age and in the evening of the world "the word was made flesh" say that the Lord is known in that flesh which he received from the virgin.[65] For no one ate that flesh of the word of God either in the morning or at noon, but in the evening. For the coming of the Lord in flesh took place in the evening as also John says, "Children, it is the last hour."[66]

But Scripture says, "And in the morning you will be filled with bread."[67] The word of God is also bread for us. For he himself is "the living bread which descends from heaven and gives life to this world."[68] But the fact that it says that this bread is given "in the morning" when we said his coming in the flesh took place in the evening, I think is to be understood as follows. The Lord came in the evening of the declining world and near the end of its appointed course, but at his coming, since he himself is "the sun of righteousness,"[69] he restored a new day for those who believe. Because, therefore, a new light of knowledge arose in the world, in a certain manner he made his own day in the morning and, as it were, "the sun of righteousness' brought forth its own morning, and in this morning those who receive his precepts are filled with bread.

Do not marvel that the word of God is said to be "flesh" and "bread" and "milk" and "vegetable" and is named in different ways for the capacity of those believing or the ability of those appropriating it.[70] This, nevertheless, also can be understood because after his resurrection, which we showed happened in the morning, he has filled those who believe with bread because he has given us those books of the Law and prophets previously unknown and unexamined, and has consigned

---

65 Jn 1.14.
66 1 Jn 2.18.
67 Ex 16.12.
68 Jn 6.51,33.
69 Cf. Mal 4.2 (LXX: 3.20).
70 Cf. Jn 1.14, 6.51; 1 Pt 2.2; Rom 14.1; Heb 5.14. The view that the word appeared to different people in different ways determined by their spiritual capacity is a common element in Origen's Christology (See Koch, 69–70). It is particularly developed in Origen *Comm. Jn.* 1.9–10(11).

these documents to the Church for our instruction, that he himself might be bread in the Gospel. In fact the other books of the Law or prophets or histories have been called more loaves from which they "who believe from the Gentiles"[71] are filled. We teach, however, that this did not happen without prophetic authority. For Isaias the prophet had predicted in this manner: "They will ascend into the mountain; they will drink wine; they will be anointed with ointment. Deliver all these things to the Gentiles for this is the will of the omnipotent Lord."[72] So, therefore, appropriately we both receive flesh in the evening and will be filled with bread in the morning because it was not possible for us to eat flesh in the morning for it was not yet time, but neither were we able at noon. For scarcely do angels eat flesh at noon and they are perhaps consigned time belonging to midday in rank.

Besides this interpretation, we can also take it to mean that for each one our morning and beginning of day is that time when we first are illuminated and approach the light of faith. At this time, therefore, when we are still in the first principles we cannot eat the flesh of the word, that is, we are not yet capable of perfect and complete doctrine. But after long exercises, after much advance, when now we are near evening and are being impelled to the goal of perfection, then at last we can become capable of solid food and the perfect word.

Let us, therefore, now hasten to receive the heavenly manna. That manna imparts the kind of taste to each mouth that each one wishes.[73] For hear also the Lord saying to those who approach him: "Be it done unto you according to your faith."[74] And, therefore, if you receive the word of God which is preached in the Church with complete faith and devotion, that word will become whatever you desire. For instance, if you are

---

71 Cf. Acts 21.25.
72 Cf. Is 57.7–9.
73 Cf. Origen *Comm. Mt.*, Ser. 100 where he relates the differing tastes of the manna to Wis 16.20–21. It was a common Rabbinic tradition that the manna had the particular taste that each person eating it wished (*Mekilta de-Rabbi Ishmael*, Vayassa' ch. V; *Midrash Rabbah*, Exod. 25.3; Yoma 75a).
74 Mt 8.13.

afflicted, it consoles you saying, "God does not despise a
contrite and humble heart."[75] If you rejoice in your future
hope, it heaps up joys for you saying, "Rejoice in the Lord and
exult, O righteous."[76] If you are angry, it calms you saying,
"Cease from wrath and leave indignation behind."[77] If you are
in pain, it heals you saying, "The Lord heals all your weak-
nesses."[78] If you are consumed by poverty, it consoles you
saying, "The Lord lifts up from the earth the helpless and
snatches the poor from the dung."[79] So, therefore, the manna
of the word of God imparts into your mouth whatever taste
you wish.

If, however, someone receives this unfaithfully and does
not eat it, but hides it, "worms come forth from it in abundance."[80] Do you think the word of God is to be withdrawn so
long that one could suppose even a worm to be born? Does this
not disturb you when you hear it? Hear the prophet say about
the person of the Lord: "I, however, am a worm and not a
man."[81] For just as it is the same one who comes "for the fall" of
some, but "for the rise" of others,[82] so also it is the same one
who now is made the sweetness of honey in the manna for the
faithful, but a worm for the unfaithful. For he is the word of
God who makes known the mind of the unjust and bores
through the conscience of sinners with the stings of reproach.
It is he who is made fire in the hearts of those for whom "He
opens the Scriptures," who say, "Was not our heart burning
within us when he opened the Scriptures to us?"[83] And for
others he is that fire which burns up the thorns of the evil
earth, that is, which consumes the evil thoughts in the heart.
And, therefore, for sinners indeed "neither does the" re-

---

75 Ps 50.19.
76 Ps 31.11.
77 Ps 36.8.
78 Cf. Ps 102.3.
79 Ps 112.7.
80 Cf. Ex 16.20.
81 Ps 21.7.
82 Cf. Lk 2.34.
83 Lk 24.32.

buking "worm ever die nor is the" consuming "fire ever extinguished."[84] He remains pleasant and sweet, however, to the righteous and faithful. For "taste and see that the Lord is sweet,"[85] God himself and our Savior Jesus Christ "to whom belongs glory and sovereignty for ever and ever. Amen."[86]

---

84 Cf. Is 66.24.
85 Ps 33.9.
86 Cf. 1 Pt 4.11.

HOMILY VIII
On the beginning of the Decalogue

OD SAYS OF EVERY SOUL WHICH HAS LEARNED how to despise the present age, which "figuratively is called Egypt,"[1] and, to use the words of the Scriptures, "has been translated" by the word of God "and is not found,"[2] because it hastens and strains to the future age: "I am the Lord your God who brought you out of the land of Egypt."[3] These words, therefore, are addressed not only to those who departed from Egypt, but much more to you, who now hear them. If only you depart from Egypt and do not further serve the Egyptians, God says, "I am the Lord your God who brought you out of the land of Egypt, out of the house of bondage."[4] See if the affairs of the world and the acts of the flesh are not "the house of bondage," just as, on the contrary, to leave wordly matters and to live according to God is the house of freedom, as the Lord also says in the Gospels: "If you continue in my word you shall know the truth and the truth shall make you free."[5] Egypt, therefore, is "the house of bondage." But Judaea and Jerusalem are the house of freedom. Hear the Apostle also proclaim about these things "according to the wisdom which was given to him in ministry":[6] "But the Jerusalem which is above is free, which is the mother of all of us."[7] As, therefore, Egypt, that earthly province, is called "the house of bondage" for the sons of Israel in comparison to Judaea and Jerusalem which become the house of freedom for them, so in com-

---

1 Cf. Rv 11.8.
2 Cf. Heb 11.5; Gn 5.24.
3 Ex 20.2.
4 Ex 20.2.
5 Jn 8.31–32.
6 Cf. 2 Pt 3.15.
7 Gal 4.26.

parison to the heavenly Jerusalem which, so to speak, is the mother of freedom, this whole world and everything which is in this world is "the house of bondage." And since man had come to the bondage of this world from the paradise of freedom for the punishment of sin, therefore the first word of the Decalogue, that is the first voice of the mandates of God, speaks of freedom saying: "I am the Lord your God who brought you out of the land of Egypt, out of the house of bondage."[8]

While you were in Egypt you could not hear this voice even if you should be ordered to celebrate the Passover, even if you "gird your loins" and put "sandals on your feet," even if you hold "a rod in your hand" and "eat unleavened bread with bitterness."[9] And why do I say that while you were in Egypt you could not hear these things? But you could not even hear these words when you advanced from Egypt immediately to the first station nor at the second or third, nor when you crossed the Red Sea; even if you come to Mara and the bitterness has become sweetness for you, even if you come to Elim to "the twelve springs of water and the seventy palm trees,"[10] even if you have passed by to Rephidim and have ascended other paths, not yet are you judged fit for words of this kind, but only when you have come to Mount Sinai. When, therefore, you have previously completed many labors and overcome many troubles and temptations, scarcely at long last will you deserve to receive the commands of freedom and to hear from the Lord: "I am the Lord your God who brought you out of the land of Egypt, out of the house of bondage." This word, indeed, is not yet a word of command, but shows who he is who commands. Now, therefore, let us see what is the beginning of the Ten Commandments of the Law, and if we do not answer everything, we shall at least set forth the beginnings as the Lord grants.

---

8 Ex 20.2. Origen's view that souls were preexistent and received bodies as punishment for sin lies behind this statement (See above *Ex. Hom.* 2.1, note 14).

9 Cf. Ex 12.3f.

10 Cf. Ex 15.23f.

(2) The first commandment, therefore, is "You shall not have other gods besides me."[11] And after this follows: "You shall not make for yourself an idol nor any likeness of anything which is in heaven above or in the earth beneath or in the waters under the earth; you shall neither adore nor worship them. For I am the Lord your God, a jealous God who avenges the sins of the fathers on the sons to the third and fourth generation for those who hate me, and shows mercy to thousands for those who love me and who keep my commandments."[12] Some think that all these words together are one commandment. But if it be thus supposed, the number ten of the commandments will not be completed—and where now will be the truth of the Decalogue? But if it be divided in that manner in which we also separated it in the preceding reading, the whole number of ten commandments will appear. The first commandment, therefore, is: "You shall not have other gods besides me."[13] The second is: "You shall not make for yourself an idol nor any likeness" etc.[14]

Let us begin, therefore, from the first commandment. But I need the help of God himself, who has given these commands, to speak, and you need purer ears to hear. If, therefore, anyone has "ears for hearing," let him hear how it has been said, "You shall not have other gods besides me."[15] If he had said, "There are no other gods besides me," the word would appear more absolute. But now because he says, "You shall not have other gods besides me,"[16] he has not denied that they exist, but he has prohibited that they exist for him to whom these commandments are given. I think the apostle Paul also assumed that because he writes to the Corinthians saying, "If indeed they exist who are called gods whether in heaven or on earth."[17] And he adds, "Just as there are many gods and many

---

11 Ex 20.3.
12 Ex 20.4–6.
13 Ex 20.3.
14 Ex 20.4.
15 Ex 20.3. Cf. Origen, *Comm. Jn.* 2.2.13–18, on the discussion in this section.
16 Ex 20.3.
17 1 Cor 8.5.

lords, but for us there is one God the Father from whom are all things and we for him, and one Lord Jesus Christ, through whom are all things and we through him."[18] But you will also find gods mentioned in many other passages of Scripture as in the passage, "Since he is the highest Lord, terrible, a great king above all gods,"[19] and, "The Lord, God of gods, has spoken,"[20] and, "In the midst he judges gods."[21] The same Apostle says of lords, "Whether thrones or dominions or powers all things have been created by him and in him."[22] "Dominions," however, are nothing other than a certain order and multitude of lords. It seems to me that the apostle Paul made the meaning of the Law clearer in this passage. For this is what he says: even if there should be "many lords" who have dominion over other nations, and "many gods" who are worshipped by others, "but for us there is one God and one Lord."

Scripture itself will be able to teach us the reason for "many gods" or "many lords" if you listen attentively and patiently. For the same Moses says in the song of Deuteronomy, "When the Most High divided the nations and scattered the sons of Adam, he set the boundaries of the nations in accordance with the number of the angels of God. And his people Jacob became the portion of the Lord, the lot of his inheritance Israel."[23] It is evident, therefore, that the angels to whom the Most High entrusted the nations to be ruled are called either gods or lords; gods as if given by God and lords as those who have been alloted power from the Lord. Whence also the Lord said to the angels who did not preserve their preeminence: "I said, 'You are gods and are all sons of the Most High. But you shall die like men and shall fall like one of the princes,' "[24] imitating, of course, the devil who became the leader of all to ruin. Whence it is evident that violation of duty, not nature, made those

---

18 1 Cor 8.5–6.
19 Ps 46.2.
20 Ps 49.1.
21 Ps 81.1.
22 Col 1.16.
23 Dt 32.8–9.
24 Ps 81.5–7.

accursed. You, therefore, O people of Israel, who are "the portion of God," who were made "the lot of his inheritance,"[25] "shall not have," the text says, "other gods besides me,"[26] because God is truly "one God" and the Lord is truly "one Lord." But on the others who have been created by him he bestowed that name not by nature but by grace.

But do not think that these words are spoken only to that "Israel" which is "according to the flesh."[27] These words are addressed much more to you who were made Israel spiritually by living for God and were circumcised in heart, not in the flesh. For although we are Gentiles in the flesh, in spirit we are Israel because of him who said, "Ask from me and I will give you the Gentiles as your inheritance and the ends of the earth as your possession,"[28] and because of him who again said, "Father all mine are yours and yours mine, I have been glorified in there,"[29] if only you so act that you may be worthy to be "a portion" of God and to walk in "the lot of his inheritance." But if you act unworthily you have for an example those who were called that they might be the "portion" of God, and by their own sins deserved to "be dispersed through all the nations."[30] And those who formerly were brought out "of the house of bondage," now again—because "he who sins is a slave of sin"[31]—are slaves no longer to the Egyptians alone, but to all nations. Therefore, to you also who went out of Egypt through Jesus Christ and were brought "out of the house of bondage," it is said, "You shall not have other gods besides me."[32]

(3) Let us see next what the second commandment also appears to contain: "You shall not make for yourself an idol nor any likeness of those things which are in heaven or which are in the earth or which are in the waters under the earth."[33] There is a great difference between idols and gods as the

---

25 Cf. Dt 32.9.
26 Ex 20.3.
27 Cf. 1 Cor 10.18.
28 Ps 2.8.
29 Jn 17.10.
30 Cf. Dt 4.27.
31 Jn 8.34.
32 Ex 20.3.
33 Ex 20.4.

Apostle himself no less teaches us. For he said of gods, "Just as there are many gods and many lords";[34] but regarding idols he says, "An idol is nothing in the world."[35] Whence it seems to me that what the Law says has not been said in passing. For it makes a distinction between gods and idols and again between idols and likenesses, for he who said that idols are nothing did not add that likenesses also are nothing. Here, however, the text says, "You shall not make for yourself an idol nor a likeness of anything."[36] Therefore, it is one thing to make an "idol," another to make a "likeness." And if the Lord should see fit to illuminate us on what is to be said, I think it is to be so interpreted that, for example, if someone with gold or silver or wood or stone should make the form of any four-footed animal or serpent or bird and set it up to be adored, he has made not an idol, but a likeness, or even if he set up a painting for this purpose he is to be said no less to have made a likeness. But he has made an idol who, according to the Apostle's word that "an idol is nothing," makes what is not. But what is that which is not? A form which the eye does not see, but which the mind imagines for itself. For example, if someone should fashion the head of a dog or a ram on human members, or again, devise two faces on one appearance of a man, or join the hindmost parts of a horse or fish to a human breast. He who makes these things and things like them does not make a likeness, but an idol. For he makes what is not, nor is there anything like it. And, therefore, knowing these things the Apostle says, "An idol is nothing in the world,"[37] for no form is adopted from existing things but that which the idle and curious mind itself perceived in itself. But it is a likeness when something is fashioned of these things which are "either in heaven or in earth or in the waters," as we said above. Nevertheless it is not easy to speak thus also about heavenly likenesses

---

34 1 Cor 8.5.
35 1 Cor 8.4.
36 Ex 20.4.
37 1 Cor 8.4. There is a similar distinction made between idols and likenesses in *Origenis adnotationes in Exodum* (PG 17.16C) and in Procopius' catena (printed in Baehrens' notes on this passage, GCS 29.221–3).

as about these likenesses which are in earth or in the sea, unless
someone should say that this can be perceived of the sun,
moon, and stars, for it is also customary for paganism to
portray forms of these. But because Moses "was learned in all
the wisdom of the Egyptians,"[38] he desired to prohibit also
those things which were in their case secret and hidden. For
example, he wished to prohibit us from using their titles,
Hecate and other forms o_ demons, which the Apostle calls
"the spiritual things of wickedness in heavenly places."[39] The
prophet also says, perhaps about the same things: "My sword is
inebriated in heaven."[40] For it is the custom with these who care
about such things to invoke demons with these forms and
likenesses either for repelling or even calling down evils. The
word of God now embracing all these things at the same time
denies and casts them out, and forbids not only the making of
an idol, but also of "a likeness of all things which are in the
earth and in the waters and in heaven."

(4) The text goes on to say, "You shall not adore them nor
worship them."[41] It is one thing to worship, another to adore.[42]
One can sometimes adore even against his will, as some fawn to
kings when they see them given to fondness of this kind. They
pretend that they are adoring idols when in their heart they are
certain that an idol is nothing. But to worship is to be subjected
to these with total desire and zeal. Let the divine word, therefore, restrain both, that you may neither worship with desire
nor adore in appearance.

Nevertheless you must know that when you decide to keep
the command of this precept and reject all other gods and
lords and have no god or lord except the one God and Lord
you have declared war on all others without treaty. When,
therefore, we come to the grace of baptism, renouncing all
other gods and lords, we confess the only God, Father, Son,

---

38 Acts 7.22.
39 Eph 6.12.
40 Is 34.5.
41 Ex 20.5.
42 The same distinction is made in *Origenis adnotationes in Exodum* (PG 17.16D).
   Cf. also Procopius' catena in Baehrens (GCS 29.223f).

and Holy Spirit. But when we confess this, unless "we love the Lord our God with our whole heart and soul" and cling to him "with our whole strength"[43] we are not made "the Lord's portion,"[44] but as though placed at some kind of boundary, we both suffer those offenses which we fled, and do not propitiate the Lord to whom we fled for refuge because we do not love him with our "whole and complete heart."[45] And, therefore, the prophet mourns over us whom he sees fluctuating in inconstancy like this and says, "Woe to the double-minded,"[46] and again, "For how long do you limp in both your knees?"[47] But the apostle James also says, "A double-minded man is unstable in all his ways."[48] We, therefore, who do not follow our Lord with complete and perfect faith and yet have withdrawn from foreign gods, stand as it were at some middle boundary. We are cut down by the foreign gods as deserters and, as unstable and doubtful men, we are not defended by our Lord.

Is this not what the prophets also imagine spiritually about the lovers of Jersualem when they say, "Your lovers themselves have become your enemies."[49] So, therefore, understand that there were also many lovers of your soul who have been seduced by its splendor with whom it has been a prostitute. It was also said of these, "I will go after my lovers who give me my wine and my oil," etc.[50] But the soul has now come to that time that it should say, "I will return to my first husband because it was better for me then than now."[51] You have returned, therefore, to your first husband; you have doubtless displeased your lovers with whom you used to commit adultery. Unless, therefore, you now remain with your husband in total faith and are joined to him in total love, because of the many evil deeds which you committed, your every movement and look and

43 Mk 12.30.
44 Dt 32.9.
45 Mk 12.30.
46 Cf. Sir 2.12.
47 Cf. 1 Kgs 18.21.
48 Jas 1.8.
49 Cf. Lam 1.2.
50 Cf. Hos 2.5.
51 Hos 2.9.

even your walk is suspected by him, if these should be too
careless. He must see nothing further in you which is playful,
licentious, or prodigal. But when you turn aside your eyes in
the slightest from your husband immediately he necessarily is
reminded of your former conduct. Therefore, that both you
may destroy the former things, and he, henceforth, may be
able to have confidence in you, not only must you do nothing
immodest, but you must not even think of such. For notice
what has been written: "When the unclean spirit has gone out
from a man, it wanders through arid places; it seeks rest and
does not find it. And then it says, 'I will return to my house
whence I came out.' And if it comes and finds it vacant, clean,
and furnished, it goes and brings with it seven other spirits
more wicked than itself and enters that house and lives in it.
And the last state of that man is worse than the first."[52] If we
give attention to these words, how can we give place to carelessness even in a small matter? For the unclean spirit dwelt in
us before we believed, before we came to Christ when our soul,
as I said previously, was still committing fornication against
God and was with its lovers, the demons. But afterward it said,
"I will return to my first husband,"[53] and came to Christ who
"created" it from the beinning "in his image." Necessarily the
adulterous spirit gave place when it saw the legitimate husband. We, therefore, have been received by Christ and our
house has been "cleansed" from its former sins and has been
"furnished" with the furnishing of the sacraments of the
faithful which they who have been initiated know. But this
house does not deserve to have Christ as its resident immediately unless its life and conduct are so holy, so pure and
incapable of being defiled that it deserves to be the "temple of
God."[54] For it ought not still be a house, but a temple in which
God dwells. If, therefore, it neglects the grace which was
received and entangles itself in secular affairs, immediately
that unclean spirit returns and claims the vacant house for

---

52 Mt 12.43–45; Lk 11.24–26.
53 Hos 2.9.
54 Cf. 2 Cor 6.16.

itself. And that it may not be able again to be expelled, "it brings with it seven other spirits more wicked and the last state of that kind of man is worse than the first,"[55] because it were more tolerable that the soul not have returned to its first husband once it became a prostitute than having gone back, after confession to her husband, to have become an adulteress again. There is, therefore, no "fellowship," as the Apostle says, "between the temple of God and idols," no "agreement between Christ and Belial."[56] If we belong to God we ought to be such that what God says about us may be fulfilled: "I will dwell in them and walk in them and they will be my people,"[57] and as a prophet says in another place: " 'Come out from their midst and be separated,' says the Lord, 'you who bear the vessels of the Lord. Come out and touch not the unclean things and I will receive you and I will be your father and you will be my sons and daughters,' says the Lord omnipotent."[58] For that reason the text says, "You shall not have other gods besides me, nor shall you make for yourself an idol nor any likeness of anything which is in heaven or in the earth or in the waters; you shall not adore them nor shall you worship them."[59]

(5) "For I am the Lord your God, a jealous God."[60] Behold the kindness of God! He himself assumes the weakness of human dispositions that he might teach us and make us perfect. For who, when he hears the phrase, "a jealous God," is not immediately astonished and thinks of the defect of human weakness? But God does and suffers all things for our sake. It is so we can be taught that he speaks with dispositions which are known and customary to us. Let us see, therefore, what this statement means: "I am a jealous God."

But that divine things may be able to be contemplated more easily, let us be instructed by human examples as those we discussed above. Every woman is either under a husband and

---

55 Cf. Lk 11.26.
56 Cf. 2 Cor 6.15–16.
57 2 Cor 6.16.
58 2 Cor 6.17–18; Is 52.11.
59 Ex 20.3–5.
60 Ex 20.5.

has been subjected to the laws of the husband or is a prostitute and uses her freedom for sinning. He, therefore, who visits a prostitute knows that he has visited a woman who is a prostitute and is accessible to all who wish, and therefore, he cannot be angry if he sees other lovers also with her. But he who adopts lawful marriage does not permit his wife to make use of her power of sinning, but is inflamed with jealousy to preserve the purity of his marriage in which he can become a lawful father.

By this example, therefore, let us understand that every soul has been prostituted to demons and has many lovers, so that the spirit of fornication now goes into it; when that spirit has left, the spirit of avarice enters, after this comes the spirit of pride, then of anger, then of envy, even later the spirit of vain glory and many others with these. All those thus commit fornication with an unfaithful soul. One does not envy another nor are they mutually moved by jealousy. And why do I say that one does not exclude the other? On the contrary they invite one another and freely call one another together, just as we already spoke a little earlier about what is written in the Gospel concerning that spirit which "went out from a man, and when it returned brought with it seven other spirits worse than itself so that they might live in one soul at the same time."[61] So, therefore, the soul which has been prostituted to demons experiences no jealousy between its lovers.

But if the soul has been united with a lawful husband, with that husband to whom Paul united and joined souls in marriage as he himself also says, "For I established you with one husband to present you as a pure virgin to Christ,"[62]—the statement in the Gospels, "A certain king made a wedding for his son,"[63] is addressed to this same subject—therefore, when the soul gives itself to the marriage of this man and receives lawful marriage with him, even if she was a sinner at some time, even if she has been a prostitute, nevertheless, if she delivers herself to this husband, she is permitted no further sin. It

---

61 Cf. Lk 11.24–26.
62 2 Cor 11.2.
63 Cf. Mt 22.2.

cannot be tolerated that a soul which has received a husband again sport with adulterers. The husband's jealousy is stirred up over her; he defends the purity of his marriage. And "God" is said to be "jealous"[64] because he does not permit the soul subjected to himself to be mingled with demons. Otherwise, if he sees the soul violating the rights of marriage and seeking occasions for sinning, then, as it is written, he gives her "a bill of divorce" and sends her away saying, "Where is your mother's bill of divorce with which I sent her away?"[65] To which he also adds: "Behold you have been sold for your sins and because of your iniquities I sent your mother away."[66] He who says these things is jealous, and because he is moved by jealousy he says these things. For he does not wish us to sin further after recognition of himself, after the illumination of the divine word, after the grace of baptism, after the confession of faith and after the marriage has been confirmed with such great sacraments. He does not permit the soul whose bridegroom or husband he himself is called to play with demons, to fornicate with unclean spirits, to wallow in vices and impurities. But even if this sometimes unfortunately should happen, he wishes, at least, that the soul be converted and return and repent.

For this is a new kind of his goodness that even after adultery he nevertheless would receive the soul which returns and repents from the heart as he also says through the prophet, "If a woman leave her husband and sleep with another man shall she return to her husband? Will she not be contaminated? You, however, have committed fornication with your many shepherds and returned to me."[67] He says the same thing elsewhere, " 'And after you committed fornication with all these, I said, "Return to me." And you have not thus returned,' says the Lord."[68]

Herein, therefore, "God is jealous": if he asks and desires that your soul cling to him, if he saves you from sin, if he

---

64 Ex 20.5.
65 Cf. Is 50.1.
66 Cf. Is 50.1.
67 Jer 3.1.
68 Cf. Jer 3.6–7.

reproves, if he chastises, if he is displeased, if he is angry and
adopts, as it were, a certain jealousy towards you, recognize
that there is hope of salvation for you. But if you do not recover
your senses when you have been chastised, if you are not
corrected when you have been reproved, if you despise when
you are beaten, know that if you go on continually sinning his
jealousy will depart from you and that which is said to Jerusalem by the prophet Ezechiel will be said to you: "Therefore
my jealousy will depart from you and I will no longer be angry
with you."[69] Behold the mercy and piety of the good God.
When he wishes to be merciful he says that he is displeased and
angry as he says through Jeremias: "You will be chastised,
Jerusalem, with pain and a scourge, lest my soul depart from
you."[70] If you understand these words it is the voice of God
having compassion when he is angry, when he is jealous, when
he brings pains and beatings. "For he scourges every son whom
he receives."[71] Do you wish to hear, however, the terrible voice
of God when he is displeased? Hear what he says through the
prophet. When he had enumerated many abominable things
which the people had committed he adds these words also:
"And for this reason I will not visit your daughters when they
fornicate nor your daughters-in-law when they commit adultery."[72] This is terrible! This is the end when we are no longer
reproached for sins, when we offend and are no longer corrected. For then, when we have exceeded the measure of sinning
"the jealous God" turns his jealousy away from us, as he said
above, "For my jealousy will be removed from you and I will no
longer be angry over you."[73] I have said these things about the
statement, "God is jealous."

(6) Now let us also see what follows, how "the sins of the
fathers" are said to be avenged "on the sons in the third and
fourth generation."[74] For the heretics are accustomed to scoff

---

69 Ez 16.42.
70 Jer 6.7–8.
71 Heb 12.6.
72 Hos 4.14.
73 Ez 16.42.
74 Ex 20.5.

at us on this word because they say it is not a word of the good God which says that one is punished for the sins of another. But according to the reasoning of those who say that the God of the Law, who commands these things, although he is not good is nevertheless just, they themselves indeed cannot show how, according to their understanding it appears to be in harmony with justice if one is punished for another's sin. It remains, therefore, that we pray that the Lord might show us how these precepts are in harmony with a just and good God.

We have often said already that not everything in divine Scripture is said to the outer man, but many things are said to the inner man. Our inner man, therefore, is said either to have God as father, if he lives according to God and does those things which are of God, or the devil, if he lives in sin and performs his wishes. The Savior shows this clearly in the Gospels when he says, "You are of your father the devil and you wish to do the desires of your father. He was a murderer from the beginning and he did not stand in the truth."[75] As, therefore, the seed of God is said to remain in us when we, preserving the word of God in us, do not sin, as John says, "He who is of God does not sin because God's seed remains in him,"[76] so also when we are persuaded to sin by the devil we receive his seed. But when we also complete the work which he urged, then he has already also begotten us; for we are born to him as sons through sin. But when we sin it scarcely happens that we sin without a helper, but we always seek either servants or helpers of sin. For example, if someone attempts adultery, he cannot commit this alone, but it is necessary that there also be an adulterous partner and companion in sin. Then besides, even if there are not several, nevertheless it is necessary that there be some man or woman in the service and partnership of sin. All of them begotten, as it were, one from the other according to the order of persuasion, have their birth in sin "from their father the devil."[77]

---

75 Jn 8.44.
76 1 Jn 3.9.
77 Jn 8.44.

And to come to those things which have been written, "the Lord of majesty,"[78] Jesus Christ our Savior has been crucified. The author of this crime and father of this wickedness is, without doubt, the devil. For it is written thus: "When, however, the devil had entered the heart of Judas Iscariot that he should betray him."[79] The devil, therefore, is the father of sin. He begot Judas as his first son in this wickedness, but Judas alone could not execute it. What then is written? "Judas departed," Scripture says, "to the Scribes and Pharisees and chief priests, and said to them: 'What will you give me and I will deliver him to you?' "[80] Therefore, the third and fourth generation of sin was born from Judas. And you will be able to detect this order even in some individual sins.

Now, therefore, let us see, according to this which we called a generation, how God "avenges the sins of the fathers on the sons even to the third and fourth generation,"[81] and does not avenge them on the fathers themselves, for nothing is said about the fathers. The devil, therefore, who has now exceeded the measure of sinning, as the prophet says, "As the garment stiffened with blood will not be clean,"[82] so also he will not be clean in this age nor is he reproached for sin nor is he scourged, for all things have been preserved for him for the future. Whence also, since he knew that that time of punishment was established for himself, he said to the Savior, "Why have you come to torment us before the time?"[83] Therefore, while this world stands, the devil, who is the father of sinners, does not receive his own sins; they are avenged, however, on his sons, that is on those whom he begot through sin. For men who are in the flesh are reproached, beaten, and scourged by the Lord. For "the Lord does not wish the death of the sinner, but that he turn back and live."[84] And because "the

---

78 Cf. Ps 28.3.
79 Lk 22.3; Jn 13.2.
80 Mt 26.14–15 and parallels.
81 Ex 20.5.
82 Cf. Is 14.19.
83 Mt 8.29.
84 Ez 33.11.

Lord is kind and merciful"[85] he avenges the sins of the fathers
on the sons, that since the fathers, that is "the devil and his
angels"[86] and other "princes of the world and rulers of this
darkness"[87]—for they also are made fathers of sin just as also
the devil—since, I say, those fathers are unworthy to be reproached in the present age, but receive what they deserve in
the future, their sons, that is those whom they persuaded to sin
and who, no less, had been received by them to the fellowship
and partnership of sin, these receive what they have done, that
they may proceed purer to the future age and not further be
made partners with the devil in punishment. Therefore, because God is merciful and "wishes all men to be saved,"[88] he
says, "I will visit their crimes with an iron rod and their sins
with whips. I will not, however, remove my mercy from
them."[89] The Lord, therefore, visits and seeks the souls which
that most wicked father begot by the persuasion of sin, and says
to each of them: "Hear, daughter, and look and incline your
ear, and forget your people and the house of your father."[90]
He, therefore, visits you after sin and disturbs you and he visits
you with a whip and a rod for the sin which your father the
devil submitted to you, that he may avenge that sin "in" your
"bosom," that is, while you continue in the body. And thus the
avenging of "the sins of the fathers in the bosoms of the sons in
the third and fourth generation" is completed.[91]

For "God is jealous" and does not wish that soul which he
betrothed to himself in faith to remain in the defilement of sin,
but wishes it immediately to be purified, wishes it swiftly to cast
out all its impurities, if it has by chance been snatched away to
some. But if the soul continues in sins and says: "We will not

---

85 Cf. Ps 102.8.
86 Cf. Mt 25.41.
87 Cf. Eph 6.12.
88 Cf. 1 Tm 2.4.
89 Ps 88.32–33, 2.9.
90 Ps 44.11.
91 Cf. Jer 32.18; Ex 20.5. This entire paragraph reflects Origen's doctrine that
   this world is a school to discipline the fallen soul and restore it to the original
   purity it possessed before its existence in the body (See, for example, *De
   Princ.* 2.8.3, 3.5.8).

hear the voice of the Lord, but we will do what we wish and will burn incense 'to the queen of heaven,' "[92] a practice reprobated by the prophet, then it is held over for that judgment of Wisdom: "Since indeed I called and you did not listen, but jeered at my words, therefore, I also will laugh at your ruin,"[93] or that judgment which has been placed on those in the Gospel when the Lord says, "Depart from me into the eternal fire which God has prepared for the devil and his angels."[94]

I choose that while I am in this world the Lord visit my sins and reform my transgressions here that there Abraham may also say of me as he said of poor Lazarus to the rich man: "Remember, son, that you received your good things in your life and Lazarus likewise evil things. Now, however, here he is at rest, but you are afflicted."[95] For this reason, when we are reproached, when we are chastised by the Lord we ought not to be ungrateful. Let us understand that we are reproached in the present age that we may attain rest in the future, as also the Apostle says, "When, however, we are chastised by the Lord we are being reproached that we might not be condemned with this world."[96] It was for this reason that blessed Job also willingly accepted all his sufferings and said, "If we have received good things from the hand of the Lord, shall we not also endure evil things?"[97] "The Lord gave, the Lord has taken away, as it pleased the Lord so it is done. May the name of the Lord be blessed."[98] However, he also returns "mercy on those thousands who love him."[99] For those who love do not need reproof for they do not sin as also the Lord says, "He who loves me keeps my commandments."[100] And, therefore, "perfect love casts out fear."[101] For this reason mercy alone has been

---

92 Cf. Jer 7.18.
93 Prv 1.24–26.
94 Mt 25.41.
95 Lk 16.25.
96 1 Cor 11.32.
97 Jb 2.10.
98 Jb 1.21.
99 Cf. Ex 20.6.
100 Cf. Jn 14.21.
101 1 Jn 4.18.

appointed to those who love, for "blessed are the merciful, because God will show mercy to them"[102] in Christ Jesus our Lord, "to whom belongs glory and sovereignty forever and ever. Amen."[103]

102 Mt 5.7.
103 Cf. 1 Pt 4.11.

HOMILY IX
On the Tabernacle

F ANYONE PROPERLY UNDERSTANDS THE DEPARTURE of the Hebrews from Egypt or the crossing of the Red Sea and this whole journey through the desert and every single campsite; if he is capable of understanding these things in such a way that he also may receive the Law of God "written not with ink, but with the spirit of the living God";[1] if anyone, I say, should give his attention to these matters in the order of their sequence and spiritually fulfilling each should acquire the growth in virtues indicated in each, that man can consequently also attain to the contemplation and understanding of the tabernacle.

The divine Scriptures speak about this tabernacle in many places. They appear to indicate certain things of which human hearing can scarcely be capable. The apostle Paul especially, however, relates to us certain indications of a more excellent knowledge about the understanding of the tabernacle, but, for some unknown reason, perhaps considering the weakness of his hearers, closes, as it were, those very things which he opens. For he says, writing to the Hebrews, "For a first tabernacle was made which contained the candlestick and the setting forth of loaves. This was called the Holy of Holies. After the second veil, however, is the tabernacle which is called Holy and contains the golden altar of incense and the ark of the covenant which contained the two tablets and the manna and Aaron's rod which had blossomed."[2] But he adds to these words: "Which are not to be spoken of now particularly."[3] Some take

---

1 Cf. 2 Cor 3.3.
2 Heb 9.2–4.
3 Heb 9.5.

the words, "Which are not to be spoken of now," to refer to that time in which he was writing the epistle to the Hebrews. But to others it appears that he asserts that the whole present life is insufficient for explaining these things because of the greatness of the mysteries. But the Apostle does not leave us completely dejected. As is his custom, he opens a few things from many so that it might be closed to the indifferent but might be discovered by those who seek and opened to those who knock.[4] He repeats, therefore, about the tabernacle and says, "For Jesus has not entered into holy places made with hands, patterns of the true, but into heaven itself, that he may appear now in the sight of God through the veil, that is his flesh."[5] He, therefore, who has interpreted the veil of the interior of the tabernacle as the flesh of Christ, the holy places themselves as heaven or the heavens, the high priest as the Lord Christ, and says that he entered "once into the holy places after he discovered an eternal redemption,"[6] from these few words if anyone knows how to understand Paul's meaning, he can observe how great a sea of understanding he has disclosed to us. But they who love the letter of the Law of Moses too much, but flee its spirit hold the apostle Paul suspect when he brings forth interpretations of this kind.

(2) Let us see, therefore, if some of the holy men of old also did not hold an opinion of the tabernacle far different than those latter now suppose. Hear how magnificently David, a distinguished man of the prophets, felt about the tabernacle: "While," he says, "it is said to me day after day, 'Where is your God?' I have remembered these things and I have poured out my soul in me, since I shall enter the place of the wonderful tabernacle, unto the house of God."[7] And again he says in the fourteenth Psalm, "Lord, who will dwell in your tabernacle? Or who will rest on your holy mountain? He who enters without a spot and works justice," etc.[8] What, then, is that "place of the

---

4 Cf. Mt 7.8; Lk 11.10.
5 Heb 9.24, 10.20.
6 Heb 9.12.
7 Ps 41.4–5.
8 Ps 14.1–2.

wonderful tabernacle" from which one enters "the house of
God," because of whose memory his soul has been poured out
in him and, as it were, has been dissipated in a kind of intol-
erable desire. Are we really to believe that the prophet, desiring that tabernacle which consisted of hides and curtains and
goat-hair coverings and other common materials was poured
out in soul and failed in his whole mind? Or certainly how will it
be true to say about that tabernacle that only "the innocent in
hands and pure in heart, who did not receive his soul in vain,"[9]
will inhabit it, when the history of the kings transmits that the
worst priests, "sons of pestilence," have dwelt in the tabernacle
of God and the ark of the covenant itself also was captured by
foreigners and detained with the impious and profane?[10] From
all of this it is evident that the prophet felt in a far different
sense about this tabernacle in which he says that only "the
innocent in hands and pure in heart, who did not receive his
soul in vain nor do evil to his neighbor and did not accept
reproach against his neighbor" will dwell.[11] It is necessary,
therefore, that the inhabitant of this tabernacle which the Lord
erected, not man, be such a person.

But let us come also to the Gospels to see if they say anything
about tabernacles, that the Lord's judgment might provide an
unquestionable answer to our question. We discover, then, the
Savior Jesus Christ himself mentioning not one tabernacle, but
many, and not temporal but eternal tabernacles when he says,
"Make for yourselves friends from mammon that when it shall
fail they may receive you into eternal tabernacles."[12] You have
heard the Lord declaring that tabernacles are eternal. Now
hear the Apostle also saying, "We desire to be clothed with our
tabernacle which is from heaven."[13]

Is a way not yet opened to you from all these words by which
you may leave earth behind, following the understanding of
the prophet and Apostle and—what is greater than all—the

---

9 Ps 23.4.
10 1 Kgs 4.
11 Ps 23.4, 14.3.
12 Cf. Lk 16.9.
13 2 Cor 5.2.

word of Christ, with your whole mind and understanding and ascend to heaven and there seek the magnificence of the eternal tabernacle whose form is imperfectly represented on earth by Moses? For thus also the Lord says to him: "See to it," the text says, "you shall make all things according to the form which has been shown to you on the mountain."[14] But the human mind, and especially ours, who know that we are the least or even nobodies in divine wisdom, can perhaps arrive at the point that it may perceive that these things which are introduced in the divine books are said not of earthly things, but of heavenly, and are forms not of present but "of future goods,"[15] not of corporeal things, but of spiritual. But how the narrative of these things can be applied to heavenly and eternal things is not in my power to say, nor, as I think, in your capacity to hear. Nevertheless, if the Lord should see fit to illuminate us by your prayers, we will attempt to make known a few things which pertain to the edification of the Church.

(3) The whole people, therefore, is ordered to construct the tabernacle, with each one contributing all he can, that in a certain sense all at the same time might be one tabernacle. The contribution itself is not made of necessity, but of free will. For God says to Moses that each one, "as it seemed good in his heart,"[16] should offer for the construction of the tabernacle gold, silver, precious stones, bronze, then in addition, linen, scarlet, blue, and purple, also red and blue hides of rams, and wood not subject to rot and goats' hair. Women wise in the skill of weaving are also required, and craftsmen who know how to prepare gold, silver, bronze, and stones and to fashion wood with gold.

Next the measurements of the courts are delivered. These courts are made secure, stretched out in curtains, erected on columns, made firm with bars, and stretched tight with ropes. There are, in addition, certain places which are separated by veils. One is called the Holy Place and the other divided no less

---

14 Ex 25.40.
15 Cf. Heb 9.11, 10.1.
16 Cf. Ex 25.1f.

by a second veil is called the Holy of Holies. The ark of the covenant is placed inside. The cherubim stand over it with wings outstretched and touching one another. A kind of base and seat, as it were, for them made from gold is placed there, which is called the place of atonement. The golden altar of incense is also there. Then in the outer place the golden candlestick is set in the southern part that it might face north. But the table and the setting forth of loaves on it is placed in the northern part. And also the altar of whole burnt offerings is placed next to the inner veil. But why am I going through these things piece by piece? We can scarcely narrate so much. It is scarcely possible that the material forms themselves be brought before our eyes, and how will anyone be sufficient to explain the mysteries hidden in these things.

Nevertheless, the reason for constructing the tabernacle is found already mentioned in the words above when the Lord says to Moses: "You shall make for me a sanctuary and thence I will be seen by you."[17] God wishes, therefore, that we make a sanctuary for him. For he promises that if we make a sanctuary for him, he can be seen by us. Whence also the Apostle says to the Hebrews, "Follow peace and the sanctuary, without which no one will see God."[18] This, therefore, is the sanctuary which the Lord orders to be constructed, which the Apostle also wishes to be present in virgins "that they may be holy in body and spirit,"[19] knowing without doubt that he who makes a sanctuary for the Lord by the purity of his own heart and body will himself see God. Let us, therefore, also make a sanctuary for the Lord both collectively and individually.

Perhaps we all make the Church which is holy, "not having spot or blemish,"[20] a sanctuary in this way, if it has as pillars its teachers and ministers about whom the Apostle says, "Peter and James and John, who appeared to be pillars, gave the right

---

17 Ex 25.8.
18 Heb 12.14. The word translated "sanctuary" both here and in the previous
    quotation is *sanctificationem*.
19 Cf. 1 Cor 7.34.
20 Eph 5.27.

hand of fellowship to me and Barnabas."[21] In the tabernacle of the Old Testament, therefore, the pillars are joined by interposed bars; in the Church the teachers are associated by the right hand of fellowship which is given to them. But let those pillars be overlaid with silver and their bases overlaid with silver. Let two bases, however, be alloted to each pillar; one, which is said to be the "capital" and is placed over it; another, which is truly called the "base" and is placed under the pillar as a foundation. Let the pillars, therefore, be overlaid with silver because those who preach the word of God shall receive through the spirit "the words of the Lord," which are "pure words, silver proved by fire."[22] But they have the prophets as the bases of their preaching, for they erected the Church "upon the foundation of the apostles and prophets,"[23] and using their testimonies they confirm the faith in Christ. The capital of the pillars, however, I believe, is he of whom the Apostle says, "The head of man is Christ."[24] I have already said above that the bars of the pillars are the right hand of the apostolic fellowship given to one another. Let the curtains, which after they have been sewn to rings and suspended in circles and tied with cords, are stretched out in the manner of curtains twenty-eight cubits in length and four in breadth, hold the remaining multitude of believers who cling to and hang on the cords of faith. For "a threefold cord is not broken."[25] This is the faith in the Trinity, from which the whole Church hangs and by which it is sustained. I think that the law introduced in the Gospels is designated by the twenty-eight cubits in length and the four in breadth which are the measure of one court.[26] For the number seven usually signifies the Law

21 Gal 2.9.
22 Ps 11.7.
23 Cf. Eph 2.20.
24 1 Cor 11.3.
25 Eccl 4.12.
26 *Atrii*. The word occurs again in this and the next section, each time in a context which suggests that it has reference to the "curtains" of Ex 26.1–2 which were ten in number and 28 x 4 in dimensions. The word in the LXX at Ex 26,1–2 is *aulaia* which the Vulgate renders *cortina*. Perhaps Rufinus connected *aulaia* in Origen's text with *aulē*, which would be correctly

because of the many mysteries of the seventh number. When
this number is united with four, four times seven consequently
makes the number twenty-eight. These ten courts, however,
were constructed that they might contain the whole number of
perfection and designate the Decalogue of the Law. But now
the appearance of scarlet and blue and linen and purple set
forth many diverse works. They disclose the curtains, the
exterior and interior veil, and the whole priestly and high
priestly attire joined with gold and gems.

But lest we linger too long on the forms of individual
virtues, we can briefly say that they indicate those things by
which the Church is adorned. Its faith can be compared to
gold; the word of preaching to silver; bronze to patience;
incorruptible wood to the knowledge which comes through the
wood,[27] or to the incorruptibility of purity which never grows
old; virginity to linen; the glory of suffering to scarlet; the
splendor of love to purple; the hope of the kingdom of heaven
to the blue. Let those, however, be the materials from which
the whole tabernacle is constructed, the priests are clothed,
and the high priest is adorned. The prophet speaks in another
passage about the nature and quality of their clothing: "Let
your priests be clothed with justice."[28] All those garments,
therefore, are garments of justice. And again the apostle Paul
says, "Put on heartfelt mercy."[29] They are also, therefore,
garments of mercy. But the same apostle no less also designates
other more noble garments when he says, "Put on the Lord
Jesus Christ, and give no attention to the flesh for lusting."[30]
Those, therefore, are the garments with which the Church is
adorned.

(4) Each one of us, however, can also build a tabernacle for
God in himself. For if, as some before us have said, this

---

rendered as *atrium*. Another possibility is that Origen himself connected the
two words and used a form of *aulē*. Fortier translates the word as "vesti-
bule."

27 *Lignum*. Probably a reference to the cross. Cf. Gal 3.13; 1 Pt 2.24.
28 Cf. Ps 131.9.
29 Col 3.12.
30 Rom 13.14.

tabernacle represents the whole world, and each individual also can contain an image of the world, why can not each one also complete a form of the tabernacle in himself? He ought, therefore, to apply the pillars of the virtues to himself, silver pillars, that is, rational patience. For it is possible indeed that a man have what appears to be patience but it is not rational. For he who feels no injury and consequently does not retaliate appears patient, but that patience is not rational. That man, therefore, has pillars, but they are not silver; but that man who suffers because of the word of God and bears it bravely is decorated and protected by silver pillars. It is also possible to extend the courts in yourself when your heart enlarges in accordance with the word of the Apostle to the Corinthians: "You also be enlarged."[31] One can also defend himself with bars when he has bound himself with the unanimity of love. One can stand on silver bases when he stations himself upon the stability of the word of God, the prophetic and apostolic word. It is possible to have a gilded capital on the pillar if the golden capital on it is the faith of Christ. "For the head of every man is Christ."[32] But one can stretch out ten courts in himself when he is enlarged not only in one or two or three words of the Law, but can extend the breadth of spiritual under-standing in the whole Decalogue of the Law, or when one produces the fruit of the spirit: joy, peace, patience, kindness, goodness, moderation, faith, temperance, when love, which is greater than all, has been added. Let that soul which will not give "sleep to its eyes" nor "sleep to its eyelids" nor "rest to its hours," "until it find a place for the Lord, a tabernacle for the God of Jacob,"[33] let that soul, I say, have further in itself also an immovable altar on which it may offer sacrifices of prayers and victims of mercy to God, on which it may sacrifice pride as a bull with the knife of temperance, on which it may slay wrath as a ram and offer all luxury and lust like he-goats and kids. But let him know how to separate for the priests even from these

---

31 2 Cor 6.13.
32 Cf. 1 Cor 11.3.
33 Ps 131.4–5.

"the right arm" and "the small breast" and the jaws, that is, good works and works of the right hand (for let him preserve nothing evil); the whole small breast, which is an upright heart and a mind dedicated to God and jaws for speaking the word of God. Let him also understand that the candlestick must be placed in his own sanctuary, that his "lamps" may be always "glowing and his loins girded" and he himself be "as a servant who awaits his master to return from a wedding."[34] For the Lord also said of these lamps, "The lamp of your body is your eye."[35]

But let him place that candlestick in the south that it may look to the north. For when the light has been lit, that is when the heart is watchful, it ought always to look to the north and watch for "him who is from the north"[36] as also the prophet says he saw "a kettle or pot kindled and its face was from the face of the north," for "evils are kindled from the north for the whole earth."[37] Watchful, therefore, apprehensive, and zealous, let him always contemplate the slyness of the devil and always watch whence temptation may come, whence the foe may invade, whence the enemy may creep up. For the apostle Peter also says, "Your adversary the devil walks around like a roaring lion seeking whom he may devour."[38]

Let the table also which has the twelve loaves of setting forth be placed in the northern part looking to the south. Let the apostolic word, in number as in power, be those loaves on it. By using it incessantly—for it is commanded that they be put "before the Lord" daily—one may again look to the south whence the Lord comes, "For the Lord will come from Theman,"[39] as it is written, which is from the south. Let him have an altar of incense in his innermost heart also, that he too may say, "We are a good odor of Christ."[40] And let him have an ark of

---

34 Lk 12.35–36.
35 Mt 6.22.
36 Jl 2.20.
37 Jer 1.13–14.
38 1 Pt 5.8.
39 Hb 3.3.
40 2 Cor 2.15.

the covenant in which are the tables of the Law, that "he may meditate on the Law of God day and night."[41] And let his memory become an ark and library of the books of God because the prophet also says those are blessed who hold his commands in memory that they may do them.[42] Let there be put back within him also a jar of manna, a fine and sweet understanding of the word of God; and let there be a rod of Aaron within him, a priestly teaching and a blooming sternness of discipline.

But over and above all this splendor let him wear the adornment of the high priest. For that part which is the most precious in man can hold the office of high priest. Some call it the overseer of the heart,[43] others, rational understanding, or intellectual substance, but whatever it is called, it is that part of us in which we can have a capacity for God. Let that part in us, therefore, as a kind of high priest, be adorned with garments and costly jewels, with a long linen priestly garment. This is the kind of garment which reaches the feet, covering the whole body. This signifies that first of all the whole man be clothed with chastity. Let him afterwards receive also the cape adorned with jewels in which the splendor of works is arranged, "that men seeing your works may magnify the father who is in heaven."[44] And let him also receive on his breast the *logion,* which can be called the oracular breastplate, which is adorned with four rows of stones. But also let the golden plate which is called *petalus* shine brightly on his forehead. "Truth" and "manifestation" are said to have been placed on both of these. In these objects which are said to be placed on the breast, I perceive the message of the Gospel which, in its fourfold order, sets out to us the truth of the faith and the manifestation of the Trinity, referring all things to the head, that is to say, to the nature of the one God. There is in these objects, therefore,

---

41 Ps 1.2.
42 Cf. Ps 105.3.
43 *Principale cordis.* Fortier translates: "l'essence du coeur." De Lubac, who wrote the introduction to Fortier's translation, notes that it is a Stoic term (SC 16.216).
44 Cf. Mt 5.16.

all truth and all manifestation of the truth. If you, therefore, wish to perform the high priesthood properly for God let the message of the Gospel and the faith in the Trinity always be held in your breast. The message of the Apostle agrees with this both in its force and estimation, so that the name of God may always be held in the head and all things may be referred to the one God.

Let the high priest also have his coverings on his inner parts; let him have his private parts covered "that he may be holy in body and spirit"[45] and pure in thoughts and deeds. Let him also have bells around the hem of his garment so that, Scripture says, "when he enters the sanctuary he may give a sound and not enter with silence."[46] And these bells, which ought always to sound, have been placed on the fringe of the garment. The purpose of this, I think, is that you might never keep silent about the last times and the end of the world, but that you might always ring forth and dispute and speak in accordance with him who said: "Remember your last end and you will not sin."[47] In this manner, therefore, our inner man is adorned as high priest to God that he may be able to enter not only the sanctuary, but also the Holy of Holies; that he may be able to approach the mercy seat where the cherubim are and thence God may appear to him. The sanctuary can be those things which a holy way of life can have in the present world. But the Holy of Holies, which is entered only once, is, I think, the passage to heaven, where the mercy seat and the cherubim are located and where God will be able to appear to the pure in heart, or because the Lord says: "Behold, the kingdom of God is within you."[48]

Let what has been said about the tabernacle suffice for the present, being all we have been able to discover cursorily and direct to the ears of our hearers, that each of us also might be zealous to make a tabernacle for God within himself. For it was

---

45 Cf. 1 Cor 7.34.
46 Cf. Ex 28.35.
47 Sir 7.40.
48 Lk 17.21.

not said in vain that the fathers dwelt in tabernacles. I understand that Abraham, Isaac, and Jacob dwelt in tabernacles as follows. For those men who adorned themselves with such great splendors of virtues built within themselves a tabernacle for God. For the royal purple was notably resplendent among them, because of which the sons of Heth said to Abraham: "You are a king from God among us."[49] The scarlet also shone, for Abraham held his right hand disposed to slay his only son for God. The blue shone when he always looked to heaven and followed the Lord of heaven. But he was also likewise adorned with the other things. I also thus understand the feast of tabernacles which the Law commands, that the people might go out on a certain day of the year and dwell in tabernacles made of palm branches and the foliage of the willow and poplar and branches of leafy trees. The palm is a sign of victory in that war which the flesh and spirit wage between themselves: but the poplar and willow tree are branches of purity as much in virtue as in name. If you preserve these things entire, you can have the branches of the bushy and leafy tree which is the eternal and blessed life when "the Lord places" you "in that green place upon the water of refreshment"[50] through Christ Jesus our Lord, "to whom belongs glory and sovereignty forever and ever. Amen."[51]

---

49 Gn 23.6.
50 Cf. Ps 22.2, 1.3.
51 Cf. 1 Pt 4.11.

HOMILY X
On the woman with child who miscarried because of two quarreling men

UT IF TWO MEN SHALL QUARREL AND STRIKE A WOMAN with child and her infant issues forth yet unformed, he shall be liable for so much damage as the woman's husband shall determine, and he shall pay it with honor. But if the infant was fully formed, he shall render life for life, eye for eye, tooth for tooth, hand for hand, foot for foot, burning for burning, wound for wound, stripe for stripe.[1]

I think the first thing to be investigated is under what category of law decrees of this kind are considered. For all things which are decreed are not, as the simple think, called law, but some for example are called law, some testimonies, others mandates and ordinances, some judgments. The eighteenth Psalm teaches this clearly in one collection of categories when it says, "The law of the Lord is blameless, converting souls; the testimony of the Lord is faithful, giving wisdom to the little ones. The ordinances of the Lord are right, rejoicing hearts; the commandment of the Lord is luminous, enlightening the eyes. The fear of the Lord is pure, enduring forever and ever; the judgments of the Lord are true, justified in themselves."[2] When we observe these differences between the decrees in the Law, the passage which we now have in hand falls under the category of ordinances or justifications. For thus the Scripture says above, "And these are the ordinances which you shall set before them."[3] We are not concerned at the present, however, to expound the differences between each of

---

1 Ex 21.22–25.
2 Ps 18.8–10.
3 Ex 21.1.

these categories, for our task is to explain these words which have been read.

It must certainly be known that part of what we are to discuss has been stated in the Gospel according to Matthew when the Lord says, "You have heard that it was said, 'An eye for an eye, a tooth for a tooth.' But I say to you, do not resist evil. But if someone strike you on the right cheek, turn to him also the other."[4] But perhaps the more attentive reader of the Scriptures may say that the words which we have related from the Gospel have not been taken from this passage in Exodus, but rather from Deuteronomy where certain words, written no less in this manner, are related: "But if an unjust witness stand against a man accusing him of impiety, both men involved in the controversy shall stand before the Lord, before the priests, and before the judges, whoever they may be in those days. And the judges shall diligently investigate and examine the matter, and behold, they shall discover that the unjust witness has testified unjustly and has risen up against his brother. And you shall do to him whatever he tried to do to his brother and you shall remove the wicked man from your midst that others, when they hear, may fear and not continue to act in this evil way among you. Your eye shall not spare him; life for life, tooth for tooth, hand for hand, foot for foot."[5] Similar things appear indeed to be said in each place. It is not clearly indicated, however, from which place in particular the statement made in the Gospel appears to have been taken: "You have heard that it was said, 'An eye for an eye, a tooth for a tooth.' "[6]

(2) Nevertheless, our discourse must now turn to those words in Exodus where two men quarrel and strike a woman with child; and so strike her that her infant issues forth from her either already "formed" or "yet unformed." First, indeed, let us consider the infant which issued forth "yet unformed." Let us consider how one of the quarreling men is ordered to be struck with a fine when Scripture refers the fault of the quarrel

---

4 Mt 5.38.
5 Dt 19.16–21.
6 Mt 5.38.

not to one, but to both. What furthermore, is it that the woman's husband "determines" or imposes on him and not them, and "he" and not rather they "shall pay it with honor"? And what is that honor?

But if an infant already formed issue forth when a woman with child has been stricken by quarreling men, we easily understand that a life is given for a life, that is, that what has been committed should be punished by death. But it is worthwhile to explain what follows: "An eye for an eye, a tooth for a tooth." For it does not seem possible that an infant which a woman aborted when she was stricken, although we understand it issued forth formed, should lose an eye in the womb because it was stricken by the foot of a quarreling man for which this man should be deprived of an eye by the judges. But assume that even this might be because it is referred to as already formed. But what shall we say about teeth? It did not have teeth in its mother's womb which the blow of the striking man knocked out, did it? But if we refer these words to the woman who had the miscarriage, again, how will it be fitting that a woman should lose an eye or be afflicted in her teeth when she miscarries? But assume that it might be said that the woman was stricken in the eye or in the teeth and this caused the miscarriage, assume that she received a stripe or a wound, but what shall we say about "burning for burning"? A woman cannot be burned, can she, when she stands with quarreling men so that "burning for burning" might be explained?

These individual phrases seem to me to be incapable of an easy solution even in the passages in Deuteronomy where laws written similarly are mentioned. For let us assume there also that "an unjust witness has risen up" falsely accusing a man of impiety. Let both be summoned to judgment; let the judges inquire diligently; let them discover that the accuser or that witness has spoken falsely. How can a judge who ought not spare a false witness also condemn the life of the guilty for the life of the innocent? How, I say, will he be able also to remove "an eye for an eye"? As if in fact he who was unjustly accused was to have been injured by the accuser in eye or tooth or hand or foot. But we have said these things wishing to show that in each passage what has been written cannot be easily explained. For it was necessary that we first discuss what is said in relation to history, and thus, since "the Law is spiritual" seek the spiritual meaning in these words.

(3) But as far as it pertains to the present, even the allegorical part itself which usually extends broadly, is narrowly reduced to us. Nevertheless, as we are able we shall attempt to explain what the passage seems to us to mean. We have frequently said that in the Scriptures parts of the soul have the same names and the same functions as parts of the body.[7] As, for example, when it is said, "You see the mote in your brother's eye, and behold you have a beam in your eye."[8] It is certain that he is not speaking about an eye of the body in which a beam lies, but about the eye of the soul. The same is true when Scripture says, "He who has ears to hear, let him hear,"[9] and, "How beautiful are the feet of those preaching peace,"[10] and many statements like these. We have pointed this out that the likeness in names may not confuse us about the members.

Let those two men, therefore, who quarrel be two discussing and examining teachings or questions of the Law with one another and, let us say as the Apostle, wrangling "over words."[11] Whence also the same Apostle, knowing that quarrels of this kind arise between brothers, anticipates it and says, "Contend not with words for it is useless and leads to the subversion of the hearers,"[12] and elsewhere, "But avoid questions of the Law, knowing that they produce quarrels. The servant of God must not quarrel."[13] Because, therefore, those who quarrel over questions quarrel "to the subversion of the hearers," on that account they strike the woman with child and expel her infant either already formed or yet unformed.

---

7 Cf. *De Princ.* 1.1.9.
8 Cf. Mt 7.3.
9 Mt 13.9.
10 Cf. Is 52.7.
11 Cf. 1 Tm 6.4.
12 2 Tm 2.14.
13 2 Tm 2.23–24.

The soul which has just conceived the word of God is said to be a woman with child. We read about such a conception also in another passage: "From your fear, Lord, we conceived in the womb and gave birth."[14] Those, therefore, who conceive and immediately give birth are not to be considered women, but men, and perfect men. For hear also the prophet saying, "Was the earth brought forth in one day, and a nation born at once?"[15] That is a generation of perfect men which is born immediately on the day that it was conceived. But lest it appear strange to you that we said men give birth, we have set forth already earlier how you ought to understand the names of the members, that you might abandon the corporeal significations and take the meaning of the inner man. But if you wish to have further satisfaction from the Scriptures on this, hear the Apostle saying, "My little children of whom I am in labor again until Christ be formed in you."[16] They, therefore, are perfect men and strong who immediately when they conceive give birth, that is, who bring forth into works the word of faith which has been conceived. The soul, however, which has conceived and retains the word in the womb and does not give birth is called woman, as also the prophet says, "The pains of birth have come upon her and she does not have the strength to give birth."[17] This soul, therefore, which is now called a woman because of its weakness, is stricken and made to stumble by two men quarreling between themselves and bringing forth stumbling blocks in the strife—which is customary in verbal dispute—so that it casts out and loses the word of faith which it had slightly conceived. This is a quarrel and contention "to the subversion of the hearers." If, therefore, the soul which has been made to stumble cast off the word yet unformed, he who made it stumble is said to suffer loss.

Do you wish to know why the word is formed in some and is yet unformed in others? The word of the Apostle which we related above teaches us clearly when it says, "Until Christ be

---

14 Cf. Is 26.17–18.
15 Cf. Is 66.8.
16 Gal 4.19.
17 Cf. Is 37.3.

formed in you."[18] But Christ is the Word of God. The Apostle shows by this that at that time at which he was writing the word of God was yet unformed in them. If, therefore, it come forth yet unformed, he will suffer loss. The Apostle also teaches about the losses of teachers when he says: "If any man's work burn, he shall suffer loss. He himself, however, shall be saved, yet so as by fire."[19] But the Lord also says in the Gospels, "For what does a man profit if he gain the whole world but lose his own soul or suffer loss?"[20] Whence it seems to be shown that certain sins pertain to loss indeed, but not to destruction, because he who has suffered loss is said, nevertheless, to be saved, although "by fire." This is the reason, I believe, the apostle John also says in his epistle that some sins are to death and others are not to death.[21] But I do not think any man can easily discern what kind of sins may be to death and what, in fact, "not to death," but to loss. For it has been written, "Who understands sins?"[22] Nevertheless, from what is mentioned in the Gospel by parables we can learn in part what sort of things are called losses when we see there certain things considered as gain which are said to have been procured by employment. For example, when another five beyond the five pounds are said to have been acquired or another two beyond the two; or when a drachma or denarius or talent is assumed and named as a specified sum of money gained in employment; but also when the master of the house is said to have a reckoning with his servants and one is brought before him who owed ten thousand talents. Such, then, is a kind of reckoning of loss, so that, for example, he who would have received ten pounds for his reward may not receive ten, but eight, or six, or even less; and he who provided a cause of stumbling to a weaker and feminine soul is said to be stricken with this loss.

(4) But he shall pay, the text says, as "her husband shall determine" or inflict, "and he shall pay it with honor." The

---

18 Gal 4.19.
19 1 Cor 3.15.
20 Cf. Mt 16.26.
21 Cf. 1 Jn 5.16.
22 Ps 18.13.

husband of the learning soul is its master. As that husband,
therefore, or Christ who is master of all, or the teacher of souls
who presides over the Church for Christ, shall determine he
who contended with words "to the subversion of the hearers"
shall suffer loss for that soul which he cast forth as an "infant
yet unformed." This can perhaps be taken of the stumbling of
a catechumen yet unformed. For it can happen that he who
injured the soul again himself instruct, repair, and restore to
the soul those things which it lost. And let him now do these
things "with honor," with modesty, and patience as the Apostle
says, "with gentleness admonishing those who resist,"[23] not
with quarreling, as formerly when he introduced the stumbling block.

"But if the infant be already formed, he shall render a life
for a life."[24] "The infant which is formed" can be seen as the
word of God in the heart of that soul which has followed the
grace of baptism or which has manifestly and clearly conceived
the word of faith. If this soul, therefore, stricken by too much
contention between teachers, should cast off the word and be
found to be a part of those of whom the Apostle said, "For some
have already turned back to Satan,"[25] "he shall render a life for
a life." Either on the day of judgment he is to be taken by that
judge "who can destroy soul and body in hell,"[26] because also
elsewhere the prophet says to Jerusalem, "I have given Egypt
as an exchange for you, Ethiopia and Saba for you."[27] Or, at
least, it is possible perhaps also to apply it so that he who was
conscious of such a stumbling block in himself might lay down
his "life for the life" of that person whom he made to stumble
and might give attention to the point of death how he may turn
back, how he may repair, how he may restore that soul to faith.

Let him also surrender "an eye for an eye" if he injured the
eye of the soul, that is, if he disturbed its understanding. Let his
own eye be removed by him who presides over the Church,

---

23 2 Tm 2.25.
24 Ex 21.23.
25 1 Tm 5.15.
26 Mt 10.28; Lk 12.5.
27 Is 43.3.

and let that turbulent and fierce intellect of him who produces a stumbling block be cut off. But also if he injured a tooth of the hearer with which he had been accustomed when receiving the food of the word to crush or grind it with his molars in order to transmit the subtle meaning from these words to the stomach of his soul; if that man damaged and tore out this tooth so that by his contention the soul cannot receive the word of God subtly and spiritually, let the tooth of that man who did not crush well and divide the foods of the Scriptures be removed. Indeed, perhaps it is for this reason that it is said elsewhere about the Lord, "You have broken the teeth of sinners";[28] and elsewhere no less it is written, "The teeth of him who eats the bitter grape will be set on edge";[29] and elsewhere, "The Lord broke the lions' teeth."[30] So, therefore, the soul is said to be injured and stricken by the members of the body. It is required also that "a hand" be given "for a hand" and a "foot for a foot." The hand is the power of the soul by which it can hold and restrain something, as if we should say its deeds and strength. The foot is the means by which it advances to good or evil. Since, therefore, if the soul experiences a stumbling block it is cast down not only in faith but also in deeds which are signified by the hands and feet, these members of that man who provided the cause of the offense are removed, the hands by which he did not work well and the feet by which he did not advance well. He will also receive "burning" in that he burned and delivered a soul to hell.

By these individual members it is shown that that striker who has been mutilated in all his members is cut off from the body of the Church, "that others" Scripture says, "might see and fear and not act in like manner."[31] The Apostle also, therefore, when he describes the teacher of the Church, among other things, admonishes that he be "no striker,"[32] lest striking pregnant women, that is beginning souls, he sur-

---

28 Ps 3.8.
29 Jer 38.30.
30 Ps 57.6.
31 Cf. Dt 19.20.
32 1 Tm 3.3.

render "a life for a life, an eye for an eye, a tooth for a tooth." Such are also those souls which the Lord too laments in the Gospels when he says, "Woe to those who are with child and who give suck in those days,"[33] in which "even the elect if possible"[34] will be made to stumble. But you should know that it is not a characteristic of the perfect to stumble, but of women or of the very small, as also the Lord says in the Gospel: "If anyone shall make one of those least little ones stumble."[35] It is the very small, therefore, and the least who can be made to stumble. "The spiritual man, however, judges all things"[36] and "proves all things and holds fast what is good and keeps himself from all appearance of evil."[37]

We have said what occurred to us in the present chapter. But let us request from the Lord that he himself may see fit to reveal to us what things are perfect through Jesus Christ our Lord, "to whom belongs glory and sovereignty forever and ever. Amen."[38]

---

33 Mt 24.19.
34 Mt 24.24.
35 Mt 18.6.
36 1 Cor 2.15.
37 Cf. 1 Thes 5.21–22.
38 Cf. 1 Pt 4.11.

HOMILY XI
On the thirst of the people in Raphidim and on the war with the Amalechites and the assistance of Jethro

INCE "EVERYONE WHO WISHES TO LIVE PIOUSLY in Christ suffers persecution"[1] and is attacked by enemies, he who travels the road of this life ought always to be armed and always to stand firm in the camp. For this reason it is also related about the people of God: "All the congregation of the sons of Israel departed from the wilderness of Sin according to their camps at the command of the Lord."[2] There is, therefore, one congregation of the Lord but it is divided into four camps. For four camps are described set up opposite the tabernacle of the Lord, as it is related in Numbers.[3] And you, therefore, if you are always watchful and armed and know that you serve as a soldier in the camp of the Lord, heed that command: "No one serving as a soldier for God entangles himself in secular affairs, that he may please him to whom he has engaged himself."[4] For if you thus serve as a soldier so that you are free from secular affairs and always keep watch in the camp of the Lord, it will also be said of you that you depart "from the wilderness of Sin at the command of the Lord" and come "to Raphidim." *Sin* is interpreted to mean "temptation," but *Raphidim* means "sound judgment."[5] That man has attained soundness of judgment who rightly departs from temptation and whom temptation renders approved. For in the day of judgment he will be sound, and soundness will be with him who has not been wounded by temptation, as it is written in the

---

1 Cf. 2 Tm 3.12.
2 Ex 17.1.
3 Cf. Nm 2.
4 2 Tm 2.4.
5 See Appendix, 34 and 35.

Apocalypse: "But to him who has overcome I will give of the tree of life which is in the paradise of my God."[6] He, therefore, who rightly "orders his words with judgment"[7] has attained soundness of judgment.

(2) But what is the meaning of that which follows? "The people thirsted for water," the text says, "and murmured against Moses."[8] It might, perhaps, appear that it was superfluous to say, "The people thirsted for water." It would have been sufficient to say that "they thirsted." What need was there to add, "They thirsted for water"? The addition is not superfluous, for there are diverse thirsts and each one has a characteristic thirst. They are blessed who, according to the word of the Lord, "thirst for justice."[9] Others no less say, "For thee, O God, my soul has thirsted."[10] But those who are sinners suffer "not a thirst for water nor a famine of bread, but a thirst of hearing the word of God."[11] For that reason, therefore, the text adds here also that "the people" who should have thirsted for God, who should have "thirsted for justice," "thirsted for water." But because God truly is "an instructor of infants" and a "teacher of the foolish,"[12] he corrects their faults and amends their errors and tells Moses to take up his rod and strike the rock and bring forth waters for them. For he wishes them now "to drink from the rock"; he wishes them to advance and attain the deeper mysteries. For "they murmured against Moses"[13] and for that reason the Lord orders him to show them the rock from which they may drink.

If there is anyone who, when he reads Moses, murmurs against him, and the Law which has been written according to the letter is displeasing to him because it seems incoherent in many things, Moses shows him the rock which is Christ and leads him to it that he may drink from it and quench his thirst.

---

6 Rv 2.7.
7 Cf. Ps 111.5.
8 Ex 17.3.
9 Cf. Mt 5.6.
10 Cf. Ps 62.2.
11 Am 8.11.
12 Cf. Rom 2.20.
13 Cf. Ex 17.3.

But this rock will not give water unless it has been struck, but when it has been struck it brings forth streams. For after Christ had been struck and crucified, he brought forth the streams of the New Testament. This is why it was said of him, "I will strike the shepherd and the sheep will be scattered."[14] He had to be struck, therefore, for unless he had been struck and unless "water and blood had gone out from his side,"[15] we all would suffer "thirst for the word of God."[16] This, therefore, is what the Apostle also understood when he said, "They all ate the same spiritual food and drank the same spiritual drink. For they drank of the spiritual rock which followed, but the rock was Christ."[17] But note that God said to Moses in this place, "Go before the people and take with you men advanced in years, that is the elders of the people."[18] Moses alone does not lead the people to the waters of the rock, but also the elders of the people with him. For the Law alone does not announce Christ, but also the prophets and patriarchs and all "those advanced in years."

(3) The war waged with the Amalechites is described next. The people are related to have fought and conquered. Before they ate the bread from heaven and drank the water from the rock, the people are not said to have fought, but it is said to them, "The Lord will fight for you and you shall hold your peace."[19] There is, therefore, a time when the Lord fights for us. "He does not permit us to be tempted above that which we are able,"[20] nor does he allow weak men to encounter "the strong man."[21] For Job too completed that whole famous struggle of his with temptation as a man already "perfect." You also, therefore, when you have begun to eat manna, the heavenly bread of the word of God, and to drink water from the rock, and when you have approached the deeper meanings

---

14 Cf. Zec 13.7.
15 Cf. Jn 19.34.
16 Cf. Am 8.11.
17 1 Cor 10.3–4.
18 Ex 17.5.
19 Ex 14.14.
20 Cf. 1 Cor 10.13.
21 Cf. Mt 12.29.

of spiritual teaching, expect battle and prepare yourself for war.

Since war is imminent, therefore, let us see what Moses commands. "He said to Jesus, 'Choose for yourself men and go out and fight with Amalec tomorrow.' "[22] Previous to this passage there has been no mention of the blessed name of Jesus. Here first the splendor of this word has appeared; here Moses first called Jesus and said to him, "Choose for yourself men." Moses calls Jesus; the Law invokes Christ that he choose for himself "strong men" from the people. Moses was not able to choose. It is only Jesus who said, "You have not chosen me, but I have chosen you,"[23] who can choose "strong men." For he himself is leader of the chosen; he himself is prince of the mighty; it is he himself who fights with Amalec, for it is he himself who "enters the house of the strong man and binds the strong man and plunders his vessels."[24]

(4) But meanwhile, let us see what the present story now discloses. "Moses went up," the text says, "to the top of the hill."[25] He did not yet go up to the top of the mountain, but "to the top of the hill." For it was reserved for him to go up to the top of the mountain at that time when Jesus was to go up, and with him Moses and Elias, and there be transformed in glory. Now, therefore, as it were, not yet glorified by the transformation of Jesus, he did not go up to the top of the mountain, but "he went up to the top of the hill."

"And it happened," the text says, "when Moses lifted up his hands Israel prevailed."[26] Moses, indeed, lifts up his hands; he does not stretch them out. Jesus, however, when he had been exalted on the cross and was about to embrace the whole earth with his arms says, "I have stretched out my hands to a people who do not believe and who speak against me."[27] Moses, therefore, lifts up his hands and, when he lifted them up, Amalec

---

22 Ex 17.9. See *Gn. Hom.* 3, footnote 45.
23 Jn 15.16.
24 Cf. Mt 12.29.
25 Ex 17.10.
26 Ex 17.11.
27 Is 65.2.

was overcome. To lift up the hands is to lift up our works and deeds to God and not to have deeds which are cast down and lying on the ground, but which are pleasing to God and raised to heaven. He, therefore, who "lays up treasure in heaven" lifts up his hands, "for where his treasure is"[28] there also is his eye, there also his hand. He also lifts his hands who says, "The lifting up of my hands is as the evening sacrifice."[29] If, therefore, our deeds are lifted up and are not on the earth, Amalec is overcome. But the Apostle also orders, "Lift up holy hands without anger and contention."[30] It was also said to some, "Lift up the hands which hang down and the feeble knees, and make straight steps with your feet."[31] If, therefore, the people observe the Law, Moses lifts his hands and the adversary is overcome; if they do not observe the Law Amalec prevails. Because, therefore, "our fight," also, "is against principalities and powers and rulers of this world of darkness,"[32] if you wish to overcome, if you wish to prevail, lift up your hands and your deeds and let not your citizenship be on the earth, but as the Apostle said, "While we walk upon the earth, we have our citizenship in heaven."[33] And thus you will be able to overcome the people who are hostile to you such as Amalec, so that it may be said also of you: "The Lord fought against Amalec with a hidden hand."[34] You also lift your hands to God; fulfill the command of the Apostle: "Pray without ceasing."[35] Then what is written will come about: "As a calf devours green grass in the plains, so this people will devour the people who are upon the earth."[36] This indicates, as we received from the elders, that the people of God were fighting not so much with force and arms as with voice and speech, that is, by pouring out prayer to God they were overthrowing their enemies. So also, therefore, if

---

28 Cf. Mt 6.20–21.
29 Ps 140.2.
30 Cf. 1 Tm 2.8.
31 Heb 12.12–13.
32 Eph 6.12.
33 Cf. Phil 3.20.
34 Ex 17.16.
35 1 Thes 5.17.
36 Cf. Nm 22.4.

you wish to conquer your enemies, lift your deeds and cry out to God as the Apostle says, "Being urgent in prayer and watching in it."[37] For this is the battle of the Christian in which he overcomes the enemy.

I think, however, that by this figure also Moses would depict an image of two peoples and would show that one is a people from among the nations who lift up Moses' hands and strengthen them, that is, who elevate on high those things which Moses wrote and establish their understanding in an elevated manner and in this way are victorious. The other is a people, who, since they do not lift Moses' hands nor elevate them from the earth nor consider anything in him to be lofty and subtle, are overcome by the adversaries and overthrown.

(5) After this Moses came to the mountain of God and there Jethro his father-in-law met him. But Moses "went out" of the camp "to meet him" and does not bring him to the mountain of God, but "brings him to his tent."[38] For the priest of Madian was not able to ascend the mountain of God. Neither could he nor Moses' wife descend into Egypt, but now he comes to Moses with his sons. For one cannot descend into Egypt and submit to the Egyptian contests unless he is a fit athlete and such as the Apostle describes: "Everyone who competes in a contest refrains from all things; those indeed that they might receive a corruptible crown, but we an incorruptible one. I therefore, so run, not as at an uncertainty; I so fight, not as one beating the air."[39] Moses, therefore, because he was a great and powerful athlete, descended into Egypt; he descended to the contests and exercises of virtues. But Abraham also descended into Egypt because he too was a great and powerful athlete. What shall I say about Jacob who by his very name is an athlete? For *wrestler* is also interpreted as "supplanter."[40] And, therefore, when Jacob had descended into Egypt with "the seventy-five souls" he became "as the stars of

---

37 Col 4.2.
38 Cf. Ex 18.7.
39 1 Cor 9.25–26.
40 See Appendix, 36.

heaven in multitude."[41] But not all who descend into Egypt fight and resolve the contests in such a way that they become a "multitude" and are multiplied "as stars of heaven." For others, to have descended into Egypt results to the contrary. I know that Jeroboam fleeing from Solomon descended into Egypt and not only did not increase "into a multitude," but both divided and corrupted the people of God because when he descended into Egypt he accepted from king Sesac "a wife, the sister of his wife Thecimena."[42]

But, meanwhile, Jethro comes to Moses bringing with him his daughter, Moses's wife, and his sons. "And Aaron came," the text says, "and all the elders of Israel to eat bread with Moses' father-in-law in the presence of God."[43] They do not all eat bread "in the presence of God," but those who are "elders," those who are older, who are perfect and approved in merits, eat bread "in the presence of God"; they are the ones who observe what the Apostle says, "Whether you eat or drink or whatever else you do, do all to the glory of God."[44] Everything, therefore, which the saints do, they do "in the presence of God." The sinner flees from the presence of God. For it has been written that Adam, after he sinned, fled "from the presence of God." When he was asked about it he answered, "I heard your voice and I hid myself because I was naked."[45] But Cain also, after he had been condemned by God for parricide, "went out," Scripture says, "from the face of God and dwelt in the land of Nain."[46] He, therefore, who was unworthy of the presence of God "went out from the face of God." The saints, however, both eat and drink "in the presence of God" and do everything they do "in the presence of God." In discussing the present passage, I see, even further, that those who receive a fuller knowledge of God and are imbued more fully with the divine disciplines, even if they do evil, do it before God and in

---

41 Cf. Gn 46.27; Heb 11.12.
42 3 Kgs 12.24e (LXX).
43 Ex 18.12.
44 1 Cor 10.31.
45 Cf. Gn 3.10.
46 Gn 4.16.

his presence just as the man who said: "To you only have I sinned and have done evil before you."[47] What advantage, then, does he have who does evil before God? That he immediately repents and says, "I have sinned." He, however, who departs from the presence of God does not know how to be converted and to purge his sin by repenting. This, then, is the difference between doing evil before God and to have departed from the presence of God when you sin.

(6) But, as I see it, Jethro did not come to Moses in vain, nor was it in vain that he ate bread with the elders of the people "in the presence of the Lord." For he gives counsel to Moses that is commendable enough and useful, that he choose and appoint leaders of the people "men who worship God, men who are mighty, and who hate pride."[48] For the leaders of the people ought to be the kind of men who not only are not proud, but also hate pride, that is, that not only are they themselves without vice, but they also hate vices in others. I do not mean that they ought to hate men, but vices.

"And you shall appoint them," the text says, "as tribunes and centurions and rulers of fifty and of ten and they shall judge the people every hour. But they shall refer the more serious matters to you."[49] Let the leaders of the people and the presbyters of the people hear that they ought to judge the people every hour, that they ought always and without intermission to sit in judgment, to settle quarrels, to reconcile those disagreeing, to recall the discordant to grace. Let each one learn his duty from the Holy Scriptures. Moses, the text says, should occupy himself in the things of God and explain the word of God to the people. But the other leaders, whom they call "tribunes"—they are called tribunes from the fact that they preside over a tribe—these others, therefore, "tribunes" or "centurions" or "rulers of fifty" should preside over lesser judgments which pertain to each individual, settling quarrels.

I think, however, that this disposition has been given to the

---

47 Ps 50.6.
48 Cf. Ex 18.21.
49 Ex 18.21–22.

Church not only in the present age but is to be preserved also in the future age. For hear what the Lord says in the Gospel: "When the Son of man shall sit on the throne of his glory you also shall sit on twelve thrones judging the twelve tribes of Israel."[50] Do you see, then, that not only does the Lord judge, to whom the Father "gave all judgment,"[51] but he appoints for himself also other leaders who judge the people about lesser causes, "but they refer the more serious matters" to himself. The Lord also, therefore, said of a certain man, "He shall be in danger of the council," but of another, "He shall be in danger of the judgment," and of another, "He shall be in danger of hell fire."[52] But we are also told that we shall render an account for an idle word and he did not say that we will render an account to God, as he says of perjury, "But you shall perform your oaths to the Lord."[53] But behold also another kind of judgment: "The queen of the south shall rise in judgment with the men of this generation and shall condemn them."[54] "He who has ears to hear, let him hear."[55] For all these things are a type and "shadow" of heavenly things and an "image" "of things to come."[56]

But as we read what has been written that "the eye is not filled with seeing nor the ear with hearing,"[57] neither can we be filled by looking and considering; from how many passages do the words which have been written edify us, in how many ways do they instruct us! For when I perceive that Moses the prophet full of God, to whom God spoke "face to face," accepted counsel from Jethro the priest of Madian, my mind goes numb with admiration. For the Scripture says, "And Moses heard the voice of his father-in-law, and did whatever he said to him."[58] He did not say, "God speaks to me and what I

---

50 Mt 19.28.
51 Cf. Jn 5.22.
52 Mt 5.22.
53 Mt 5.33.
54 Mt 12.42.
55 Mt 13.43.
56 Cf. Col 2.17.
57 Cf. Eccl 1.8.
58 Ex 18.24.

ought to do is delivered to me by a word from heaven," and, "How shall I receive counsel from a man, and a Gentile at that, an alien from the people of God?" But he listens and does everything which he says. He hears not the one who speaks, but what he says. Whence also we, if perhaps now and then we discover something said wisely by the Gentiles, ought not immediately to despise what is said because we despise the author. Nor is it appropriate, because we hold a law to be given by God, for us to swell with pride and despise the words of the prudent, but as the Apostle says, we should "prove all things and hold fast that which is good."[59] But who today of those who preside over the people—I do not mean if he has already received revelations from God, but if he has some merit of knowledge of the Law—sees fit to accept counsel from even a lower priest, much less from a layman or a Gentile? But Moses, who was "meek above all men,"[60] accepted the counsel of a lower man both that he might give a model of humility to the leaders of people and represent an image of the future mystery. For he knew that at some future time the Gentiles would offer good counsel with Moses, that they would bring a good and spiritual understanding to the Law of God. And he knew that the Law would hear them and do all things as they say. "For the Law cannot be effective," as the Jews affirm, because "the Law is weak in the flesh,"[61] that is, in the letter, and can accomplish nothing according to the letter, "for the Law brought nothing to perfection."[62] In accordance with this counsel, however, which we offer to the Law, all things can come about spiritually. Sacrifices which cannot now be offered in a fleshly manner can be offered spiritually; and the law of leprosy which cannot be kept according to the letter can be spiritually observed. So, therefore, as we understand, as we perceive and give counsel, the Law accomplishes all things; but according to the letter it does not accomplish all things, but very few things.

---

59 1 Thes 5.21.
60 Nm 12.3.
61 Rom 8.3.
62 Heb 7.19.

(7) After this, however, when Jethro had departed and
Moses had come "out of Raphidim into the desert of Sinai"[63]
and there the Lord had descended to Moses "in a column of
cloud,"[64] that the people, when they saw, might believe in him
and hear his words, the Lord says to Moses: "Descend, testify to
the people and purify them today and tomorrow, and let them
wash their garments and let them be prepared for the third
day."[65] If there is anyone who has assembled to hear the word
of God, let him hear what God has ordered. After he has been
sanctified he ought to come to hear the word; he ought to wash
his garments. For if you bring dirty garments to this place you
too will hear: "Friend, how did you enter here, not having
wedding garments?"[66] No one, therefore, can hear the word of
God unless he has first been sanctified, that is, unless he is
"holy in body and spirit,"[67] unless he has washed his garments.
For a little later he shall go in to the wedding dinner, he shall
eat from the flesh of the lamb, he shall drink the cup of
salvation. Let no one go in to this dinner with dirty garments.
Wisdom also has commanded this elsewhere saying: "Let your
garments be clean at all times."[68] For your garments were
washed once when you came to the grace of baptism; you were
purified in body; you were cleansed from all filth of flesh and
spirit. "What," then, "God has cleansed, you shall not make
unclean."[69] Hear, therefore, now also the kind of
sanctification: "You shall not approach," the text says, "your
wife today and tomorrow, that on the third day you may hear
the word of God."[70] This is what the Apostle also says: "It is
good for a man not to touch a woman."[71] Marriage, nevertheless, is a sound remedy for those who need its remedy for
their weakness. But, nevertheless, let us hear the counsel of the

---

63 Ex 19.2.
64 Ex 19.9.
65 Ex 19.10–11.
66 Mt 22.12.
67 Cf. 1 Cor 7.34.
68 Eccl 9.8.
69 Cf. Acts 10.15, 11.9.
70 Cf. Ex 19.15.
71 1 Cor 7.1.

Apostle: "Because the time is short, it remains that those who have wives be as those who do not, and those who buy as not possessing, and those who use this world as not using it. For the outward form of this world is passing away."[72] The temporal kingdom is passing away that the perpetual and eternal one may come, as we are also ordered to say in the prayer, "Your kingdom come,"[73] in Christ Jesus our Lord "to whom belongs glory and sovereignty forever and ever. Amen."[74]

---

72 1 Cor 7.29–31.
73 Mt 6.10.
74 Cf. 1 Pt 4.11.

HOMILY XII

On the glorified countenance of Moses and on the veil which he placed on his face

HE TEXT OF EXODUS HAS BEEN READ TO US which either stimulates us to seek understanding or repels us. It stimulates zealous and open minds; it repels idle and occupied minds. For it is written: "Aaron and all the sons of Israel saw Moses, and his face and the appearance of his countenance had been glorified, and they were afraid to approach him."[1] And the text says a little further on: "Moses placed a veil on his face. But whenever he went into the presence of the Lord to speak to him he laid the veil aside."[2] But the Apostle in discussing these things with that noble understanding which he uses in other matters of which he said, "But we have the mind of Christ,"[3] said: "But if the ministration of death engraven with letters upon stones was glorious, so that the sons of Israel could not steadfastly behold the face of Moses for the glory of his countenance, which is passing away, how shall not the ministration of the spirit be rather in glory?"[4] And again a little later he says, "And not as Moses placed a veil on his face that the sons of Israel might not steadfastly look at the appearance of his countenance. For their senses were made dull, for until this present day when Moses is read, the veil is upon their heart."[5] Who would not marvel at the magnitude of the mysteries? Who would not greatly fear the sign of a dulled heart? Moses' face was glorified, but "the sons of Israel" were not able "to look at the appearance of his countenance"; the people of

---

1 Ex 34.30.
2 Ex 34.33–34.
3 1 Cor 2.16.
4 2 Cor 3.7–8.
5 2 Cor 3.13–15.

the Synagogue were not able "to look." But if anyone can be superior in conduct and life to the multitude, he can look at the glory of his countenance. For even now, as the Apostle says, "The veil is placed on the reading of the Old Testament";[6] even now Moses speaks with glorified countenance, but we are not able to look at the glory which is in his countenance. We are not able, therefore, because we are still the populace and we have no zeal or merit more than the common crowd. But because the holy Apostle says, "But that same veil remains in the reading of the Old Testament,"[7] the expressed opinion of such a great apostle would have cut off all hope of understanding for us if he had not added: "But when anyone shall turn to the Lord, the veil shall be removed."[8] He says, therefore, that the cause of the removal of the veil is our turning to the Lord. We should draw the conclusion from this that as long as we read the divine Scriptures without understanding, as long as what has been written is obscure to us and closed, we have not yet turned to the Lord. For if we had turned to the Lord, without doubt the veil would have been removed.

(2) But let us also see what it means "to turn to the Lord." And that we might be able to know more clearly what *turned to* means, we must first say what *turned away* means. Everyone who is occupied with common stories when the words of the Law are read is turned away. Everyone who is concerned about affairs of the world, about money, about profits "when Moses is read" is turned away. Everyone who is tied up with concerns for possessions and distracted by the desire for riches, who is zealous for the glory of the age and honors of the world is turned away. But he also is turned away who appears to be a stranger to the attitudes we have just mentioned; who stands and hears the words of the Law intent both in countenance and eyes, but wanders in his heart and thoughts.

What, then, does it mean to *turn to*? If we turn our backs on all these things and give attention to the word of God with zeal, actions, mind, and care; if "we meditate on his Law day and

---

6 2 Cor 3.14.
7 2 Cor 3.14.
8 2 Cor 3.16.

night"[9]; if, all things having been disregarded, we devote ourselves to God; if we are exercised in his testimonies, this is to *turn to* the Lord. If you wish your son to have a liberal education, to know the grammatical or rhetorical discipline, do you not grant him freedom from all other things, do you not make him give his attention to this one study, all others having been disregarded, do you not see to it that he lacks nothing at all in paedogogues, teachers, books, and expenses, until he brings back completed the work of the proposed study? Who of us has so turned himself to studies of the divine Law; who of us has thus given attention to it? Who seeks a divine education with as much zeal and work as he sought a human education? And why do we complain if we are ignorant because we do not learn? Some of you leave immediately as soon as you have heard the texts which are selected read. There is no mutual investigation of these words which have been read, no comparison. There is no remembrance of that command which the divine Law impresses upon you: "Ask your fathers and they will tell you, your elders and they will declare to you."[10] Some do not even patiently wait while the texts are being read in church. Others do not even know if they are read, but are occupied with mundane stories in the furthest corners of the Lord's house. I have dared to speak about these matters because, "when Moses is read" "a veil" is no longer placed "on their heart," but a kind of partition and wall. For if he who is present, who hears and is intent and reconsiders and discusses what he hears, and investigates and becomes acquainted with what he cannot follow, can scarcely arrive at freedom of knowledge, how is that man, who covers his ears lest he hear and turns his back to the reader, to be said to have a veil imposed on his heart, when not even the veil of the letter which is the sound of the voice in which the meaning is wrapped has approached him? The figure, therefore, is clear, in what manner Moses' face became glorious; for the words which he speaks are full of glory, but these words are covered and concealed and all his glory is internal.

9 Cf. Ps 1.2.
10 Dt 32.7.

(3) Consider also what it means that in the Law Moses' face indeed is related to have been glorified although it is covered with a veil, but his hand is said to have been placed "in his bosom" and "made leprous as snow."[11] It seems to me that the design of the whole Law is fully described in this, for the word of the Law is designated in his face; the works in his hand. Because, therefore, "no one was to be justified by the works of the Law"[12] nor could the Law bring anyone "to perfection,"[13] for that reason Moses' hand becomes "leprous" and is hidden "in his bosom" as it would have no perfect work. His face, however, is glorified, but is covered with a veil because his word has the glory of knowledge, but a hidden glory. Whence also the prophet says, "If you will not hear in secret, your soul will weep,"[14] and David says, "You have shown me the uncertain and hidden things of your wisdom."[15]

In the Law, therefore, Moses has only his face glorified; his hands have no glory, nay rather they have even reproach; nor do his feet have glory. He is ordered to remove his sandal, so there was no glory in his feet. This also, of course, did not happen apart from the figure of some mystery, for the feet are the last part of a man. It was shown, therefore, that in the last times Moses would remove his sandal that another might take a bride and she would be called "the house of the unshod"[16] "to this day."[17] Moses has, therefore, nothing else glorious in the Law except his face. In the Gospels, however, the whole Moses is glorified anew. For hear what it says in the Gospels: "When Jesus had ascended a high mountain, taking with him Peter and James and John, and was transformed there before them, and behold Moses and Elias appeared in glory talking with him."[18] Here it does not say that his countenance is glorified, but that the whole man "appeared in glory" talking with Jesus.

---

11 Ex 4.6.
12 Cf. Rom 3.20.
13 Cf. Heb 7.19.
14 Jer 13.17.
15 Ps 50.8.
16 Cf. Dt 25.10.
17 Cf. 2 Cor 3.15.
18 Cf. Mt 17.1–3.

There that promise was fulfilled to him which he received on Mt. Sinai when it was said to him, "You shall see my back parts."[19] He saw, therefore, his back parts, for he saw what had happened in the later and last days and he was glad. For as Abraham longed to see the day of the Lord "and he saw it and was glad,"[20] so also Moses longed to see the day of the Lord "and he saw it and was glad." "He was glad" necessarily because no longer does he descend from the mountain glorified only in his face, but he ascends from the mountain totally glorified. Moses "was glad" without doubt because of him about whom he had said: "The Lord your God will raise up to you a prophet of your brothers like me. You shall hear him in all things."[21] Now he saw that he was present and lent credence to his words. And lest he doubt in anything, he hears the Father's voice saying, "This is my beloved son in whom I am well pleased, hear him."[22] Moses earlier said, "You shall hear him"; now the Father says, "This is my son, hear him," and he shows that he is present of whom he speaks. Moses seems to me to rejoice also for this reason: he himself also now, in a sense, puts aside "the veil having turned to the Lord,"[23] when those things which he predicted are clearly fulfilled or when the time arrived that those things which he had concealed might be revealed by the Spirit.

(4) Nevertheless we must examine the understanding of the holy Apostle and consider what he meant when he said, "But if anyone shall turn to the Lord, the veil shall be removed," that he should add, "But the Lord is a spirit,"[24] by which, as it were, he appears to explain what the Lord is. Who indeed does not know that the "Lord is a spirit"? But was either the nature or substance of the Lord discussed in this passage, that he should say, "The Lord is a spirit"? Let us beware, therefore, lest not only "when Moses is read," but also when Paul is read "a veil"

---

19 Ex 33.23.
20 Jn 8.56.
21 Dt 18.15.
22 Mt 17.5.
23 Cf. 2 Cor 3.16.
24 2 Cor 3.16–17.

be "placed over" our "heart." And clearly, if we hear negligent-
ly, if we bring no zeal to learning and understanding, not only
are the Scriptures of the Law and prophets but also of the
apostles and Gospels covered for us with a great veil. I fear,
however, lest by too much negligence and dullness of heart the
divine volumes be not only veiled to us, but also sealed, so that
"if a book should be put into the hands of a man who cannot
read to be read, he would say, 'I cannot read'; if it should be put
into the hands of a man who can read, he would say, 'It is
sealed.' "[25] Whence it is shown that we must not only employ
zeal to learn the sacred literature, but we must also pray to the
Lord and entreat "day and night"[26] that the lamb "of the tribe
of Juda" may come and himself taking "the sealed book" may
deign to open it.[27] For it is he who "opening the Scriptures"
kindles the hearts of the disciples so that they say, "Was not our
heart burning within us when he opened to us the Scriptures?"[28] May he, therefore, even now see fit to open to us what
it is which he inspired his Apostle to say, "But the Lord is a
spirit, and where the spirit of the Lord is, there is freedom."[29]

So far as I, at least, can perceive with my limited understanding, I think that the word of God differs for the sake of
the hearers. As we have often already said, he is called at one
time "way," at another "truth," now "life,"[30] again "resurrection,"[31] now also "flesh,"[32] and now "spirit."[33] For although
he truly received the substance of flesh from the virgin in
which he also endured the cross and initiated the resurrection,
nevertheless there is a passage where the Apostle says, "And if
we have known Christ according to the flesh; but now we know
him so no longer."[34] Because, therefore, even now his word

---

25 Is 29.12,11.
26 Cf. Ps 1.2; Jos 1.8.
27 Cf. Rv 5.5.
28 Lk 24.32.
29 2 Cor 3.17.
30 Jn 14.6.
31 Cf. Jn 11.25.
32 Cf. Jn 1.14.
33 Cf. 2 Cor 3.17.
34 2 Cor 5.16.

calls the hearers forth to a more subtle and spiritual understanding and wishes them to perceive nothing carnal in the
Law, he says that he who wishes the "veil to be removed" from
his heart "may turn to the Lord"; not, as it were, to the Lord as
flesh—he is, to be sure, this also because "the Word became
flesh"[35]—but, as it were, to the Lord as spirit. For if he turns, as
it were, to the Lord as spirit, he will come from fleshly to
spiritual things and will pass over from slavery to freedom, for
"where the spirit of the Lord is, there is freedom."[36]

Let us also use some other ideas of the Apostle to make his
meaning even clearer. He says to some men whom he considered incapable, "I decided to know nothing else among you
except Christ Jesus and him crucified."[37] He did not say to such
men, "The Lord is a spirit,"[38] nor did he say to them that Christ
is the "wisdom" of God.[39] For they were not able to know Christ
in so far as he is "wisdom," but in so far as he was "crucified."
But those to whom he said, "We speak wisdom among the
perfect, not, however, the wisdom of this world nor of the
princes of this world who come to nought, but we speak the
wisdom of God hidden in a mystery,"[40] did not need to receive
the Word of God in so far as he "became flesh," but in so far as
he is "wisdom hidden in a mystery." So, therefore, it is said also
in this passage to these who are called forth from a carnal to a
spiritual understanding: "But the Lord is a spirit, and where
the spirit of the Lord is, there is freedom."[41] That, however, he
might show that he himself has already attained freedom of
knowledge and has divested himself of the slavery of the veil he
adds to these words: "But we all beholding the glory of the
Lord with unveiled face."[42]

If, therefore, we also pray to the Lord that he see fit to
remove the veil from our heart, we can receive spiritual under-

35 Jn 1.14.
36 2 Cor 3.17.
37 1 Cor 2.2.
38 2 Cor 3.17.
39 1 Cor 1.21,24.
40 1 Cor 2.6–7.
41 2 Cor 3.17.
42 2 Cor 3.18.

standing if only we turn to the Lord and seek after freedom of knowledge. But how can we attain freedom, we who serve the world, who serve money, who serve the desires of the flesh? I correct myself; I judge myself; I make known my faults. Let those who hear see what they perceive about themselves. I, meanwhile, say that as long as I am devoted to any of these things I have not turned to the Lord nor have I followed freedom as long as such affairs and cares bind me. I am a slave of that affair and care to which I am bound. For I know that it is written that "by what each one is conquered, to this also he is delivered as a slave."[43] Even if love of money does not overcome me, even if the care of possesssions and riches does not bind me, nevertheless I desire praise and follow human glory, if I depend on the expressions and words of men, what this man feels about me, how that man regards me, lest I displease this man, if I please that one. As long as I seek those things I am their slave. But I would want to try at least, if I might be able to be freed from this, if I might be able to be released from the yoke of this foul slavery and attain freedom in accordance with the admonition of the Apostle who says: "You have been called to freedom; do not become the slaves of men."[44] But who will give me this manumission? Who will free me from this most unseemly slavery except him who said, "If the son shall make you free, you shall be free indeed"?[45] But indeed I know that a slave cannot be given freedom unless he serves faithfully and loves his master. And for this reason, let us also serve faithfully and "let us love the Lord our God with our whole heart and with our whole soul and with our whole strength,"[46] that we might deserve to be given freedom by Christ Jesus, his son, our Lord, "to whom belongs glory and sovereignty forever and ever. Amen."[47]

---

43 Cf. 2 Pt 2.19.
44 Gal 5.13; 1 Cor 7.23.
45 Jn 8.36.
46 Cf. Mk 12.30.
47 Cf. 1 Pt 4.11.

HOMILY XIII
On those objects which are offered for the tabernacle

E HAVE ALREADY INDEED PREVIOUSLY SPOKEN about the tabernacle as we were able, but the description is often repeated in the book of Exodus. It is related both when God commanded Moses how it ought to be made and again when Moses commanded the people to present the materials for the work's construction, as contained in the text just read to us. But also afterwards the individual objects are enumerated when they are prepared by Beseleel and other wise men, and again when they are brought before Moses, and again when they are dedicated by the command of the Lord. Moreover these things are mentioned also in other books or passages and are frequently repeated because of what they necessarily bring to mind.

Now, therefore, that passage has been read to us where it says, "And Moses spoke to all the congregation of the sons of Israel saying, 'This is the word which the Lord has commanded, saying: "Take from yourselves an offering for the Lord. Let everyone who has understood in his heart bring the firstfruits to the Lord: gold, silver, bronze, blue, purple, scarlet doubled, twisted linen, goats' hair, rams' skins dyed red, blue colored skins, wood not subject to decay, sardian stones, and stones for sculpture on the cape and robe. And let everyone wise in heart among you come and prepare everything which the Lord has commanded." ' "[1]

In the first place, when I consider and examine myself, I am chagrined to attempt an explanation of this. For I fear that even if the Lord should see fit to reveal it to anyone—I have not dared to speak on my own—I fear, I say, and have grave

---

1 Ex 35.4–10.

doubts that he would find an audience. And since this is the case, I fear that perhaps it may be required of him who shall attempt to explain it, where or how or before whom the pearls of the Lord may be cast.[2] But since you earnestly expect that something be discussed from these words which have been read, and my Lord has commanded me saying, "You should have given my money to the bank and at my coming I should have exacted it with interest,"[3] I shall ask him that he might see fit to make my word his money, that I might not lend my money, nor my gold to you, but his, that I might speak to you with his word and his "mind"[4] and bring these things to the bank of your hearing. You who receive the Lord's money have already seen how you should prepare its interest for the Lord when he comes. Interest on the word of God is to have in the practice of life and deeds those things which the word of God has commanded. If, then, when you hear the word, you use it and act according to those words which you hear and live according to these words, you are preparing interest for the Lord. Each of you can make ten talents from "five talents" and hear from the Lord, "Well done, good and faithful servant, you shall have power over ten cities."[5] But beware of this, lest any of you either gather "in a napkin" or bury "in the earth" the money which has been received,[6] because you know well the nature of the outcome for this kind of man when the Lord comes. We shall attempt, therefore, to make some observations on many things, or rather, even fewer on a few points, that our discourse and your attention might be balanced.

(2) First of all, therefore, let us see what it is that Moses says to the sons of Israel: "Take from yourselves an offering for the Lord. Let everyone who has understood in his heart offer the firstfruits to the Lord."[7] Moses does not want you to offer God something which is outside yourself. "Take from yourselves,"

---

2 Cf. Mt 7.6.
3 Mt 25.27.
4 Cf. 1 Cor 2.16.
·5 Cf. Mt 25.21; Lk 19.17.
6 Cf. Lk 19.20; Mt 25.25.
7 Ex 35.5.

he says, "and bring the firstfruits to the Lord, as each one has understood in his heart." It is ordered that gold, silver, bronze, and other materials be brought. How can I bring this from myself? Is gold produced within me, or silver and the other things which are ordered? Does not each one bring these things forth from his storerooms and boxes? What does Moses mean, then, when he says, "Bring from yourselves and each one as he has understood in his heart"? It is evident that the gold and silver and other materials from which the tabernacle was constructed were brought forth from the boxes and storerooms of each person.

The spiritual law, however, demands gold which is within us for the tabernacle, and requires silver which is within us, and all those other materials which we can both have within us and bring forth from ourselves. For the Scripture says, "The word is near you, in your mouth and in your heart; for if you confess the Lord Jesus and believe in your heart that God has raised him from the dead, you shall be saved."[8] If, therefore, "you believe in your heart," your heart and your understanding is gold, therefore, you have offered the faith of your heart as gold for the tabernacle. But if you also "confess" in word, you have offered the word of confession as silver. For that reason Moses, who is the spiritual Law, says, "Take from yourselves." You take these things from yourself. They are within you. Even if you should be destitute you can have these things. But what he adds also bears on this point: "Each one as he has understood in his heart," For you cannot offer God anything from your understanding or from your word unless first you have understood in your heart what has been written. Unless you have been attentive and have listened diligently your gold or silver cannot be excellent, for it is demanded that it be "purged." Hear the Scripture saying, "The words of the Lord are pure words, as silver purged by the fire, refined seven times."[9] If, therefore, you have understood in your heart what has been written, your gold, that is your understanding, will be

---

8 Rom 10.8–9.
9 Ps 11.7.

excellent, and your silver, which is your word, excellent.

What also shall we say about bronze? Bronze is also needed for the construction of the tabernacle. It seems indeed that bronze can be taken to mean strength and can take the place of strength and endurance. But lest someone say that this is to conjecture rather than to explain, where what is said is not supported by the authority of the Scriptures, I think, therefore, that bronze can be taken to represent sound. For speech is one thing, the sound another.[10] Speech is said to be language supported by reason; but the sound is, for example, whether it be said in Latin or Greek, whether elevated or subdued. But you also necessarily demand that we prove these things from the Scriptures. Hear what the Apostle says: "If I speak with the tongues of men and of angels, but have not love, I am as sounding bronze or a tinkling cymbal."[11] So, therefore, to speak in tongues and to interpret from one tongue to another is an offering of bronze. For it is necessary that the tabernacle of the Lord have all things and nothing be lacking in the house of God. The sound is, therefore, as we said, an offering of bronze. It is the sound on the one hand which changes the thought from one language into another, but it is speech which brings forth the proper thought. These are all, therefore, offered to God: thought, speech, and sound.

(3) What shall we say about the other things? They are many and it would be a huge taks to discuss them individually. But what would it profit should they be discussed by our vast toil indeed, but be despised by hearers who are preoccupied and can scarcely stand in the presence of the word of God a fraction of an hour, and come to nothing. For "unless the Lord build the house, they have labored in vain who build it."[12] Nevertheless, as we already said above, we deliver the Lord's money to the bank. Let each hearer take heed how he receives what is

---

10 Origen makes the same kind of distinction between voice (*phonē*) and speech (*logos*) in *Comm. Jn.* 2.32.193; C. Blanc, *Origène: Commentaire sur st. Jean*, vol. 1, SC 120 (Paris: les Éditions du Cerf, 1966), 338, notes an analogous distinction in Aristotle.

11 1 Cor 13.1.

12 Ps 126.1.

delivered. "Let each one," the text reads, "as he has understood in his heart, bring the firstfruits to the Lord."[13]

Because the text spoke of "firstfruits," I ask, "What are the
firstfruits of gold or silver? And how do firstfruits appear to be
gathered from scarlet and purple and linen? Or how does
anyone offer 'as he has understood in his heart' "? This now
strikes each of us. Let us see at the same time both how we who
are now present here have understood in heart and how the
word of God is handled. There are some who understand in
heart what is read; there are others who do not at all understand what is said, but their mind and heart are on business
dealings or on acts of the world or on counting their profit.
And especially, how do you think women understand in heart,
who chatter so much, who disturb with their stories so much
that they do not allow any silence? Now what shall I say about
their mind, what shall I say about their heart, if they are
thinking about their infants or wool or the needs of their
household? I truly fear that they follow those women of whom
the Apostle says, "Who learn to go about from house to house
not only tattlers but also busybodies, saying things which they
ought not."[14] How, then do such women understand in heart?
No one understands in heart unless his heart is untrammeled,
unless he be open-minded and totally intent. Unless one be
watchful in heart he cannot understand in heart and offer gifts
to God. But even if we have been neglectful thus far let us
immediately, starting now, be more attentive and give attention carefully, that we can understand in mind.

It is just, indeed, that each one be found to have his own
portion in the Lord's tabernacle. For what each one offers does
not escape the Lord's notice. How glorious it is for you if it be
said in the Lord's tabernacle: "That gold," for example, "with
which the ark of the covenant is covered, is his; the silver from
which the bases and the columns are made is his; the bronze
from which the rings and laver and some bases of the columns
have been made is his; but also those stones of the cape and

---

13 Ex 35.5.
14 1 Tim 5.13.

breastplate are his; the purple with which the high priest is adorned is his; the scarlet is his" and so on for the other things. And again how shameful, how miserable it will be if the Lord, when he comes to inquire about the building of the tabernacle, should find no gift from you in it; if he should perceive nothing offered by you. Have you lived so irreligiously, so unfaithfully that you have desired to have no memorial of your own in God's tabernacle? For just as "the prince of this world"[15] comes to each one of us and seeks to find some of his own deeds in us and if indeed he find anything he claims us for himself, so also, on the contrary, if the Lord, when he comes, should find something of yours in his tabernacle, he claims you for himself and says you are his.

Lord Jesus, grant that I may deserve to have some memorial in your tabernacle. I would choose, if it be possible, that mine be something in that gold from which the mercy seat is made or from which the ark is covered or from which the candlestick and the lamps are made. Or if I do not have gold, I pray that I be found to offer some silver at least which may be useful in the columns or in their bases. Or may I certainly deserve to have some bronze in the tabernacle from which the hoops and other things are made which the word of God describes. Would that, moreover, it be possible for me to be one of the princes and to offer precious stones for the adornment of the cape and breastplate of the high priest. But because these things are beyond me, might I certainly deserve to have goats' hair in God's tabernacle, lest I be found barren and unfruitful in all things.

"Each one," therefore, "as he has understood in his heart."[16] See if you understand, see if you retain, lest perhaps what is said vanish and come to nothing. I wish to admonish you with examples from your religious practices. You who are accustomed to take part in divine mysteries know, when you receive the body of the Lord, how you protect it with all caution and veneration lest any small part fall from it, lest anything of the

---

15 Cf. Jn 12.31.
16 Ex 35.5.

consecrated gift be lost. For you believe, and correctly, that you are answerable if anything falls from there by neglect. But if you are so careful to preserve his body, and rightly so, how do you think that there is less guilt to have neglected God's word than to have neglected his body?

They are ordered, therefore, to offer the first things, that is, the firstfruits. He who offers what is first by necessity has what is left for himself. See how much we ought to abound in gold and silver and all the other things which are ordered to be offered so that we might both offer to the Lord and have something left over for us. For first of all my mind ought to understand God and offer to him the firstfruits of its understanding so that when it shall have understood God well, it might consequently know the other things. Let speech also do this and all these things which are in us.

But let us also consider the other things. "Blue and purple and scarlet doubled and twisted linen."[17] Those are four materials from which either the garments of the high priest or other things which are prepared for the sacred adornment are made. Some also before us have spoken about these things and as it is not fitting to steal words belonging to another, so it is appropriate, I think, to use words said well by another and acknowledge their source. Therefore, as it appeared to men before us, these materials represent the four elements of which both the world and the human body consist, that is, air, fire, water, and earth. The blue, therefore, refers to the air—for the color itself indicates this—as also scarlet refers to fire. Purple represents water, which, as it were, receives its color from the waters; linen corresponds to the earth because it springs from the earth.[18] We also, therefore, have all these materials in us and since we are ordered to offer firstfruits from these things to the Lord, the text says: "Take from yourselves and offer firstfruits to the Lord."[19]

(4) But I think we must consider why Moses, when he spoke

---

17 Ex 35.6.
18 Cf. Philo *Mos.* 2.88; Josephus *Ant.* 3.183; *Bell.* 5.2.2; Clement *Strom.* 5.6.
19 Ex 35.5.

simply about the other materials, added only to scarlet, "doubled," and to linen, "twisted." It is asked, therefore, why he spoke simply about the other materials by which the other elements are indicated, but with scarlet alone, by which fire is designated, he placed "doubled." These matters are difficult to understand and much more difficult to express. Nevertheless, as the Lord may grant, we shall attempt to explain . For it is necessary that some things be said and some be passed over.

Let us see, therefore, why he said "scarlet doubled." That color, as we said, indicates the element of fire. Fire, however, has a double power: one by which it enlightens, another by which it burns. This is the historical reason. Let us come also to the spiritual reason. Even here fire is double. There is a certain fire in this age and there is fire in the future. The Lord Jesus says, "I came to cast fire on the earth."[20] That fire enlightens. Again the same Lord says in the future to the "workers of iniquity": "Go into everlasting fire which my Father has prepared for the devil and his angels."[21] That fire burns. Nevertheless, that fire which Jesus came to cast "enlightens," indeed, "every man coming into this world."[22] But it has something also which burns, as those acknowledge who say, "Was not our heart burning within us when he opened to us the Scriptures?"[23] Therefore, "by opening the Scriptures" he both burned and enlightened at the same time. I do not know, however, whether that fire in the world to come which burns also has power to enlighten. The nature of fire, therefore, as we have shown is double and, for that reason, it is ordered that "scarlet doubled" be offered.

Let us see, therefore, how we can offer that doubled fire for the building of the tabernacle. If you are a teacher you are erecting a tabernacle when you edify the Chruch of God. God, therefore, says to you also what he said to Jeremiah: "Behold I have made my words in your mouth as fire."[24] If, therefore,

---

20 Lk 12.49.
21 Cf. Lk 13.27; Mt 25.41.
22 Jn 1.9.
23 Lk 24.32.
24 Jer 5.14.

when you teach and edify the Church of God, you rebuke only and reprove and censure and upbraid the sins of the people, but you offer no consolation from the divine Scriptures, you explain nothing obscure, you touch nothing of more profound knowledge, you do not open any more sacred understanding, you have offered scarlet, indeed, but not doubled. For your fire burns only and does not enlighten. And again, if, when you teach, you open the mysteries of the Law, you discuss hidden secrets, but you do not reprove the sinner nor correct the negligent nor hold severity of discipline, you have offered scarlet, to be sure, but not doubled. For your fire enlightens only; it does not burn. He, therefore, who "offers rightly" and "divides rightly"[25] offers scarlet doubled, so that he mixes the small flame of severity wth the light of knowlege.

(5) Let us consider also what "twisted linen" means. For here also he makes an addition to the other elements. We said that linen represents the earth which is our flesh. Therefore, he does not wish flesh to be offered to God wallowing in luxury and enfeebled by pleasures, but he orders it to be twisted and restrained. Who, therefore, is it who twists his flesh? He, doubtless, who said, "I torment my body and bring it into subjection, lest perhaps when I have preached to others I myself should become a castaway."[26] So, therefore, to offer also twisted linen is to weaken the flesh by abstinence, by vigils, and by the exertion of meditations.

Goats' hair is also offered. This kind of animal is ordered in the Law to be offered for sin. Hair is a dead, bloodless, soulless form. He who offers this animal shows that the disposition to sin is already dead in himself, nor does sin further live or rule in his members. The skins of rams are also offered. Some before us suggested that the ram represents madness. And because a skin is an indication of a dead animal, he who offers the skins of rams to the Lord shows that madness is dead in himself.

Next the text says, "And all the men to whom it seemed

---

25 Cf. Gn 4.7 (LXX).
26 Cf. 1 Cor 9.27.

good in their understanding received from their wives and brought jewels and earrings and rings and hairpins and bracelets."[27] You see here also how those offer gifts to God who see in their heart, who conceive understanding in their heart, who have their mind intent and given to the word of God. Those, therefore, bring gifts and they bring them also from their wives, the text says, "earrings and jewels and bracelets." We have already often said that woman, according to the allegorical sense is interpreted as flesh and man as the rational understanding. Those, therefore, are good wives who obey their husbands; the flesh is good which no longer resists the spirit, but submits and agrees. Therefore, "if two or three of you agree, whatever you shall ask shall be done to you" the Lord said.[28] They offer, therefore, "earrings from their wives." You see how the hearing is offered to the Lord. But bracelets also are offered to the Lord which refer to skillful and good works which are performed through the flesh. The rational understanding offers these things to the Lord. But hairpins are also offered. He offers hairpins who knows well how to discern what is to be done, what to be avoided, what is pleasing to God or what displeasing, what is just, what unjust. Those are the hairpins which are offered to the Lord. Here, therefore, the women offer earrings to the Lord because they are wise women. For the text says wise women came and made whatever things were necessary for the garments of the high priest. But those women who offered their earrings to make a calf were foolish, who "turned away their hearing from the truth and turned to fables and impiety,"[29] and, therefore, offered their earrings to make the head of a calf. But also in the book of Judges we find another idol no less made from the earrings of women. Those women, therefore, are blessed, that flesh is blessed, which offers to the Lord its earrings and its hairpins and its rings and all the works of its hands which it performs in the commandments of the Lord.

---

27 Ex 35.22.
28 Cf. Mt 18.19.
29 2 Tim 4.4.

(6) After this the text adds that he "with whom was found wood not subject to rot,"[30] brought it to the Lord. If anyone loves Christ the Lord "in incorruption,"[31] he offers wood not subject to rot to God. Blessed, therefore, is he with whom is found either an uncorrupted understanding or an uncorrupted body and he offers this to God. Whence also the text said very well, "With whom wood not subject to rot was found." For "wood not subject to rot" is not found with all. He did not say about gold or silver, "with whom it has been found," for understanding and speech can be found with all. But neither did he say this about the four colors, for all people consist of the four elements in the body. "Wood not subject to rot," however, that is, the grace of incorruption and virginity, can be found only rarely, as also the Lord says: "All men take not this word, but they to whom it is given."[32]

(7) But the text also says, "the princes offered"[33] their gifts. What are those gifts which the princes offer? "They offered jewels," it says, "emeralds, stones of fulfillment, and stones for the cape."[34] They are called stones of fulfillment which are placed on the *logion,* that is, which are arranged on the breast of the high priest, inscribed with the names of the tribes of Israel. This which is said to be the *logion,* that is, the oracular breastplate,[35] which is arranged on the breast of the high priest represents the rational understanding which is in us. The "stones of fulfillment" are said to be placed on this, which nevertheless cohere and are joined together with the stones of the cape and, bound together, are supported from these. The adorned cape is an indication of good deeds. Action, therefore, is associated with reason and reason with actions, that there might be harmony in both, "for he who shall do and teach, he shall be called great in the kingdom of heaven."[36] Let

---

30 Ex 35.24.
31 Eph 6.24.
32 Mt 19.11.
33 Cf. Ex 35.27.
34 Cf. Ex 35.27.
35 *rationale.*
36 Mt 5.19.

our speech, therefore, rest upon actions and let actions adorn
our speech, for this is related as the adornment of the high
priest. But the princes are required to execute these things;
that is the adornment of those who have advanced so far that
they deserve to preside over the people.

The princes also offer oil which will be beneficial for twofold uses: for lamps and for anointing. For the lamp of those
who preside over the people ought not to be hidden or "placed
under a bushel, but on a candlestick that it may shine to all who
are in the house."[37] But the princes also offer "a mixture of
incense" which is mixed by Moses "for a savor of sweetness to
the Lord,"[38] that they themselves also might say, "We are the
good odor of Christ."[39] And after the people made their
offering the text says, "Moses called every wise man"[40] in
constructing and building that they might put together and
construct the individual things which were described."But,"
the text says, "he also called the wise women,"[41] that they might
make the things which were proper in the tabernacle of the
Lord.

You see, therefore, that everything which was made was
made by the wise; both women and men are called wise. For
"all the works of the Lord" are done "in wisdom."[42] Each one,
therefore, "wise in understanding"[43] comes and does the works
of the Lord. It is not sufficient for us if we only make an
offering, but we must also work with wisdom those things
which are in us: we must know how to mix gold with linen and
to double scarlet or to mix it with purple. For what does it
profit you, if you have these things and do not know how to use
them nor know how you ought to fit each one in its time and
place and bring it forth. And, therefore, we must work that we
may be wise and able to bring forth in their time these things

---

37 Cf. Mt 5.15.
38 Ex 35.28, 29.41.
39 2 Cor 2.15.
40 Ex 36.2.
41 Cf. Ex 35.25.
42 Ps 103.24.
43 Cf. Ex 35.25 (LXX).

which we hear from the Holy Scriptures and to fit them and put them together and from them to adorn "a tabernacle for the God of Jacob"[44] through Christ Jesus our Lord, to whom belongs "glory and sovereignty forever and ever. Amen."[45]

---

44 Ps 131.5.
45 Cf. 1 Pt 4.11.

APPENDIX
The Interpretation of Names in the Genesis and Exodus
Homilies

Etymological exegesis of names is one of the techniques of Origen's allegorical interpretation of Scripture. This is his attempt to draw spiritual significance from the meaning of the names of various persons and places in the Scriptural narrative by relating the names to words from which they are derived or, what is often the case, which they resemble.[1]

In this practice Origen stands in the tradition of allegorical interpretation reaching back through the Jewish and Greek allegorists before him. The Stoic Cornutus, for example, from whose works Porphyry says Origen learned to interpret the Jewish writings figuratively,[2] works through the names of the gods in Greek mythology in this way.

> Sky (*ouranos*)...encircles the earth and the sea and all things on the earth and in the sea, and for this reason acquired this name, being watcher (*ouros*) over all and forming the boundaries (*horizōn*) of nature. But some say he has been called Sky (*ouranos*) because he takes care of (*ōrein* or *ōreuein*) what exists...But others derive the etymology from his observing (*horasthai*) on high.[3]

Philo, whose influence on Origen in this respect is frequently apparent, applies this technique to the names of persons and places in the Pentateuch. He treats the name of the first river mentioned in Gn 2.11, for example, as follows. "One species of the four virtues is prudence, which he has called 'Pheison,'

---

1 Ancient etymologists were notoriously careless in their etymologies. See, for example, Plato's *Cratylus*.
2 Eusebius *H.E.* 6.19.8.
3 C. Lang, ed., *Cornuti Theologiae Graecae Compendium* (Leipzig: Teubner, 1881), 1–2.

owing to its 'sparing' (*pheidesthai*) and guarding the soul from deeds of wrong."[4]

The most comprehensive study of this phenomenon among the early Christians is that of Franz Wutz.[5] He lists all the names in Origen along with the interpretations he gives to them and the places where they are found in Origen's works. His interest is not primarily in how the various meanings are derived, however, but in whether or not Origen compiled an onomasticon of Biblical names. His conclusion is that he did not compile such a work and that no such complete work existed in Origen's day. R. P. C. Hanson has done a much narrower study in which he focuses on seven lists of names derived from the fragments of Origen on Genesis and his homilies on Numbers.[6] His concern is to demonstrate that Origen was drawing on onomastica, some of which, he thinks, may have come from the Rabbis of Caesarea.[7]

Our purpose in this appendix is not to argue for or against the existence of onomastica which Origen may have used, but simply to show how the etymologist, whether Origen himself or someone else, derived the meaning he attaches to the name.

The names will be treated in the order in which they appear in the homilies. Rufinus' Latin text will be quoted showing how the name was spelled, followed by the Hebrew word or words from which the etymologist derived the name.

1. Noe, qui interpretatur requies vel iustus, qui est Christus Jesus (*Gn. Hom.* 2.3; GCS 31.15–16). See Wutz, *OS*, 102, 115. Origen seems to be dependent on Philo for this interpretation: "Noah means rest (*anapausis*) or just (*dikaios*)." See Philo, *L.A.* 3.24.77; *Abr.*5.27. The association of rest (*nûah*) with the name *Noah* goes back as early as Gn 5.29.

2. "Mambre" in nostra lingua interpretatur visio sive per-

---

4 Philo *L.A.* 1.20.66. Translation by F. Colson and G. Whitaker, *Philo*, vol. 1 (Cambridge: Harvard University Press, 1962), 191.

5 *Onomastica Sacra* (Leipzig, 1914). Hereinafter cited as Wutz, *OS*.

6 "Interpretation of Hebrew Names in Origen," *Vigiliae Christianae* 10 (1956), 103–123.

7 Ibid., 122.

spicacia (*Gn. Hom.* 4.3; GCS 53.22–23).[8] Philo *Mig.* 165, says, "Mambre, which translated is 'from seeing'. . . ." This treats Mambre as a combination of the Hebrew preposition "from," *m(in)* and the verb "to see," *rā'āh.* Wutz, *OS*, 416, thinks *perspicuus* may represent the Hebrew noun, *mār'eh* ("sight," "vision").

3. Puto ergo Sarram, quae interpretatur princeps vel principatum agens, formam tenere *aretēs*, quod est animi virtus (*Gn. Hom.* 6.1; GCS 66.18–20). Philo frequently interprets Sara as *archē* or *archousa* (*Cher.* 3.5; *Cong.* 2). In *QG.* 3.53 he says that spelled with one *rho* the name means "my rule" (*archē mou*), but spelled with two it means "ruler" (*archousa*) (See Wutz, *OS*, 91). In *Abr.* 99 Philo refers to some natural philosophers who said Abraham's wife was "virtue," her Chaldean name "Sarra" meaning "ruler" (*archousa*) in Greek, because nothing is fitter for ruling or more capable of commanding than virtue. These meanings are derived from the Hebrew noun *śar* ("ruler") and its derivative verb *śārar* ("to rule").

4. Nec enim poterat cum exterminatore—hoc enim interpretatur in lingua nostra Pharao—virtus habitare (*Gn. Hom.* 6.2; GCS 67.16–18). Philo *Som.* 2.211, equates Pharao with

---

8 It should be noted that several of the names are interpreted by doublets in the Latin text (cf. 1, 3, 8, 11, 12, 13, 17, 18, 22, 28, 31, 35). Wagner, *Rufinus the Translator*, 35–36, has shown that the expansion of one word into two is a characteristic practice of Rufinus. She notes several types of expansions that Rufinus employs. That most relevant to our purposes is the explanation of the first concept by the second. For example, he translates the Greek *idiōtou* by *idiotae et simpliciori*. Lacking a Greek text for comparison, one cannot be sure that the doublets used to interpret the various names in the Genesis and Exodus homilies are the work of Rufinus and not Origen. Given his tendency, however, as proven by Wagner, one should be alerted to the possibility that Origen himself used only one term. We can be certain at least in number eight where Rufinus has preserved the Greek term *thymiama* as the meaning of Chettura and then translates it into Latin with the doublet, *incensum vel bonus odor*, following the pattern noted by Wagner of explaining the first concept by the second. Most of the doublets in relation to names appear to fall into this category of an explanatory nature and so would seem to be the work of Rufinus. The double meaning given to the name Noah by Philo (number one above), however, demonstrates that some of the doublets may go back to the original text of Origen.

skedasmos ("a scattering," "dissipating") (Wutz, *OS*, 173). The Hebrew verb *pāra^c*, to which Hebrew *par^cōh* is related, means "to let go." Given the methods of ancient etymologists, it appears more likely that the word has been regarded as if derived from the verb *pārar* which means "to break" or "to make ineffectual."

5. Abimelech interpretatur pater meus rex (*Gn. Hom.* 6.2; GCS 67.27–28). See Wutz *OS*, 64. This etymology correctly interprets the Hebrew name: *'ābî* ("my father") *melek* ("[is] king").

6. Isaac risus vel gaudium interpretatur (*Gn. Hom.* 7.1; GCS 70.23–24). Wutz, *OS*, 585, notes that this interpretation is frequently given to the name Isaac. This etymology, too, correctly derives the name from the Hebrew root *ṣāḥaq* ("to laugh").

7. Rebecca, quae interpretatur patientia (*Gn. Hom.* 10.2; GCS 95.24–25). Cf. *Gn. Hom.* 10.3 (GCS 96.23–24): Habetote patentiam, quia de Rebecca nobis, id est de patientia, sermo est. Wutz, *OS*, 92, notes that the Hebrew name *Ribqāh* ("Rebekah") is treated as composed of *rab* ("much") and the verb *qāwāh* ("to wait for"). He notes further that Philo and his followers always omit the "much." See Philo *Som.* 1.46 (*hypomonē*); *Fug.* 45, *Cher.* 41 (*epimonē tōn kalōn*); *QG.* 4.97; Clement of Alexandria *Strom.* 1.5.31.3.

8. Chettura . . . *thymiama* interpretatur, quod est incensum vel bonus odor (*Gn. Hom.* 11.1; GCS 102.6–8). Cf. Wutz, *OS*, 457, who refers to Philo *Sac.* 43, where Cetura is taken to mean *thymiōsa*. The Hebrew name *Qeṭûrāh* ("Cetura") in this etymology is given the meaning of the noun *qeṭōrāh* ("the smoke of sacrifice" or "incense").

9. Phennana . . ., id est conversio (*Gn. Hom.* 11.2; GCS 102.26). Cf. Wutz, *OS*, 743. The etymologist seems to have the name (*Peninnāh*) from the verb *pānāh* ("to turn").

10. Anna . . ., id est . . . gratia (*Gn. Hom.* 11.2; GCS 102.26). Cf. Wutz, *OS*, 106, 740. Philo, *Deus* 5, takes *Anna* to mean *charis*. This etymology correctly derives the Hebrew name *Ḥannāh* from the verb *ḥānan* ("to be gracious") and its derivative noun *ḥēn* ("grace").

11. Jacob a luctando vel supplantando nomen accepit. Philo, *Mig.* 200, relates Jacob's name to "wrestling" (*palaiontos*) and "catching by the heel" (*pternizontos*), i.e. "deceiving" or "tripping up" someone. The Hebrew verb ʿ*āqab* from which the name *Jacob* (*Yaʿăqōb*) is derived means "to follow at the heel" or "to overreach." Wutz, *OS*, 19, suggests that the meaning "wrestler" is derived by associating the name with the somewhat similar verb *ʾābaq* ("to wrestle"). Cf. Wutz, *OS*, 74–75.

12. Esau vero—ut aiunt qui Hebraea nomina interpretantur—vel a rubore vel a terra, id est rubeus vel terrenus vel, ut aliis visum est, factura dictus esse videatur (*Gn. Hom.* 12.4; GCS 110.5–8). See Wutz, *OS*, 74,431. Philo, *Deus* 144 and 148, refers to the "earthly" (*gēinos*) Edom. This linking of Edom and Esau goes back to Gn 25.30. The name *ʾĕdôm* ("Edom") is derived from the verb *ʾādōm* ("to be red"). The meaning "earthly" connects the word with the noun *ʾădāmāh* ("ground"). Philo, *Cong.* 61, also attests the association of "something made" (*poiēma*) with the name *Esau*. This relates ʿ*ēśāw* ("Esau") to the verb ʿ*aśah* ("to make").

13. Intuere nostrum Isaac . . . venientem in valle Gerarum, quam interpretantur maceriam sive saepem (*Gn. Hom.* 13.2; GCS 114.15–17). See Wutz, *OS* 22,767. The etymologist appears to have connected the Hebrew *Gĕrār* with the root *gādar* ("to wall up") and its derivative noun *Gĕdērāh* ("a wall" or "hedge").

14. Interpretatur autem Ochozath 'tenens' (*Gn. Hom.* 14.3; GCS 124.15–16). Wutz, *OS*, 580. This etymology correctly derives *ʾăḥûzat* ("Ochozath") from the root *ʾāḥaz* ("to grasp," "take possession").

15. Interpretatur . . . et Philcol 'os omnium' (*Gn. Hom.* 14.3; GCS 124.16). Wutz, *OS*, 743. The etymologist has treated the name *Pikōl* as if it were composed from the words *peh* ("mouth") and *kōl* ("all").

16. Interpretatur . . . Abimelech 'pater meus rex' (*Gn. Hom.* 14.3; GCS 124.17). See number 5 above.

17. Istrahel scribitur, tamquam qui mente videat veram vitam, qui est verus Deus Christus (*Gn. Hom.* 15.3; GCS 130.

1–2). Wutz, *OS*, 88–89, notes that Philo refers to Israel as "he who sees God" (*horōn theon*). See, for example, Philo *Ebr.* 82 where he says the name Israel reveals a vision (*horasin*) of God. The etymologist has broken the Hebrew word *Yiśrā'ēl* into syllables. The final syllable is *'ēl* ("God"). His derivation of the first part of the word, however, is obscure. Perhaps he saw a connection with the verb *šûr* ("to behold" or "look").

18. Interpretatur...Gessen proximitas vel propinquitas (*Gn. Hom.* 16.7; GCS 144.16–17). Wutz, *OS*, 744. The etymologist may have seen some connection between *Gōšen* ("Gessen") and the root *nāgaš* ("to draw near"). Cf. number 34 below where the etymology involved a metathesis of consonants.

19. "Phiton" quae in nostra lingua significat os defectionis vel os abyssi (*Ex. Hom.* 1.5; GCS 152.16–17). Wutz, *OS*, 369. Philo, *Post.* 55, says *Pithom* means "oppressing mouth." To arrive at *os abyssi* the etymologist has taken the Hebrew name *Pitōm* to be a combination of *peh* ("mouth") and *tĕhôm* ("abyss"). The former meaning was perhaps attached to the name because of its similarity to *pit'ōm* ("suddenness"), which was usually associated with "calamity" and "terror."

20. "Ramesse" quae interpretatur commotio tineae (*Ex. Hom.* 1.5; GCS 152.17–18). Wutz, *OS*, 140. Cf. Philo *Post.* 55. Hanson, "Interpretation," 115, shows that *ra'ĕmsēs* has been regarded by the etymologist as consisting of *ra'am* ("thunder") and *sās* ("moth").

21. "On, id est Heliopolis," quae dicitur civitas solis (*Ex. Hom.* 1.5; GCS 152.18–19). Wutz, *OS*, 429. The etymologist has here interpreted the Greek name, *Heliopolis* in place of the Hebrew *On*. Philo, *Post.* 55, does the same.

22. "Sephora"...interpretatur passer (*Ex. Hom.* 2.1; GCS 156.13–14). Philo, *Her.* 128, says *Sephora* means "sparrow" (*ornithion*). The midwife's Hebrew name in Ex. 1.15 is *Šiprāh*, which means "fairness" or "clearness." Moses' wife was named *Ṣipōrāh* (Ex 2.21, 4.25, 18.2) which means "bird." The LXX translated both of these names as *Sepphōra*. The etymologist is either relying on the LXX, or is associating the two words on the basis of their similarity, and gives the meaning of the name of Moses' wife to both names.

23. "Phua" . . . apud nos vel rubens vel verecunda dici potest (*Ex. Hom.* 2.1; GCS 156.14–15). Philo, *Her.* 128, says *Phoua* means "red." *Pûʿāh*, the name of the second midwife in Ex 1.15, and Pû ăh, a proper name occurring in Jgs 10.1 and elsewhere are both rendered *Phoua* by the LXX. The second name, *Pûʾāh*, occurs in rabbinic Hebrew meaning "red dye" (Cf. Wutz, *OS*, 647). Here, as in number 21, the etymologist has either relied on the LXX or has himself brought the two different words together and given the meaning of the one to the other.

24. "Ramesse" . . . interpretatur commotio tineae (*Ex. Hom.* 5.2; GCS 185.7). See number 20 above.

25. "Sochoth" tabernacula intelligi apud Hebraeos tradunt interpretes nominum (*Ex. Hom.* 5.2; GCS 185.16–17). Cf. Wutz, *OS*, 821, 937, 1039, where he cites Syriac, Armenian, and Slavic onomastica which give this meaning to the name. This etymology correctly relates *Sukkôt* ("Socoth") to *sukkōh* ("booth"). Cf. Hanson, "Interpretation," 115.

26. "Othon" vero in nostram linguam verti dicunt signa iis (*Ex. Hom.* 5.2; GCS 185.24–25). This fanciful etymology appears to be based on the resemblance between the Hebrew term in Ex 13.20, *ʾētām*, which the LXX rendered *Othom*, and the Hebrew noun *ʾōt* ("sign") with the masculine plural suffix *m* added, i.e. *ʾōtam*. For a completely different etymological connection in the *Homilies on Numbers,* see Hanson, "Interpretation," 115.

27. Haec autem interpretantur: "Epauleum" quidem adscensio tortuosa (*Ex. Hom.* 5.3; GCS 186.24–25). Wutz, *OS*, 743. The relationship the etymologist saw between *Epauleum* and *adscensio tortuosa* is obscure. The Hebrew *Pîhahîrōt* provides no help. See Hanson, "Interpretation," 115, where this Hebrew word is taken to mean "os iroth" in the *Homilies on Numbers.* The LXX *epauleōs* translates the Hebrew term *hăsērôt* ("enclosures"). The etymologist appears to have done here what Hanson, "Interpretation," 105, has noted in other places. He seems to have started with the word in Greek, divided it into syllables, translated these syllables into Hebrew, and then drawn his etymology from the Hebrew word he constructed

from the Greek word. If we assume this process here, then he may have related the syllable *aul* of the Greek word to the Hebrew root ʿ*ālâh* ("to ascend").

28. Interpretantur. . . Magdolum "turris" (*Ex. Hom.* 5.3; GCS 186.25). Wutz, *OS*, 587. The translation of *Magdol* as "*turris*" is correct. The Hebrew text in Ex 14.2 has *migdōl* which is from the same root as *migdāl* ("tower"). Hanson, *Interpretation*, 116, notes that *Migdōl* is given the meaning "*magnificentia*" in the *Homilies on Numbers*, based on the Hebrew root *gdl*.

29. Interpretantur. . . "Beelsephon" adscensio speculae vel habens speculam (*Ex. Hom.* 5.3; GCS 186.26). The Hebrew text has *baʿal ṣĕpōn*. Wutz, *OS*, 59, notes that the Hebrew root *baʿal* often means "to have." The Hebrew root *ṣapāh* means "to look about" or "keep watch" and has a derivative noun *mispeh* ("watchtower"). The meaning *adscensio speculae* was probably derived by regarding *baʿal* as related to the verb ʿ*ālāh* ("to ascend"). Cf. Hanson, *Interpretation*, 116, and Wutz, *OS*, 59, 140, 593.

30. "Philistiim" id est cadentes populi (*Ex. Hom.* 6.8; GCS 198.20–21). Wutz, *OS*, 187, 743. The etymologist seems to have connected the Hebrew *Pĕlištî* ("Philistine") with the verb *nāpal* ("to fall") on the basis of the two consonants *p l*.

31. "Edom"qui interpretatur terrenus (*Ex. Hom.* 6.8; GCS 198.21). See number 12 above.

32. "Omnes habitantes Chanaan" qui mutabiles interpretanur et mobiles (*Ex. Hom.* 6.8; GCS 198.26–199.1). Wutz, *OS*, 157, suggests that the etymology has been derived from the Hebrew *nûʿa* ("to tremble" or "totter").

33. Manna enim interpretatur "quid est hoc" (*Ex. Hom.* 7.5; GCS 212.1). Wutz, *OS*, 328. Philo, *L.A.* 2.86; 3.175, says *manna* means "what?" (*ti*). This relates the Hebrew *mān* ("manna") to the question *mān hûʾ* ("what is this"). This etymology goes back to Ex 16.15.

34. Sin enim tentatio interpretatur (*Ex. Hom.* 11.1; GCS 253.2–3). Wutz, *OS*, 489. The Hebrew verb "to tempt" is *nāsāh*. In order to relate *Sîn* to this verb the etymologist has had to transpose the consonants *s* and *n*.

35. Raphidin vero sanitas iudicii (*Ex. Hom.* 11.1; GCS 253.3). Wutz, *OS*, 456. The interpretation of the Hebrew *Rĕpîdîm* as *"sanitas iudicii"* was reached by dividing the word in the middle and then relating the two parts to the Hebrew words *rāpāʾ* ("to heal") and *dîn* ("judgment"). Cf.Hanson, "Interpretation," 116.

36. Nam de Jacob quid dicam, qui ipso nomine athleta est? Luctator enim et supplantator interpretatur (*Ex. Hom.* 11.5; GCS 257.13–14). See number 11 above.

INDICES

INDEX OF PROPER NAMES

INDEX OF HOLY SCRIPTURE

(Books of the Old Testament)

(Books of the New Testament)

THE FATHERS
OF THE CHURCH

(A series of approximately 100 volumes when completed)

The City of God (books 1–7)
translated by D. Zema, G. Walsh

OCLC 807084

Volume 9:   SAINT BASIL ASCETICAL WORKS   (1950)
translated by M. Wagner

OCLC 856020

Volume 10:   TERTULLIAN APOLOGETICAL WORKS   (1950)
Tertullian Apology
translated by E–J. Daly
On the Soul
translated by E. Quain
The Testimony of the Soul
To Scapula
translated by R. Arbesmann
Minucius Felix: Octavius
translated by R. Arbesmann

OCLC 1037264

Volume 11:   SAINT AUGUSTINE   (1957)
Commentary on the Lord's Sermon on the Mount
Selected Sermons (17)
translated by D. Kavanagh

OCLC 2210742

Volume 12:   SAINT AUGUSTINE   (1951)
Letters (1–82)
translated by W. Parsons

OCLC 807061

Volume 13:   SAINT BASIL   (1951)
Letters (1–185)
translated by A–C. Way

OCLC 2276183

Volume 14:   SAINT AUGUSTINE   (1952)
The City of God (books 8–16)
translated by G. Walsh, G. Monahan

OCLC 807084

Volume 15:   EARLY CHRISTIAN BIOGRAPHIES   (1952)
Life of St. Ambrose by Paulinus
translated by J. Lacy
Life of St. Augustine by Bishop Possidius

Life of St. Cyprian by Pontius
   translated by M. M. Mueller, R. Deferrari
Life of St. Epiphanius by Ennodius
   translated by G. Cook
Life of St. Paul the First Hermit
Life of St. Hilarion by St. Jerome
Life of Malchus by St. Jerome
   translated by L. Ewald
Life of St. Anthony by St. Athanasius
   translated by E. Keenan
A Sermon on the Life of St. Honoratus by St. Hilary
   translated by R. Deferrari

OCLC 806775

Volume 16:   SAINT AUGUSTINE   (1952)
The Christian Life
Lying
The Work of Monks
The Usefulness of Fasting
   translated by S. Muldowney
Against Lying
   translated by H. Jaffe
Continence
   translated by M–F. McDonald
Patience
   translated by L. Meagher
The Excellence of Widowhood
   translated by C. Eagan
The Eight Questions of Dulcitius
   translated by M. Deferrari

OCLC 806731

Volume 17:   SAINT PETER CHRYSOLOGUS   (1953)
Selected Sermons
Letter to Eutyches
       SAINT VALERIAN
Homilies
Letter to the Monks
   translated by G. Ganss

OCLC 806783

Volume 18:   SAINT AUGUSTINE   (1953)

Letters (83–130)
> *translated by W. Parsons*

OCLC 807061

Volume 19: EUSEBIUS PAMPHILI (1953)
Ecclesiastical History (books 1–5)
> *translated by R. Deferrari*

OCLC 708651

Volume 20: SAINT AUGUSTINE (1953)
Letters (131–164)
> *translated by W. Parsons*

OCLC 807061

Volume 21: SAINT AUGUSTINE (1953)
Confessions
> *translated by V. Bourke*

OCLC 2210845

Volume 22: FUNERAL ORATIONS (1953)
Saint Gregory Nazianzen: Four Funeral Orations
> *translated by L. McCauley*
Saint Ambrose: On the Death of His Brother Satyrus I & II
> *translated by J. Sullivan, M. McGuire*
Saint Ambrose: Consolation on the Death of Emperor
> Valentinian
> Funeral Oration on the Death of Emperor Theodosius
> *translated by R. Deferrari*

OCLC 806797

Volume 23: CLEMENT OF ALEXANDRIA (1954)
Christ the Educator
> *translated by S. Wood*

OCLC 2200024

Volume 24: SAINT AUGUSTINE (1954)
The City of God (books 17-22)
> *translated by G. Walsh, D. Honan*

OCLC 807084

Volume 25: SAINT HILARY OF POITIERS (1954)
The Trinity
> *translated by S. McKenna*

OCLC 806781

Volume 26: SAINT AMBROSE (1954)

Letters (1–91)
translated by M. Beyenka

The Divination of Demons
translated by R. Brown
Faith and Works
The Creed
In Answer to the Jews
translated by L. Ewald

Adulterous Marriages
translated by C. Huegelmeyer
The Care to be Taken for the Dead
translated by J. Lacy
Holy Virginity
translated by J. McQuade
Faith and the Creed
translated by R. Russell
The Good of Marriage
translated by C. Wilcox

Letters (186–368)
translated by A–C. Way

Ecclesiastical History
translated by R. Deferrari

Letters (165–203)
translated by W. Parsons

Sermons (1–8)
translated by M–M. Mueller

Letters (204–270)
   translated by W. Parsons

                                        OCLC 807061

Volume 33:   SAINT JOHN CHRYSOSTOM   (1957)
   Commentary on St. John The Apostle and Evangelist
   Homilies (1–47)
      translated by T. Goggin

                                        OCLC 2210926

Volume 34:   SAINT LEO THE GREAT   (1957)
   Letters
      translated by E. Hunt

                                        OCLC 825765

Volume 35:   SAINT AUGUSTINE   (1957)
   Against Julian
      translated by M. Schumacher

                                        OCLC 3255620

Volume 36:   SAINT CYPRIAN   (1958)
   To Donatus
   The Lapsed
   The Unity of the Church
   The Lord's Prayer
   To Demetrian
   Mortality
   Works and Almsgiving
   Jealousy and Envy
   Exhortation to Martyrdom to Fortunatus
   That Idols Are Not Gods
      translated by R. Deferrari
   The Dress of Virgins
      translated by A. Keenan
   The Good of Patience
      translated by G. Conway

                                        OCLC 3894637

Volume 37:   SAINT JOHN OF DAMASCUS   (1958)
   The Fount of Knowledge
   On Heresies
   The Orthodox Faith (4 books)
      translated by F. Chase, Jr.

                                        OCLC 810002

429

The Sacrament of the Incarnation of Our Lord
The Sacraments
translated by R. Deferrari

OCLC 2316634

Volume 45:   SAINT AUGUSTINE   (1963)
The Trinity
translated by S. McKenna

OCLC 784847

Volume 46:   SAINT BASIL   (1963)
Exegetic Homilies
translated by A–C. Way

OCLC 806743

Volume 47:   SAINT CAESARIUS OF ARLES II   (1963)
Sermons (81–186)
translated by M. M. Mueller

OCLC 2494636

Volume 48:   THE HOMILIES OF SAINT JEROME   (1964)
Homilies 1–59
translated by L. Ewald

OCLC 412009

Volume 49:   LACTANTIUS   (1964)
The Divine Institutes
translated by M–F. McDonald

OCLC 711211

Volume 50:   PAULUS OROSIUS   (1964)
The Seven Books of History Against the Pagans
translated by R. Deferrari

OCLC 711212

Volume 51:   SAINT CYPRIAN   (1964)
Letters (1–81)
translated by R. Donna

OCLC 806738

Volume 52:   THE POEMS OF PRUDENTIUS   (1965)
The Divinity of Christ
The Origin of Sin
The Spiritual Combat
Against Symmachus (two books)
Scenes from Sacred History Or Twofold Nourishment
translated by C. Eagan

431

433

Rule for the Monastery of Compludo
General Rule for Monasteries
Pact
Monastic Agreement
translated by C. Barlow

OCLC 718095

Volume 64:   THE WORKS OF SAINT CYRIL   (1970)
OF JERUSALEM II
Lenten Lectures (Catcheses) 13–18
translated by L. McCauley
The Mystagogical Lectures
Sermon on the Paralytic
Letter to Constantius
translated by A. Stephenson

OCLC 21885

Volume 65   SAINT AMBROSE   (1972)
Seven Exegetical Works
Isaac or the Soul
Death as a Good
Jacob and the Happy Life
Joseph
The Patriarchs
Flight from the World
The Prayer of Job and David
translated by M. McHugh

OCLC 314148

Volume 66:   SAINT CAESARIUS OF ARLES III   (1973)
Sermons 187–238
translated by M. M. Mueller

OCLC 1035149; 2494636

Volume 67:   NOVATIAN   (1974)
The Trinity
The Spectacles
Jewish Foods
In Praise of Purity
Letters
translated by R. DeSimone

OCLC 662181

THE FATHERS
OF THE CHURCH

A NEW TRANSLATION

VOLUME 71

THE FATHERS
OF THE CHURCH

A NEW TRANSLATION